A Nation of Widening Opportunities

A Nation of Widening Opportunities

Opportunities

The Civil Rights Act at 50

Edited by Ellen D. Katz and Samuel R. Bagenstos

Michigan Publishing

Published in the United States of America by
Michigan Publishing
Manufactured in the United States of America

978-1-60785-368-8

An imprint of Michigan Publishing, Maize Books serves the publishing needs of the University of
Michigan community by making high-quality scholarship widely available in print and online. It
represents a new model for authors seeking to share their work within and beyond the academy,
offering streamlined selection, production, and distribution processes. Maize Books is intended as a
complement to more formal modes of publication in a wide range of disciplinary areas.

http://www.maizebooks.org

This book was produced using Pressbooks.com, and PDF rendering was done by PrinceXML.

To our families

Contents

Preface and Acknowledgments ix

1. Performative Citizenship in the Civil Rights and Immigrant Rights Movements 1
   Kathryn Abrams

2. Discriminatory Animus 29
   Cary Franklin

3. Civil Rights 3.0 46
   Nan D. Hunter

4. Toward a Jurisprudence of the Civil Rights Acts 70
   Robin L. West

5. On Class-Not-Race 105
   Samuel R. Bagenstos

6. The Diversity Feedback Loop 119
   Patrick Shin, Devon Carbado, and Mitu Gulati

7. Is the Future of Affirmative Action Race Neutral? 144
   Brian T. Fitzpatrick

8. The Judicial Repeal of the Johnson/Kennedy Administration's "Signature" Achievement 165
   Judge Nancy Gertner (Ret.)

9. Taking Seriously Title VII's "Floor, Not a Ceiling" Invitation 184
   Craig Gurian

10. Leveraging Antidiscrimination 211
    Olatunde Johnson

11. A Signal or a Silo? Title VII's Unexpected Hegemony 234
    Sophia Z. Lee

12. Labor Unions and Title VII: A Bit Player at the Creation   251
     Looks Back
     Theodore J. St. Antoine

13. Justice Ginsburg's Umbrella   264
     Ellen D. Katz

14. Disparate Impact Abroad   283
     Julie Suk

     List of Contributors   307

Preface and Acknowledgments

The Civil Rights Act of 1964 was an extraordinary achievement of law, politics, and human rights. On the fiftieth anniversary of the Act's passage, it is appropriate to reflect on the successes and failures of the civil rights project reflected in the statute, as well as on its future directions. This volume represents an attempt to assess the Civil Rights Act's legacy.

On October 11, 2013, a diverse group of civil rights scholars met at the University of Michigan Law School in Ann Arbor to assess the interpretation, development, and administration of civil rights law in the five decades since President Lyndon Baines Johnson signed the Civil Rights Act. In the volume that follows, readers will find edited versions of the papers that these scholars presented, enriched by our lively discussions at and after the conference. We hope that the essays in this volume will contribute to the continuing debates regarding the civil rights project in the United States and the world.

This volume, and the conference from which it emerged, would not have existed without the generous financial support of the Anti-Discrimination Center. We thank the Anti-Discrimination Center and its executive director, Craig Gurian, for their tremendous assistance. The current and former deans of the University of Michigan Law School, Mark West and Evan Caminker, also were especially supportive of this project. We thank Jenny Rickard, Jenny Whalen, and Jessica Hanes for their tireless staff work to make the conference and volume a success. And last but not least, we very much appreciate the editorial assistance of two terrific students, Cali Cope-Kasten and Rachel Goldberg.

Performative Citizenship in the Civil Rights and Immigrant Rights Movements

Kathryn Abrams

In August 2013, Maria Teresa Kumar, the executive director of Voto Latino, spoke alongside civil rights leaders at the fiftieth anniversary of the March on Washington. A month earlier, immigrant activists invited the Reverend Al Sharpton to join a press conference outside the federal court building as they celebrated a legal victory over Joe Arpaio, the anti-immigrant sheriff of Maricopa County. Undocumented youth organizing for immigration reform explained their persistence with Martin Luther King's statement that "the arc of the moral universe is long, but it bends toward justice."[1]

The civil rights movement remains a potent reminder that politically marginalized groups can shape the law through mobilization and collective action. This has made the movement a crucial source of symbolism for those activists who have come after. But it has also been a source of what sociologist Doug McAdam has called "cultural innovations"[2]: transformative strategies and tactics that can be embraced and modified by later movements. This chapter examines the legacy of the Civil Rights Act by revisiting the social movement that produced it and comparing that movement to a recent and galvanizing successor, the movement for immigrant rights.[3] This movement has not simply used the storied tactics of the civil rights movement; it has modified them in ways that render them more performative: undocumented activists implement the familiar tactics that enact, in daring and surprising ways, the public belonging to which they aspire.[4] This performative dimension would seem to distinguish the immigrant rights movement, at the level of organizational strategy, from its civil rights counterpart, whose participants were constitutionally acknowledged as citizens. However, focusing instead on the legal consciousness and self-conception of individual activists may unveil greater similarities between participants in the two movements. As the individual narratives elicited by sociologists and historians of the civil rights movement demonstrate, participants in many civil rights campaigns were asserting a citizenship in which they did not feel secure, notwithstanding its formal recognition in law. In this respect, both movements relied on what Patricia Williams has called the "alchemy" of claiming rights that may be emergent or precarious as a means of securing their formal recognition.

Part I of this chapter examines the civil rights movement and the immigrant rights movement from the standpoint of organizational strategy and tactics. It focuses on two "cultural innovations" that have become hallmarks of the civil rights movement: the use of direct action, particularly civil disobedience, to protest Jim Crow laws in Southern states, and the campaigns that sought to prepare and register black residents for the franchise in rural communities of the Deep South, such as Mississippi. Both direct action and civic engagement campaigns have been central to the emerging movement for immigrant rights. But they have been implemented with distinctive variations, which enable the assertion of belonging by one visible and compelling segment of the immigrant population—undocumented youth. Part II reconsiders the claim advanced in Part I, that the immigrant rights movement is distinct in its performative dimension, by focusing on the individual legal consciousness of participants. This analysis suggests that early civil rights activists also performed a citizenship they did not experience as secure in order to bring it more fully into being. The work of social scientists such as Francesca Polletta and Charles Payne, who have studied the civil rights movement at the level of individual legal consciousness, demonstrates that the sense of belonging experienced by grassroots activists in the movement was shaped as much by the pervasive threat of state-sanctioned violence as by the formal rights of citizenship they were seeking to enforce. The role of "first-class citizens," which activists undertook to secure the enforcement of their rights, may have felt to them as uncertain or aspirational as the civic roles embraced by undocumented immigrants.

I. Organizational Tactics: Adoption and Adaptation

A. Direct Action and Civil Disobedience

The civil rights movement deployed a range of direct action tactics, whose moral impetus and visual imagery became synonymous with the movement in the public mind. Boycotts brought coordinated economic pressure to bear on those who followed segregationist laws or practices.[5] Sit-ins violated Jim Crow laws, which protesters viewed as inconsistent with federal guarantees of equal protection.[6] Freedom riders exercised the federal right to integrated public accommodations in state contexts where that act of integration sparked violent resistance.[7] These actions made visible to the public that constitutional guarantees of equal protection and full citizenship were being flouted by Jim Crow laws and Southern resistance. Direct action tactics also highlighted the moral resolve of protesters and their willingness to endure hardship in order to communicate their message.[8]

But these tactics served an additional purpose: they exposed the regime of often-violent enforcement that held segregative practices in place.[9] The dogs and firehoses that Bull Connor loosed on student protesters in Birmingham and the angry mobs who attacked Freedom Riders as they debarked at interstate bus terminals set in motion several responses that were critical to movement strategy. These repressive responses often triggered court challenges, which enabled federal judges to articulate the federal guarantees applicable to African Americans.[10] Moreover, where state officials targeted protesters with violence, or failed to restrain the violent response of their citizens, protesters could demand—and occasionally received—federal intervention and protection.[11] Finally, and perhaps most importantly, confrontations between nonviolent protesters and violent state officials or citizens elicited broad media coverage, which could incite empathy, indignation, and outrage across broad swaths of the American public.[12] Campaigns targeting communities that combined Jim Crow laws with volatile law enforcement were particularly effective in influencing a legislative response.[13] The meetings, trainings in nonviolent protest, and mass arrests that surrounded direct action events also built deep solidarity among protesters.[14]

The immigrant justice movement has deployed many of these tactics with a full awareness of the expressive value of their legacy. Protests over the enactment of Arizona's S.B. 1070, the first in a spate of anti-immigrant state laws, utilized many of the direct action tactics that had helped civil rights activism to gain purchase. The enactment of the law was swiftly followed by the announcement of an economic boycott of the state, organized by coalition of immigrant groups and endorsed by Rep. Raul Grijalva, a proimmigrant member of Congress.[15] A cascade of protests, including a one-hundred-day vigil at the state capital, followed.[16] Protesters held sit-ins on public streets and at state and federal buildings; they occasionally blocked the vehicles of anti-immigrant Sherriff Joe Arpaio of Maricopa County. A group of undocu-mented activists boarded the Undocubus for an interstate journey to the 2012 Democratic National Convention (DNC).[17] However, the contexts in which movement activists utilized these tactics, and the ways in which they were executed, often diverged from those of the civil rights move-ment.

First, the appeal to the federal government implicit in these tactics was a more ambivalent undertaking. While the Obama administration ultimately challenged S.B. 1070 on the grounds that it was preempted by federal authority over immigration, a complex array of laws and programs, such as section 287(g) of the Immigration and National Act (287(g)) and Secure Communities, created partnerships between state and local officials and the federal government in the enforcement of immigration law. This meant the federal government was often directly implicated in the very patterns of enforcement to which protesters objected. Second, although direct action tactics have been similar, they have been directed toward different targets and have reflected different kinds of strategies. Because enforcement of federal immigration law rests substantially in the discretion of state and federal law enforcement agents, it is more difficult to stage a protest that targets a particular law, or captures its symbolism, in the way that the lunch counter sit-ins, for example, captured the quotidian yet corrosive character of segrega-tion. Early examples of direct action by immigrants were often staged to manifest generalized resistance, with protesters sitting on a banner in the middle of a busy street or in a courtyard in front of a state or federal building. More recently, activists have sought to target the oper-ation of immigration enforcement by chaining themselves to buses car-rying immigrants toward deportation or buildings where the detention or processing of those subject to deportation occurs.[18] Moreover, direct action tactics by immigrant groups have not predictably provoked the repressive response that sparked widespread publicity during the civil rights movement. Although a sea of cell phones has been raised to cap-ture each encounter between police and protesters,[19] there have been few incidents of brutality in the confrontation or arrests of those prac-ticing civil disobedience. This may be partly because law enforcement officials have learned the lessons of the civil rights protests. But it may be because officials have had a different weapon to wield against protesters, particularly as undocumented activists began to join in acts of protest and civil disobedience. The fact that undocumented activists taken into custody in connection with civil disobedience or other acts of protest could be subject to detention or deportation on the basis of their immigration status has introduced a new dynamic into direct action events. The fear of deportation and family separation is present for undocumented protesters, as the fear of violence had been for civil rights demonstrators. But it is a less visible fear, and when realized in the context of an "off-camera" administrative process, it has not subjected law enforcement to publicity or to comparably widespread moral judgment. Consequently, activists have been required to develop additional tactics to turn direct action protests to their strategic advantage.

One particularly powerful tactic was introduced by DREAMers, undocumented youth who were among the first undocumented activists to assume visible leadership in the larger immigrant justice movement. Beginning in 2010, as they mobilized for a federal law that would have granted a path to citizenship for childhood arrivals, DREAMers began to "come out" as "undocumented and unafraid."[20] This tactic drew inspiration from the self-disclosures that became paradigmatic for the LGBT movement as a vehicle for fighting isolation and generating both community and public awareness.[21] It also drew on the practices of self-narration common in feminist consciousness raising and in mass meetings of the civil rights movement.[22] This self-narration had several functions in immigrant activism. The first was raising consciousness and conveying information. The stories of undocumented activists communicated what it was like to be a person without legal status, thus conveying a reality that was starkly unfamiliar to most Americans. Young activists described surviving day to day without even the assurance provided by a legal presence that a family would not be deported or separated; they described the difficulties of trying to make a living or get an education any of the government-conferred benefits—from a social security number to in-state tuition or scholarships—that many with legal status take for granted.[23] But the stories of undocumented youth were not simply narratives of suffering. They were also stories about progress made in confronting and transcending these limitations, both through individual effort and through political solidarity. Finally, there was also a persuasive and performative dimension of "stories of self" that was directed at the larger public. Coming out as "undocumented and unafraid" reflected an almost Austenian performativity. Those who declared their fearlessness in coming "out of the shadows" may well have felt fear, yet they found energy, strength, and resolve in their own declarations, the parallel actions of others, and the responsive shouts of "undocumented and unafraid" that surrounded them as they exposed their identities, crossed borders, or chained themselves to public property. By speaking directly and candidly to the public and petitioning the government for redress of grievances, they were claiming the role of citizens—a role that felt both earned and precarious.[24] They were also enacting, in salient respects, the political reality to which they aspired: a political world in which they could engage, as members, over critical questions of national policy. But because undocumented immigrants did not yet enjoy, as a matter of formal law, the role that they were claiming, these disclosures had persuasive as well as performative value. They showcased DREAMers as participants with moral courage and political responsibility who were willing to take risks to win a role for which they were otherwise prepared, much as the willingness to endure violent attacks with nonviolent perseverance had distinguished civil rights protesters.

Whether activists were mobilizing for federal reforms or resisting oppressive state laws, practices of "coming out of the shadows" and "telling your story" had a flavor of civil disobedience. They made visible an ongoing violation of the law and exposed violators to potential consequences[25] in order to change the law. When these practices of self-disclosure[26] were combined with familiar forms of direct action, the combination made the risk-taking of undocumented activists visible and generated visibility for the movement. For example, in July 2012, during the federal civil rights trial of Sherriff Joe Arpaio, four undocumented Phoenix activists held a press conference announcing their status and sat down in the street in front of the federal court building, subjecting themselves to arrest.[27] Or, later that summer, several dozen undocumented activists rode the Undocubus across several states that had enacted or considered anti-immigrant legislation, en route to the in the Democratic National Convention in Charlotte, North Carolina.[28] These protests used tactics popularized by the civil rights movement: the sit-in, the freedom ride, the confrontation at the Democratic National Convention. But in each case, protesters used a new and innovative tactic—self-disclosure and self-narration by undocumented activists—to attain the visibility and mount the kind of moral claim that civil rights protesters had achieved by exposing themselves to state-sponsored violence.

B. Voter Registration and Civic Engagement

As a movement of citizens who were, for all practical purposes, disenfranchised, the civil rights movement embraced twin imperatives.

First, it sought to enable African Americans to exercise their right to vote, which would signal the advent of "first-class citizenship" and would be integral in securing future legislative reforms. Second, because that right, and any future reforms, would likely require legislative action for its vindication, the movement sought to elicit the political mobilization of those who were already able to exercise the franchise—namely, sympathetic whites. The vote was sometimes the object of direct action campaigns, such as the Southern Christian Leadership Conference's (SCLC) efforts in Selma in 1964,[29] but it was also the focus of a second kind of campaign. In the counties of the Deep South, activists from groups like the Student Nonviolent Coordinating Committee (SNCC) sought to persuade black residents to register to vote. This was no modest undertaking. Blacks who attempted to register suffered economic retaliation and physical violence from employers, neighbors, and state actors.[30] Yet organizers sought to highlight voter participation as a vehicle for full citizenship and to impart to participants the knowledge and civic responsibility that would sustain it. For example, in SNCC's "Mississippi Project," organizers not only sought to facilitate black voter registration but also provided registrants and residents of local communities with the experience of electoral participation through the Mississippi Freedom Democratic Party (MFDP).[31] The MFDP conducted its own primaries and conventions for local African American participants, giving those who had not previously participated direct experience of the electoral process. The project also enabled some MFDP activists to communicate their experience and commitment to a dubious white public as a result of claiming their right to be seated at the 1964 Democratic National Convention. Another innovation of the Mississippi Project (sometimes referred to as "Freedom Summer") was to bring hundreds of elite, white college students to work with local organizers in rural Mississippi.[32] The role of whites in promoting registration in Mississippi, which built on years of organizing by SNCC activists, was more than an injection of relief troops in a sharply embattled region. The dangers to which both black and white activists were exposed—captured chillingly by the murders of organizers Goodman, Cheney, and Schwerner in the summer of 1964—made the meaning of massive resistance, and of second-class citizenship, stunningly concrete to the students and their well-connected parents. Their concrete understanding of the ways that racial hierarchy was maintained by state-supported violence prompted demands for protective federal intervention in Mississippi and created a body of influential allies for the movement as a whole.[33]

Civic engagement has also played a large role in the movement for immigrant rights, but it has been structured by a different set of dynamics. Undocumented immigrants face a barrier to the franchise that is different from the registrars and sheriffs of Mississippi. With no legal status (and for most no legal presence), undocumented immigrants cannot assert even a formal right to the franchise. Legislative reform providing some path to citizenship is necessary before such a claim can be made. To enlist support for such legislation, immigrant activists, like their civil rights counterparts, have been required to mobilize voters beyond the group who stands directly to benefit. The immigrant rights movement, however, can draw on a group of Latino voters that is more proximate than the general population of whites and far larger than the group of "Freedom Summer" parents whose familial connection to segregationist violence spurred their political participation. Many Latino voters have firsthand exposure to the struggles of undocumented family members, friends, and neighbors or have experienced their own fear of family separation. The challenge, however, has been to reach and mobilize a group of voters who have not historically turned out in high numbers[34] and help them make the connection between the changes they want to see, and their own electoral participation.

A pivotal innovation in this effort has been the recruitment of undocumented youth to register and mobilize Latino voters. A series of civic engagement campaigns in Arizona demonstrate the potential of this practice. Undocumented youth have been volunteering in civil engagement campaigns in Arizona since at least 2011 when Randy Parraz and Citizens for a Better Arizona mounted a recall campaign against Russell Pearce, the legislative sponsor of S.B. 1070.[35] Youthful volunteers signed on to challenge a politician who had exposed their communities to fear, surveillance, and harassment. Both those who had already been active in politics, such as members of the Arizona Dream Act Coalition and those who were entirely new to organizing, came out for the effort to register voters. When voters seemed reluctant about registering or doubted that their vote could make a difference, undocumented volunteers engaged them by narrating their own experience under S.B. 1070, arguing that if they could make a difference when they could not even cast a ballot, surely a registered voter could make a contribution to bringing about change.[36] This tactic was given a powerful boost when Pearce was defeated by an unlikely combination of Latino voters, moderate business interests, and concerned Mormons. Both Latino voters and undocumented volunteers saw that they could make a difference in the direction of state politics.[37] Perhaps the most striking example of this approach occurred in the summer and fall of 2012, when a coalition between a proimmigrant civic engagement organization and a local union recruited more than two thousand teenage volunteers and organizers, many of them undocumented, to register voters for the November 2012 election. Calling their campaign "Adios Arpaio," the activists used the reelection campaign of the sheriff of Maricopa County as a hook for registering and motivating Latino voters.[38] Through a systematic training process supported by nationwide organizations such as the Center for Community Change, young activists learned to share their stories of racial profiling and family separation perpetuated by Arpaio's forces and to engage creatively with apathetic or reluctant voters. A DREAM Act organization supplemented their efforts with the "I am a DREAM Voter" campaign, in which DREAMers asked registered voters to cast their ballots on in support of pro-DREAMer candidates and policies. Although Arpaio was reelected, his margin was very narrow, and the campaigns registered tens of thousands of new Latino voters in the greater Phoenix area.[39]

The civic engagement campaigns reflected another dimension of the performative strategy of the immigrant rights movement. The volunteers who canvassed in Arizona's civic engagement campaigns became deeply involved not only with the principal goal of replacing particular elected officials but also with the mechanics of the vote, the issues facing particular neighborhoods, and the concept of political accountability.[40] In many cases they taught citizens either about the substantive issues or about filling out a ballot. Placing undocumented youth in an integral facilitative role in relation to one of the most central rights of citizenship created a new political reality just as the meetings, caucuses, and elections of the MFDP created a new political reality in which mainstream participants could see the knowledge and commitment of the new participants differently. Yet, if anything, the inauguration of new political relations—the improbable claiming of the "space of citizenship"—was even more striking in the case of young immigrants. Theirs was not a parallel process: they were integrally involved with citizens in their registration to vote and the casting of their ballots. And the young people who performed this role were not American citizens brutally deprived of their voting rights but residents with no legal status and, in some cases, no legal right to be present. Both the efficacy and the transformative symbolism of this strategy were such that it was perhaps no surprise that the Arizona legislature soon began to enact legislation regulating the roles of volunteers in the early balloting process.

II. Rights Consciousness, Emergent Rights, and Performative Rights Assertion

Thus far the civil rights movement and the immigrant justice movement have been considered as constellations of actors on the public stage. This lens reveals that the discourse, the strategies, and the specific tactical repertoires of the civil rights movement have become symbols and templates for the immigrant justice movement and for many other movements. This perspective also highlights the ways that immigrant activists have revised these strategies and tactics to encompass new practices. These practices of self-narration and multifaceted civic engagement are performative along several dimensions. First, they enable immigrants to reject the fear and the resulting posture of hiding that governmental officials have sought to impose on them through anti-immigrant legislation and enforcement efforts. Second, these tactics have enabled undocumented activists to "claim the space of citizenship" while simultaneously developing and manifesting the skills and attributes that serve to unsettle public understanding of undocumented immigrants and their belonging. Finally, these performances create an outside—a public impression—that emanates more from desire and imagination than from legal foundation or subjective self-conception. In concrete and socially transformative ways, immigrants undertake the tasks of a citizenship they have not yet been granted and manifest a confidence and self-possession that may belie a far more ambivalent set of feelings and expectations. These performative dimensions of the recent immigrant mobilization might seem to distinguish it from a civil rights activism that was grounded in the guarantees of the Civil War Amendments and sought to make good on their incomplete promise through federal legislation and enforcement.

But the literature of social movements suggests another way to look at these two efforts: not as movements engaging with legal institutions in carefully choreographed repertoires but as situated groups of individual actors, asserting or negotiating rights claims. From this perspective, the question is how actors in these two movements think about their rights, or how they see their relation to the polity as they go about their day-to-day work. Viewed in this way, taking the individual activist and his or her legal or rights consciousness as the focus,[41] the difference between the movements is not as stark as one might initially suspect. For many grassroots participants in the civil rights movement, the formal rights to citizenship and to equal protection that were conferred on African Americans by the Civil War Amendments were less constitutive of their sense of rights and of belonging than the regimes of social and institutional exclusion, economic retaliation, and public-private violence that structured their daily existence. In pivotal contexts such as movement organizing in Mississippi, the self-assertion of African American activists had aspects of performativity that, in some respects, resemble those of the immigrant justice movement.

A. Rights Consciousness and Emergent Rights among Immigrant Activists

As noncitizens who lack a legal status and, in most cases, a legal right to be present, immigrant activists do not instinctively regard their "rights" as formal claims that can be directed to courts or enforced by legislatures.[42] The experience of mobilizing without legal status, and indeed the experience of navigating American society without many formal rights, has engendered in many immigrant activists an attitude of improvisatory self-reliance. They view progress as more likely to arise from their own organizing than from the declarations of the courts.[43] Consequently, groups often operate orthogonally to formal occasions of rights declaration.[44] Immigrant activists have used major court dates as opportunities for rallying, marching, or direct action—for reminding public officials that "we are still here and we are watching."[45] Activists across the country marched on the day that the Supreme Court heard argument in *Arizona v. United States*.[46] Activists in Arizona held a press conference and engaged in civil disobedience on the day that Sherriff Joe Arpaio testified before the district court in *Melendres v. Arpaio*.[47] Participants also seem to understand their activism as working parallel to formal adjudicative processes. For example, activists sometimes say that the *Melendres* decision simply confirmed what they knew about Joe Arpaio when they sat down in front of his trucks or conducted the "Adios Arpaio" campaign.[48]

One primary way in which undocumented activists seem to understand their own rights, however, is as claims to be negotiated or extended through assertion in encounters with law enforcement officials. One starting point for this assertion of rights is the "Know Your Rights" sessions that have been held throughout Arizona and other states, often sponsored by legal organizations such as the ACLU in conjunction with local proimmigrant organizations. These forums have been frequent and well-attended events that have served as both a basis for organizing and a vehicle for preventing panic in the face of legislation like S.B. 1070.[49] They advise members of the community about what they should do in preparation for a stop, detention, or deportation. The range of rights that undocumented immigrants can assert in encounters with state law enforcement officials or with agents of Immigration and Customs Enforcement (ICE) is, in a formal sense, limited.[50] For example, they can decline to tell law enforcement officials where they are from (though this information may become available if they are ultimately held and fingerprinted). They can ask for a lawyer if they are detained. They can create an advance directive specifying who will be responsible for their children (or pets or property) if they are deported. None of these rights, however, will predictably prevent detention or deportation. Yet some immigrant activists report that knowing about these rights can make a difference in the way they engage law enforcement if they are actually stopped and the way they live their daily lives.[51] This greater confidence is an advantage to the movement because it may prevent daunted immigrants from returning to their countries of origin in the face of restrictive state legislation. Some report that simply having made arrangements for the care of their children gives them greater peace of mind as they travel from home to work and back.[52] Others say that they feel less panic when they are stopped, and they are less likely to make costly errors. One young woman explained that this kind of preparation helped her assert her rights over a thirty-six-hour period of detention. She noted, moreover, that the calm and persistent way that she responded when questioned helped persuade Immigration and Customs (ICE) officials that she was "a good person"—the kind of person who should be released rather than deported even though officials ultimately understood that she was in the United States without authorization.[53]

This example points to a peculiar feature of immigration enforcement, particularly in a period of legislative stalemate, in which many important decisions related to detention and deportation rest on a broad and differentially applied set of enforcement priorities. In the gray area of intersection between immigration law and discretionary enforcement priorities such as those contained in the Morton memorandum,[54] one's de facto "right" to remain—which is not a formal legal right but an experientially grounded judgment about the acts for which, or circumstances under which, one will *not* be deported—may ultimately be established or extended by tendentious efforts to push the envelope. One young man, a naturalized citizen who had been active in the early formation of Arizona's DREAM Act movement, described his disbelief when he heard that the first DREAMers had identified themselves publicly as undocumented. "My God, I thought, those kids are going to be deported. But then they were not. And soon others joined them," making similar self-disclosures.[55] Had those initial DREAMers not disclosed their status, the entire community might still believe that their self-identification would trigger deportation. After their action, many began to believe that it might not—at least not predictably—do so. Hundreds of DREAMers began to live their lives and conduct their politics differently as a result.[56] This assertion of emergent rights[57] was performative in the sense that it reflected neither a foundation in established law nor a grounding in the subjective expectations of the participants, who likely also assessed the risk of deportation as great. Perhaps more important, this act was performative in the sense that activists' willingness to suffer the consequences of a previously untested form of political conduct helped establish this form of engagement as a plausible strategy—a lower-risk activity than had previously been believed. Because activists' legal status has not changed, these acts of self-assertion continue to occupy a gray area of hazard. Although the DREAMers themselves may not be deported for coming out as "undocumented and unafraid," there are cases in which their family members have been detained or have come close to deportation in the wake of this form of activism.[58] But, due in large part to this purposeful pressing of the envelope, the scope of the de facto "right to remain" has expanded a bit.

Activists explain the resolve that has animated these risk-taking acts in many ways.[59] Some point to a feeling of necessity—that is, they must attempt to press boundaries because there is no other choice. "When your back is to the wall, you come out swinging" is a phrase that emerges regularly among Arizona activists. Another kind of explanation that reflects some tension with the preceding explanation is that undocumented youth often feel like they belong to American society. "We are citizens without the papers," activists frequently say.[60] A sense of authorization may also come from a subset of families who approach being undocumented matter-of-factly and teach their children that it should not be a barrier to their aspirations.[61] A feeling of authorization may also be generated through solidaristic activity within the movement through which activists learn that "it doesn't have to be this way: we can empower ourselves to make a change"[62] or that "the safest place for anyone targeted by these laws is out, proud, and part of an organized community."[63] But performative assertion of emergent rights—asserting oneself and/or one's right to remain in a negotiation with a state or federal official acting in a gray area of enforcement discretion—may have value in establishing new boundaries for the activity of undocumented immigrants.

B. Emergent Rights and Performative Citizenship in the Civil Rights Movement

One might expect this pattern of rights-consciousness and rights-assertion to distinguish the immigrant justice movement from the civil rights movement, which is grounded on a conception of rights as legally established entitlements. No less a document than the Constitution declares the rights of former slaves and their descendants to citizenship and to the nondiscriminatory exercise of the right to the vote. These rights faced adamant resistance; they required articulation by the courts and enforcement by the elected branches, neither of which was a foregone conclusion as the civil rights movement waged its early campaigns. But the specific rights asserted by the movement had a basis in written law. Moreover, as citizens and as federal rights holders, African Americans assumed a plausible role when they petitioned their government for the redress of their grievances.[64] The notion of rights as formal constitutional guarantees, which had only to be enforced by the federal government against state and local resistance, was central to the discourse of the movement. As Martin Luther King Jr. told a mass meeting at the beginning of the Montgomery Bus Boycott, "We are not wrong...[and] if we are wrong, the Supreme Court is wrong, and if we are wrong, the Constitution is wrong."[65]

But if we move from the public discourse and group-based tactics of the movement to the self-understandings of participants doing the work of the movement on a daily basis, a different picture emerges. For the mother sending her child to the first integrated school in her city or the Mississippi sharecropper mustering the courage to register to vote, for countless movement participants facing administrative intransigence, employer retaliation, and the ever-present threat of state-sanctioned violence, rights were never simply constitutionally established objects of federal enforcement.[66] In individual and family conversations and in mass meetings at black churches, participants had to persuade themselves and each other that they could claim the role of citizens, a role that was as much a product of their persistent, if uneasy, self-assertion as of the declarations of federal courts.

This dimension of the civil rights struggle can be glimpsed, for example, in Francesca Polletta's analysis of rights consciousness among SNCC activists in Mississippi from 1961 to 1966.[67] Studying the sharecroppers and domestic workers who risked their lives and livelihoods to register to vote, Polletta did not find actors who felt that their constitutionally established rights simply had to be vindicated by federal intervention and affirmation. She saw people whose daily lives drove home the lessons of their marginality and second-class citizenship, and whose struggle, as they put it, to achieve "first-class citizenship" was fraught with retaliation, harassment, and pervasive physical danger. These activists, Polletta explained, played an active role in unsuccessful lawsuits against registrars who denied their rights or sheriffs who beat them. They spent hours giving statements or testifying in court because they experienced a pride in being able to tell their stories. They gathered at the courthouse each day for the trials, fueled by a sense of wonder at witnessing efforts—however unsuccessful—to hold white men to account. In much the same way as immigrant activists in Arizona, these activists saw moments of adjudication as opportunities for community organizing, for relating their own experience, for bearing witness to the possibilities of an ongoing struggle rather than simply as occasions of rights declaration.

Civil rights organizing in Mississippi was also characterized by moments of improvisatory rights assertion, which sometimes provided activists with greater room to maneuver. Neither the groups of prospective voters who presented themselves to registrars in rural Greenwood County, nor the African American organizers who made a practice of attending the white movie theater every Wednesday, nor the registrants who defended themselves with words or the occasional shotgun against neighbors or officials who came to intimidate them, knew what awaited them in these encounters.[68] As the courage of these actors became contagious in a county or a region, the tide of violent enforcement would sometimes recede a little.

While participants may have drawn the courage for these moments of rights assertion from the knowledge of their formal constitutional rights, scholars of movement organizing point to other sources with greater parallels to the experience of undocumented students. Some of those in the movement drew their strength from the instruction and support of family. Charles Payne quotes one Mississippi organizer: "I think somehow you've always had families who were not afraid...they just talked to their immediate family and let them know, you know 'You're somebody. You can't express it right now but you keep this in mind. You're just as much as anybody, you keep it in mind.' And then when the time for this came, we produced."[69]

Also crucial in fueling this impetus were mass meetings, often held in local black churches.[70] At these meetings, participants were exhorted by leader-organizers like Fanny Lou Hamer or Aaron Henry.[71] They sang together[72] and they narrated to each other the burdens and dangers of trying to comport themselves like "first-class citizens" by surmounting the many perils of registering to vote.[73] By sharing and witnessing each other's stories they began to earn the status of first-class citizens in each other's eyes, if not yet in the eyes of the law.[74] This attainment enabled them to push forward, much like the DREAMers who have celebrated each other's "stories of self," both in public and in smaller, organizational settings. Participants in Mississippi organizing campaigns had formal citizenship, but their daily lives were a constant reminder of its unaccomplished status. Their rights were emergent[75] and their participation as citizens—though constitutionally warranted—was, in important ways, performative. It inaugurated a new political reality in which African Americans in the rural South emerged from the constraints imposed by threats and fear to be participants in public life, and it created a powerful external impression that fueled rather than reflected a subjective sense of entitlement. Their "first-class citizenship"—like the undocumented immigrants' de facto right to remain—was always in the process of being forged by activists' often excruciating efforts.

III. Conclusion

When immigrant justice activists employ the tactical forms or the broad equal opportunity frames of the civil rights movement, this may in fact be part of their performative strategy. They embrace the paradigmatic example of citizens vindicating their rights in the face of brutal opposition and uncertain enforcement as yet another way of modeling the citizenship that they hope to attain. Perhaps the recapitulation of the tactics or frames of the civil rights movement in a more pointedly performative register is the ultimate example of creative adaptation. It demonstrates that the conceptual and tactical vocabulary developed to claim the full measure of citizenship can also be deployed by those who lack even its formal guarantees. But immigrant justice activists may also glimpse something about the civil rights movement that much of the public (and many legal scholars) has tended to miss—namely, that for African Americans fighting for civil rights, their recognition was never a *fait accompli*. Their first-class citizenship was always at stake, something that had to be contended for every day.[76] These parallels suggest an insight that may be applicable not only to the civil rights movement but to many movements for inclusion through law. Even as we most firmly assert our claims to belonging, we are performing, with a fragile mix of hope and insistence, our entitlement to exercise them.

About the Author

Herma Hill Kay Distinguished Professor of Law, UC-Berkeley School of Law. This chapter draws not only on the secondary literatures I cite but on my own ongoing empirical study of the immigrant justice movement in the state of Arizona. The Arizona Immigrant Justice Project (Kathryn Abrams, P.I.) draws on interview data and ethnographic observation of proimmigrant organizations in Phoenix and Tucson to answer questions about the mobilization, legal consciousness, and emotion management of immigrant activists—particularly those who are undocumented—during a period bracketed by the enactment of S.B. 1070 (2010) and the congressional debate over comprehensive immigration reform (2013–14). (Interview data and other relevant materials on file with author.) I want to thank colleagues in the UC-Berkeley Immigration, Framing, and Rights Workshop for helpful comments on an early draft of this chapter and colleagues in the UC-Berkeley Law and Humanities Workshop and Center for the Study of Law and Society for lively discussions of some of the ideas elaborated here.

Notes

1. Martin Luther King, Jr. used this phrase in a number of speeches. When he first published it in a 1958 article in *The Gospel Messenger*, Dr. King placed the expression in quotes, indicating his belief that the phrase was in circulation at the time he used it. See Martin Luther King, *Out of the Long Night*, GOSPEL MESSENGER, February 8, 1958, p. 3, p. 14 col 1, https://archive.org/stream/gospelmessengerv107mors#page/n177/mode/2up. A similar phrase is attributed to the American Transcendentalist and abolitionist, Theodore Parker, who said, "I do not pretend to understand the moral universe, the arc is a long one and my eye reaches but little ways...But from what I see I am sure it bends towards justice." See http://quoteinvestigator.com/2012/11/15/arc-of-universe/.

2. Doug McAdam, *"Initiator" and "Spinoff" Movements: Diffusion Processes in Protest Cycles*, in REPERTOIRES AND CYCLES OF COLLECTIVE ACTION 217, 236 (Mark Traugott ed., 1995).

3. The term that those activists in the movement use to refer to themselves is still a work in progress. Some activists, particularly those fighting for federal reform, use the term "immigrant rights movement" perhaps as part of the effort to underscore similarities to the civil rights movement and to emphasize the aspiration to formal rights for immigrants, such as those reflected in S. 744's path to citizenship. In Arizona, activists refer to their struggle with the term "immigrant justice movement." (They may also describe their work less globally and more specifically as "advocating for the community" or "fighting deportations.") The term "immigrant justice" may reflect the fact that resistance to legislation such as Arizona's anti-immigrant law S.B. 1070 may be more a matter of justice than of presently enforceable rights: there are not many rights that an undocumented immigrant can assert in the face of an official demand to show his or her papers. Perhaps more to the point, this term seems intended to emphasize the moral imperative behind the movement. There is value in both

terms—the latter for its moral impetus, the former for its performative self-assertion (participants in the civil rights movement, one might argue, could point to a range of formal rights whose recognition and enforcement comprised the goals of their movement). Both terms, as appropriate, will be used in this chapter.

4.   The term "performative," which has attained broad theoretical usage in the last two decades, is subject to different kinds of understandings or interpretations. In this chapter, I will have recourse to three distinct though sometimes interrelated understandings. The first draws on J. L. AUSTIN, HOW TO DO THINGS WITH WORDS (1962). Austin distinguishes "performative utterances" from "constative utterances," the latter of which purport to describe or report on phenomena in the world and may be true or false. *Id.* at 1. Performative utterances "do not 'describe' or 'report' or constate any thing at all...[and] the uttering of a sentence is, or is part of, the doing of an action." *Id.* at 5. Paradigmatic examples include saying "I take this woman to be my wife" in the context of a wedding ceremony or "I name this ship the Queen Elizabeth" while smashing a bottle across the stern. Austin clarifies that the uttering of the words is not "the *sole* thing necessary if the act is deemed to have been performed...it is always necessary that the *circumstances* in which the words are uttered should be in some way, or ways, *appropriate*, and it is very commonly necessary that either the speaker himself or other persons should *also* perform certain *other* actions, whether 'physical' or 'mental' actions or even acts of uttering further words." *Id.* at 8. The second draws on the work of Judith Butler. Butler, who has written on this concept famously and extensively, contrasts an "expressive" understanding of gender, as a "core or identity...[that] is prior to the various acts postures and gestures by which it is dramatized and known" with a "performative" understanding of gender in which "these attributes [acts postures and gestures] effectively constitute the identity they are said to express or reveal." Judith Butler, *Performative Acts and Gender Constitution: An Essay in Phenomenology and Feminist Theory*, 40 THEATER J. 519, 527–28 (1988). This understanding may be viewed as having an Austenian resonance in the sense that those acts which might conventionally be understood to describe actually bring into being. Butler uses this understanding *inter alia* to challenge what she views as a pervasive notion of gender as an ontology, its external signs functioning as an expression of an internal essence. Through her contrasting notion of gender as "repeated acts within a highly rigid regulatory frame that congeal over time to produce...a natural sort of being," JUDITH BUTLER, GENDER TROUBLE: FEMINISM AND THE SUBVERSION OF IDENTITY 33 (1990), she suggests the ways that we intuitively make use of the social scripts and the materials through which gender is constructed in mainstream culture, and the possibility of using gender performance to disrupt those scripts. This understanding has certain parallels with the third notion of performativity, which draws on recent work on immigrant activism in particular by Cristina Beltrán. In her article *Going Public: Hannah Arendt, Immigrant Action, and the Space of Appearance*, 37 POL. THEORY 595 (2009), Beltrán uses the work of Hannah Arendt and Michael Warner to offer a provocative characterization of the proimmigrant marches of 2006. By appearing in the public domain to march in large numbers, undocumented immigrants constituted themselves as a Warnerian "counterpublic," forging a resistant collectivity and creating individual subjectivities that had not existed before. As Beltrán notes, "when subjects enter the public realm, they are not simply enacting their already-existing commitments. Instead, subjectivity is produced and transformed through these civic encounters." *Id.* at 616. In this way, the marchers of 2006 exercised what Arendt called the "power of beginnings": "the freedom to call something into

being, which did not exist before, which was not given, not even as an object of cognition or imagination, and which therefore, strictly speaking, could not be known." *Id.* at 601 (quoting Hannah Arendt, *What Is Freedom?*, in BETWEEN PAST AND FUTURE: EIGHT EXERCISES IN POLITICAL THOUGHT 151 (2006)). In evoking Arendt's performativity, Beltrán is not marking a contrast between a public performance and some ostensibly expressed interior state; rather, her vision is confluent with Butler's in its sense of the way a public performance creates conforming or resistant meaning through its iteration of familiar and unfamiliar elements. "By elaborating new citizenships, new privacies, and new critical languages," Beltrán argues, "this plurality of counterpublics challenged familiar scripts regarding the undocumented, unsettling traditional notions of sovereignty and blurring the boundaries between legal and illegal, assimilation and resistance, civic joy and public outrage." *Id.* at 598.

5. For an interesting history of the Montgomery Bus Boycott from a legal scholar's perspective, see Randall Kennedy, *Martin Luther King's Constitution: A Legal History of the Montgomery Bus Boycott*, 98 YALE L.J. 999 (1989) [hereinafter *MLK's Constitution*].

6. *See, e.g.*, Michael Walzer, *A Cup of Coffee and a Seat*, DISSENT, 112 (1960). For a discussion of the range of tactics employed by the civil rights movement, see Doug McAdam, *Tactical Innovation and the Pace of Insurgency*, 48 AM. SOC. REV. 735 (1983) [hereinafter *Tactical Innovation*].

7. For a comprehensive history of the 1961 Freedom Rides, see RAYMOND ARSENAULT, FREEDOM RIDERS: 1961 AND THE STRUGGLE FOR RACIAL JUSTICE (2006).

8. *See, e.g.*, *MLK's Constitution*, *supra* note 4, at 1023 (ability of African Americans in Montgomery to create alternatives to bus use during the boycott reflected "the extraordinary sense of political commitment that suffused and mobilized the black community"). *See also* Jeff Goodwin & Steven Pfaff, *Emotion Work in High-Risk Social Movements: Managing Fear in the U.S. and East German Civil Rights Movements*, in PASSIONATE POLITICS: EMOTIONS AND SOCIAL MOVEMENTS 282 (Jeff Goodwin et al. eds., 2001) (describing process through which protesters learned to manage the fears created by high-risk tactics in civil rights movement) [hereinafter *Emotion Work in High-Risk Social Movements*].

9. *See* Doug McAdam, *The Framing Function of Movement Tactics: Strategic Dramaturgy in the American Civil Rights Movement*, in COMPARATIVE PERSPECTIVES ON SOCIAL MOVEMENTS: POLITICAL OPPORTUNITIES, MOBILIZING STRUCTURES, AND CULTURAL FRAMINGS 338 (Doug McAdam et al. eds., 1996) [hereinafter *Strategic Dramaturgy*].

10. *See, e.g.*, *MLK's Constitution*, *supra* note 4, at 1001 (describing First Amendment decisions on rights of protesters that emanated from civil rights movement).

11. *See Tactical Innovation*, *supra* note 5, at 745 (1983) (quoting James Farmer, architect of the Freedom Rides, as saying the intention was "to provoke the Southern authorities into arresting us and thereby prod the Justice Department into enforcing the law of the land").

12. *See Strategic Dramaturgy*, *supra* note 8.

13. *Tactical Innovation*, *supra* note 5, at 748–50 (describing role of community-wide protest campaigns in Birmingham and Selma in passing civil rights legislation).

14. For vivid discussions of the sense of purpose, intimacy, and solidarity that emerged among movement participants, see CHARLES PAYNE, I'VE GOT THE LIGHT OF FREEDOM: THE ORGANIZING TRADITION AND THE MISSISSIPPI FREEDOM

STRUGGLE 236–64 (2007); DOUG MCADAM, FREEDOM SUMMER 66–115 (1988); *Emotion Work in High-Risk Social Movements*, *supra* note 7.

15.　*See* Randall C. Archibold, *In Wake of Immigration Law, Calls for an Economic Boycott of Arizona*, N.Y. TIMES, Apr. 26, 2010. *See also* Randall C. Archibold, *Phoenix Counts Big Boycott Cost*, N.Y. TIMES, May 11, 2010.

16.　Daniel González, *SB 1070 Protesters Hold Vigil, Pray Court Overturns Law*, AZCENTRAL.COM (June 21, 2012, 10:58 PM), http://www.azcentral.com/12news/ news/articles/2012/06/21/20120621sb-1070-protesters-hold-vigil-pray-court- overturns-law.html (describing vigil held at state capitol for 103 days, from the signing of S.B. 1070 to the decision of federal district court to enjoin several of its provisions, and subsequent vigil between Supreme Court argument and decision on constitutionality of S.B. 1070).

17.　Griselda Nevarez, *The Undocubus: DREAM Activists Arrive in Charlotte to Make Their Voices Heard at the Democratic National Convention*, HUFFINGTON POST (Sept. 3, 2012, 12:36 PM), http://www.huffingtonpost.com/2012/09/03/undocubus-dream- activists-democractic-convention_n_1852019.html. For an array of opinions on the politics of the Undocubus, see *Is Getting on the "UndocuBus" a Good Idea?*, THE OPINION PAGES: ROOM FOR DEBATE, NYTIMES.COM (Aug. 1, 2012), http://www.nytimes.com/roomfordebate/2012/08/01/is-getting-on-the- undocubus-a-good-idea. For the travelers' own blog relating the events and images of their journey, see *No Papers No Fear: Ride for Justice*, NOPAPERSNOFEAR.ORG (last visited Feb. 11, 2014).

18.　*DREAMers Switch to Civil Disobedience to Help Cause*, UPI.COM (Aug. 26, 2013, 3:09 PM), http://www.upi.com/Top_News/US/2013/08/26/Dreamers-switch-to-civil- disobedience-to-help-cause/UPI-95551377544151 (describing shift in strategy suggested by direct action protests at ICE building and immigration facility). Perhaps the most controversial direct-action protest to date has been the return of the DREAM 9, a group of undocumented activists who reentered the United States after either experiencing deportation or leaving to be reunited with family in Mexico. Although they were initially taken into custody at the border and detained, they were subsequently released and have cleared the initial, comparatively low hurdle (a "credible fear" screening) in their claims for asylum. Aura Bogado, *Undocumented Activists Take a Giant Risk to Return Home*, COLORLINES (July 23, 2013, 8:30 AM), http://colorlines.com/archives/2013/07/ Undocumented%20Activists%20Take-a-Giant-Risk-to-Return-Home.html. *See also* Julia Preston & Rebekah Zemansky, *Demonstration at Arizona Border Divides Supporters of Immigration Overhaul*, N.Y. TIMES, Aug. 4, 2013, *available at* http://www.nytimes.com/2013/08/05/us/demonstration-at-arizona-border- divides-supporters-of-immigration-overhaul.html?_r=0; David Leopold, *The Dream 9's Misguided Protest*, FOX NEWS LATINO (Aug. 9, 2013), http://latino.foxnews.com/latino/opinion/2013/08/09/david-leopold-dream-s- misguided-protest/#ixzz2dfw3ygPj.

19.　Conventional media sources also covered these protests and were tuned into potential sites of conflict. However, the use of cell phones to capture potential confrontations (which was vigorously encouraged both by activist groups and by allies such as the ACLU as protests unfolded) signaled the increasing contribution of movement-generated coverage and social media in communications strategies of the movement.

20.　*See* Dream Activist: Undocumented Students Action & Resource Network, *National Coming Out of the Shadows Week*, DREAMACTIVIST.ORG, http://webcache.googleusercontent.com/search?q=cache:http://www.

dreamactivist.org/comeout/. For sociological discussions of "coming out" in the DREAM Act movement, see WALTER J. NICHOLLS, THE DREAMERS: HOW THE UNDOCUMENTED YOUTH MOVEMENT TRANSFORMED THE IMMIGRANT RIGHTS DEBATE (2013); Hinda Seif, *"Unapologetic and Unafraid": Immigrant Youth Come Out from the Shadows, in* YOUTH CIVIC DEVELOPMENT: WORK AT THE CUTTING EDGE 59–75 (C. A. Flanagan & B. D. Christens eds., 2011).

21. For an analysis of the relation between LGBT and undocumented "comings out," see Rose Cuison Villazor, *Coming Out of the Undocumented Closet*, 92 N.C. L. REV. 1 (2013).

22. A public form of this kind of self-narration in the civil rights movement was Fanny Lou Hamer's statement to the Credentials Committee at the Democratic National Convention in 1964.

23. DREAMer narratives sometimes also had additional goals. They may have been aimed at dispelling stereotypes, such as those that circulated among supporters of anti-immigrant state legislation that undocumented immigrants were associated with Latin American drug cartels or had come to the United States to draw on public benefits. Some early DREAMer narratives also involved a claim that, because they had been brought to the United States as children, undocumented youth had violated immigration regulations through no fault of their own. This "no fault" strategy has more recently been criticized within the movement as divisive and hierarchizing and has been muted as undocumented youth have sought to make claims on behalf of the eleven million, and to explain and celebrate, rather than stigmatize, the sacrifices of their parents. *See* NICHOLLS, *supra* note 19, at 127–29.

24. Many undocumented immigrants, particularly those who have been in the United States since early childhood, express the feeling that they are "citizens in every way but the papers." Arizona Immigrant Justice Project, *supra* (interview transcripts and notes on file with author). On the other hand, they understand that this experience of familiarity and cultural belonging can be shattered at any moment by an encounter with a law enforcement official or the detention of a family member. This contradictory reality was captured vividly by the experience of Arizona DREAMer Erika Andiola, a cofounder of the Arizona Dream Act Coalition, and a highly visible and effective activist. Her home was raided by ICE agents on the evening of January 10, 2013, and her mother and older brother were taken into custody. Stephen Lemons, *DREAM Activist Erika Andiola Says Mom and Brother Taken into Custody by ICE*, PHOENIX NEW TIMES BLOGS (Jan. 11, 2013, 9:00 AM), http://blogs.phoenixnewtimes.com/bastard/2013/01/dream_activist_erika_andiola_s.php. Andiola made a video that was then circulated nationwide through social media in which she related her mother's and brother's detentions and sought help. Relating the circumstances of the ICE raid and her family members' arrests, Andiola wept and said, "I need everyone to stop pretending that nothing is wrong, stop pretending that we're just living normal lives, because this can happen to any of us any time." Carla Chavarria, *Erika Andiola's Family Separated*, YOUTUBE (Jan. 11, 2013), http://www.youtube.com/watch?v=FVZKfoXsMxk. The national outcry prompted by Andiola's video resulted in her mother's release, and the video petition has become a powerful tool in immigrant activists' arsenal for fighting detentions and deportations.

25. The risk to which an undocumented activist was exposed through such self-revelation depended, in part, on the context in which he or she made it. Sharing one's status or one's story at an organization meeting created less risk of consequences than sharing one's status at a public rally, which in turn was less

risky than sharing one's status at public rally at which one was about to be arrested for sitting down in a public thoroughfare. The varying consequences of self-disclosure permitted activists some ability to regulate the risk to which they were exposing themselves.

26. Over time, self-narration in the context of direct action enabled demonstrators who might not possess the familiar credentials of DREAMers to engage in similar performative, persuasive acts. They highlighted their civic courage and commitment by talking about their work or family—implicitly, the jobs they would imperil or the children who would have to be cared for by others—while they took the risk of coming out in the context of likely arrest.

27. *"No Papers, No Fear": As Arpaio Fights Arizona Suit, 4 Undocumented Immigrants Reveal Their Status*, DEMOCRACY NOW! (July 26, 2012), http://www.democracynow.org/2012/7/26/no_papers_no_fear_as_arpaio [hereinafter *"No Papers, No Fear"*].

28. The riders of the Undocubus did not seek to be seated at the DNC, but they staged a sit-down in protest of the Obama administration's record of deportation, during which ten protesters were arrested. The arrests were not violent and protesters were released the following day. However, this example of civil disobedience still entailed substantial risks given the undocumented status of all the arrested protesters, many of whom were not DACA-eligible (Deferred Action for Childhood Arrivals). *See* Elise Foley, *DNC Protest Leads to Arrest of 10 Undocumented Immigrants*, HUFFINGTON POST (Sept. 5, 2012, 2:50 PM), http://www.huffingtonpost.com/2012/09/05/dnc-protest-undocumented-immigrants_n_1858331.html?1346871007. Another focus for riders of the Undocubus was organizing with members of the undocumented communities in targeted cities and states along their route. This organizing was also fueled by events where undocumented activists publicly disclosed their statuses and subsequently exchanged stories with members of the communities they visited. For an evocative narrative of this experience, see Marco Flores, *Letter to My Mother*, NO PAPERS NO FEAR: RIDE FOR JUSTICE (Sept. 18, 2012), http://undocubus.org/blog/post.php?s=2012-09-18-letter-to-my-mother (from CULTURESTRIKE (Sept. 18, 2012), http://culturestrike.net/letter-to-my-mother).

29. *Tactical Innovation, supra* note 5, at 749–50 (describing community-wide protests at Selma as pivotal in the passage of the Voting Rights Act).

30. Francesca Polletta, *The Structural Context of Novel Rights Claims: Southern Civil Rights Organizing, 1961–1966*, 34 LAW & SOC'Y REV. 367, 384 (2000).

31. For two accounts of this campaign with contrasting foci, see DOUG MCADAM, FREEDOM SUMMER (1988) (focusing on the experience of white volunteers who went south for SNCC's Mississippi Project); Polletta, *supra* note 29 (focusing on the experience of rural African Americans taking part in SNCC's voter registration campaigns). *See also* DOUG MCADAM, POLITICAL PROCESS AND THE DEVELOPMENT OF BLACK INSURGENCY 1930–1970 (1982).

32. *See* DOUG MCADAM, FREEDOM SUMMER (1988); SALLY BELFRAGE, FREEDOM SUMMER (1965).

33. *See* DOUG MCADAM, FREEDOM SUMMER 157–60 (1988).

34. Mark Hugo Lopez & Ana Gonzalez-Barrera, *Inside the 2012 Latino Electorate*, PEW RESEARCH HISPANIC TRENDS PROJECT (June 3, 2013), http://www.pewhispanic.org/2013/06/03/inside-the-2012-latino-electorate/ (finding that despite record Latino turnout in absolute numbers, the rate of Latino turnout has lagged behind African Americans and whites in last two presidential elections).

35. Jeff Biggers, *Arizona Topples Senate President Russell Pearce, SB 1070 Immigration Law Architect, in Historic Recall Vote*, Huffington Post (Nov. 8, 2011, 11:02 PM), http://www.huffingtonpost.com/jeff-biggers/breaking-arizona-topples-_b_1083202.html (noting that Citizens for a Better Arizona registered 1,150 new voters in the district).

36. *See* Arizona Immigrant Justice Project, *supra* (interview transcripts and notes on file with author).

37. A similar approach applied in the 2011 city council elections resulted in a 500 percent increase in Latino registration in one city council district and the election of a proimmigrant, Latino council member, Daniel Valenzuela. *See* Monica Alonzo, *SB 1070 Fuels a Movement of New Voters*, Phoenix New Times, July 5, 2012, *available at* http://www.phoenixnewtimes.com/2012-07-05/news/sb-1070-fuels-a-movement-of-new-voters/2.

38. *See* Joe Bernick, *"Adios Arpaio" Campaign Heats Up in Arizona*, People's World (Oct. 1, 2012), http://peoplesworld.org/adios-arpaio-campaign-heats-up-in-arizona/?utm_medium=twitter&utm_source=twitterfeed. *See also* Alonzo, *supra* note 36. This campaign used the voter registration process to accomplish the kind of "political jujitsu" that civic rights activists achieved through direct-action confrontations with officials like Bull Connor—the more unreasonable, violent, or suppressive the official response, the more successful the activist effort. For a discussion of political jujitsu in the civil rights movement, see *Strategic Dramaturgy, supra* note 8.

39. Stephen Lemons, *Joe Arpaio Still Won, Arizona Vote Count Over*, Phoenix New Times Blogs (Nov. 21, 2012), http://blogs.phoenixnewtimes.com/bastard/2012/11/joe_arpaio_still_won_democrats.php (contrasting Arpaio's 6.02 point victory over main challenger Paul Penzone, and 1.4 percent margin of victory over all opposing candidates, with 13 point victory in previous election).

40. Arizona Immigrant Justice Project, *supra* (interview transcripts and notes on file with author).

41. For an excellent example of this focus in the sociolegal literature, see Leisy J. Abrego, *Legal Consciousness of Undocumented Latinos: Fear and Stigma as Barriers to Claims-Making for First- and 1.5-Generation Immigrants*, 45 Law & Soc'y Rev. 337 (2011).

42. There are obvious exceptions, such as when a state actor clearly violates some rights that those without formal legal status enjoy as "persons" under the U.S. Constitution. For example, when Governor Jan Brewer enacted an executive order stating that undocumented youth who had just received Deferred Action for Childhood Arrivals (DACA) were ineligible to obtain driver's licenses, the Arizona Dream Act Coalition sued the governor in federal court. *Arizona Dream Act Coalition et. al* [sic] *v. Brewer*, ACLU (Sept. 18, 2013), https://www.aclu.org/immigrants-rights/arizona-dream-act-coalition-et-al-v-brewer (lawsuit claiming that Brewer's executive order violates supremacy clause and equal protection clause of Fourteenth Amendment).

43. Carlos Garcia, *Arizona, Arpaio and SB1070 Spur Crusade for Immigrant Rights*, Politic 365 (June 20, 2012, 5:46 AM), http://politic365.com/2012/06/20/arizona-arpaio-and-sb1070-spur-crusade-for-immigrant-rights. In a call to action framed around the Supreme Court's opinion in *Arizona v. United States*, Garcia, the head organizer of a leading immigrant justice organization in Phoenix, stated the following:

For more than a decade, we petitioned Congress for immigration reform only to be kicked around as a political football by both parties. We hoped things would change with President Obama but instead of feeling our pain, he caused more of it. Instead of executive action to grant us relief, he gave us record deportations and unprecedented quotas. When all else failed, we looked at the courts but even they seem ready to deny us our humanity...migrant communities have responded by losing our fear and peacefully defending ourselves. By learning our rights and more importantly, how to defend them when law enforcement tries to ignore them, we have created networks of protection that are prepared for the raids and the wrongful arrests.

Id.

44.   Enabling the exercise of rights by Latino citizens and other allies may be another way that undocumented activists work indirectly in relation to rights. Activists involved in the civic engagement campaigns discussed previously may draw satisfaction and experience civic investment by enabling (while not being able to exercise) the franchise. "I may not be able to vote," one volunteer explained, "but I can empower other people to vote." Arizona Immigrant Justice Project, *supra* (interview transcripts and notes on file with author).

45.   Arizona Immigrant Justice Project, *supra* (interview transcripts and notes on file with author).

46.   *Cities across Country to Protest SB1070, Call for Federal Action to Reject "Arizonification" as Supreme Court Hears SB1070 DOJ Case in Washington*, NDLON: NATIONAL DAY LABORER ORGANIZING NETWORK (April 23, 2012, 1:30 PM), http://www.ndlon.org/en/pressroom/press-releases/item/479-sb1070-2012-marches.

47.   *"No Papers, No Fear," supra* note 26.

48.   Arizona Immigrant Justice Project, *supra* (interview transcripts and notes on file with author). *See also "No Papers, No Fear," supra* note 26 (organizer Carlos Garcia observing of DOJ lawsuit against Arpaio,"[t]his just means more evidence of the things we've known for the last four years").

49.   Arizona Immigrant Justice Project, *supra* (interview transcripts and notes on file with author).

50.   ACLU of Arizona makes available a small, portable card that describes the rights immigrants have when they are stopped by a law enforcement agent and provides advice for managing the encounter. The rights enumerated include a right to remain silent, a right to deny consent to search beyond a manual "pat-down," a right to leave if you are not under arrest, and a right to a lawyer if you are under arrest. *See What to Do If You're Stopped by Police, Immigration Agents or the FBI*, ACLU.ORG (June 2010), http://www.acluaz.org/sites/default/files/documents/bustcard_eng_20100630.pdf.

51.   Arizona Immigrant Justice Project, *supra* (interview transcripts and notes on file with author).

52.   *Id.*

53.   *Id.* Another example of this kind of self-assertion yielding results was a story told by an Arizona DREAMer in a recent op-ed. Daniel Rodriguez, *Dear Governor: I'm Legal, So Why Can't I Legally Drive Yet?*, AZCENTRAL.COM (Feb. 22, 2013), http://www.azcentral.com/opinions/articles/20130214rodriguez-dear-governor-im-legal-why-cant-legally-drive-yet.html. Soon after receiving his DACA, he was stopped by a local law enforcement agent as he drove across Phoenix. This was one encounter in which displaying his new work permit, which he did, was unlikely to be availing, as DACA-mented Arizonans are prohibited by state

executive order from getting drivers' licenses. He explained to the officer the purpose of his trip—namely, he was going to a scholarship luncheon "with a bunch of lawyers." *Id.* The officer, who could have cited him for driving without a license at minimum, "basically let [him] go." *Id.* While both of these examples represent forms of "envelope-pushing" that draw in various ways on the distinctive (and arguably more privileged) profile of the paradigmatic DREAMer, they nonetheless illustrate the potential value of the performative assertion of emergent rights.

54.   Memorandum from John Morton, Dir., U.S. Immigration & Customs Enforcement, to All Field Office Dirs., All Special Agents in Charge, & All Chief Counsel, *Exercising Prosecutorial Discretion Consistent with the Civil Immigration Enforcement Priorities of the Agency for the Apprehension, Detention, and Removal of Aliens,* ICE.GOV (June 17, 2011), http://www.ice.gov/doclib/secure-communities/pdf/prosecutorial-discretion-memo.pdf. The memorandum identifies a range of factors that enforcement agents should take into account when deciding whether to exercise discretion to apprehend, remove, or detain undocumented immigrants. Among those which militate in favor of apprehension, detention, and removal are commission of serious felonies, repeat offenses, unlawful reentry into the United States, gang membership, and clear risks to national security. Among those which militate against such enforcement are military service, presence in United States since childhood, victimization through domestic violence or trafficking, and being a minor or an elderly person. *Id.*

55.   Arizona Immigrant Justice Project, *supra* (interview transcripts and notes on file with author).

56.   Similarly, before the DREAM 9 asserted their right to reenter the United States after deportation or voluntary departure to join family members, no one knew that they would be permitted, even temporarily, to do so; some immigration experts had expressed the view that Mexican nationals were unlikely to be granted the opportunity to make out claims for asylum. *Cf.* Jason Dzubow, *Mexican Asylum Seekers Need Not Apply,* THE ASYLUMIST (Nov. 13, 2013), http://www.asylumist.com/2013/11/13/mexican-asylum-seekers-need-not-apply (examining reasons that the rate of Mexican asylum claims granted is disproportionately low when violence in Mexico is high).

57.   The term "emergent rights" is used to designate rights that activists are contending for but have not been formally recognized or enforced by governmental actors. These might be formal rights that have not been enforced, such as the voting rights of African Americans prior to the enactment of the Voting Rights Act of 1965, or they might be de facto rights that emerge in a discretionary zone of enforcement, such as the de facto right to remain that may be enjoyed by undocumented immigrants when enforcement officials decline to detain or deport them under particular circumstances. The point made about "emergent" rights is that when protesters assert these rights by registering to vote or coming out as undocumented in public settings, their acts are more performative (aimed at inaugurating a new political reality or bringing such rights into being) than descriptive of a set of entitlements that have been enforced or an expectation about governmental recognition of such rights.

58.   The family of undocumented student activist Tam Tran was taken into custody only days after she testified before Congress in support of the DREAM Act. (After Tran mobilized the intervention of Representative Zoe Lofgren of California, they were released.). *See* Emma Stickgold, *Tam Tran, Brown Student, Fought for Immigrant Rights,* BOS. GLOBE, May 17, 2010. Erika Andiola also questioned

whether the arrest and detention of her family members was related to her activism, particularly after her brother reported that an ICE agent had said to him, "[W]e know about your sister, we know what she does, and you need to stay away from that." Lemons, *supra* note 23.

59.   What feelings, experiences, or self-conceptions give rise to these forms of political self-assertion among undocumented activists is one of the central research questions of the Arizona Immigrant Justice Project, *supra*. Because the empirical research that forms the basis of the project is not yet complete, only a survey of some of the answers that have emerged most prominently from the research thus far—in part to demonstrate their correspondence to some of the feelings, experiences, and self-conceptions articulated by participants in the civil rights movement—can be provided.

60.   Arizona Immigrant Justice Project, *supra* (interview transcripts and notes on file with author). This contradictory sense of belonging and precariousness seems to be a feature of the legal consciousness of undocumented youth. *See infra* at note 23 (footnote on Erika Andiola's mother's detention).

61.   Arizona Immigrant Justice Project, *supra* (interview transcripts and notes on file with author).

62.   *Id.*

63.   Carlos Garcia, *supra* note 42.

64.   The First Amendment, in fact, prohibits Congress from making any law that abridges "the right *of the people*...to petition the Government for a redress of grievances." U.S. CONST. amend. I (emphasis added). But while First Amendment rights in this context are guaranteed to "the people," members of the public may see petitioning for redress of grievances as an action more properly taken by citizens whose electoral relation to governmental actors gives them the power to hold the government accountable.

65.   The concluding sentence of this sequence, "If we are wrong, then God Almighty is wrong," suggests that there were rhetorical as well as strictly legal dimensions to this argument. Nonetheless, a view of the constitution as the ground of civil rights claims comes through in his statement. *See MLK's Constitution, supra* note 4, at 1000 (quoting speech by Martin Luther King Jr. at Holt Street Baptist Church, Montgomery, Alabama, December 5, 1955). Another example of this way of thinking about rights can be found in a recent statement by Justice Ruth Bader Ginsburg. As a litigator for the Women's Rights Project of the ACLU, she played a leading role in the movement for sex equality, briefing and arguing many of the landmark cases in the Supreme Court. This movement was premised on the same kind of immanent critique as the civil rights movement: the notion that the United States, a constitutional democracy based on equal opportunity, was obligated to extend that equality to a group which did not yet fully enjoy it—women. Asked about her role in bringing about constitutional change, Ginsburg replied, "I didn't change the equality principle; it was there from the start. *I was just an advocate for securing its full realization." The Take Away with John Hockenberry: Interview with Supreme Court Justice Ruth Bader Ginsburg* (KQED radio broadcast Sept. 16, 2013) (transcript available at http://www.thetakeaway.org/story/transcript-interview-justice-ruth-bader-ginsburg/) (emphasis added).

66.   *See, e.g.*, Polletta, *supra* note 29, at 384 ("The names of those who registered were published in the local paper [ostensibly to give others an opportunity to challenge their 'good character'], so black residents knew that once they made the trip to

the courthouse they would be fair game for reprisals. They were verbally harassed and often subjected to physical violence."").

67. *See id.* In this article, Polletta used archival and interview-based data from civil rights activists to assess the rights critique mounted by Peter Gabel and other critical legal studies scholars. Polletta offered this study to demonstrate that, far from being ineffectual, atomizing or limiting, rights talk could be powerfully connected to an imaginative reinvisioning of unequal structural conditions and to intragroup solidarity. But her interview data also demonstrate the emergent character of rights—even for those who could point to constitutional declarations of citizenship—and the performative strand of their activism.

68. PAYNE, *supra* note 13, at 207-64.

69. *Id.* at 207.

70. *Id.* at 256–64, 260–61 (mass meetings "created a context in which individuals created a public face for themselves, which they then had to try to live up to"); Polletta, *supra* note 29, at 390–91; *Emotion Work in High-Risk Social Movements, supra* note 8, at 288–93.

71. PAYNE, *supra* note 14, at 256–64.

72. *Id.* at 261–63; *Emotion Work in High-Risk Social Movements supra* note 7, at 291–93.

73. Polletta, *supra* note 29, *Emotion Work in High-Risk Social Movements, supra* note 7, at 290–91.

74. Polletta notes, "First-class citizenship was an identity in the making, something claimed now, rather than a means to an end. Such an identity required recognition, but recognition not necessarily from the state (which was outright hostile at the local level and unreliable at the national level). Instead, recognition of first-class citizenship came from kinfolk, congregation, community, and movement." *Id.* at 390.

75. The rights of both civil rights and immigrant rights activists were emergent in another sense as well. Their public performances of civic commitment, discussed previously, helped persuade Congress to enact the Civil Rights and Voting Rights Acts in the mid-1960s, and helped persuade the Senate, in 2013, to enact S. 744 (the comprehensive immigration reform legislation). In this chapter, however, references to performativity or the emergent character of rights refer to the more immediate effects of these performances in transforming participants' sense of their circumstances (undocumented students became, as a result of their political posture, less fearful), their role in the polity (as participants engaged with the electoral process), and their de facto rights or political horizons (members of both groups discovered by pushing the boundaries of the politically possible that they could engage publicly in ways that they might previously have assumed they could not).

76. Patricia Williams is one of the few legal scholars who has specifically taken this vantage point on the civil rights movement. In an early article in which she, like Polletta, sought to answer the critical legal studies critique of rights, she highlighted the performative character of black Americans' assertion of civil rights:

> To say that blacks never fully believed in rights is true; yet it is also true to say that blacks believed in them so much and so hard that we gave them life where there was none before. We held onto them, put the hope of them into our wombs, and mothered them—not just the notion of them. We nurtured rights and gave rights life...The making of something out of nothing took immense alchemical fire: the fusion

of a whole nation and the kindling of several generations. The illusion became real only for a very few of us; it is still elusive and illusory for most. But if it took this long to breathe life into a form whose shape had already been forged by society...imagine how long would be the struggle without even that sense of definition, without the power of that familiar vision.

Patricia J. Williams, *Alchemical Notes: Reconstructing Ideals from Deconstructed Rights*, 22 Harv. C.R.-C.L. L. Rev. 401, 430 (1987). In her understanding, the form of rights did for African Americans in the civil rights movement what the civil rights movement is now doing for immigrant activists: it gave them a template with a legitimating grounding in law that activists, by force of will and determination, could extend into uncharted areas. Williams may be able to access a perspective not available to many legal scholars because her approach, although not systematically empirical, draws—as does Polletta's—on the narratives and perspectives of actors engaging in the process of asserting and defending their rights.

2

Discriminatory Animus

Cary Franklin

In addition to barring employers from discriminating on the basis of race, sex, and a number of other protected categories, Title VII of the 1964 Civil Rights Act provided for the creation of a new federal agency, the Equal Employment Opportunity Commission.[1] The EEOC's powers were relatively limited in the years immediately after Title VII was enacted, and the political compromises necessary to secure the law's passage deprived the agency of any real enforcement authority.[2] From the very beginning, however, the EEOC had the power to collect data from employers regarding the number of women and racial and ethnic minorities in their workforce.[3] One of the first regulations the EEOC issued required large employers and government contractors to submit annual EEO-1 reports supplying this information to the agency.[4] The EEOC continues to require EEO-1 reports from employers to this day, meaning the agency now has data from nearly half a century documenting changes and fluctuations in the racial and gender composition of a substantial percentage of American workplaces.[5]

Sociologists Kevin Stainback and Donald Tomaskovic-Devey recently decided to analyze four decades of EEO-1 reports to determine what these reports could tell us about the successes and failures of the project of racial and gender integration inaugurated by Title VII.[6] They found that from the time Title VII went into effect until 1980, American workplaces were desegregating, sometimes significantly, in terms of both race and gender, due in no small part to the implementation and enforcement of antidiscrimination law.[7] At the start of the 1980s, however, progress began to stall—and it has not picked up since then.[8] In fact, over the past decade or two, numerous industries in the United States have begun to resegregate. Thus far in the twenty-first century, nearly a third of all industries have witnessed racial resegregation among white and black men;[9] racial resegregation among white and black women has been even more "disturbingly widespread."[10] Moreover, resegregation and exclusion have tended to rise with higher income opportunities[11]—a trend that has contributed to growing economic inequality and led Stainback and Tomaskovic-Devey to the rather dispiriting conclusion that "[t]he United States is no longer on a path to equal opportunity."[12] Put succinctly, the EEO-1 reports tell a story of early success and subsequent decline: Title VII got off to a promising start, but progress under the statute began to stall within two decades of its enactment and has not yet shown much sign of reviving.[13]

Stainback and Tomaskovic-Devey attribute the decline in Title VII's efficacy as a tool for desegregating American workplaces to the major political and policy changes that accompanied Ronald Reagan's ascendance to the White House.[14] They argue that white voters' exhaustion with, and frustration over, civil rights projects such as affirmative action, busing, and government aid to the poor helped contribute to Reagan's victory in the presidential election of 1980, and that the new administration's stance toward civil rights enforcement mirrored the attitudes of these constituents.[15] The policy implications of this new stance were immediately apparent in the sections of the federal government tasked with enforcing Title VII and other civil rights provisions. The Reagan administration reduced the budget of the Office of Federal Contract Compliance Programs (OFCCP)—the office within the Department of Labor charged with ensuring that federal contractors comply with the government's affirmative action and equal employment guarantees—so significantly that the OFCCP was forced to cut more than half its staff and drastically reduce the number of compliance reviews it conducted; this resulted, inter alia, in a 77 percent reduction in back pay awards between 1980 and 1982.[16] The scene at the EEOC was similar. In the first two years of the Reagan administration, the EEOC's budget was reduced by 10 percent, its staff was cut by 12 percent, and travel funds for EEOC investigations were eliminated.[17] The agency's new head, Clarence Thomas, declared himself "unalterably opposed to programs that force or even cajole people to hire a certain percentage of minorities"[18] and suggested that employment policies that have a disparate impact on protected groups ought not to count as discrimination under Title VII.[19] By

1983, the EEOC was bringing less than half the number of Title VII lawsuits it had brought during the mid-1970s, despite the fact that the number of discrimination claims it received was substantially greater in the later period.[20]

Stainback and Tomaskovic-Devey use numbers (EEO-1 reports and data regarding agency funding and staffing) to tell a story about the history of Title VII over the past fifty years. This essay tells a similar story about the history of Title VII over the past half-century, not by analyzing vast demographic shifts in the workplace but by focusing on the shifting meaning of a single word—"animus"—over the same period of time. The concept of "discriminatory animus" plays a central role in the interpretation of Title VII.[21] Thus, examining how the meaning of this phrase evolves over time can provide additional purchase on the historical trajectory documented in the EEO-1 reports. It can help illuminate the change in mind-set and understanding that accompanied the cessation of progress the EEO-1 reports reveal. It can tell us something about how courts and regulators thought about the concept of discrimination in the decade or two after Title VII was enacted, and how these actors came to think about discrimination after what Stainback and Tomaskovic-Devey call the "short regulatory decade"[22] from 1973 to 1980 came to an end.

One of the reasons the word "animus" functions as such a useful barometer for measuring attitudinal change over time is that it admits of multiple meanings. In this sense, it is like the word "age."[23] The Supreme Court has noted that "the word 'age' standing alone can be readily understood either as pointing to any number of years lived, or as common shorthand for the longer span and concurrent aches that make youth look good."[24] So, for instance, the word may mean something very different in "a sentence like 'Age can be shown by a driver's license,' [than it does in]...the statement, 'Age has left him a shut-in.'"[25] The Court has been highly attentive to these variations in the meaning of the word "age" when interpreting the Age Discrimination in Employment Act.[26]

As we shall see, however, courts have not been as attentive to such semantic differences when deploying the word "animus" in Title VII cases. They almost never take note of the fact that "animus" also has two primary, and quite distinct, meanings. It can mean basic attitude, governing spirit, or motivation; this meaning carries no negative connotations. But it can also mean prejudiced or spiteful ill will, hostility, dislike, or hatred. Animus, in this second sense, connotes something far less innocuous. To harbor animus against someone, or against an entire group of people, is to actively wish them harm and—in the context of antidiscrimination law—seems tantamount to bigotry.

From the perspective of a plaintiff in a Title VII lawsuit, it matters very much which type of animus one is required to prove. It is not easy to prove that an employer's actions were motivated by hatred or animosity toward a protected group, if only because most contemporary employers are too savvy to confess openly to harboring such attitudes, and judges are often hesitant to find employers guilty of outright bigotry.[27] If animus, defined in this way, were the legal standard, few plaintiffs would win Title VII suits. Officially, of course, it is not the standard. Plaintiffs alleging disparate treatment under Title VII are not required to prove that an employer acted out of hostility toward a protected class but simply that race or sex or one of the other protected categories animated, or played a role, in the employer's decision.

In practice, however, courts in Title VII cases have not always maintained a clear division between these two meanings of the word "animus." As frustration with the traditional project of antidiscrimination law mounted in the late 1970s and throughout the 1980s, Americans increasingly began to view race and sex discrimination as phenomena of an earlier era, which surfaced now only as aberrant conduct perpetrated by a few malevolent employers in a generally egalitarian labor market. Against this backdrop, Title VII increasingly came to be seen not as a tool for combating the kinds of structural problems that continue to generate vast racial and gender-based inequalities in the labor market but rather as a mechanism for policing outliers. Today, this is all too often precisely how Title VII functions. This essay argues that if Title VII is to accomplish the broader, more structural purposes for which it was enacted, we need to engage in a new conversation—or really, reinvigorate an older conversation—about what constitutes discrimination under the law.

I. The Emergence of "Animus" in Title VII Law

The word "animus" does not appear in the text of Title VII. Nor does it appear in early Title VII case law. From the mid-1960s through the mid-1970s, judicial opinions almost never use the word when discussing discrimination by employers.[28] For the first decade of Title VII's existence, "animus" simply did not play a significant role in the law's implementation or the adjudication of employment discrimination cases.

This is not to say, however, that the word "animus" never surfaces in discourse about Title VII in the years after the statute was enacted. Legal scholars and lawyers at the EEOC sometimes used the term during this period to refer to the old, outdated conception of discrimination Title VII was designed to replace. Alfred Blumrosen, who assisted in the organization of the EEOC in 1965 and served as its first chief of conciliations and director of federal-state relations from 1965 to 1967, asserted that, in the post–World War II era, before the enactment of Title VII, "[d]iscrimination was seen as the evil act of the misguided,"[29] or as "conduct [that was] motivated by the dislike of the group or class to which the victims of discrimination belonged."[30] Blumrosen noted that governmental actors who attempted to police this form of discrimination were not terribly successful, in part because "evil motive" was extremely difficult to prove, even in midcentury America.[31] Neither employees nor judges have access to employers' minds, and courts were generally loath to find that employers had acted with malice or ill will toward racial minorities. For this reason, among others, antidiscrimination law in the postwar period did little to improve the status of racial minorities at work.[32]

Commentators—and courts—in the late 1960s agreed that Title VII had moved antidiscrimination law beyond this search for animus.[33] The House Report that recommended passage of Title VII asserted that the law was necessary not in order to protect minorities from racial animosity on the part of employers but to ameliorate the following three problems: (1) black unemployment rates were double those of whites; (2) black workers were concentrated in the lowest paid, least stable job classifications; and (3) given comparable age, education, and experience, the median annual wage and salary income of black workers was 60 percent that of white workers.[34] Commentators pointed to these passages as evidence that Congress had identified the racial stratification of the American labor market as a pervasive and urgent social problem and had passed Title VII to ameliorate it.[35] They asserted that the law's goal is to ensure that those who had historically encountered discrimination and exclusion would now be full and equal participants in the workplace. The law aimed to accomplish this goal, they argued, by providing American workers and lawyers advocating on their behalf with tools to dismantle structural practices that perpetuate inequality—not simply to identify and censure a few renegade employers with sinister motives.[36]

In keeping with this understanding of Title VII's purpose, the lawyers tasked with enforcing the statute in the years after its enactment targeted the kinds of structural practices, such as employment tests and seniority systems,[37] that locked historically subordinated groups out of good jobs. In the late 1960s and early 1970s, a number of federal courts issued key rulings holding that such practices violate Title VII because they continue to freeze out members of the groups the law is designed to protect.[38] The reasoning in these decisions reveals that there was not a sharp conceptual divide between discriminatory effects and discriminatory intent in this period.[39] If an employer's policy had the effect of depriving members of protected classes of employment opportunities, that was considered sufficient—by courts, by the EEOC, and by many academic commentators—to show intent. Courts in this era repeatedly explained that if an employer implements a policy or practice it can reasonably foresee will have a deleterious effect on the job prospects of minorities protected by Title VII, its cognizance of the probable outcome of its actions satisfies any intent requirement in the statute.[40] In other words, courts held, it is fair to assume that an employer intends the likely consequences of its actions. Foreseeable effects were deemed sufficient to show intent in this period because interpreters of the law were not focused on what was transpiring inside the employer's head. They had a *thin* conception of intent: the focus was on eradicating instances in which race or sex was functioning as a barrier to employment, not on plumbing the depths of employers' minds to determine their motivations.[41]

In the mid- to late 1970s, in the constitutional context, courts began to define discriminatory intent differently, and more narrowly, than they had in the preceding decade. By 1980, evidence that a decision maker could reasonably foresee the deleterious effects a particular policy or practice would have on a protected class was no longer deemed sufficient evidence of discriminatory intent. The Court suggested in *Washington v. Davis*[42] that discriminatory intent and discriminatory effects were conceptually distinct categories that involved separate structures of proof.[43] A few years later, the Court held in *Personnel Administrator of Massachusetts v. Feeney*[44] that to prove discriminatory intent for the purposes of equal protection law, a plaintiff was required to demonstrate that the state had adopted a particular course of action not simply "in spite of" its adverse effects on a protected group but at least in part "because of" those effects.[45] In other words, *Feeney* defined "intent" as acting not simply with an awareness of impending harm but also out of a base desire to cause such harm. As a result, courts began to understand discriminatory intent, for purposes of equal protection law, as a "state of mind akin to malice."[46]

Davis and *Feeney* were not Title VII cases; they concerned state action and the meaning of discrimination under the Constitution. But they reflected a turn inward—a turn toward the mental state of the discriminator—that was also occurring in Title VII law.[47] By this time, courts had made it clear that disparate treatment and disparate impact were also to be treated as distinct doctrines under Title VII. And it was at this moment, in the late 1970s, that the word "animus" first entered Title VII case law. For the first decade of the law's existence, "animus" played no role in judicial discourse about employment discrimination. But by the late 1970s, courts began to assert, in dozens of Title VII cases each year, that an allegation of disparate treatment requires proof of "discriminatory animus."[48] By the 1980s and 1990s, the word "animus" started to appear in hundreds of Title VII cases each year.[49] After the turn of the century, such appearances began to number in the thousands.[50] Today, it has become routine for courts in disparate treatment cases to ask whether an employer has acted with "discriminatory animus."[51]

II. The Double Meaning of "Animus" and Its Implications for Title VII

To be perfectly clear: Title VII doctrine does not require the plaintiff in a disparate treatment case to demonstrate that an employer acted with animus defined as hostility or ill will.[52] A plaintiff is required to show only that an employer acted with discriminatory intent. Thus, when courts assert, as they frequently do, that proof of "discriminatory animus" is required under Title VII, they are ostensibly using the word "animus" as a synonym for "intent." In the late 1970s, when courts first began to deploy the word "animus" in antidiscrimination cases, they sometimes took care to explain this. One court explained, for instance, that when it used "[t]he term 'animus,' [it meant that term] to be synonymous with 'motivation,'"—as in, race animated the decision—and did not mean to refer to "animus" in its secondary sense of personal hostility or enmity.[53]

In practice, however, it has proven difficult to maintain a strict separation between these two senses of the word. It is difficult to hear the word "animus" without also hearing its negative connotations. The phrase "discriminatory animus," or "racial animus," seems to point to a thicker conception of intent. So when courts routinely declare that disparate treatment claims under Title VII require evidence of "discriminatory animus," this cannot help but shade our understanding of the kind of conduct that violates the law. Whatever the formal doctrine says, the term "animus" seems to describe a particular mental state, with overtones of ill will or hostility toward a particular group. Indeed, this usage is far more common in normal everyday discourse than the more innocent use of the word "animus" to mean, simply, intent.

Not surprisingly, courts often seem to find it difficult to eradicate the negative connotations of the word "animus" from their thought process when determining whether a plaintiff has succeeded in meeting the burden of proof in a Title VII case. This second layer of meaning seems regularly to spill over into judges' consideration of what constitutes discriminatory intent and, thus, what counts as discrimination under the law. Consider, for instance, the rhetoric the First Circuit deployed when discussing discrimination in *Candelario Ramos v. Baxter Healthcare*,[54] a Title VII case in which the Puerto Rican employees of a health-care products manufacturer alleged they had been discriminated against on the basis of their national origin. The court rejected this claim on the ground that "there is simply no evidence that Baxter management acted out of animus to Puerto Ricans."[55] The court noted that "there are no statements by Baxter management disparaging Puerto Ricans,"[56] nor any evidence that the reasons proffered by the employer for its actions were pretexts for "wicked motives."[57] There is simply no evidence, the court concluded, that the company's management "harbored animus toward Puerto Ricans."[58]

My point is not that the plaintiffs in *Candelario Ramos* should have won their case but rather that this kind of rhetoric, in which there seems to be considerable slippage between the two meanings of the word "animus," subtly or not-so-subtly affects our understanding of what constitutes discrimination. Such rhetoric is not unusual in contemporary Title VII cases.[59] Courts today sometimes reject disparate treatment claims on the ground that the plaintiff failed to produce any evidence of "racial animus"[60] or "sex-based animus,"[61] and it is hard not to conclude that the word "animus" does some work in these instances. For example, when courts find for an employer on the ground that the plaintiff has "offer[ed] no evidence...of antipathy toward Hispanics"[62] or "anti-Hispanic animus"[63]—or when a court observes that a plaintiff has failed to show that an employer acted with "invidious racial animus"[64]—it seems clear that the more negative connotations of the word "animus" have conditioned the way adjudicators think about the kind of conduct Title VII prohibits. Doctrinally speaking, these courts must simply mean that there is no evidence in these cases that race or sex played a role in the adverse employment actions the plaintiffs allege. But by framing intent as "animus," courts may allow a lack of evidence of group-based hatred or ill will to bring them most of the way to a decision. Thus, although Title VII law has not formally incorporated the notion that plaintiffs must prove evil motive (indeed, the law explicitly rejects this idea[65]), the word "animus" can nonetheless muddle the meaning of "intent" in a way that allows it to slide in that direction.

It is not a coincidence that the word "animus" began to appear in Title VII case law with increasing frequency at precisely the same moment workplace integration began to stall. The emergence of this word coincided with a new (or, perhaps, renewed) understanding of discrimination as conduct perpetrated by bad apples—a relatively circumscribed number of employers with evil motives—rather than the pervasive and deeply entrenched social problem Title VII was designed to address. The hunt for animus makes sense if one believes discrimination is largely a thing of the past—if one believes there may still be isolated bad actors, but conditions in the workplace are now generally fair, and any inequalities along lines of, say, race are likely attributable to factors other than discrimination. In fact, by the late 1970s, the Court *had* started to reason about discrimination in this way. This conception of discrimination led the Court, in the context of affirmative action, to invalidate a series of programs designed to integrate institutions of higher education and sectors of the labor market previously reserved for whites.[66] In the context of public education, it motivated the Court to curtail the pursuit of desegregation through busing and other race-conscious integrative measures.[67] Today, this narrative features quite prominently in Supreme Court jurisprudence: it recently played a central role in the Court's decision to eviscerate § 5 of the Voting Rights Act.[68] Title VII law has not formally incorporated the more restrictive definitions of discrimination that historically subordinated groups now confront in the context of equal protection law. But as the past several decades of EEO-1 reports reveal, employment discrimination law has not remained untouched by these conceptual shifts.[69]

The only way to revive the project of workplace integration inaugurated by the passage of Title VII is to begin to tell a different story about discrimination than the one that has currently captured the Court's imagination. It is not a new story, exactly—it is the story that lawyers at the EEOC and academic commentators told in the 1960s, just after the enactment of the Civil Rights Act. These commentators looked to the 1963 House report as a guide to the statute's interpretation. That report concluded that discrimination in the workplace was an urgent social problem—and that a new federal employment discrimination law was necessary—because (1) black unemployment rates were double those of whites; (2) black workers were concentrated in the lowest paid, least stable job classifications; and (3) given comparable age, education, and experience, the median annual wage and salary income of black workers was 60 percent that of white workers.[70] Statistics like these do not come about through the conduct of a few bad actors. They are evidence of major structural problems. Early proponents of Title VII, and indeed, many courts, viewed the law as a means of combating such problems—not by targeting employers with bad motivations but by dismantling policies and practices that impede equality in the workplace.

Today, fifty years after the passage of Title VII, (1) black unemployment rates remain double those of whites;[71] (2) blacks, and other racial minorities, are still concentrated in the lowest paying, least stable job classifications;[72] and (3) black households earn on average just 59 percent as much as white households.[73] Thus, we might echo the academics and EEOC lawyers of the 1960s in saying that workplace inequality is an urgent social problem. Statistics like these do not come about through the conduct of a few bad actors. They are evidence of major structural problems. I believe antidiscrimination law still has a role to play in addressing these sorts of problems, but it will not—it cannot—do so if we conceive of its goal as the policing of outliers who harbor "animus" against protected groups.

About the Author

Professor of law, University of Texas School of Law. Many thanks to Sam Bagenstos and Ellen Katz for conceiving of and editing this volume and for organizing the conference out of which it came.

Notes

1. Civil Rights Act of 1964, Pub. L. No. 88-352, § 705, 78 Stat. 241, 258–59 (codified as amended at 42 U.S.C. § 2000e-4 (2000)) (providing for the creation of the EEOC).

2. Initially, the statute gave the Commission the power to receive, investigate, and conciliate complaints where it found reasonable cause to believe that discrimination had occurred but not to file lawsuits. In 1972, Congress extended to the EEOC the power to initiate lawsuits when it believed an employer had engaged in a discriminatory pattern or practice in violation of Title VII. *See* Equal Employment Opportunity Act of 1972, Pub. L. No. 92-261, § 5(e), 86 Stat. 107 (codified at 42 U.S.C. § 2000e-6(c)).

3. Section 709(c) of Title VII of the Civil Rights Act of 1964 (codified as amended at 42 U.S.C. § 2000e-8(c)) requires employers to make and keep records relevant to a determination of whether unlawful employment practices have been or are being committed, to preserve such records, and to produce reports as the Commission prescribes.

4. *See* Alexandra Kalev & Frank Dobbin, *Enforcement of Civil Rights Law in Private Workplaces: The Effects of Compliance Reviews and Lawsuits over Time*, 31 LAW & SOC. INQUIRY 855, 870 (2006) (The EEOC requires EEO-1 reports from private sector employers with 100 or more employees and from government contractors and subcontractors with 50 or more employees and contracts worth at least $50,000.).

5. *See* Corre L. Robinson et al., *Studying Race or Ethnic and Sex Segregation at the Establishment Level: Methodological Issues and Substantive Opportunities Using EEO-1 Reports*, 32 WORK & OCCUPATIONS 5, 16 (2005) (noting that EEO-1 reports cover more than 40 percent of private sector employees nationwide).

6. *See* KEVIN STAINBACK & DONALD TOMASKOVIC-DEVEY, DOCUMENTING DESEGREGATION: RACIAL AND GENDER SEGREGATION IN PRIVATE-SECTOR EMPLOYMENT SINCE THE CIVIL RIGHTS ACT (2012). Stainback and Tomaskovic-

Devey analyze EEOC-1 reports from 1966 to 2005, a data set that includes more than 5 million American workplaces.

7. *Id.* at xxiv; *see also id.* at 118–54.

8. *Id.* at 167–69. Progress stalled earlier for African Americans than it did for white women, but even the gradual increases in workplace integration between white men and white women had petered out by the turn of the century. *Id.* at 168–69.

9. *Id.* at 232; *see also id.* at 233 tbl.7.9.

10. *Id.* at 235; *see also id.* at 234 tbl.7.10; *id.* at 245 ("[S]egregation between white women and black women shows the most disturbing industry-specific trends. We found only eight industries in which the average workplace was systematically hiring or promoting white women and black women into equal-status employment. These were the exceptions...[T]he long list of industries...in which the average workplace was hiring or promoting white women and black women into increasingly segregated roles is a bleak testament to the widespread reversal of racial desegregation among women.").

11. *Id.* at 238–39.

12. *Id.* at xxxiv; *see also id.* at 320 ("At this point in the history of private-sector equal opportunity, the dominant pattern is inertia. Little or no national aggregate progress is being made in terms of either desegregation or access to good jobs. Nationally, progress toward workplace equal opportunity has stalled. Moreover, it is disturbing to note that in many workplaces, communities, and industries segregation is increasing...").

13. In fact, Stainback and Tomaskovic-Devey suggest that their account likely understates the amount of segregation in the American workforce because it takes into account only large firms subject to EEOC reporting requirements and government contractors, which are required to have affirmative action programs. Small private firms, which account for nearly 60 percent of private sector employment, are more segregated along both race and gender lines than larger firms, and since the 1960s, white men have increasingly been moving out of the government and regulated private sector into this nonregulated private sector. *Id.* at 41–44.

14. *Id.* at 155.

15. *Id.* at 157–59.

16. STAINBACK & TOMASKOVIC-DEVEY, *supra* note 6, at 158; *see also*FRANK DOBBIN, INVENTING EQUAL OPPORTUNITY 136–37 (2009) (noting that after 1980, contractor debarments and findings of violations dropped, and those who were charged with violations were less likely to be required to take any action in response); James P. Sterba, *Completing Thomas Sowell's Study of Affirmative Action and Then Drawing Different Conclusions*, 57 STAN. L. REV. 657, 667 (2004) (book review) ("During the Reagan era, affirmative action under the federal government's contract compliance program virtually ceased to exist except in name only.")

17. *See* Peter H. Schuck, *Affirmative Action: Past, Present, and Future*, 20 YALE L. & POL'Y REV. 1, 51 (2002); Sterba, *supra* note 16, at 667.

18. Ernest Holsendolph, *Skills, Not Bias, Seen as Key for Jobs*, N.Y. TIMES, July 3, 1982, at A5.

19. *See* Clarence Thomas, *The Equal Employment Opportunity Commission: Reflections on a New Philosophy*, 15 STETSON L. REV. 29, 35–36 (1985).

20. David L. Rose, *Twenty-Five Years Later: Where Do We Stand on Equal Employment*

Opportunity Law Enforcement?, 42 VAND. L. REV. 1121, 1159 (1989); *see also* STAINBACK & TOMASKOVIC-DEVEY, *supra* note 16, at 158 (noting that this era also witnessed the virtual demise of the class action lawsuit, as the number of class actions fell from 1,106 in 1975 to a mere 51 in 1989).

21. *See, e.g.,* Ledbetter v. Goodyear Tire & Rubber Co., Inc., 550 U.S. 618, 637 (2007) (rejecting plaintiff's claims under Title VII and the Equal Pay Act in part because she failed to adduce any evidence that her employer "initially adopted its performance-based pay system in order to discriminate on the basis of sex or that it later applied this system to her within the charging period with any discriminatory animus"); Price Waterhouse v. Hopkins, 490 U.S. 228, 271 (1989) (O'Connor, J., concurring) (concurring in the holding that the plaintiff had established a claim of sex discrimination under Title VII in part because she adduced "direct evidence of discriminatory animus" on the part of her employer).

22. STAINBACK & TOMASKOVIC-DEVEY, *supra* note 16, at xxxii (describing the years from 1973 to 1980 as "an era of relatively strong federal regulatory oversight, increased legislative, judicial, and regulatory emphasis on women's employment rights, effective legal challenges to employer discrimination, and the institutionalization of equal opportunity human resource practices").

23. Gen. Dynamics Land Sys., Inc. v. Cline, 540 U.S. 581, 596 (2004) (observing that some words, such as "age," have "several commonly understood meanings among which a speaker can alternate in the course of an ordinary conversation").

24. *Id.*

25. *Id.*

26. *See, e.g.,* Smith v. City of Jackson, 544 U.S. 228 (2005); *General Dynamics*, 540 U.S. at 595–98.

27. *See, e.g.,* Chad Derum & Karen Engle, *The Rise of the Personal Animosity Presumption in Title VII and the Return to "No Cause" Employment*, 81 TEX. L. REV. 1177, 1233–36 (2003) (discussing courts' tendency to characterize even blatantly racist and sexist comments by employers as "stray remarks" or evidence of personal animosity rather than evidence of a Title VII violation); *cf.* U.S. v. Clary, 846 F. Supp. 768, 779 (E.D. Mo. 1994) ("When counsel first argued that overt racism was really the basis for the discriminatory crack penalties, this Court rejected that approach out-of-hand, for the Court did not believe that such outrageous and outmoded ideas would affect legislators of this day and age...There is a realization that most Americans have grown beyond the evils of overt racial malice..."), *rev'd* 34 F.3d 709 (8th Cir. 1994). The district court in this case went on to find that race had actually influenced the legislators responsible for the vast distinction in the way criminal law treats crack as opposed to powder cocaine, but that finding was later overturned by the Eighth Circuit. *Id.*

28. A review of all Title VII cases decided in the first decade of Title VII's existence (and available in Westlaw) indicates that the word "animus" appears only a handful of times.

29. Alfred W. Blumrosen, *Quotas, Common Sense, and Law in Labor Relations: Three Dimensions of Equal Opportunity*, 27 RUTGERS L. REV. 675, 679 (1974).

30. *Id.* at 681; *see also* Linda Hamilton Krieger, *The Content of Our Categories: A Cognitive Bias Approach to Discrimination and Equal Employment Opportunity*, 47 STAN. L. REV. 1161, 1175 (1995) ("After World War II...prejudice was seen as stemming from a particular pathological personality structure. Thus the problem confronting

students of intergroup relations became identifying the prejudice-prone personality—the bigot.'").

31. Alfred W. Blumrosen, *The Crossroads for Equal Employment Opportunity: Incisive Administration or Indecisive Bureaucracy?*, 49 NOTRE DAME L. REV. 46, 53 (1973) ("The concept of 'discrimination' historically was that of conduct animated by an 'evil motive' of distaste for the group to which the individual victim of the discrimination belonged. This search for 'evil motive' was difficult, and in the period 1945–1965 meant that there was little law enforcement activity by the state civil rights agencies.").

32. Indeed, Congress cited the failure of antidiscrimination laws to ameliorate the vast economic disparities between whites and racial minorities in the postwar period as a central reason for enacting Title VII. *See* S. REP. NO. 88-867, at 6–8 (1964) ("[T]he vast amount of work yet to be done is apparent from the economic facts developed in the course of the hearings on the bill. Gross disparities in earnings and employment opportunities continue to prevail in States having fair employment practice legislation and statewide unemployment rates do not appear to differ substantially from those in States without such legislation."); *see also* Note, *Title VII, Civil Rights Act of 1964: Present Operation and Proposals for Improvement*, 5 COLUM. J.L. & SOC. PROBS. 1, 2 (1969) ("Title VII...was designed to inaugurate a full-scale attack on racial discrimination in employment. Twenty years of experience under state fair employment practice laws had proved them to be of little efficacy in most cases...").

33. i>See, e.g., Newsweek Mag. v. D.C. Comm'n on Human Rts., 376 A.2d 777, 785–86 (D.C. 1977) ("Prior to the early 1960's courts viewed racial discrimination as an attitude based on an 'evil motive,' 'mens rea,' or 'state of mind.' Under this concept it was necessary to show that a person was actively motivated by dislike or hatred of the group to which the complainant belonged...When Title VII of the Civil Rights Act of 1964...was being considered it was argued that some earlier concepts [such as this] were too restrictive."); United States v. Gulf-State Theaters, Inc., 256 F. Supp. 549, 552 (N.D. Miss. 1966) ("The Civil Rights Act is not concerned with the subjective racial prejudices of the people affected."); George Cooper & Richard B. Sobol, *Seniority and Testing under Fair Employment Laws: A General Approach to Objective Criteria of Hiring and Promotion*, 82 HARV. L. REV. 1598, 1670–71 (1969) (arguing that "[t]his shift away from a restrictive focus on the state of mind of the employer is essential to the effective enforcement of fair employment laws," in part because seniority and testing practices—not necessarily enacted with explicit or provable discriminatory animus—are "the most important contemporary obstacles to the employment and promotion of qualified black workers").

34. H.R. REP. NO. 88-914, pt. 2, at 26–27 (1963); *see also* S. REP. NO. 88-867, at 6–8 (1964) (making similar observations about the relative position of racial minorities and whites in the labor market and the need for a federal law designed to address this problem).

35. *See, e.g.*, Alfred W. Blumrosen, *The Duty of Fair Recruitment under the Civil Rights Act of 1964*, 22 RUTGERS L. REV. 465, 473 (1968) [hereinafter Blumrosen, *Duty of Fair Recruitment*] ("Both House and Senate committee reports cited the unemployment statistics and indicated that these were the fundamental grounds for the adoption of [T]itle VII."); Blumrosen, *supra* note 29, at 684 (asserting that antidiscrimination laws enacted in the postwar period did little to improve the employment opportunities of racial minorities as measured by income, unemployment ratio, or occupational distribution, and that Title VII was intended to address these "three indices of minority exclusion and

subordination"); *see also* Owen M. Fiss, *A Theory of Fair Employment Laws*, 38 U. CHI. L. REV. 235, 240 & n.7 (1971) (citing commentary asserting that the goal of Title VII is "to improve the relative economic position of blacks" and to equalize "the actual distribution of employment opportunities").

36. *See* Blumrosen, *Duty of Fair Recruitment*, *supra* note 35, at 475 ("Title VII is not a criminal statute requiring *mens rea*.").

37. *See*HUGH DAVIS GRAHAM, THE CIVIL RIGHTS ERA 248 (1990) ("High on such a list [of targets for the EEOC] were two formidable barriers to black advancement: employee tests and seniority systems."); Margaret H. Lemos, *The Consequences of Congress's Choice of Delegate: Judicial and Agency Interpretations of Title VII*, 63 VAND. L. REV. 363, 397, 395 (2010) (asserting that the EEOC in the 1960s "focus[ed] on 'systems and effects' rather than tort-like individual wrongs" and quickly "identified seniority systems as one of the major causes of systemic racial disparities in many sectors of the workforce").

38. *See, e.g.*, Robinson v. Lorillard Corp., 444 F.2d 791 (4th Cir. 1971); Jones v. Lee Way Motor Freight, Inc., 431 F.2d 245 (10th Cir. 1970); United States v. Dillon Supply Co., 429 F.2d 800 (4th Cir. 1970); Local 189, United Papermakers v. United States, 416 F.2d 980 (5th Cir. 1969); Armstead v. Starkville Mun. Separate Sch. Dist., 325 F. Supp. 560 (N.D. Miss. 1971); Quarles v. Philip Morris, Inc., 279 F. Supp. 505 (E.D. Va. 1968); *see also*, of course, Griggs v. Duke Power Co., 401 U.S. 424, 430 (1971) ("Under the Act, practices, procedures, or tests neutral on their face, and even neutral in terms of intent, cannot be maintained if they operate to 'freeze' the status quo of prior discriminatory employment practices.").

39. For more on the lack of differentiation between discriminatory effects and discriminatory intent in Title VII law in the 1960s and early 1970s, see Michael Selmi, *Was the Disparate Impact Theory a Mistake?*, 53 UCLA L. REV. 701 (2006); *see also* Reva B. Siegel, *The Supreme Court, 2012 Term—Foreword: Equality Divided*, 127 HARV. L. REV. 1, 9–15 (2013) (discussing the parallel lack of differentiation in this period between discriminatory effects and discriminatory purpose in the context of equal protection law).

40. *See, e.g.*, *United Papermakers*, 416 F.2d at 997 ("The requisite intent may be inferred from the fact that the defendants persisted in the conduct after its racial implications had become known to them. Section 707(a) demands no more."); *see also*ALFRED W. BLUMROSEN, BLACK EMPLOYMENT AND THE LAW 176 (1971) (explaining that "the intent requirement in Title VII is the intent requirement of a civil action in tort—that the defendant be aware of the consequences of his action which are reasonably certain to flow from his behavior").

41. *See* Ian Haney-López, *Intentional Blindness*, 87 N.Y.U. L. REV. 1779, 1798 (2012) (arguing that "[d]uring the civil rights era, the Court was not on the hunt for individual bigots," and that "'[i]ntent,' if it is to be used to describe the Court's racial jurisprudence through at least 1977, must not be construed as a reference to the motives of particular individuals...[but rather] as a term of art, connoting a judicial conclusion regarding the illegitimacy of certain racial practices").

42. 426 U.S. 229 (1976).

43. *But see id.* at 253–54 (Stevens, J., concurring) ("Frequently the most probative evidence of intent will be objective evidence of what actually happened rather than evidence describing the subjective state of mind of the actor...My point in making this observation is to suggest that the line between discriminatory purpose and discriminatory impact is not nearly as bright, and perhaps not quite as critical, as the reader of the Court's opinion might assume.").

44. 442 U.S. 256 (1979).

45. *Id.* at 279.

46. *See* Haney-López, *supra* note 41, at 1783; Reva B. Siegel, *Why Equal Protection No Longer Protects: The Evolving Forms of Status-Enforcing State Action*, 49 STAN. L. REV. 1111, 1135 (1997).

47. *See* Krieger, *supra* note 30, at 1168 (observing that as disparate treatment law developed, discrimination came to be understood as the product of "discriminatory animus towards members of the plaintiff's racial or ethnic group").

48. *See, e.g.*, Turner v. Tex. Instruments, Inc., 555 F.2d 1251, 1257 (5th Cir. 1977) ("Title VII…[does] not protect against unfair business decisions—only against decisions motivated by unlawful animus.").

49. *See, e.g.*, Zachery v. Texaco Exploration & Prod., Inc., 185 F.R.D. 230, 236 (W.D. Tex. 1999) ("An allegation of disparate treatment requires proof of racial animus.").

50. *See, e.g.*, Candelario Ramos v. Baxter Healthcare Corp. of Puerto Rico, Inc., 360 F.3d 53, 61 (1st Cir. 2004) ("Even with reasonable inferences drawn in plaintiffs' favor, the district court correctly held that there was no evidence of animus—and that means that the discriminatory treatment claim fails.").

51. *See, e.g.*, Allen v. Radio One of Tex. II, LLC, 515 F. App'x 295, 300 (5th Cir. 2013) (rejecting plaintiff's claim on the ground that she failed to "demonstrate her termination was motivated by sex-based animus").

52. Rebecca Hanner White & Linda Hamilton Krieger, *Whose Motive Matters?: Discrimination in Multi-Actor Employment Decision Making*, 61 LA. L. REV. 495, 501 (2001) ("For years, it has (or should have) been clear that discriminatory intent or motive is not coextensive with hostile animus.").

53. Local No. 1 v. Int'l Bhd. of Teamsters, 419 F. Supp. 263, 277 n.23 (E.D. Pa. 1976). This case did not involve a Title VII claim, but the court's observations regarding the term "animus" are perfectly applicable in the context of Title VII.

54. 360 F.3d 53 (1st Cir. 2004).

55. *Id.* at 61.

56. *Id.* at 57.

57. *Id.*

58. *Id.* at 59.

59. *See* White & Krieger, *supra* note 52, at 501 (noting that "the equation of discriminatory intent with hostile animus still powerfully shapes the decisions of many lower courts").

60. Grillo v. N.Y.C. Transit Auth., 291 F.3d 231, 234–35 (2nd Cir. 2002).

61. Allen v. Radio One of Tex. II, LLC, 515 F. App'x 295, 300 (5th Cir. 2013).

62. Castro v. City of N.Y., No. 05 Civ. 593(LAK)(MHD), 2009 WL 2223037, at *8 (S.D.N.Y. July 22, 2009).

63. *Id.*

64. Hyman v. Atlantic City Med. Ctr., No. Civ. A. 97-795(JEI), 1998 WL 135249, at *12 (D.N.J. Mar. 16, 1998).

65. *See, e.g.*, EEOC v. Joe's Stone Crab, Inc., 220 F.3d 1263, 1283–84 (11th Cir. 2000) ("To prove the discriminatory intent necessary for a disparate treatment or

pattern or practice claim, a plaintiff need not prove that a defendant harbored some special 'animus' or 'malice' towards the protected group to which she belongs."); Doe v. City of Belleville, 119 F.3d 563, 583 n.19 (7th Cir. 1997) ("[W]e have expressly rejected the argument that proof of a gender-based animus is required to make a claim of sex discrimination."); King v. Bd. of Regents of the Univ. of Wis. Sys., 898 F.2d 533, 539 (7th Cir. 1990) ("All that is required is that the action taken be motivated by the gender of the plaintiff. No hatred, no animus, and no dislike is required.").

66. *See, e.g.,* Regents of the Univ. of Cal. v. Bakke, 438 U.S. 265, 292, 295 (1978) (asserting that the United States is now "a Nation of minorities" and that "[t]he clock of our liberties...cannot be turned back to 1868," when African Americans faced more discrimination than other groups); City of Richmond v. J.A. Croson Co., 488 U.S. 469, 499–500, 503 (1989) (finding no evidence of discrimination in a Southern city where blacks comprise 50 percent of the population and minority-owned prime contractors are awarded .67 percent of city construction contracts because "[t]here are numerous explanations for this dearth of minority participation, including past societal discrimination in education and economic opportunities as well as both black and white career and entrepreneurial choices," in addition to the possibility that "[b]lacks may be disproportionately attracted to industries other than construction").

67. *See, e.g.,* Milliken v. Bradley, 418 U.S. 717 (1974) (striking down a remedial interdistrict busing plan designed to integrate a highly segregated metropolitan area on the ground that it pulled students from white suburbs innocent of any responsibility for the current state of segregation); Mo. v. Jenkins, 515 U.S. 70 (1995) (striking down a court-ordered intradistrict remedy on the ground that it attempted to attract students from white suburbs that did not bear any responsibility for school segregation in the metropolitan area).

68. Shelby County v. Holder, 570 U.S., 133 S. Ct. 2612, 2625, 2626 (2013) (finding the Voting Rights Act's preclearance formula hopelessly outdated in part because "things have changed dramatically," and "our Nation has made great strides" since the Act was passed); *id.* at 2626 (suggesting the burdens § 5 places on the South are no longer fair or necessary because the nation has come a long way since 1965, when police "in Selma, Alabama...beat and used tear gas against hundreds marching in support of African-American enfranchisement").

69. Indeed, the trajectory of integration and resegregation documented by the EEO-1 reports parallels almost exactly the trajectory of integration and resegregation in public schools documented by political scientist Gary Orfield. *See*ERICA FRANKENBERG, CHUNGMEI LEE, & GARY ORFIELD, A MULTIRACIAL SOCIETY WITH SEGREGATED SCHOOLS: ARE WE LOSING THE DREAM? 30–31 & fig. 5-6 (2004) (showing that the desegregation of black and white school children ended in the early 1980s and that schools have been resegregating along racial lines in the decades since then); *id.* at 18 (arguing that school desegregation ended and resegregation began in the early 1980s due in large part to the Reagan administration's new ideas about discrimination and the law's proper role in combating it).

70. *See supra* note 34 and accompanying text.

71. *See* Brad Plumer, *These Ten Charts Show the Black-White Economic Gap Hasn't Budged in Fifty Years,* WASH. POST, Aug. 28, 2013 (noting that "[t]he black unemployment rate has consistently been twice as high as the white unemployment rate for 50 years" and that "this gap hasn't closed at all since 1963"); *see also* Michael A. Fletcher, *Fifty Years after March on Washington, Economic Gap between Blacks,*

Whites Persists, WASH. POST, Aug. 27, 2013 (noting that "racial economic disparities are mostly unchanged [since the 1960s] and in some cases are growing" and discussing the role of discrimination in perpetuating these disparities).

72. *See* U.S. DEP'T OF LABOR, THE AFRICAN-AMERICAN LABOR FORCE IN THE RECOVERY (2012), *available at* http://www.dol.gov/_sec/media/reports/BlackLaborForce/BlackLaborForce.pdf.

73. PEW RESEARCH CTR., KING'S DREAM REMAINS AN ELUSIVE GOAL; MANY AMERICANS SEE RACIAL DISPARITIES (2013), http://www.pewsocialtrends.org/2013/08/22/kings-dream-remains-an-elusive-goal-many-americans-see-racial-disparities/ ("Expressed as a share of white income, black households earn about 59% of what white households earn, a small increase from 55% in 1967."). Neither of these figures controls for variables such as age, education, and experience.

3

Civil Rights 3.0

Nan D. Hunter

> *President Obama's endorsement of gay marriage...was by any measure a watershed.*
> *A sitting United States president took sides in what many people consider the last*
> *civil rights movement...*
> —New York Times, May 9, 2012[1]

The LGBT (lesbian, gay, bisexual, and transgender) rights movement owes an immeasurable debt to the advocates for racial justice who created the modern American idea of civil rights as well as its doctrinal foundation. Perhaps an even greater debt is owed to those midcentury civil rights leaders for creating one of the nation's most compelling cultural narratives: a scripture-like account of suffering, Exodus, and redemption that has inspired every campaign for social justice since that time. The quasi-mythologized history of civil rights in the 1960s has created the sense of the eventual inevitability of victory over the most extreme forms of irrational bias and the achievement of formal equality.

This narrative now attaches to LGBT rights, as evidenced by how frequently LGBT equality is being described as the last, or the next, or today's, preeminent civil rights issue.[2] Indeed, it was this background narrative that gave such rhetorical power to President Obama's phrasing of his support for LGBT equality in his second inaugural address, a passage that cements the place of LGBT rights squarely in the civil rights heritage, in implicit equivalence to its forebears.[3] But the march-of-progress narrative, while not entirely untrue, is deeply misleading.

In this chapter, I will explore what it means, for better and for worse, to be (arguably) this generation's emblematic civil rights campaign. What does the label tell us about the civil rights paradigm itself? If the achievement of marriage equality is the great civil rights achievement of this generation, what does that suggest about a future for equality more generally? How have new forms of, and technologies for, movement-building affected the idea and practice of civil rights? Does the civil rights paradigm have a future? Or are we on the cusp of reaching the civil rights version of the end of history?[4]

This chapter addresses three aspects of the social meaning of civil rights: legal doctrine and legal institutions, especially as they relate to statutory mandates for equal treatment; social movement strategies, with a focus on the professionalization and corporatization of a civil rights campaign; and the tension between the discourse of social hierarchy and that of civil rights.

The gay story began with what many saw as an upstart, even faux, civil rights movement as compared to the traditional civil rights movements that were thought to be the real thing. Until recently, LGBT rights advocates struggled to join the informal alliance of constituency-based rights groups, to get a place at the civil rights table and entrée to the diversity industry that flourishes among large employers, and to build their own niche as part of the base of the Democratic Party. Those goals have been achieved, along with a broad public recognition that the LGBT movement counts as a civil rights struggle.

As other movements in the American civil rights tradition have each brought new insights, approaches, and problems to the fore, so too has the LGBT movement. Over time, the movement itself has changed, acquiring greater resources and responding to changes in the broader political climate. LGBT organizations have utilized increasingly sophisticated technologies to achieve fundamental social movement objectives of framing issues, mobilizing a constituency, forging alliances, and interacting with political parties and state actors.

LGBT legal rights work began in earnest after the ascent of Reagan-Bush era conservatives whose elections were fueled by the coalition of social issues and probusiness policies. For many of the current leaders—in all civil rights movements—that Reagan-Bush political culture forms the baseline for goals and expectations.[5] This context of backlash and retrenchment contributed to the growth of multidimensional advocacy: LGBT rights advocates have moved, or been forced, into a variety of lawmaking venues—state and federal courts and legislatures, elections, and advertising. The result is a melding of new and old models of persuasion in which themes developed in nonjuridical contexts may migrate to courts and legislatures. The hyperinvestment in litigation during the height of the Warren Court era has ceased. Advocates now routinely develop campaigns to eliminate discriminatory laws consciously using litigation as only one component of an array of techniques.

Underlying the chapter is an understanding that the social meaning of civil rights in the United States is extraordinarily rich, with issues being framed and reframed in a continuous iterative process. Every marginalized group seeks pathways and portals into greater power, whether through institutions of the state, the market, or civil society. The discourse of civil rights has been productive in both jurisgenerative and culture-generative terms.

Examining the meaning of civil rights through the prism of the LGBT rights movement provides a window into strengths, weaknesses, and dynamism of the struggle for social justice in the United States. What we learn is that LGBT advocates have contributed to the overall project of formal equality under law primarily by developing an extraordinary strategic and tactical dexterity, uniquely so at the state level and in their alliance with the business sector. Particularly as to the latter, however, there are major trade-offs that have yet to become manifest. Meanwhile, because of a broader retrenchment in civil rights law generally, the possibility of advances in substantive equality law—either statutory or constitutional—has shrunk. Even as LGBT rights groups make breakthroughs in achieving goals such as marriage equality, they will have to contend with conservative pressure to dismantle overarching protections such as the disparate impact principle or heightened scrutiny under the Equal Protection Clause. For the future, the big question for this movement—and all other social justice movements in the United States—is whether it will deploy its talents and resources to meet the more difficult challenge of dislodging embedded, structural forms of discrimination and social hierarchy.

I. The Law: Equality and Containment

I got nothing but homage an holy thinkin for the ol songs and stories
But now there's me an you.
    —Bob Dylan[6]

The project that civil rights movements and arguments framed under the rubric of equality do best, and for which the law is perfectly suited, is ending exclusions and categorical inequalities. What civil rights movements and equality arguments more broadly do not do so well is dismantling hierarchies.[7] The fundamental critique of formal equality is that its very achievement perpetuates more deeply embodied patterns of stratification, in part because the existence of civil rights laws tends to legitimate the hierarchy that remains. Whether constitutional or statutory, formal equality rights are differentially deployed by differently situated subjects in a complex stratified society.

To date, LGBT equality has been overwhelmingly framed as being about ending exclusions—currently and most dramatically the exclusion from marriage, but prior to that, a series of other categorical exclusions: from legal shelter for the exercise of sexual intimacy, from protection of one's parental rights, and often from employment. So in that structural sense at least, LGBT rights should be an easy fit for a civil rights paradigm. And indeed there is truth in this parallel construction: the LGBT movement does offer its own narrative of progress in ending exclusions. Gay sex is no longer criminal in the United States, even in the most conservative jurisdictions. Several million Americans have achieved at least a bounded liberty to live honest lives that are more economically and physically secure than was imagined possible fifty years ago. Prospectively, a demographically driven tectonic shift in public opinion suggests that more progress is on the way.

Yet it is also true that the LGBT equality movement has not yet attained the two traditional markers of formal equality in law. One is adoption by the Supreme Court of an equal protection analysis under which laws differentiating on the basis of a specific characteristic are presumptively unconstitutional under a heightened scrutiny analysis. The other is national legislation that regulates the private as well as the public sectors and that prohibits discrimination based on the given characteristic in a variety of contexts. Neither has occurred in the field of LGBT rights.

From a political point of view, we must ask whether this institutional reluctance by both the Supreme Court and Congress stems from something more than hostility to a particular and relatively "new" minority. Doubtless some part of it derives from controversies specific to homosexuality and gender identity, but it also reflects a shrinking of the vision of equality. Mapping civil rights legal doctrine from the perspective of a constituency that seems to stand on the cusp of crossing the finish line into formal equality can tell us much about how the dialog between law and politics has constructed the evolving social meaning of "civil rights." LGBT groups are poised to follow in the footsteps of older movements based on race and gender, but the parameters of what is possible have narrowed.

In both constitutional and statutory law, the Supreme Court has cut back on the promise that law would serve as a tool to achieve racial, and to a lesser extent gender, justice. These examples of retrenchment are easy to overlook in the LGBT rights context because, for this group, they stunt forward progress, which is less dramatic than forcing a group backward, as has occurred with people of color and women. Since Congress enacted the Civil Rights Act in 1964, an increasingly conservative Supreme Court has in effect discounted the value of achieving equivalent protection by interpretations that have undermined the efficacy of the underlying statute.[8] Together, these changes have redefined equality under law in more limited ways, even if the number of constituencies protected under civil rights law has expanded.

The shrinkage of the civil rights paradigm is evident in comparing the Civil Rights Act of 1964 to its closest analog in the field of sexual orientation or gender identity that has gotten to a floor vote in Congress. The Senate adopted a version of the Employment Non-Discrimination Act (ENDA) in November 2013[9] but the bill died in the House of Representatives.[10] In this section, I will describe how ENDA and the current law on the standard of review for sexual orientation discrimination under the Equal Protection Clause illustrate ways in which constrictions of existing civil rights law are channeling future law. Ironically, the strongest protection against discrimination for LGBT persons may come not from a twenty-first-century civil rights bill but instead from a dynamic reading of the fifty-year-old Title VII.

A. A Cabined Vision

As its name indicates, the ENDA legislation covered only one of the realms—employment—that fall within the scope of the 1964 Civil Rights Act. Congresswoman Bella Abzug introduced omnibus legislation in 1974 that would have added sexual orientation protection to a range of issues covered in the Civil Rights Act, but Washington-based advocates decided in 1993 that redrafting the bill to cover only employment would increase the possibility of legislative success, because the workplace was the context that drew the greatest level of popular support for an antidiscrimination law.[11] More recently, hoping to build on the momentum from the Supreme Court's ruling on same-sex marriage, rights groups introduced a new version of the omnibus approach. Its future appears dim, however, as long as Republicans control Congress.

Despite the increased numbers in public opinion polls voicing agreement that LGBT persons should not be fired based on that characteristic,[12] the needle has not moved for twenty years on advancing federal antidiscrimination legislation in this area. In addition to the power of social conservatives who view homosexuality with distaste, forward

progress is stymied by hostility toward civil rights and government regulation more generally.

Compare the United Kingdom, which enacted a new civil rights law
in 2010. The Equality Act unified dozens of laws and policies into one
comprehensive statute, eliminating fragmented coverage for race, gender, disability, and sexual orientation.[13] The new British law is designed
to modernize and clarify, rather than expand, the reach of the civil rights
paradigm, in an effort to render the overall concept more accessible to
the public and to eliminate areas of confusion for employers and other
institutions that must comply. Civil rights law in the United States has
expanded since 1964 only through a series of one-off measures, each
increasing the complexity of the legal edifice of antidiscrimination.[14]
Despite the political modesty of the British law, enacting its equivalent
here seems impossible in the current political environment.

The second telling characteristic of the version of ENDA that passed
the Senate is that it explicitly forbade claims based on disparate impact
theory.[15] The disparate impact doctrine allows proof of discrimination
without the need to prove the defendant's intent to discriminate. While
disparate impact claims in the context of sexual orientation or gender
identity have so far been rare,[16] the insistence by business interests on
the inclusion of its prohibition in ENDA[17] reflects a much larger campaign against the underlying concept.

In *Griggs v. Duke Power Co.*,[18] the Supreme Court held that proof of
the disparate impact on racial minorities of facially neutral employment
rules constituted a violation of Title VII. Its effect was a powerful boost
to the continued efficacy of that statute after employers discarded once
explicitly discriminatory policies. More than one scholar has characterized *Griggs* as the Court's most important civil rights decision aside from
Brown.[19] The disparate impact principle comes the closest of any aspect
of antidiscrimination law to reaching structural patterns of stratification.[20] In other words, at least in theory, disparate impact claims have
the potential to achieve more than formal equality, something more like
concrete steps toward disestablishing hierarchy.

Since *Griggs*, the battle over disparate impact has become a central
point of back-and-forth dispute between those who seek to expand the
concept of civil rights and those who seek to shrink it. The Supreme
Court has ruled that disparate impact does apply to claims filed under
the Fair Housing Act and the Age Discrimination in Employment Act,[21]
but it has precluded disparate impact claims under Title VI of the Civil
Rights Act,[22] Section 1981,[23] and the Fourteenth[24] and Fifteenth[25]
Amendments. In *Wards Cove Packing Co. v. Atonio*,[26] the Court severely
limited disparate impact by its ruling on allocation of burden of proof

and the scope of the business necessity defense. Congress responded to *Wards Cove* with the Civil Rights Act of 1991,[27] which effectively reversed most of the Court's decision, returning the burden of proof to the defendant and requiring the defendant to show that practice with disparate effects was job related and consistent with business necessity.[28] In one of the most recently enacted antidiscrimination laws, the Genetic Information Nondiscrimination Act, the issue arose again. Congress barred disparate impact claims pending review by an Advisory Commission.[29]

In light of this ongoing battle, it is a mistake to consider the disparate impact exclusion in ENDA as turning on gay-specific issues or as of trivial significance. The enactment of a prohibition on disparate impact in LGBT civil rights legislation would contribute to a precedent against it in future legislative debates beyond LGBT issues.

A third weakness of the version of ENDA that passed the Senate was its overly broad exemption for religious organizations. In contrast to Title VII, which allows religious employers to give preference to employees based on religion (but not based on other characteristics), the 2013 iteration of ENDA would have given such employers a blanket exemption from antidiscrimination requirements based on sexual orientation and gender identity and prohibited the denial of federal contracts on the ground of noncompliance. The acceptance of this provision as part of the negotiations with Senate leadership produced a split among the LGBT rights groups; ultimately, all the LGBT groups opposed the version of ENDA that emerged from the Senate.[30]

B. Equal Protection

Many people use the term "civil rights" to encompass equal protection law as well as the statutory antidiscrimination prohibitions. In this aspect of equality law, the Supreme Court has struck down forms of sexual orientation discrimination, most recently and importantly in the marriage decision.[31] Remarkably, however, it has done so without articulating a clear standard of review for such classifications, leaving lower courts to conclude that some form of a rational basis test was used, even though there is little possibility that the outcomes would have been the same had the traditional and highly deferential version of rational basis been the operative standard.[32]

The Court's treatment of this next, last, or most contemporaneous civil rights issue signals that, like the scope of antidiscrimination statutes, the future likely holds only the possibility of additional one-off invocations of constitutional equality. The Court has become allergic to any extension of a more stringent standard for scrutiny beyond the groups to which it has traditionally been applied.[33] I read the Court's message in the gay cases as indicating that the Justices accept that they will have to address whether sexual orientation exclusions violate the Constitution but are determined to do so without articulating standards for equal protection scrutiny that will have broader application.

C. Sex Discrimination Claims: A Return to the Future?

With the failure to enact national legislation prohibiting employment discrimination, advocates have turned to the prohibition on sex discrimination in Title VII to reach adverse workplace actions against LGBT persons. To date, the progress is uneven but promising. The majority of circuits have ruled that adverse actions that result from sex stereotyping based on gender nonconformity can constitute sex discrimination against LGBT people.[34] Courts increasingly accept that antipathy toward homosexuality or transgender status is vulnerable because it hinges on stereotypes of masculinity or femininity.[35] These rulings reopen the possibility of using sex discrimination theories, regardless of whether new legislation is enacted.

The EEOC has led the movement forward on this front by issuing decisions finding that gender identity and sexual orientation discrimination are both covered under Title VII as per se sex discrimination.[36] As a result, the EEOC accepts claims of both forms of discrimination for investigation and conciliation and has also initiated or supported litigation on these theories.[37] Thus administrative agency enforcement of Title VII as it applies to discrimination based on either sexual orientation or gender identity is already occurring nationwide, and hundreds of persons have sought redress through this channel.[38]

In many respects—the availability of disparate impact claims and a more targeted religious exemption—Title VII is a stronger law than was ENDA.[39] Thus, ironically, the best hope for the future of civil rights protection for LGBT Americans, at least in the workplace, may well lie in the 1964 Civil Rights Act, a law that is older than most of the lobbyists who are working on this issue.

II. The Law Reform Movement: Mobilization in an Era of Retreat

While there are lots of lessons that we have learned from chapters one and two of the civil rights movement, we're in a new day. We need a little boost. There is so much to be learned from [the LGBT forces].
—Judith Browne Dianis, quoted in *San Francisco Magazine*, 2012[40]

One cannot understand the ways in which legal claims for LGBT equality signal both continuity and change in the civil rights paradigm without understanding the historical context and legal culture in which those claims were formulated, debated, and adjudicated. Lawyers who brought LGBT rights claims beginning roughly in the 1980s had the advantage of well-established constitutional law doctrines and equal rights statutes that were in their infancy for an earlier generation of civil rights lawyers working in the 1950s and 1960s. Ironically, however, the LGBT rights lawyers who sought to build on the legal foundations set in place by earlier social justice lawyers discovered that the foundations themselves were eroding. The adaptations made by the legal wing of the LGBT civil rights movement offer a window into changes in strategy and innovations in tactics that other civil rights movements can learn and utilize.

LGBT rights strategies emerged on a large scale only after—indeed, long after—the end of the Warren and early Burger Courts. LGBT rights litigation got off the ground not in the afterglow of *Brown v. Board of Education*,[41] but in the midst of a rights counterrevolution. The result was a strange disconnect. Many of us grew up with civil rights movement lawyers as heroes and with an aspirational understanding of the potential for using law to achieve justice that grew out of experiencing the 1960s during childhood. When baby boomers (including the first generation of women in significant numbers) began attending law school, public interest law was already a recognized field. Some of us studied with civil rights lawyers who had become law professors. We took courses designed to train us as advocates for disadvantaged groups, an opportunity that did not exist when the older generation had been in law school. Upon graduation, many of us secured jobs with public interest and civil rights groups or worked with civil rights units of government agencies—organizations that were available for young lawyers to join, rather than to have to invent.

The legal culture into which we graduated, however, had changed dramatically in a conservative direction. The single most prominent issue in legal politics grew out of a backlash movement rather than a civil rights movement: the continuing effort to reverse *Roe v. Wade*,[42] a goal adopted as official policy by the Department of Justice after President Ronald Reagan took office.[43] As the Reagan administration brilliantly used the power of judicial appointment to deepen the conservative nature of the federal bench that had begun under President Nixon,[44] a new consensus emerged among progressives: that federal courts had become unreliable, at best, as allies in struggles for equality. In response to Reagan's policies and appointments, traditional civil rights groups were drawn to Congress, where Democrats controlled both chambers from 1986 to

1994.[45] Congress, rather than the courts, became the site for expansions of rights to new groups and for legislation effectively reversing Supreme Court decisions that had narrowly interpreted civil rights statutes.[46]

Advocates seeking to establish equality protections for LGBT persons adopted the adjustments made by the older groups and developed new ones. The federal courts almost literally closed to equal protection claims based on sexual orientation after the Supreme Court upheld the legitimacy of a state law that criminalized same-sex intimacy. In *Bowers v. Hardwick*,[47] the Court torpedoed what was then the movement's legal priority—eliminating sodomy laws, upon which so much antigay discrimination was based. Although grounded in liberty rather than equality analysis, that decision prevented any significant victory for a class understood as being defined by criminal conduct until the Court's decision in *Romer v. Evans* ten years later.

LGBT advocates turned to state courts as an alternative. When *Hardwick* was decided, a deliberate shift to litigation strategies based on state constitutional claims had already occurred among progressive lawyers engaged with issues such as school financing.[48] Building on this base, LGBT rights lawyers began identifying and litigating challenges to state sodomy laws in state courts. The successes in the campaign to invalidate sodomy laws eventually became the most successful use of state constitutions to expand rights. Half of the sodomy laws that had been in existence at the time of *Hardwick* were eliminated, which paved the way for the Supreme Court's repudiation of *Hardwick* in the 2003 *Lawrence v. Texas* decision.[49]

On the national level, LGBT rights lawyers joined other civil rights groups in seeking relief in Congress, but to a lesser extent. Their major success was the inclusion of HIV/AIDS as a presumptively covered disability in the Americans with Disabilities Act adopted in 1990.[50] Most of the Washington-based LGBT lobbying addressed issues that arose from the first decade of the HIV/AIDS crisis.[51] The movement's greatest congressional setback was the enactment of Don't Ask Don't Tell legislation following President Clinton's failed attempt to allow openly gay persons to serve in the military.[52]

What the LGBT legal groups did much more extensively than traditional civil rights groups was to focus on state legislatures. During the 1980s, this strategy was defensive—driven primarily by the need to respond to proposals for coercive restrictions on persons with HIV/AIDS that arose as amendments to state public health laws.[53] LGBT organizations often formed alliances with public health officials, who understood that prevention and treatment efforts would be more successful if patients and those at risk trusted them. To a large extent, the strategy worked; the kinds of quarantines and forced testing that many had feared did not materialize.[54]

A second, positive rather than defensive, factor drew LGBT rights advocates to state legislatures: campaigns to add protection based on sexual orientation—and later gender identity—to state antidiscrimination laws. The initial adoption of laws prohibiting discrimination based on race and religion had also begun with state legislatures. The pace of enactment of sexual orientation protection between 1990 and today resembles that of the race discrimination laws between 1945, when New York adopted the nation's first such law, and 1963, just before the federal statute was enacted.[55] With their attention appropriately directed to national civil rights laws, the traditional racial justice constituency groups had little ongoing engagement with state legislatures. As a result, the discourse of civil rights in state legislatures since the 1980s has focused almost exclusively on LGBT issues, together with contests over abortion laws.

The turn to the state level of lawmaking—in both courts and legislatures—has been a distinguishing characteristic of LGBT rights lawyering, and it has served the movement well. The mutual familiarity between state lawmakers and LGBT rights advocates that has developed since the 1980s has probably contributed significantly to legal progress in moderate to liberal regions of the United States. On the biggest issue of family law—marriage equality—the extent of legislative success was dramatic. Of the twelve jurisdictions where same-sex marriage was authorized under state law at the time of the Supreme Court decision requiring the federal government to accept those expanded definitions of marriage for the purpose of federal benefits, the change in law occurred by legislative action in ten.[56] Marriage equality was forced by a judicial decision in only two states.[57]

Some scholars, most prominently Gerald Rosenberg,[58] continue to assert an old critique of civil rights lawyers, now adding to it the lawyers in marriage equality cases: that they have been blind to the lack of social progress achieved by litigation and the risk of backlash it generates. In fact, civil rights groups long ago began to develop multidimensional forms of advocacy that are not dependent on litigation.[59] The LGBT rights movement provides the strongest refutation of Rosenberg's arguments. Although some marriage equality litigation undoubtedly has triggered backlash in the short term, advocates have adeptly managed a complex overall strategy, relying on organizing and education and coordinating lawsuits with lobbying in state legislatures and even with anticipated referenda.[60] Litigation is no longer seen as the rifle-shot path to equality but rather as merely one device in an increasingly high-tech set of tools. Litigation, in other words, has become radically decentered in civil rights strategy.

In this environment, LGBT lawyering groups have developed an extraordinary level of sophistication with regard to nonjuridical modes and technologies of advocacy. If the emblematic movement tactic during the late 1980s and early 1990s was an ACT-UP (AIDS Coalition to Unleash Power) sit-in or demonstration, the core tactic now is polling. Today, LGBT groups commission their own polling, the results of which often shape their messaging strategies, which in turn suggest the parameters of "story banks" that solicit and authorize the collection of accounts of certain kinds of experiences, stories that one often finds summarized in the opening portions of the complaints that initiate litigation, in legislative testimony, and in media feature stories.[61] Until recently, a nonprofit group's media strategy consisted of efforts to attract media attention and coverage of its issues; today it is likely to be an intentional and data-driven set of techniques to change public opinion, the success or failure of which can be measured.

Use of new technologies of social change is not unique to the LGBT civil rights movement,[62] but LGBT groups have been early adopters of mechanisms generated by broader technological change. One reason is necessity: the frequency of antigay ballot initiatives has forced LGBT groups into the electoral arena more often than other civil rights groups.[63] This experience has required LGBT advocates to develop more sophisticated methods for persuading voters—not simply judges or legislators—to reject antigay arguments.

Direct electoral political battles over LGBT rights issues culminated in the unsuccessful effort to defeat Proposition 8 in California in 2008. Approximately 53 percent of a total of 13.4 million voters supported a state constitutional amendment to prohibit same-sex marriage.[64] Each side raised and spent more than $40 million, making it second only to the presidential contest that year in the amount of money spent on an election campaign.[65] The scale of fundraising and the nature of the political expertise required to compete in that kind of electoral environment creates an immediate need for the capacity to play to win in the big leagues, and its urgency simultaneously discourages any instinct to challenge the structures of wealth that distort the electoral system. Just as civil rights groups learn from each other, so, of course, do conservatives, and this history of repeated ballot initiatives may be predictive of continuing antiequality campaigns on other issues, such as immigration.

Combined, these interventions outside the courtroom have helped shape new constitutional meanings of LGBT equality. In an ironic full circle return to Rosenberg's criticism, high-stakes court challenges on the issue of marriage have become virtually a no-lose proposition. Messaging campaigns do not explain all of this success, and there were some aspects of the marriage equality campaign that fell short. The litigation to invalidate Proposition 8 succeeded but only for California; it did not produce the nationwide ruling that plaintiffs had sought.[66] And even in requiring all states to allow same-sex marriage, the Supreme Court declined to adopt heightened scrutiny in analyzing the constitutionality of sexual orientation discrimination more generally.[67] But public opinion shifts surely did pave the way for the remarkable number of lower court opinions that struck down exclusionary marriage laws in the wake of *Windsor*,[68] despite the lack of guidance in that opinion.[69] In the spring of 2013, *Time Magazine* declared on its cover that "gay marriage [has] already won."[70] For the marriage equality campaign, it would be only a slight exaggeration to say that the Supreme Court became a very, very important opinion poll.

These nonlitigation skills are not unique to LGBT groups, but multidimensional advocacy has been formative in its impact on relatively newer rights organizations like the LGBT groups and on a younger generation of leaders in all groups. The by-products of new technologies of advocacy and the blurred lines between legal advocacy and election campaigns will shape the future dimensions of civil rights practice in American political culture.

III. Social Change: Civil Rights + Corporate Social Responsibility = Corporatist Civil Rights

> *Struggles for human rights always begin with brave men and women who stand up, isolated, against the forces of oppression. But, in the United States, victory really arrives on the glorious day when the people with money decide discrimination is bad for business.*
> —New York Times, Feb. 26, 2014[71]

Law is not an autonomous realm, least of all when one seeks social justice reforms. Other dimensions of movement advocacy interact with the kinds of legal work described in the prior section. The meaning of constitutional principles and the aspiration to equality are shaped by many actors—not only courts and legislatures, or even only those in the legal profession more broadly.

One distinguishing mark of the LGBT civil rights movement is the extent to which the corporate business sector has become an important nonjuridical voice. More so than in other civil rights movements,[72] gay advocates have negotiated directly with employers to obtain internal policies against discrimination and have enlisted corporate support to stress economic reasons for greater equality. Out of these efforts, a major coalition has emerged: an alliance between LGBT rights and corporate interests that has become one of the most effective movement resources for combating the arguments of moral conservatives.

Again, historical context is everything. The LGBT civil rights movement grew up under and into a Reagan-Bush-Clinton-Bush-Obama corporatist political culture. Throughout that period, the political and economic dynamics of globalization weakened the power of government to regulate multinational enterprises and to mitigate the localized externalities of downward pressure on wages and benefits. The balance of power between business on the one hand and labor and environmental interests on the other shifted dramatically from what it was in 1964. It should not be surprising that the significance and presumed legitimacy of business interests would be baked into any overall strategy for achieving civil rights that essentially began during this era.

The alliance with corporate interests in the LGBT rights movement grew out of the effort to eliminate workplace discrimination. Outside of municipalities, usually in either large urban or university-dominated areas, most of the early successes in securing protection came through negotiations with large corporate employers rather than from legislation.[73] As more employers agreed to adopt antidiscrimination rules, the Human Rights Campaign began a Corporate Equality Index that itself has become a major factor in further driving adoption of these policies, fostering a competition among human relations and diversity professionals as they sought the 100 percent score awarded to entities that satisfied each of the HRC's indicia of "corporate equality."[74]

The larger political context for this effort was the rise of a Corporate Social Responsibility (CSR) concept within the business sector roughly coexistent with the rise of the LGBT rights movement.[75] CSR consists of voluntary, nonenforceable practices by which companies use methods of self-regulation to integrate social and environmental concerns in their business operations and in their relations with stakeholders.[76] The power of internal corporate law has grown as firms have been able to bargain with public authorities and to relocate in search of less restrictive legal regimes. Implicit in the CSR concept is recognition that corporations comprise a privatist layer of sovereignty, with internal law that crosses traditional political boundaries of state and nation.

Antidiscrimination agreements for LGBT employees are a classic CSR strategy. Especially in sectors such as technology and tourism, corporations have long viewed the LGBT population as an important source of skilled labor or an important market segment for their products, or both.[77] Today, with popular support for LGBT equality increasing,

88 percent of Fortune 500 companies have adopted policies that prohibit discrimination and provide benefits for LGBT employees.[78] LGBT employee groups exist at nearly three hundred large employers.[79]

The corporate-friendly approach has brought cascading benefits to the LGBT civil rights movement, at least among elites. Most significantly, it has produced a mutually legitimating discourse that can be deployed in multiple settings. Advocacy groups repeatedly invoke a "business leads the way" theme in efforts to persuade Congress or other legislatures to enact antidiscrimination protections.[80] When the leading corporate actors in a state, region, or nation have endorsed equal treatment, it is much easier to depict companies that continue to discriminate as laggards or outliers. Corporate support extended to marriage as well. Amicus briefs were filed by a number of large corporate employers in both the challenge to the "Defense of Marriage Act" and the challenge to state laws prohibiting same-sex marriage. Employers argued that businesses were harmed by the unnecessary complexities in personnel-related laws caused by their inability to treat married same-sex couples in the same way as married different-sex couples under federal laws.[81] A Wikipedia entry lists almost 125 corporations that have issued statements in support of same-sex marriage.[82]

The power of corporate support for LGBT rights burst into public view in 2014 when Arizona Governor Jan Brewer vetoed legislation that would have allowed persons with religious objections to same-sex marriage to decline service to gay customers.[83] Behind her decision was a business-led lobbying effort that stressed the potential of antigay laws to harm prospects for economic development.[84] The episode illustrated the value to LGBT rights advocates of using corporate interests to peel off economic from social conservatives. Indeed, LGBT rights, including marriage, seems to have become a reverse wedge issue that once fueled support for conservative politicians but is now weakening the free market-traditional values coalition on which the Republican Party has depended.

There are three major costs to this alliance, however. First, it is contingent on a discourse of cultural and political sameness—that is, that the achievement of LGBT equality would change very little in the broader society, in family dynamics and certainly in the economic structure.[85] As Patricia Cain has noted, every civil rights movement has relied on sameness arguments to allay fears about the effects of eliminating legal stigma,[86] but such arguments, by their very nature, tend to de-radicalize a social movement and distance it from broader efforts to rectify injustice.

Second, the mutual legitimation effect of an LGBT-corporate alliance strengthens a discourse promoting privatization of social costs and risks. In family law, for example, the tendency to shift the cost associated with vulnerable populations (unemployed homemakers, children, the elderly) to individual caretakers has long been criticized by feminist theorists but was largely unexamined in LGBT advocates' proposals for new family status forms of domestic partnerships and same-sex marriage.[87] More generally, the effort to allocate to individuals the expenditures that flow from increasingly unregulated corporate discretion in hiring, firing, and compensation of employees has become a major theme in conservative politics in the United States.[88] This development conflicts with all but the narrowest conception of equality.

Lastly, the man-bites-dog narrative that results when well-known conservatives, such as Theodore Olson, endorse LGBT rights issues tends to garner an outsize amount of media attention and public interest. This can provide a powerful mechanism for breaking through media noise and clutter to convey a message that equality is a demand with broad support, but it can also be used to reinforce old stereotypes that the LGBT community is almost exclusively composed of affluent white males.

IV. The Future: Toward Antihierarchy

For years groups seeking equality for gays drew inspiration from the civil-rights era...[After the adoption of Prop 8], Gay campaigners concluded that their approach had been wrong. With their talk of discrimination, they had been appealing to voters' heads...[The new strategy] involves persuading voters that their existing values allow them to accept gay marriage...because same-sex couples are asking to join the institution, rather than to change it.
—The Economist, Feb. 2014[89]

The future of the civil rights paradigm turns on what "civil rights" means in a political and legal environment in which formal equality has been incorporated into institutions of governance and cultural authority, although structural forms of subordination continue and even worsen. The gains of race and gender civil rights movements have reshuffled those hierarchies, benefiting most the women and people of color who are socially advantaged in terms of class. Those least likely to benefit have been persons with intersecting vectors of social disadvantage, for whom the indicia of social inequality have hardened or condensed at the bottom of the social pyramid. The prospect that formal equality will fail to achieve social equality, which is so evident with regard to race and gender,[90] looms for the LGBT civil rights movement as well.

Liberal equality discourse may provide an essential tool in a long-term effort to more fundamentally alter patterns of social stratification. But there is an inevitable temptation to declare victory, paired with a tendency to run out of steam (not to mention donors), when a civil rights movement has achieved a dramatic success such as marriage. The big question for LGBT advocates is whether, when that point is reached on these issues, "today's civil rights movement" will take on the project of challenging the economic and social hierarchy associated with sexuality.

The paradoxical effect of securing formal equality can be to strengthen the subordination of those at the bottom of the pyramid. Progress in ending sex discrimination, for example, can reinforce (and not merely pass by) the oppression of low-income women and women of color by creating a mutually reinforcing dynamic of invisibility.[91] If harms disproportionately affecting LGBT people of color or who have low incomes are not challenged as such and if privileged sectors of the LGBT community turn their attention away from a seemingly completed set of goals, the least powerful groups will become even more vulnerable. The entrenched nature of discrimination against some women and some LGBT people not only will remain but also will worsen.

There are ideological consequences as well as material harms associated with the condensation of social hierarchy. The resilience of stratification along lines of race and poverty, in the face of civil rights progress, creates a naturalization effect—a sense that there are intractable, irremediable causes associated with the very nature of the people who suffer the worst that explains why they have not succeeded.

Let me close by briefly sketching two possible futures for the social meaning of "civil rights." The first model is civil rights as a cultural commodity. LGBT equality is a global brand, grounded in the most desirable market demographic: young adults (gay and straight) who are in the process of developing public policy loyalties, as they do product loyalties, that they will continue to favor for the rest of their lives. LGBT equality is a stakeholder-governed, public-private partnership. It is both consumer friendly and a consumer durable. It combines value and growth. It is market-friendly equality, embedded in the concepts associated with CSR.

The second model of civil rights is grounded in egalitarianism and the project of dismantling hierarchy. It is made visible by demographic data documenting the LGBT individuals at greatest risk of harm, such as low-income parents who—even if entitled to lawfully marry—routinely engage with a variety of hostile public and private institutions. Such persons are at high risk of HIV infection, of police harassment, of incarceration, and of inadequate educations—all for reasons that are not limited to, but are related to, their sexuality or gender identity.[92] They are concentrated not in the well-known gay strongholds of D.C., Fort Lauderdale, and San Francisco but in San Antonio, Memphis, and Virginia Beach.[93]

One does not have to strain to identify intersectionality in such situations. Relatively advantaged LGBT people experience modified, usually mitigated systems of stratification, often sheltered by race or gender privilege. Those without such shelters are trapped in complex hierarchies, mutually constituted by multiple vectors of subordination. Exclusions can be attacked one by one. But it is not possible to engage any hierarchy—whether sexual, racial, or other—without addressing this complexity. Heteronormativity is a layered set of interlocking hierarchies, not just a collection of exclusions. It is not merely straight—it has a race, a class, and even a geography.

One of these models of civil rights—perhaps even a mixture of both—will comprise Civil Rights 3.0.

About the Author

Professor of law, Georgetown University Law Center, and Distinguished Scholar, Williams Institute, UCLA.

Notes

1. Adam Nagourney, *A Watershed Move, Both Risky and Inevitable*, N.Y. TIMES, May 9, 2012, at A-1, *available at* http://www.nytimes.com/2012/05/10/us/politics/obamas-watershed-move-on-gay-marriage.html?_r=2&ref=todayspaper&.

2. *See, e.g.*, Emily Bazelon, *The Civil Rights Case of Our Generation*, SLATE, Dec. 7, 2012 (referring to same-sex marriage case), *available at* http://www.slate.com/articles/news_and_politics/jurisprudence/2012/12/supreme_court_to_hear_gay_marriage_cases_the_justices_agree_to_hear_windsor.html;   Susan Kellerher, *Gregoire: Same Sex Marriage "the Civil Rights Issue of This Generation,"*SEATTLE TIMES, Nov. 6, 2012, *available at* http://blogs.seattletimes.com/politicsnorthwest/2012/11/06/gregoire-same-sex-marriage-the-civil-rights-issue-of-this-generation/; N.Y. Times, *Next Civil Rights Landmark*, Dec. 7, 2012, *available at*   http://www.nytimes.com/2012/12/08/opinion/next-civil-rights-landmark.html?hp=&adxnnl=1&adxnnlx=1354980094-hDkQU/vtqN8Lt9ZR0xd8cw&_r=0; Monique Ruffin, *It's Official: Gay Is the New Black*, HUFFINGTON POST, Dec. 28 2011, *available at* http://www.huffingtonpost.com/monique-ruffin/gay-civil-rights_b_1168897.html.

3. President Barak Obama, Second Inaugural Address (Jan. 21, 2013) ("We the people declare today that the most evident of truths—that all of us are created equal—is

the star that guides us still; just as it guided our forebears through Seneca Falls, and Selma, and Stonewall; just as it guided all those men and women, sung and unsung, who left footprints along this great Mall, to hear a preacher say that we cannot walk alone; to hear a King proclaim that our individual freedom is inextricably bound to the freedom of every soul on Earth."), available at http://www.whitehouse.gov/the-press-office/2013/01/21/inaugural-address-president-barack-obama.

4. The reference is to FRANCIS FUKUYAMA, THE END OF HISTORY AND THE LAST MAN (1992), which argued that the fall of the Soviet Union left classic Western liberal thought as the only viable paradigm in global politics.

5. To make this concrete, if you were ten years old when Ronald Reagan was elected president in 1980, you are forty-five years old today.

6. Bob Dylan, "For Dave Glover" available at http://www.bjorner.com/WFMH%20-%20Poems%20&%20Other%20Pieces.htm#_Toc515002067, *quoted in*SEAN WILENTZ, BOB DYLAN IN AMERICA 277 (2010).

7. For a comparison of the impact of *Lawrence v. Texas* with that of *Roe v. Wade* using this analytical framework, see Nan D. Hunter, *Reflections on Sexual Liberty and Equality: "Through Seneca Falls and Selma and Stonewall,"* 60 UCLA L. REV. DISCOURSE 172 (2013).

8. *Seeinfra.*

9. Jeremy W. Peter, *Senate Approves Ban of Antigay Bias in the Workplace*, N.Y. TIMES, Nov. 7, 2013, *available at* http://www.nytimes.com/2013/11/08/us/politics/senate-moves-to-final-vote-on-workplace-gay-bias-ban.html?emc=etal.

10. Chris Johnson, *Boehner Tells LGBT Caucus "No Way" ENDA Will Pass*, WASHINGTON BLADE, Jan. 29, 2014, *available at* http://www.washingtonblade.com/2014/01/29/boehner-tells-lgbt-caucus-way-enda-will-pass/. A different version of ENDA had passed the House in 2007 but was not considered by the Senate.

11. Chai R. Feldblum, *The Federal Gay Rights Bill: From Bella to ENDA, in*CREATING CHANGE: SEXUALITY, PUBLIC POLICY AND CIVIL RIGHTS 178–79 (John D'Emilio et al. eds., 2000).

12. JEFF KREHELY, CTR. FOR AM. PROGRESS, POLLS SHOW HUGE PUBLIC SUPPORT FOR GAY AND TRANSGENDER WORKPLACE PROTECTIONS (2011), http://www.americanprogress.org/wp-content/uploads/issues/2011/06/pdf/protection_poll.pdf.

13. Equality Act 2010: Guidance, https://www.gov.uk/equality-act-2010-guidance (last updated June 16, 2015).

14. Since the Civil Rights Act of 1964, Congress has enacted laws to protect the aged, Pub. L. No. 90-202, 81 Stat. 602 (1967); pregnant women, Pub. L. No. 95-555, § 1, 92 Stat. 2076 (1978); persons with disabilities, Pub. L. No. 101-336, 104 Stat. 327 (1990); and persons with genetic markers for serious medical conditions, Pub. L. No. 110-233, 122 Stat. 881 (2008).

15. ENDA, S. 815, § 4(g), *available at* https://www.govtrack.us/congress/bills/113/s815/text.

16. Before same-sex marriage was recognized nationwide, some courts found that limiting health insurance coverage to married couples would have a disparate effect on lesbian and gay employees who could not marry. Diaz v. Brewer, 656 F.3d 1008 (9th Cir. 2012); Irizarry v. Bd. Educ. City of Chicago, 251 F.3d 604 (7th Cir. 2001).

17. *Employment Non-Discrimination Act of 2009: Hearing on H.R. 3017 before the H. Comm. on Educ. & Labor*, 111th Cong. 32 (2009) (statement of Camille A. Olson, Partner, Seyforth Shaw, LLP).

18. 401 U.S. 424 (1971).

19. Robert Belton, *Title VII at Forty: A Brief Look at the Birth, Death, and Resurrection of the Disparate Impact Theory of Discrimination*, 22 HOFSTRA LAB. & EMP. L.J. 431, 433 (2005); Alfred W. Blumrosen, *The Legacy of* Griggs: *Social Progress and Subjective Judgments*, 63 CHI.-KENT L. REV. 1, 1–2 (1987).

20. *See* Reva Siegel, *Why Equal Protection No Longer Protects: The Evolving Forms of Status-Enforcing State Action*, 49 STAN. L. REV. 1111, 1145 (1997).

21. Texas Dep't of Housing and Community Affairs v. Inclusive Communities Project, Inc., 135 S.Ct. 2507 (2015) (Fair Housing Act); Smith v. City of Jackson, 544 U.S. 228 (2005) (Age Discrimination Act).

22. Alexander v. Sandoval, 532 U.S. 275 (2001).

23. Gen. Bldg. Contractors Ass'n v. Pennsylvania, 458 U.S. 375 (1982).

24. Washington v. Davis, 426 U.S. 229 (1976).

25. City of Mobile v. Bolden, 446 U.S. 55 (1980).

26. 490 U.S. 642 (1989).

27. Pub. L. No. 102-166, 105 Stat. 1071 (1991).

28. Neal Devins, *Reagan Redux*, 68 NOTRE DAME L. REV. 955, 990–95 (1993).

29. 42 U.S.C. 2000ff-7(a)–(b) (Supp. V 2012).

30. S. 815, supra note 15 at Section 6. See Tierney Sneed, Why LGBT Groups Turned on ENDA, US News, July 9, 2014 (available at http://www.usnews.com/news/articles/2014/07/09/why-lgbt-groups-turned-on-enda).

31. Obergefell v. Hodges, 576 U.S. _____, 135 S.Ct. 2584 (2015); United States v. Windsor, 570 U.S., 133 S. Ct. 2675 (2013); Lawrence v. Texas, 539 U.S. 558 (2003); Romer v. Evans, 517 U.S. 620 (1996).

32. In *Windsor*, for example, the Court intertwined equality and federalism grounds to conclude that "no legitimate purpose overcomes the purpose and effect to disparage and to injure those whom the State, by its marriage laws, sought to protect in personhood and dignity." 133 S. Ct. at 2696. *See* Michael J. Klarman, *Comment*: Windsor *and* Brown: *Marriage Equality and Racial Equality*, 127 HARV. L. REV. 127, 140–42 (2013) (explaining why *Windsor* opinion is "unconvincing as a doctrinal matter").

33. City of Cleburne v. Cleburne Living Ctr., 473 U.S. 432, 445–46 (1985) (reasoning that if the class in question was deemed suspect, it would broaden the landscape of suspect classification in a way that the Court was unwilling to do).

34. Higgins v. New Balance Athletic Shoe, Inc., 194 F.3d 252 (1st Cir. 1999); Dawson v. Brumble & Brumble, 398 F.3d 211, 218 (2d Cir. 2005); Prowel v. Wise Bus. Forms, Inc., 579 F.3d 285, 287 (3d Cir. 2009); EEOC v. Boh Bros. Constr. Co., 689 F.3d 458, 457–60 (5th Cir. 2013) (en banc); Barnes v. Cincinnati, 401 F.3d 729, 737 (6th Cir. 2005); Hamm v. Weyauwega Milk Prods., Inc., 332 F.3d 1058, 1062 (7th Cir. 2003); Scmedding v. Tnemec Co., 187 F.3d 862, 865 (8th Cir. 1999); Schwenk v. Hartford, 204 F.3d 1187, 1202 (9th Cir. 2000); Glenn v. Brumby, 663 F.3d 1312, 1316–17 (11th Cir. 2011) (Equal Protection Clause analysis).

35. Cary Franklin, *Inventing the "Traditional Concept" of Sex Discrimination*, 125 HARV. L. REV. 1309, 1375–78 (2012).

36. Baldwin v. Foxx, No. 0120133080, 2015 WL 4397641 (E.E.O.C., July 15, 2015); Macy v. Holder, No. 0120120821, 2012 WL 1435995 (E.E.O.C. Apr. 20, 2012).

37. U.S. Equal Employment Opportunity Commission, "What You Should Know About EEOC and the Enforcement Protections for LGBT Workers," *available at* http://www.eeoc.gov/eeoc/newsroom/wysk/enforcement_protections_ lgbt_workers.cfm; U.S. Equal Employment Opportunity Commission, Office of Field Programs, "Intake and Charge Processing of Title VII Claims of Sex Discrimination by LGBT Individuals," Nov. 9, 2012.

38. U.S. Equal Employment Opportunity Commission, "What You Should Know About EEOC and the Enforcement Protections for LGBT Workers," *available at* http://www.eeoc.gov/eeoc/newsroom/wysk/enforcement_protections_ lgbt_workers.cfm.

39. *See* 42 U.S.C. § 2000e-2(k) (2006); 42 U.S.C. § 2000e-1(a) (2006). *Compare* to ENDA, S. 815 §§ 4(g) and 6, *available at* https://www.govtrack.us/congress/bills/113/s815/ text.

40. Nina Martin, *Pride of the Left*, SAN FRANCISCO MAGAZINE, Oct. 17, 2012, *available at* http://www.modernluxury.com/san-francisco/story/pride-of-the-left.

41. 347 U.S. 483 (1954).

42. 410 U.S. 113 (1973).

43. Amy Goldstein & Jo Becker, *Alito Helped Craft Reagan-Era Move to Restrict "Roe,"* WASH. POST, Dec. 1, 2005, http://www.washingtonpost.com/wp-dyn/content/ article/2005/11/30/AR2005113000723.html.

44. Jon Gottschall, *Reagan's Appointments to the U.S. Court of Appeals: The Continuation of a Judicial Revolution*, 70 JUDICATURE 48, 49 (1986) ("Nixon's administration pledged to reverse a purported liberal tide in federal criminal justice through the appointment of judicial 'strict constructionists...'"); Joan Biskupic, *Reagan's Influence Lives on in U.S. Courts*, USA TODAY, May 12, 2008, http://usatoday30.usatoday.com/news/washington/judicial/ 2008-05-11-appellate-judges_N.htm.

45. *See* STEPHEN G. CHRISTIANSON, FACTS ABOUT CONGRESS 514, 521, 530, 539 (1996). (showing Democratic majorities in the 100th through 103rd Congresses).

46. Congress expanded coverage beyond what the Court had allowed in narrow statutory interpretations in the Civil Rights Restoration Act, Pub. L. No. 100-259, 102 Stat. 28 (1988), and the Civil Rights Act of 1991, Pub. L. No. 102-166, 105 Stat. 1071 (1991). During the same time period, advocates used the same strategy to preserve important components of the Voting Rights Act. Hugh Davis Graham, *The Civil Rights Act and the American Regulatory State*, *in* LEGACIES OF THE 1964 CIVIL RIGHTS ACT 55–60 (Bernard Grofman ed., 2000).

47. 478 U.S. 186 (1986).

48. John Dayton, *Serrano and Its Progeny: An Analysis of 30 Years of School Funding Litigation*, 157 WEST'S EDUC. L. REP. 447, 447 (2001) ("When the U.S. Supreme Court largely foreclosed the option of federal funding equity challenges in *San Antonio v. Rodriguez*,...plaintiffs...turn[ed] to state courts for relief."). *See also* William J. Brennan, *The Bill of Rights and the States: The Revival of State Constitutions as Guardians of Individual Rights*, 61 N.Y.U. L. REV. 535 (1986).

49. Lawrence v. Texas, 539 U.S. 558, 578 (2003).

50. Roger N. Braden, *AIDS: Dealing with the Plague*, 19 N. KY. L. REV. 277, 319–21 (1992).

51. William B. Turner, *Mirror Images: Lesbian/Gay Civil Rights in the Carter and Reagan Administrations*, inCREATING CHANGE,*supra* note 11 at 22–28.

52. National Defense Authorization Act for Fiscal Year 1994, Pub. L. No. 103-160, § 571, 107 Stat. 1547, 1670 (1993); Mark Thompson, *"Don't Ask, Don't Tell" Turns 15*, TIME MAG., Jan. 28, 2008, http://content.time.com/time/nation/article/0,8599,1707545,00.html (citing Clinton's campaign pledge to reverse an executive order barring gays and lesbians from serving).

53. *See* Ronald Bayer, *The Continuing Tensions between Individual Rights and Public Health: Talking Point on Public Health versus Civil Liberties*, 8 EMBO REPORTS 1099, 1100 (2007).

54. *See* Ronald Bayer & Amy Fairchild-Carrino, *AIDS and the Limits of Control: Public Health Orders, Quarantine, and Recalcitrant Behavior*, 83 AM. J. PUB. HEALTH 1471 (1993).

55. *Compare* the sequence of adoption of pre-1964 state civil rights statutes, ANTHONY S. CHEN, THE FIFTH FREEDOM: JOBS, POLITICS AND CIVIL RIGHTS IN THE UNITED STATES 1941-1972, at 118 (2009) *with* that of amendments adding sexual orientation protection, WILLIAM N. ESKRIDGE, JR., & NAN D. HUNTER, SEXUALITY, GENDER AND THE LAW 567 note a (3d ed. 2011).

56. United States v. Windsor, 133 S.Ct. at 2690 (Connecticut, Delaware, District of Columbia, Maryland, Minnesota, New Hampshire, New York, Rhode Island, Vermont, and Washington).

57. Iowa and Massachusetts,.

58. GERALD N. ROSENBERG, THE HOLLOW HOPE: CAN COURTS BRING ABOUT SOCIAL CHANGE? 415–19 (2d ed. 2008).

59. ALAN K. CHEN & SCOTT L. CUMMINGS, PUBLIC INTEREST LAWYERING: A CONTEMPORARY PERSPECTIVE 515–19 (2013); Deborah L. Rhode, *Public Interest Law: The Movement at Midlife*, 60 STAN. L. REV. 2027, 2042–46 (2008).

60. CHEN & CUMMINGS, *supra* note 59, at 501–07; Mary L. Bonauto, Goodridge *in Context*, 40 HARV. C.R.-C.L. L. REV. 1, 2–21 (2005); Douglas Nejaime, *Winning through Losing*, 96 IOWA L. REV. 941 (2011).

61. CHEN & CUMMINGS, *supra* note 59 at 267–68, 520–21, 530.

62. *See e.g.*, Amy Kapczynski, *The Access to Knowledge Mobilization and the New Politics of Intellectual Property*, 117 YALE L.J. 804 (2008); Seth F. Kreimer, *Technologies of Protest: Insurgent Social Movements and the First Amendment in the Era of the Internet*, 150 U. PA. L. REV. 119 (2001).

63. Barbara S. Gamble, *Putting Civil Rights to a Popular Vote*, 41 AM. J. POL. SCI. 245 (1997).

64. Institute of Governmental Studies, "Proposition 8," *available at* https://igs.berkeley.edu/library/elections/proposition-8.

65. Justin Ewers, *California Same-Sex Marriage Initiative Campaigns Shatter Spending Records*, U.S. NEWS & WORLD REP., Oct. 29, 2008, http://www.usnews.com/news/national/articles/2008/10/29/california-same-sex-marriage-initiative-campaigns-shatter-spending-records.

66. Hollingsworth v. Perry, 570 U.S. , 133 S. Ct. 2652 (2013).

67. Hollingsworth v. Perry, 570 U.S. , 133 S. Ct. 2652 (2013).

68. *See, e.g.*, DeLeon v. Perry, No. CA-00982, 2014 WL 715741 (W.D. Tex. Feb. 26, 2014); Bourke v. Beshear, No. 3:13-cv-750-H, 2014 WL 556729 (W.D. Ky. Feb. 12, 2014); Bishop v. United States *ex rel.* Holder, No. 04-CV-848-TCK-TLW, 2014 WL 116013 (N.D. Okla. Jan. 14, 2014); Lee v. Orr, 13-CV-8719, 2014 WL 683680 (N.D. Ill. Feb. 21, 2014); Bostic v. Rainey, No. 2:13cv395, 2014 WL 561978 (E.D. Va. Feb. 13, 2014); Kitchen v. Herbert, No. 2:13–cv–217, 2013 WL 6697874 (D. Utah Dec. 20, 2013); Garden State Equality v. Dow, 82 A.3d 336 (N.J. Super. Ct. Law Div. 2013); Griego v. Oliver, 316 P.3d 865 (N.M. 2013).

69. *Windsor*, 133 S. Ct. 2675.

70. *See* David Von Drehle, *Gay Marriage Already Won. The Supreme Court Hasn't Made Up Its Mind—but America Has*, TIME MAG., Apr. 8, 2013, *available at* http://content.time.com/time/covers/0,16641,20130408,00.html.

71. Gail Collins, *The State of Arizona*, N.Y. TIMES, Feb. 26, 2014, http://www.nytimes.com/2014/02/27/opinion/collins-the-state-of-arizona.html?partner=rssnyt&emc=rss&_r=0.

72. *Compare*GAVIN WRIGHT, SHARING THE PRIZE: THE ECONOMICS OF THE CIVIL RIGHTS REVOLUTION (2013). Business leaders now argue that discrimination in any form is bad for economies. Jim Yong Kim, *Discrimination by Law Carries a High Price*, WASH. POST, Feb. 27, 2014, http://www.washingtonpost.com/opinions/jim-yong-kim-the-high-costs-of-institutional-discrimination/2014/02/27/8cd37ad0-9fc5-11e3-b8d8-94577ff66b28_story.html.

73. *See*NICOLE CHRISTINE RAEBURN, CHANGING CORPORATE AMERICA FROM INSIDE OUT: LESBIAN AND GAY WORKPLACE RIGHTS 23–52 (2004).

74. *See*HUMAN RIGHTS CAMPAIGN, CORPORATE EQUALITY INDEX, http://www.hrc.org/campaigns/corporate-equality-index.

75. Jerome J. Shestack, *Corporate Social Responsibility in a Changing Corporate World*, *in*CORPORATE SOCIAL RESPONSIBILITY: THE CORPORATE GOVERNANCE OF THE 21ST CENTURY 114–18 (Ramon Mullerat ed., 2d ed. 2011).

76. LUC FRANSEN, CORPORATE SOCIAL RESPONSIBILITY AND GLOBAL LABOR STANDARDS: FIRMS AND ACTIVISTS IN THE MAKING OF PRIVATE REGULATION 4–7 (2012); Orly Lobel, *The Paradox of Extralegal Activism: Critical Legal Consciousness and Transformative Politics*, 120 HARV. L. REV. 937, 966–70 (2007).

77. Steve Friess, *Big Tech and Gay Rights Have Evolved Together*, POLITICO, June 25, 2013, http://www.politico.com/story/2013/06/big-tech-and-gay-rights-have-evolved-together-93361.html; Edward Iwata, *More Marketing Aimed at Gay Consumers*, USA TODAY, Nov. 2, 2006, http://usatoday30.usatoday.com/money/advertising/2006-11-02-gay-market-usat_x.htm. *See generally*FRANSEN, *supra* note 76, at 189–91; Shestack, *supra* note 75, at 120–22.

78. *See*HUMAN RIGHTS CAMPAIGN, LGBT EQUALITY AT THE FORTUNE 500, https://www.hrc.org/resources/entry/lgbt-equality-at-the-fortune-500.

79. *See*OUT AND EQUAL, http://outandequal.org/employee-resource-groups-corps.

80. *See, e.g.*, Kevin Bogardus, *Gay Rights Activists Turn to Fortune 500*, THE HILL, Nov. 6, 2013, http://thehill.com/business-a-lobbying/business-a-lobbying/189361-gay-rights-activists-tap-fortune-500-for-support; *Gay Marriage Advocates Gain Corporate Support*, ONE COMMUNITY BLOG (June 5, 2012, 3:24PM), http://www.onecommunity.co/blog/2012/23/gay-marriage-advocates-gain-corporate-support.

81. Brief of 278 Employers and Organizations Representing Employers as Amici

Curiae in Support of Respondent, United States v. Windsor, No. 12-307, 2013 WL 823227, 570 U.S. (2013). There, LGBT rights advocates were following the lead of racial justice advocates who secured amicus briefs from a number of large corporations and from retired military leaders making the argument that affirmative action is necessary for the competitiveness of U.S. firms in the context of global capitalism and for national security. Grutter v. Bollinger, 539 U.S. 306, 330–31 (2003). Tomiko Brown-Nagin sharply criticized this litigation tactic as enhancing the role of elites in determining the attention given by the Supreme Court and the media to justifications for affirmative action. Tomiko Brown-Nagin, *Elites, Social Movements and the Law*, 105 COLUM. L. REV. 1436, 1516–17 (2005).

82. WIKIPEDIA, LIST OF ORGANIZATIONS THAT SUPPORT SAME-SEX MARRIAGE IN THE UNITED STATES, http://en.wikipedia.org/wiki/List_of_organizations_that_support_same-sex_marriage_in_the_United_States.

83. Fernanda Santos, *Arizona Vetoes Right to Refuse Service to Gays*, N.Y. TIMES, Feb. 27, 2014, http://www.nytimes.com/2014/02/27/us/Brewer-arizona-gay-service-bill.html?_r=0.

84. *Id.*; Alexander Burns & M.J. Lee, *How Business Went "DEFCON 1" in Arizona*, POLITICO, Feb. 27, 2014, http://www.politico.com/story/2014/02/businesses-arizona-sb1062-104058.html; Adam Nagourney, *Arizona Bill Stirred Alarm in the G.O.P.*, N.Y. TIMES, Feb. 28, 2014, http://www.nytimes.com/2014/02/28/us/arizona-bill-allowing-refusal-of-service-to-gays-stirred-alarm-in-the-gop.html.

85. *See generally* Nan D. Hunter, *The Future Impact of Same-Sex Marriage: More Questions Than Answers*, 100 GEO. L.J. 1855 (2012).

86. PATRICIA A. CAIN, RAINBOW RIGHTS: THE ROLE OF LAWYERS AND COURTS IN THE LESBIAN AND GAY CIVIL RIGHTS MOVEMENT 277–81 (2000).

87. Nan D. Hunter, *Marriage, Law and Gender: A Feminist Inquiry*, 1 LAW & SEXUALITY 9 (1991).

88. JACOB S. HACKER, THE GREAT RISK SHIFT: THE NEW ECONOMIC INSECURITY AND THE DECLINE OF THE AMERICAN DREAM (2008).

89. Lexington, *Heads and Hearts: What Victorious Gay-Marriage Campaigners Can Teach Others*, THE ECONOMIST, Feb. 1, 2014, at 26.

90. Louise G. Trubek, *Public Interest Law: Facing the Problems of Maturity*, 33 U. ARK. LITTLE ROCK L. REV. 417, 424–33 (2011).

91. MARTHA CHAMALLAS, INTRODUCTION TO FEMINIST LEGAL THEORY 81–83 (2d ed. 2003).

92. See, for example, a series of reports from the Williams Institute, including M.V. LEE BADGETT ET AL., NEW PATTERNS OF POVERTY IN THE LESBIAN, GAY AND BISEXUAL COMMUNITY (June 2013), *available at* http://williamsinstitute. law.ucla.edu/wp-content/uploads/LGB-Poverty-Update-Jun-2013.pdf; ANGELIKI KASTANIS & BIANCA WILSON, RACE/ETHNICITY, GENDER AND SOCIOECONOMIC WELLBEING OF INDIVIDUALS IN SAME-SEX COUPLES, *available at* http://williamsinstitute.law.ucla.edu/wp-content/uploads/Census-Compare-Feb-2014.pdf; MOVEMENT ADVANCEMENT PROJECT, A BROKEN BARGAIN FOR LGBT WORKERS OF COLOR (Nov. 2013), *available at* http://www.lgbtmap.org/workers-of-color.

93. KASTANIS & WILSON, *supra* note 92; WILLIAMS INSTITUTE, INFOGRAPHIC: % OF SAME-SEX COUPLES RAISING CHILDREN IN TOP METRO AREAS (2013).

4

Toward a Jurisprudence of the Civil Rights Acts

Robin L. West

What is the nature of the "rights," jurisprudentially, that the 1964 Civil Rights Act[1] legally prescribed? And, more generally, what is a "civil right"? Today, lawyers tend to think of civil rights, and particularly those that originated in the 1964 Act, as antidiscrimination rights: our "civil rights," on this understanding, are our rights not to be discriminated against, by employers, schools, landlords, property vendors, hoteliers, restaurant owners, and providers of public transportation, no less than by states and state actors, on the basis of race, gender, ethnicity, age, sexuality, or disability. Contemporary civil rights scholarship overwhelmingly reflects the same conception: our civil rights are quasi-constitutional rights to be free of discrimination in the private as well as public world.[2] But this conventional lawyerly understanding—basically, that "civil rights" are "antidiscrimination rights"—is clearly inadequate, certainly with respect to civil rights generally but also, and more tellingly, even with respect to the rights created and then protected by the 1964 Act itself.

First, on the general point: some of the "civil rights" sought or held across our history have not been antidiscrimination rights of any sort at all—labor rights, welfare rights, free speech rights, and the constitutional rights of criminal defendants have all, at various times, been championed as "civil rights," and these rights are neither logically nor jurisprudentially tied to any conception of antidiscrimination.[3] But furthermore, even the "civil rights" that are defined and then protected against discrimination by the 1964 Civil Rights Act, as well as by various Civil Rights Acts both before and subsequent to it, are not, in circular fashion, simply our rights not to be discriminated against on the basis of impermissible characteristics. Rather, the "civil rights" of which we cannot be discriminatorily deprived, whether originating in the 1964 Act or elsewhere, are, after all, rights *to* something: to vote,[4] to physical security,[5] to enter contracts,[6] to own, buy, or sell property,[7] to legal recourse in the aftermath of a wrong committed against us, [8] to write a will,[9] to be considered for or to hold down a job and to be paid fairly for our labor,[10] to the use of a restaurant or a hotel or a city bus,[11] to a public education,[12] and to marry whom we love.[13] And these are just some of the public goods that have been recognized at various times as "civil rights," of which we cannot be deprived by discriminatory action.

Even if just that much is correct, then the "civil right" protected by all of our Civil Rights Acts, including the 1964 one, is considerably more complex, jurisprudentially, than the conventionally legalistic and formulaic equation of "civil rights" with "antidiscrimination rights" suggests. Minimally, the "civil right" recognized or protected by the various Civil Rights Acts is almost invariably a *multilayered* right, or a "right to a right": it is a right to not be discriminatorily deprived of some underlying right. Only the first right in that phrase "a right to a right" is the antidiscrimination right. The second "right," though, is the underlying civil right of which we cannot be discriminatorily deprived, and it is both itself complex and highly variable. It might be a common law right, such as a right to enter contracts or sell property, or a statutory right, such as a right to vote, or simply a right to a social or public good, such as employment or educational opportunities, or the protection of a trustworthy police force against private violence. And while we have generated a library of writing, and jurisprudence, and judicial opinions on the nature of the first "right" in that phrase—the right not to be deprived of various rights on the basis of race, sex, and so forth—we have devoted much less to the second: the nature of the underlying right of which we cannot be deprived. So what is the jurisprudential nature of that right? What is a "civil right," jurisprudentially, both with respect to the rights protected against discrimination by the Civil Rights Act of 1964 and more broadly? Again, and more generally, what is a "civil right"?

Oddly, I believe, and in spite of their unquestioned importance in our contemporary public life, we are woefully short on a jurisprudential understanding of civil rights, both with respect to the Civil Rights Act of 1964, whose fiftieth anniversary we celebrated last year, and more broadly. Although we have recently seen an explosion of scholarship on the history, or histories, of both the civil rights movement of the 1950s through 1970s and the Civil Rights Acts they produced,[14] there has not been, either during or following our various "legislative moments" ushering in civil rights laws, a body of scholarly work engaged in reflective debate over the jurisprudential nature of the civil rights they sought to win and then to protect. We simply do not have a scholarly jurisprudential canon that seeks to encompass not only the nature of the antidiscrimination norm that our various Civil Rights Acts codify but also the nature of the substantive underlying rights that all of those rights against discrimination protect. Legal scholars have, for better or worse, focused on judge-made law, and particularly judge-made constitutional law, when engaging in the work of discerning the overarching principles of rights-based jurisprudence. Nowhere is this clearer than in the areas of law and life touched by the Civil Rights Acts themselves. I will return to this problem below. Here, I just want to note that for whatever reason, our scholarship on civil rights has shortchanged the complexities of both the Civil Rights Acts and civil rights movements and their product—civil rights—more broadly construed. We have focused our jurisprudential scholarship almost entirely on the rights to nondiscrimination our Civil Rights Acts created. But we have neglected the need to understand the nature of the underlying rights of access to the social goods, systems of law, or institutions—contractual freedom and powers, property ownership, education, employment opportunities, public accommodation, family life, and so on—that those nondiscrimination rights were designed to protect.

This is a neglect that matters, beyond the obvious problem that the neglect itself fosters confusion, with disputants and debaters often talking at cross-purposes.[15] There are at least two deeper worries. First, the lack of a jurisprudence of the Civil Rights Acts that centers the underlying civil rights, and not just the antidiscrimination norm, likely reflects as well as contributes to a lack of appreciation of the civil society and of the law that facilitates it that "civil rights," historically and today, both depend upon and produce. We have a well-developed jurisprudential scholarship on the nature of rights, including natural rights, human rights, legal rights, and constitutional rights.[16] And we have a well-developed body of scholarship concerning civil society—but it is a peculiarly legally denuded civil society that, thus far, we have studied: it is the "civil society" of voluntary bowling leagues and private associations, often by definition set apart from or in opposition to the legal society of the courthouse and City Hall.[17] We do not have much, if any, scholarship seeking to understand the civil society structured, and facilitated, by positive law, and we have virtually none centering the nature of our rights to participate in it.

But second, the lack of jurisprudential study of the underlying civil rights protected by our various Civil Rights Acts throughout our history has quite possibly skewed, and perhaps truncated, our inherited civil rights traditions, as well as possibilities for their creative regeneration. Civil rights, as well as the civic and participatory life they facilitate, can be threatened not only by discriminatory private practices of the sort prohibited by the Civil Rights Acts but by much else as well. Our natural rights to participate in family life can be threatened not only by discriminatory state marriage law that grants rights to form families or marriages to some but not others but also by private or intimate violence within those marriages that goes unaddressed by states, by a punitive criminal justice system that overincarcerates marriageable men for trivial or victimless offenses, and by a lack of community support for our caregiving obligations. Our civil rights to a healthy and physically secure life can be threatened not only by sexually discriminatory medical treatment or racially discriminatory policing and profiling but also by a lack of affordable health care, a lack of trustworthy police protection against private or neighborhood violence, and an unhealthy and polluted planet. Our rights to decent employment opportunities can be denied us not only by intentional discrimination or neutral rules with discriminatory impacts but also by a lack of skills and skills training, jobs outsourcing, plant relocations, capital strikes, and high unemployment. Our rights to education are frustrated by a lack of preschool readiness and lack of community support for parents of newborns, infants, and toddlers as much as by racially discriminatory admissions or school districting policies. To secure these rights, then, to family life, education, employment, and physical security (assuming for the moment we have such rights), we do indeed need to enforce laws against discrimination. But we need to do much else as well. The scholarly focus of the last fifty years on the nature of discrimination and its unlawfulness, rather than on the full array of obstacles that stand as barriers to the enjoyment of civil rights, and without insisting on the point that discrimination is but one such obstacle among others, has shrunk our understanding and appreciation of our own civil rights tradition, as well as its regenerative potential.

This chapter seeks to begin such a conversation. In Part I, I introduce, or reintroduce, and then endorse a definition of civil rights put forward by Thomas Paine more than two hundred years ago—well before the idea of "nondiscrimination" had taken hold—in his famous and indeed iconic pamphlet *Rights of Man*.[18] "Civil rights," Paine argued in that world-changing document, are, first, "natural rights"—by which he meant that they are rights that attach by virtue of our humanity,[19] what we today sometimes call "human rights" and what were then sometimes called "fundamental rights." But, he went on to explain, natural rights and civil rights are not *coterminous*, for two reasons. First, while natural rights attach to a man by virtue of his humanity, civil rights, Paine argued, are those natural rights that distinctively attach not just by virtue of his humanity but also by virtue of his "member[ship] in society."[20] That is what makes "civil" rights civil. Second, and relatedly, "civil rights" are that subset of natural rights that a man cannot enforce on his own: rights, in Paine's own language, "to the enjoyment of which his individual power is not, in all cases, sufficiently competent."[21] Unlike the natural rights "of the mind," or of conscience, or of behavior that does not harm others, Paine argued, civil rights distinctively require the presence of the state for their perfection and enforcement.[22] Civil rights, in other words, unlike other (noncivil) natural rights, are not rights *from*, but rather are rights *to*: "civil rights," distinctively, are rights *to* state action, *to* state law, *to* state institutions, *to* a functioning government, and basically, *to* community. Paine's definition, I will argue, penned well before the idea of a legal or constitutional right against discrimination had taken hold, may provide a better account of both our oldest and our most contemporary civil rights than the modern idea of civil rights as simply rights of nondiscrimination. But more to the point, Paine's account highlights just the feature of civil rights—the necessity of the state, and of law, to the perfection of the rights at the heart of civil society—that we have most failed to center in our scholarship.

Paine's quite formal definition, however, does not give us much help in developing the content of our civil rights, beyond his fecund and prescient suggestion that they must include rights of "security and protection."[23] Beyond reintroducing Paine, therefore, my second general goal in the first part of this chapter will be to marry, or synthesize, the formal definition of "civil rights" he provided with the modern and very substantive account of the content of "human rights" propounded by Martha Nussbaum and Amartya Sen over the last thirty years in their exposition of the "capabilities approach" to rights and human welfare.[24] The capabilities approach, as developed by Sen and Nussbaum, I believe, fills the gap in a way that is resonant with Paine's overall political philosophy: we have human rights, Nussbaum and Sen argue, to enjoy those human capabilities that are most conducive to our individual flourishing—including, for example, our "capability" for a healthy and long life, for sociability, for intimacy, for play, for cultural and intellectual engagement, and for interaction with our natural environment.[25] Protection of these capabilities and the human flourishing they nurture may, sometimes, require that the state leave us alone and let us develop and enjoy our capabilities according to our own lights, without interference from an overly intrusive community or censorial state actors. Often, though—more often, in fact—the individual flourishing that Sen and Nussbaum identify as the end of human welfare requires a state actively promoting those fundamental capabilities that produce it. States, therefore, sometimes have an obligation to promote and protect those capabilities, as well as an obligation to sometimes leave them be, and individuals have rights—human rights—to states that do both.

The various human capabilities Sen and Nussbaum identify that require active state promotion and protection, rather than state restraint, suggest the premises of a moral argument for Painean civil rights as well as a foundation for at least some of the interests protected against discrimination by our Civil Rights Acts, of both centuries. At the same time, a (modified) Nussbaum-Senian "capabilities approach" to welfare and rights suggests a moral argument for those civil rights we might believe we should have but do not yet fully enjoy: rights to decent work that is safe, meaningful, and fairly compensated; rights to greater community support for parents caring for young children or grown children caring for sick or dying parents; a high-quality education that prepares us for citizenship as well as gainful employment; a trustworthy and effective police force that protects us against violence without violating our rights of privacy and dignity; and so on. I will therefore try to supplement Paine's bare-boned account of the political logic of civil rights—how and where they fit, so to speak, in the pantheon of natural, fundamental, legal and constitutional rights—with Nussbaum and Sen's rich, substantive account of human welfare and what states are obligated to do to promote it. This blended account, I will conclude, suggests what is distinctive about "civil rights" against the backdrop of both our legal rights and human rights. Against the former, civil rights are those legal rights that promote fundamental human capabilities and protect our enjoyment of them against unjust impediments, including public and private discrimination. Against the latter, civil rights are those natural rights that, more specifically, attach by virtue of membership in society, which a man cannot enforce on his own and therefore require active state involvement for their protection, much as Paine argued two centuries ago.

Putting this together, I will ultimately argue in the first part below that "civil rights" are rights to be free of unjust impediments—such as, as per the 1964 Act, public or private discriminatory practices—to the underlying rights we all should enjoy to some set of legally constructed or legally protected social goods or institutions: private property, contractual freedom and powers, dignified and fairly compensated labor, public accommodation and transportation, high-quality public education, civil marriage, family life, and religious practice, among others. These civil rights and the underlying rights both facilitate participation in civic life and permit us to enjoy our most fundamental human capabilities. So my claim will be that "civil rights," jurisprudentially, are those rights that give us access to the legal apparatus of civil life, which in turn facilitates the enjoyment of basic, universally shared human capabilities. I will sometimes call my account a Painean-Nussbaumean, or Painean for short, account of the jurisprudential nature of a civil right. In the first part of this chapter, I will argue that the Painean account illuminates features of the Civil Rights Act and shows its continuity with other civil rights we possess or should possess, as well as with civil rights movements from our history.

In Part II, I elaborate a bit on my constructed Painean conception of civil rights by contrasting civil rights, so understood, with what I believe is an emerging and new paradigm of constitutional rights, which I have called elsewhere "exit rights."[26] These relatively new and newly constitutionally recognized "exit rights," I will argue briefly here and have argued at length elsewhere, are not classically individual rights, justified on traditionally liberal grounds; they are not simply rights to enjoy some measure of privacy, or religious freedom, or freedom of conscience, or to individuate ourselves in some other way, within civil society. Rather, exit rights—which include, inter alia, the rights to own and use a gun in self-defense, to procure an abortion, to die, to homeschool one's children, and to not purchase health insurance, as well as, possibly, the rights of religious corporations or nonprofit entities to exemptions from the mandate of antidiscrimination laws—are radically libertarian rights to effectively "exit" civil society, the social contract, or some substantial part of it. Our "civil rights," understood in the Painean sense, by contrast, can fairly be called "rights to enter" that compact or to garner the benefit of it, and to do so, specifically, through accessing some aspect of its legal architecture. The exit rights increasingly protected by the Constitution, as construed by our courts, are rights to exit the same civil society to which civil rights protect entrance. Constitutional rights and civil rights, then, contrary to the claims of a number of constitutional law theorists, are not only not the same thing and not mutually constitutive of our "fundamental law," but they also are more often than not, these days, on a collision course.

The contrast between civil and constitutional rights that I will explore in Section II below is at heart aesthetic and ethical. Our relatively new array of constitutionally inscribed "exit rights" have, I will suggest, a tragic arc. As in the last act of a classic or Shakespearean tragedy, their exercise often culminates with characters splayed dead across the stage: individuals exercising their rights to die, to kill, and to abort are, after all, severing earthly as well as communitarian coils; they are all dealing in death. Even when not lethal, however, the exercise of an exit right culminates almost invariably in the spectacle of an isolated individual, shrouded in his various constitutional rights to be left alone, with the community from which he is so willfully estranged in shatters. The intruder is killed by the homeowner, rather than captured by a trustworthy constable; the fetus is expunged, rather than borne into a supportive community; the child is educated in isolation at home, rather than at a public school and in a community of peers; the suicidal patient is dead, rather than cared for in hospice. Civil rights have, by contrast, what I call a "comedic arc." As in Shakespearean and classical comedy, the exercise of a civil right culminates in a communal ritual or event, such as a couple's wedding celebration, where they are joined by their community's representatives of faith and state, or a new day in a well-functioning and integrated schoolroom or workplace, or the cure of an illness and restoration to health, financed by a community of coinsureds who have spread and shared risks, or the joyous arrival of a new birth accompanied by responsible attendant care and not threatened by the specter of a lost job. In the last act of a comedy, the state as well as the community and its worth are reconfirmed, and the individual's role within it, as well as his distinctiveness from it, is celebrated. Part II below draws the obvious inference that centering comedic civil rights rather than the tragic constitutional rights we have obsessed over for the last thirty years, in our understanding of rights and in our ongoing attempts to take them seriously, might give us a more balanced jurisprudence and a sliver of hope for a more balanced community likewise.

The conclusion revisits the Trayvon Martin killing and its aftermath in light of some of these distinctions.

I. Tom Paine's Civil Rights

According to an influential and much-quoted definition provided in Thomas Paine's canonical late-eighteenth-century essay *Rights of Man*, "civil rights" are those natural rights that are owed by a government to the people—*all* of them—by virtue of their membership in civil society.[27] "Civil rights," Paine held, are a subspecies of "natural rights"—a claim repeated and embraced, indeed insisted upon—by proponents of the 1866 Civil Rights Act, three-quarters of a century after Paine wrote.[28] Natural rights, in turn, are rights we enjoy solely by virtue of our humanity; we hold them regardless of the accident of the geographic details of our birth. We hold them against our own sovereign, whether or not he recognizes them, and would hold them likewise against any sovereign. And we *all* hold them, Paine thought—slaves and American Indians no less than free men.[29] That "natural rights" underpinning of our civil rights and civil rights tradition is no historical relic; it is, rather, a vital connection between both the reconstruction and revolutionary era use of the phrase and our modern antidiscrimination law today. From the very beginning, civil rights have been grounded in natural rights, meaning they are owed everyone, without regard to race, sex, disability, and so on—again, they are owed by virtue of one's humanity. By virtue of their origin as natural rights, civil rights have always connoted some version of an antidiscrimination norm.

Civil rights were not, however, viewed by Paine and his contemporaries as coterminous with the natural rights man possesses by virtue of his humanity, when both phrases were part of the ordinary vocabulary of lawyers and constitutionalists. Rather, they were a subset, with two characteristics differentiating them from the larger class of natural rights, of which, again, they are a part (all civil rights are natural rights, all natural rights, however, are not civil rights). First, civil rights, unlike other natural rights, are rights that attach by virtue of one's "member[ship] in society," rather than solely by virtue of one's humanity. But second, although civil rights *originate* as natural rights, Paine explained, unlike some of those natural rights, such as rights to the mind and conscience or rights to behavior that does not harm others, "civil rights" are those rights that cannot be perfected by individuals standing alone, so to speak, or outside civil society and law:[30]

> Natural rights are those [rights] which appertain to man in right of his existence. Of this kind are all the intellectual rights, or rights of the mind, and also all those rights of acting as an individual for his own comfort and happiness, which are not injurious to the natural rights of others. Civil rights are those which appertain to man in right of his being a member of society. Every civil right has for its foundation, some natural right pre-existing in the individual, but to the enjoyment of which his individual power is not, in all cases, sufficiently competent. Of this kind are all those which relate to security and protection.[31]

Civil rights, then, to the founding generation, at least if Paine's understanding was representative, were natural rights that require, distinctively, civil society, including both positive law and legal institutions for their perfection. Unlike other natural rights, we cannot enforce civil rights on our own. We need the affirmative assistance of positive law. So defined, "civil rights" included, for Paine, quintessentially, those rights pertaining to protection of the physical security of the individual. The security of and protection of the physical body are examples, then, of foundational rights that are only imperfectly, at best, enforceable through self-help. We "trade in" our natural rights to self-protection and security, so to speak, for the "civil right" of the protection of our physical security by the state.

How does Paine's account of "civil rights"—penned long before the Civil Rights Acts of either of the two centuries following and before the idea of antidiscrimination as an actionable wrong had gained traction—as "natural rights" that "appertain to man in right of his being a member of society" but "of which his individual power is not, in all cases, sufficiently competent"[32] stand up, as a jurisprudential account of civil rights, both those passed into law fifty years ago and those in various statutory provisions before and since? Better, I think, than our current lawyerly equation of "civil rights" with "antidiscrimination rights." At least echoes of Paine's definition can be heard not only in the Civil Rights Act of 1964 but also in virtually all of the various Civil Rights Acts and movements of both the nineteenth and twentieth centuries. Thus, according to the framers and advocates of the seminal Civil Rights Act of 1866, "civil rights" include rights to enter and enforce contracts; to buy, hold, rent, and sell property; to sue, be parties, or give evidence in judicial proceedings; and to enjoy the protection of the state and its laws pertaining to the security of persons and property[33]—all of which readily fit Paine's description of civil rights as that subset of natural rights that should attach by virtue of membership in society and that require legal definition and institutions to perfect. These "civil rights," as they were then called (in part to distinguish them from "political rights," such as rights to vote or serve on juries) clearly required positive law for their perfection—the power to make and enforce contracts requires contract law, enjoyment of property obviously requires property law, rights to sue and give evidence require the law of procedure, rights pertaining to the security of persons and property require the criminal law, and so forth. As such, these civil rights, which had long been granted by law to white men through the combined effect of common law or statute, should, according to the framers of the nineteenth-century Civil Rights Act of 1866, be granted to African Americans as well.[34]

The Civil Rights Act of 1871, one of the "enforcement acts" passed in the wake of the Reconstruction Amendments and popularly known as the Ku Klux Klan Act, explicitly added personal security from various private conspiracies to commit, among other wrongs, acts of domestic violence to the list of civil rights to be enforced by the federal government, rather than state militias.[35] Here too, the extension fits Paine's understanding. The civil and natural right to be protected against private violence had been granted to some by the criminal laws prohibiting it and their enforcement by state authorities, but that protection had not been extended to the protection of the freed slaves against private conspiracies contemplating violence (such as lynchings) against them; thus the need for the Ku Klux Klan Act. The civil right to protection against private violence, according to the framers of that Act, must be extended to freed slaves. For the authors of the constitutionally doomed Civil Rights Act of 1875, "civil rights" also included the right to use public accommodations such as hotels and restaurants, to employ public transportation, and to enjoy and participate in public amusements such as in theatres.[36] Here as well, these rights to participate sociably in these public spaces of civil society, which attach by virtue of membership in that society, require law for their creation and enjoyment, and the Act of 1875 created a nondiscrimination right to enjoy those participatory rights. The 1875 Act as well, then, fits Paine's definition. The major Civil Rights Acts of the nineteenth century all put into law an inclusive, universalist, and profoundly Painean impulse: to ensure that civil rights—to contract, own property, sue for private wrongs, enjoy the state's protection against violence, and make use of public accommodations—that had been granted to some would be guaranteed to all, conditioned solely on one's membership in civil society rather than on one's racial heritage or one's earlier identification as free or slave.

In the twentieth century, the phrase took on new meanings but nevertheless held close to the jurisprudential core of Paine's definition. Virtually all of our twentieth-century civil rights—both those recognized in law and those still fought over—can easily be described as natural rights that attach, or should attach, by virtue of both one's humanity and one's membership in civil society but that cannot be enforced by an individual standing alone. Thus, as told in Risa Goluboff's groundbreaking scholarship from ten years ago,[37] but as intimated as well in much of William Forbath's early work,[38] the idea of "civil rights" in the post-*Lochner* era included, foundationally, labor rights, including not only rights to be free of peonage and involuntary servitude, derived directly from the Thirteenth Amendment, but also, eventually, the right to join a union and to strike, as well as rights to minimum wages and safe work conditions.[39] Participation in the labor economy as a free and equal citizen, Goluboff shows, was viewed as key to a shared civic life, according to the New Deal–inspired, Justice Department–housed lawyers of the

1940s Civil Rights Section, who were responsible for giving content and meaning to the "civil rights" they were charged to enforce.[40] This usage continued in popular discourse throughout much of the century: as late as 1968, Martin Luther King himself spoke of rights to jobs, to strike, to organize, and to unionize as "civil rights," and scores of labor activists since have followed suit.[41]

In a now much-studied history, during the middle and second half of the twentieth century, the content of "civil rights" shifted from labor rights per se to rights of minorities to enjoy employment and educational opportunities free of discrimination, and it was during this time that the lawyerly identification of "civil rights" with "antidiscrimination rights" apparently took hold, at least according to historians of the era.[42] Here as well, though, the underlying civil rights—to employment and education opportunities—no less than the underlying nineteenth-century civil rights of contract, property, security, and access to civil justice—are fairly described as natural rights owed to individuals by virtue of their membership in civil society and cannot be enforced by individuals standing alone. Fair employment and decent education both are social institutions that are heavily dependent upon an array of laws, both statutory and common, for their realization. In the last few decades, by dint of at least occasional if not common usage, the phrase "civil rights" is sometimes understood as including various statutorily or constitutionally created rights that facilitate family life, such as the "right to marry" without regard to sexual orientation;[43] the right to family or medical leave from work necessitated by the birth of a child or the illness of a family member, as protected by the Family Medical Leave Act (FMLA);[44] the right to be free of intimate violence, as protected by the Violence Against Women Act (VAWA);[45] rights derived from various sources to a high-quality as well as integrated public education, as imperfectly echoed in statutes such as No Child Left Behind (NCLB)[46] and the Individuals with Disabilities Education Act (IDEA);[47] as well as a right to health care, the existence of which is strongly suggested by the Affordable Care Act (ACA).[48] Here too, the underlying natural rights—to family, parentage, marriage, safe intimacy, quality education, and access to health care—are owed to all of us by virtue of societal membership. And here as well, they are rights that cannot be enforced by any individual without the aid of considerable positive law. They all look like Painean civil rights.

Thus, all of these early, mid-, and late twentieth and early twenty-first-century civil rights laws, or, in some cases, still unfinished civil rights campaigns, recognize, create, advocate for, or protect civil rights that loosely fit Paine's definition. Most, although not all, protect those civil rights against some form of race, sex, disability, age, or sexuality dis-crimination. What they *all* do, though, is protect various civil rights against some sort of unjust social ill—either discrimination, poverty, joblessness, lack of insurance, private violence, or unequal allocations of unpaid intimate labor, with its consequent disparate impacts in work-places—that in turn hampers enjoyment of underlying civil rights. In all of them, the underlying "civil right" protected against these perni-cious forces is a right to engage or participate in some aspect of civil society—employment, education, marriage and family life, access to health care, physical security and the mobility that goes with it, con-tract exchanges, and ownership of property—that is in turn facilitated through legal processes. And in all of them, again echoing Paine, the underlying right that is being protected, extended, or guaranteed is not simply *natural*, although it is that—a right that should attach to one by virtue of one's humanity—but it is also, distinctively, *civil*—it attaches or should attach by virtue of one's membership in society.

Let me try to extract four definitional principles of the jurisprudential nature of a "civil right" from this application of Paine's definition of civil rights to the examples surveyed above, of the rights protected by our various Civil Rights Acts. First: a civil right is a natural right, mean-ing it is a right that attaches by virtue of one's humanity. In contempo-rary terms, we might restate the same point in this way, drawing on Sen and Nussbaum's universalist account of human well-being: civil rights, like all natural rights, protect or nurture our fundamental "human capa-bilities"—the capabilities we have, by virtue of being human, for long and healthy lives, for cultural and intellectual engagement, for play, for interacting with our natural environments, and so on—enjoyment of which are the preconditions, universally, for living a good life.[49] Some of those human capabilities, of course, are nurtured by familial direc-tion during childhood and then furthered and directed by individual effort. They require nothing more than benign neglect from the state for their flowering. Some of them are also, though, furthered by social institutions and the laws that structure them, and some of them are fully dependent on those social institutions and laws.[50] Thus, our capability for health and longevity is furthered not only by a sensible diet and plenty of exercise growing up in a healthy household but also by access to health care throughout life.[51] Our capability for mobility and phys-ical freedom is furthered not only by strong limbs developed by nat-ural and healthy maturation but also by protection against violence and the policing that provides it; our capability for intimacy not only by the flowering of private lives that seek it and the emotional health that sus-tains it but also by the promise of a family life that will be protected by sound policing against external threat and internal abuse; our capability for sociability not only by a natural capacity for language but also by access to our legally structured public accommodations and public spaces; and our capability for a stimulating mental life in adulthood not only by being left alone to discover (or not) Pythagorean theorems on our own but also by a high-quality public education, with sound curriculum and pedagogy and the law that structures it. The "civil right," in all of these cases, is the right to access those institutions and to enjoy the laws that structure them, which protect and nurture these natural capabilities. The various Civil Rights Acts, in turn, provide that those rights cannot be discriminatorily denied.

The 1964 Civil Rights Act itself, of course, directly and explicitly guarantees rights to some of the legal structures that facilitate various capabilities, notably, for employment opportunities, education, sociability, and community. These capabilities are quite directly furthered by fair jobs offered at nondiscriminatory wages, the hospitality of restaurants and hotels and the convenience and mobility of public transportation, decent educational opportunities, and the buying and selling of property to allow for both mobility and choice of residence and also the enjoyment or production of consumer goods. The same relation holds, though, for our newer civil rights. The Affordable Care Act directly protects, through a complex regime of rights and responsibilities, the individual capability to live a healthful life,[52] while NCLB and the IDEA[53] protect, again through rights, the fundamental capacities we all share for exploring the world and enjoying a lively mental and cultural life. The Family and Medical Leave Act (FMLA)[54] encourages our capabilities for both work and family, and state gun safety laws and the Violence Against Women Act (VAWA)[55] aim to do the same for our capabilities for intimacy, mobility, physical security, safe sociability, and freedom from fear. All of these are human capabilities that are essential to a good life, on Nussbaum and Sen's account, and all of these capabilities are protected through the social and civil life that law and society both aim to structure. Our civil rights can be understood as the rights to enjoy the fruits of all of that law, and our Civil Rights Acts can be understood as laws that guarantee that those civil rights will not be discriminatorily denied.

My second principle also tracks Paine: "civil rights" are natural rights that attach not only by virtue of man's humanity but also by virtue of his "member[ship] in society." Briefly: civil rights center our rights *to participate* in community rather than rights to be free from it. Professor Rebecca Zeitlow is entirely right, for just this reason, to refer to the antidiscrimination rights created by the 1964 Civil Rights Act as "rights of belonging."[56] Antidiscrimination rights that attach by virtue of one's "member[ship] in society," as Paine put the point, are "rights of belonging," in Zeitlow's near-biblical usage.

The point can, however, be substantially broadened beyond Zeitlow's intended meaning. It is not only the antidiscrimination rights created by the 1964 Act that can be fruitfully described as "rights of belonging" for two reasons. First, the underlying civil rights protected against discrimination by both the 1964 Civil Rights Act as well as the various Civil Rights Acts that came after it are *themselves* "rights of belonging." They are all rights to "belong to" or participate in various communities: communities of employers and employees, of landlords and tenants, of buyers and sellers, of students, of teachers and administrators, of neighbors, and of officials in polling places. The Acts protect the civil rights of workers, buyers, sellers, tenants, voters, citizens, students, teachers, producers, and consumers to participate in these various communal workplaces, neighborhoods, markets, schools, city halls, courthouses, sites of public gathering and transportation, and voting sites and to do so through accessing the legal forms, rules, and entitlements that structure those locales. As Zeitlow argues, the nondiscrimination right those Acts create brings people together in real space and time.[57] They do not just create an abstract right in an individual to be free of an invidious discriminatory intention in the minds of state actors: the antidiscrimination rights originating in the Civil Rights Acts prohibit policies that adversely impact actual rates of participation and encourage or mandate affirmative actions and related remedies that aim directly for more inclusive workplaces and neighborhoods. But the same is true of the underlying civil rights themselves. The civil rights protected against discrimination by the Civil Rights Acts, in other words, and not just the antidiscrimination norm itself, concern the terms of our actual communal interactions with each other; they are not about the terms of our individual relationship with the minds of state actors. They aim to bring us together contractually, educationally, civilly, and so on. The aim of those laws in toto, then, is a participatory community, by virtue of not only the antidiscrimination norm but also the underlying rights. All of those rights seek to build trust between classes of strangers once indifferent or implacably hostile, and all do so, toward the end of strengthening the community's civic bonds.

Zietlow's provocative metaphor—that the civil rights of the Civil Rights Acts are "rights of belonging"[58]—can be extended in a second direction as well. Other rights won or fought for as "civil rights" in our history, outside the parameters of those Acts, and whether protected against the pernicious effects of discrimination or some other social ill, can also be described as "rights of belonging." The civil right to form a labor union and to decent wages for safe labor, for example, prompted by the labor struggles of the 1910s, 1920s, and 1930s, were "rights of belonging," aiming for a more decent, fair, and democratically participatory workplace. Those rights contrasted—and in ways that parallel the contrast between the constitutional and statutory antidiscrimination norms—with the bare and sterile right to "individual liberty" presupposed by rights to contract: contract rights, at best, create freer individuals, unbound by paternalistic states and empowered, at least in theory, to set terms and conditions of their own individual employment by virtue of their power to exit.

The Family and Medical Leave Act directly aims to strengthen actual communities in the home and in the workplace by pooling the costs of early infant care or the care of sick family members, and the ACA likewise strengthens ties of responsibility among those who share risks in insurance pools. Gun control laws aim to build on mutual trust rather than rely on mutually assured destruction–styled individual antagonism to protect us each against the threat of violence posed by each other, and VAWA aims to protect physical security similarly, toward the end of enhancing the protection of women's mobility and safety in the communities of home and civil life. NCLB- and IDEA-styled laws aim for stronger communities, both in schools and in neighborhoods that indirectly benefit from the floor of quality they establish, rather than leaving parents and their children to their own individualistically fashioned means, needs, and desires. Some of these laws can be (and have been) fairly described as antidiscrimination laws—VAWA corrects prior discriminatory policing policies, FMLA corrects an indirect form of gender discrimination on the job, and IDEA corrects for prejudicial educational policies against children with learning disabilities. But they obviously cannot be *simply* described as antidiscrimination laws, and they might not be *best* described in that way. VAWA most directly targets *violence* against women, not discrimination against them; IDEA aims to *educate*, not eradicate invidious distinctions; and FMLA likewise directly aims to *support parents*, rather than abolish discrimination against women on the job. All of these laws, whether they can fairly be described as antidiscrimination norms, directly aim to strengthen civic, communal, or neighborly bonds.

Third: civil rights distinctively aim to protect those individual fundamental capabilities that are facilitated *by law* and that, as per Paine, cannot be perfected or enforced by the individual standing alone. The "civil right" is a positive right of access to the laws, legal structures, legal forms, and legal entitlements that in turn protect or nurture fundamental capabilities that cannot be protected without societal and civil interaction, encouragement, or involvement. So the civil rights acts of both the nineteenth and twentieth centuries empower individuals who would be otherwise barred by dint of private discrimination from various social institutions that depend upon civil society, and its law, for their very definition: buying and selling property, contracting for and then occupying hotel rooms, eating in restaurants, and working at jobs under the same terms as white coworkers.

Likewise, the Accordable Care Act protects the human capabilities of health and longevity through pooling risk and thereby ensuring improved health, which is facilitated not by individual effort but by an intricate and interpersonal jurisprudence interweaving statute, contract, and property law. Gun safety laws and the Violence Against Women Act protect the individual capabilities of safety, intimacy, and mobility by seeking to limit the isolating fears and inhibitions associated with excessive private violence and do so through a set of laws and legal institutions, rather than through arming everyone or engaging in exhortations toward individual empowerment. The Family and Medical Leave Act protects individual capabilities for both work and family life, not through cheerleading heroically individualized parenting—exhorting us all to "lean in"—but through mandated employer-provided assistance with the costs of child care. The underlying individual capabilities in all of these cases require legal structures, law, and social institutions, not just unimpeded individual initiative. Without the ACA, our ability to live a healthy life is frustrated by poverty that prevents the purchase of insurance; without FMLA, our ability to care for dependents and remain employed—our ability to participate in both family and work life—is hampered by our inability to share the burden of caring for newborns; without gun control laws, our ability to move freely through our neighborhoods is hampered by our fears for our own physical security; without education laws, our abilities to participate in high culture as well as in an educated workforce and public sphere is severely limited by ignorance and illiteracy. We cannot do any of this on our own, basically, and, per Paine, that is where and why civil rights enter the picture.

Finally, civil rights are aspirational rather than positivistic. They are not a listing of what the state has provided through law. Rather, they are rights the state should protect, even if it does not. The positivistic civil rights we have, in other words, are an imperfect and incomplete recordation of the civil rights we are owed. Thus, while we have perfected, more or less, the right to contract, which the 1866 Civil Rights Act aimed to guarantee to freed slaves as well as white men, we have clearly not perfected, in our labor law, a fully recognized legal right to good and decently paid labor.[59] We may have a "civil right," then, to a decent job at decent wages, but we clearly do not have a legal right to one. Quite the contrary: the antidiscrimination right to employment opportunities exists against the backdrop of an employment-at-will regime that in fact guarantees very much the opposite. Likewise, we may have a "civil right" to a high-quality education, as evidenced in part by the rhetoric and justifications given our rights to "individualized educational plans" if we suffer disabilities, our rights "not to be left behind" if we suffer impoverished school placements, and the inclusion of a constitutional right to a good education in most state constitutions, which guarantees some measure of intrastate—although not interstate—equality. But we do not have a secure and legally recognized legal right to a high-quality education across the board. We may have a civil right to health care, as evidenced in part by a right we now have to purchase insurance at reasonable rates under the Affordable Care Act, but that is obviously a highly contingent as well as contested and vulnerable right: we do not have a robust legally recognized right to either health or health care. We have various legal rights under the Violence Against Women Act, but we do not yet have anything like a full recognition of a civil right to be free of intimate violence. Yet the civil rights to employment, education, safe intimacy, and health are nevertheless the aspirational rights that we "have," even if only imperfectly secured by these statutes.

Now, let me contrast this conception of civil rights—Paine's understanding, basically—with the conventional and truncated understanding of a civil right that I believe wrongly dominates our civil rights conversations. Civil rights, as I believe they should be defined, facilitate forms of individual participation in the civic community that promote fundamental individual capabilities, such as our capabilities for intimacy, work, physical security, health, engagement in mental and cultural life, and neighborliness, and they do so through guaranteeing access to the laws that structure the civic institutions that promote or protect them. Rights to contract, property, employment, and so on facilitate participation in aspects of civic life that enhance our individual capabilities for work, family, health, and sociability. Civil rights to nondiscrimination guarantee that access to those rights is equally shared, regardless of race and gender. This much of the Painean view is consistent with what I have labeled the conventional view.

The differences, however, are significant. First, and as I have stressed throughout, the Painean conception, unlike the traditional, centers rather than ignores the content of the underlying civil rights protected by the antidiscrimination norm: rights to contract, employment opportunities, education, and so on. Second, the Painean conception is aspirational, meaning rooted in natural as well as positive law: the civil rights we have are those rights we should have, not just the rights we have already won. Our civil rights are not exhausted by the rights to contract, property, employment, and educational opportunities protected by extant Civil Rights Acts but also include rights to marriage, physical security, safe intimacy, health and longevity, participation in family life, and our capacity for meaningful work, all of which are intimated but nevertheless only imperfectly protected by existing law. Third, and as I will elaborate below, civil rights, so understood, are neither constitutional rights nor quasi-constitutional rights: their recognition might be necessary to further particular constitutional guarantees, but their meaning, their reach, and their jurisprudential implications are not defined or limited by those guarantees or the constitutional texts that provide them. They are determined by our nature, not by our law, constitutional or otherwise. Fourth, "civil rights" so understood are rights *to* the state support, state law, and state institutions that are necessary to their enjoyment. Under the Painean view as I have constructed it here, this positivity is a central feature of those rights definitionally rather than an awkward and contingent feature that clumsily contrasts with the overwhelming negativity of the constitutional rights with which civil rights are often grouped under the traditional view.

Last, the barriers to the full development of our capabilities that relate to community participation and that require law for their perfection, on the Painean conception, do not end with discrimination, either public or private. Poverty, poor education, poor health care, and vulnerability to violence are also barriers. Laws that seek to counter those barriers, no less than laws that seek to counter discrimination, on this understanding of the rights at the heart of "civil rights," are core, not peripheral, examples of Civil Rights Acts. Collectively, civil rights laws all guarantee rights to which we are entitled by virtue of our membership in society. Some, but not all, do so by providing "rights to those rights" against private or public discrimination. They all, though, confer rights to participate in civic structures that are products of law: public education, public markets in insurance, secure and safe unarmed communities protected by a trustworthy police force, and structured and legally mandated support in the aftermath of a child's birth. Laws that do so, such as the VAWA, ACA, NCLB, IDEA, FLSA, and FEMA, whether or not they aim at discriminatory public or private conduct, are also, quintessentially, civil rights laws.

II. Constitutional and Civil Rights: One Contrast

Are civil rights, both those protected by the Civil Rights Acts and civil rights more generally, best understood as constitutional or quasi-constitutional rights? A number of commentators over the last ten years, including Bruce Ackerman in his Holmes lectures on the subject, have suggested, or argued, as much.[60] It is easy to see why this collapsing of civil and constitutional rights is a prudentially attractive suggestion: if the passage of the Civil Rights Act can be regarded as an extended constitutional moment and civil rights, therefore, as constitutional rights, then neither the courts nor subsequent congresses should trim them, cut them back, repeal them, or find them unconstitutional for any but the gravest of reasons. Constitutionalizing them, in effect, gives them some measure of permanence as well as stature against potentially hostile future configurations of congresses and courts. It is also a doctrinally logical suggestion, particularly if we think of civil rights as antidiscrimination rights: understood as antidiscrimination rights, civil rights, like the Court's equal protection doctrine, are attempts to give content to the general promises of equality embedded in the Constitution's Fourteenth Amendment. And antidiscrimination is now the heart of the Court's equal protection doctrine. So: if civil rights are antidiscrimination rights, and antidiscrimination rights are constitutional rights, then, ergo, civil rights must be constitutional rights, or at least quasi-constitutional rights, as well.

It is important to note that the doctrinal syllogism just spelled out does not work: even if the framers of the Civil Rights Acts were reinterpreting section 1 of the Fourteenth Amendment in devising rights of antidiscrimination, it by no means follows that that is *all* they were doing. And indeed, it is not all they were doing, as I hope I have already shown. There are, however, prudential reasons as well to resist what is essentially a rhetorical and strategic conflation of civil rights on the one hand with constitutional rights on the other. The major reason is simply this: even if constitutional and civil rights are overlapping categories—some civil rights are also constitutional rights, and vice versa—and even though civil rights also target the inequality prohibited by the Fourteenth Amendment, which of course they do, nevertheless, there are vast differences between civil rights, at least on the Painean conception I have outlined above and particularly our contemporary constitutional rights. Those differences are simply obscured, or muted, if we blur the distinctions between them. Once we include within the scope of "civil rights" the underlying rights those civil rights acts protect—if, that is, we examine civil rights in the Painean sense as to include the rights protected against discrimination rather than just the antidiscrimination right itself—it is clear that civil rights contrast, far more than they compare, with constitutional rights and particularly with the newly discovered constitutional rights that have been recognized, argued for, or contemplated over the last twenty or so years. Painean civil rights and constitutional rights so understood are not only, then, not co-constitutive of constitutional law. They are also, increasingly, on a collision course, and it might be wise not to obscure that fact. Let me just draw out this contrast.

The civil rights I have focused on in this chapter—both the historic nineteenth-century civil rights to enjoy property, contract, physical security, and public accommodations, and rights to sue for wrongs, and also our modern civil rights to a high-quality publicly funded education, family and medical leave, access to health insurance, trustworthy police protection against intimate, private, or neighborhood violence, rights to marry, and rights to decent labor and employment opportunities—are all rights to be included in a participatory public life. As noted above, Professor Zeitlow calls the antidiscrimination rights the Acts created "rights of belonging"; I would say, I think more inclusively, that the civil rights protected by those antidiscrimination rights are *rights toenter*. They are rights to enter schoolhouses, workplaces, homes, marriages, neighborhoods, and so on. Understood as such, civil rights contrast—not compare—with a group of constitutional rights that cover much of the same lived geography; that have been sought, recognized, or argued for over the last thirty years; and that I have elsewhere called "rights to exit": the still-contested but increasingly recognized constitutional right to homeschool one's children;[61] the constitutional right to die[62] and the right to not buy health insurance;[63] the Second Amendment right to own a gun and use it in self-defense;[64] the ever-embattled constitutional right to procure an abortion;[65] and, most recently, the right of religious schools to exemptions from antidiscrimination law for the hiring of their "ministerial" teachers[66] and the right of religious employers to exemptions from the ACA to protect the sensitivities of conscience.[67] The contrast between the civil right to enter and the constitutional right to exit can be drawn most sharply one by one. Thus, the civil right to public education, in contrast to the constitutional right to withdraw one's children from school and homeschool them, reflects values of shared sacrifice and common purpose, both in the ways in which it is funded and in the content of what is conveyed. The civil right is a right to enter a public world of education, while the constitutional right is a right to exit it. The civil right to unpaid leave during a child's infancy is aimed at permitting a parent to enter a familial and parental relation rather than providing a constitutional right to exit such a relation through abortion. It imposes a responsibility on the community of shareholders, customers, and co-employees for the shared burden of the costs of the care required to nurture newborns or sick family members, rather than an individual right to avoid those costs by aborting the fetus. Again, it is a right to enter a world of shared responsibility for parenting, while the constitutional right is a right to exit both the biological relationship with the fetus and with other potential caregivers. The civil rights to physical security implied by VAWA and decent gun control laws create a community of trust and shared interest among community members who have laid down their arms and a state's police force, rather than a distrust of either the competency or the desires of the police to provide that protection, reflected in the Second Amendment's right to arms. The civil right is a right to enter that social compact of protection for forbearance, while the constitutional right is a right to exit it. The civil right to health care spreads the burden of sickness and illness over a community through the mechanism of shared risk rather than on an individual's constitutional right to either self-insure, self-help, or commit suicide. The civil right to health care is a right to enter a civil world of shared risk, cross-subsidizing insurance, and, at the end of life, communal hospice care, while constitutional rights to die and to refuse insurance are rights to exit just those worlds. And of course, the civil rights to nondiscrimination—the rights of belonging, as Zeitlow dubs them—protect rights to enter employment and education institutions, while the "freedom of the church" now being pressed by scholars and to some extent by courts protects the rights of churches and the schools and hospitals they sponsor to exit those laws, through blanket exemptions and various "ministerial exceptions." In each of these examples, the civil right, unlike the constitutional one, not only envisions a community constituted by the civil right to enter but also rests on an assumption of trust and common purpose between the individual holder of the civil right and his co-citizens—parents, teachers, neighbors, and taxpayers sharing the burden of educating children; employers, coworkers, and customers of an enterprise as partners in the financing and support of new parents; a community of insured individuals and medical professionals sharing the burdens and risks of sickness of each member—and between neighborhoods and police empowered to minimize violence in responsible and humane ways.

In other work,[68] I have put forward the claim that these constitutional "exit rights" represent the first wave of an emerging new paradigm of constitutional individual rights. Unlike earlier First, Fourteenth, and Fourth Amendment rights valorized during the first two-thirds of the last century, this new generation of rights—rights to homeschool, to own and use a gun in self-defense, to procure an abortion, to die, to refuse health insurance, and to exempt oneself from antidiscrimination law by referencing one's conscience or ministerial role—are rights that facilitate not just the liberty of individuals within the confines of civic life but also a quite extreme form of "exit" from civic life and from the community and the state that structure it. They guarantee exit from some aspect of the social contract that defines civil society. The constitutional right to own a gun and to use it in self-defense is a right to not participate in—to exit—the traditional liberal social compact by which we disarm—relinquish our right to self-help—in exchange for the sovereign's duty to protect us from private violence. It envisions an erected wall of distance, difference, and lethality not only between the individual gun owner and the intruder who endangers his life and interrupts his solitude but also between the individual gun owner and the state and its police force who have failed to protect him, the community from which intruders come, and neighbors who must be kept at bay. It is a right to exit that part of the social contract constituted by the trade of one's right to self-help in exchange for the civil right to protection from private violence. The constitutional right to die is a right to exit not just life itself and all of its biological ties but also the social compact by which that life is protected against self-abnegation. It protects the most isolated, solitary, noncommunitarian act an individual can possibly make against the paternalistic interventions of community, family, medicine, or state. The abortion right, as well, obviously older but consistent with these newer rights, is a right to exit an unwanted relationship not only with the fetal life within but also from the community, family, or state that seeks to protect it. Both killing oneself and aborting fetal life do, after all, like killing an intruder in justified self-defense, sever earthly coils. The right to homeschool one's children with no supervision from a school or school board, recognized by some lower courts as well as by school districts in several cash-strapped states, is similarly a "right to exit" from the civic and shared project of intergenerational public education with its shared liberal norms of tolerance, pluralism, and feminism. The homeschooling parent seeks to exit the shared communal project of education as well as, oftentimes, its shared goal: a civic life informed by norms of tolerance, gender and racial equality, and individual, but civic, autonomy. The right to not buy health insurance, heartily insisted upon by Chief Justice Roberts as well as numerous commentators is likewise a "right to exit"—this time, from the shared societal project of pooling health risks through the mandatory purchase of insurance. All of these newfound rights (the oldest of the group being the abortion right) are echoes of the much older *Lochner*-era contract right, which, within the context of employment, confers an explicit right to "exit," at will, the employment relation.

In all of these cases, the individual's constitutional exit right is, in form, a negative right protecting individual liberty against an intrusive state. But they are not only that. Exit rights protect not just an individual's liberty within a community but, more radically, an individual's willed separation from the community or from some threatening part of it: a moralistic state with its intrusive sonograms and impediments to reproductive choice; a totalitarian state with its threatening black helicopters; an incompetent state with its ineffectual police force and poor educational pedagogy; a liberal state with its offending teachers preaching noxious norms of inclusion and respect; or a nanny state with its mandatory insurance policy and its forced sharing of risk and coshouldering of costs. In every one of these cases, the constitutional right found by the Supreme Court or ardently desired by advocates is not only *not* a civil "right of belonging," quasi or otherwise. It is the antithesis of one. The constitutional right protects the individual's right to exit the very community that the civil right, at least on the Painean conception, protects, nurtures, and seeks to promote. Civil rights and constitutional rights are not mutually constitutive. They are on a collision course.

Let me draw out one further contrast. Part of what is distinctive about exit rights—rights to homeschool, to kill oneself, to abort a pregnancy, to refuse to buy health insurance, to exercise lethal self-help against violence—is their tragic hue. They protect a radical separation of the self from others or, at best, an extreme alienation from the civic national community: the homeschooled child is homeschooled precisely in order to maintain or erect a strict separation from that community; the health insurance holdout wants nothing to do with an obligation to support co-citizens in a mutual web of obligation toward a mutual goal of a healthier community; the gun owner risks his own death and that of loved ones as the price he willingly pays for his rights of self-defense against hostile outsiders and an ineffectual (or worse) police force; the "free contractor" from the *Lochner* era deals with unhelpful co-contracting employees or employers through the right to exit at will; the suicidal individual and the woman obtaining an abortion are both dealing in death. And, in each case, the constitutional exit right separates the individual from some feared part of the physical, biological community: from a fetus that may threaten a woman's life or well-being, a threatening intruder that endangers a homeowner's life, a public school teacher with liberal norms of forced ideological inclusion and equality, and, most poignantly, the suicidal individual from his own pained body. All of this recalls, if nothing else, classical definitions of tragedy: in the last act of Shakespearean or classical tragedy, the characters wind up dead on the stage, with the community or state from which they came torn asunder. In constitutional tragedies, those dead individuals as well as those who killed them are shrouded in rights.

Painean civil rights, by contrast, are comedic rather than tragic. The last act of a comedy typically culminates in a community ritual, such as a wedding celebration or the birth of a child, that reaffirms the value of a shared, communal life, both for the individuals involved and for the larger society. Our civil rights are "comedic" in precisely this way. If Title VII of the Civil Rights Act is working properly, then the last scene of the last act of that legal drama is a workplace that is actually integrated, not a society of atomistic individuals who have rights against irrational state classifications. If Title IX is functioning properly, then in the last act, universities and colleges are healthier communities: women are actually playing on sports teams and African Americans are actually participating in classrooms. When the Family Medical Leave Act is working properly, actual workers tend to dependents in their real-life families, creating stronger communities in both homes and workplaces. The parent nurtures the newborn child, or the adult child cares for the parent, without fear of losing her place in the workforce. When civil rights to education are secured, then the classroom is public, in all senses of the word—publicly funded, publicly supported, open to all comers, and serving the public that funds it. It educates for citizenship and fulfilling lives. When labor rights are enjoyed, workplaces are healthier, better paid, and more participatory. With the civil right to marry secured, the couple weds, in a ritual of communal reaffirmation, toward the end of a communally recognized shared life. With the civil right to gun safety and gun control, the neighborhood is safe, and the individual and her community are supported and healthy. In the last act of comedy, not just individuals but also the communities in which they live are on stage, celebrating the civil rights that unite and support them.

There is, it is important to note, nothing Dionysian or even romantic about any of this. These rituals are made possible *by law*, and lots of it—not by an inherently sociable nature. All of these rituals—a marriage, the opening of a school, the integration of a workplace, the care of a newborn, the policing of a neighborhood—are not just dependent upon but fully constituted by law and legalism. The workplace is a product of contract, property, and labor law; the parent's nurturance of a newborn without fearing loss of employment is a product of an act of Congress; the safe neighborhood is the end result of the social compact that exchanges, at its core, the natural right of self-help with the mutual obligations of a communally funded and manned police force; the healthy individual owes her health to the pooling of risk, itself facilitated by a set of tax and spending acts of Congress; and civil marriage, as commentators on all sides of the debates surrounding its expansion have noted,[69] is a product of law and legalism, not of faith traditions. There is nothing particularly romantic, and certainly nothing anarchic, about any of these rights. Health care is not something we enjoy by nature's bounty; it is something we enjoy if we have structured our community and its laws in a way that is conducive to pooled risk. Education is not something that a child will pick up willy-nilly if we would but leave him to his own devices; it is a highly structured product of law, bureaucracy, deliberation, compromise, and pedagogy. Safe neighborhoods are not the spontaneous flowering of a natural Homo sapiens community in Walden Pond; they are the deliberate outcome of a self-motivated contract through which we exchange our own natural rights of self-defense for a web of communal protection. Our own health is not something we will enjoy in a state of nature; quite the contrary, our lives in such a state would be both nasty and short, even without the brutishness of others. It is something that is produced through effective law facilitating the production and distribution of effective medicine and medical care. An integrated workforce and access to fair labor is not the natural product of a primitive instinct to bargain or unstructured, spontaneous contracts without need of public enforcement. Rather, it is the product of legalistic constraints on those instincts. Civil rights speak to our capabilities, our respect for community, and our recognition of how law is in service to those communal instincts. They speak to law's virtue and law's necessity, not to law's mendacity or irrelevance. They are, in short, rights *to* law, not rights to be free of it. We would not enjoy the goods they promise or the capabilities they protect—health, education, welfare, safe neighborhoods, decent work, family, and marriage—without law's presence.

III. Conclusion: Civil Violence, Civil Rights

In contemporary usage, we tend to conflate civil rights and the idea of civil rights with the antidiscrimination laws that protects those rights. This is a mistake. Antidiscrimination laws protect us from unequal enforcement of our civil rights, particularly where that unequal enforcement is due to racial discrimination or classification on the basis of irrational criteria. Our civil rights, though, are not simply the rights we have to that nondiscrimination. Rather, they are rights to participate in our community in all of the ways peculiarly facilitated by law, which we have a right to enjoy free of the discrimination that would deprive us of them. By conflating the antidiscrimination norm with the civil rights that norm protects, we have unnecessarily truncated the natural development of our understanding of the contribution our very civil law makes to our very civil society, and to the aspects of the good life that civil law facilitates, and for which law is so architecturally central.

By way of conclusion, look again at the killing of Trayvon Martin, the trial of George Zimmerman for that death, and its aftermath. The failure to find Zimmerman guilty of second-degree murder[70] may or may not be attributable, in part or whole, to either intentional or unintentional racism on the part of the jury, the judge, the community, the prosecutors, the expert witnesses, the police force, and the defense team. If it was, then there may have been a violation of not only the antidiscrimination norm in the abstract but also Martin's civil rights, both as I have defined them here and as traditionally defined, primarily to security and protection. But whether that is the case or not, there is another violation of Trayvon Martin's civil rights revealed by that tragedy that is *not* fundamentally a function of racism—although it is certainly exacerbated by it. "Stand your ground" laws,[71] as well as newly broadened self-defense laws that expand the scope of permissible violence in altercations,[72] basically expand the scope of justified lethal force to include all scenarios in which a combatant is in fear for his life, regardless of who or what triggered the fight that put him there. You can, that is, stalk someone so long as your "stalking" is itself legal, pick a fight with him, find yourself losing that fight, consequently fear for your own life, and then fire a gun with the intent and hope to kill, all in justified self-defense. That is what Zimmerman did. Martin's mistake was to fight his stalker, and effectively.

Zimmerman's justified lethal violence, because it was lawful "self-defense," was not criminal. That which is not criminal is legal. So, when we expand self-defense law with stand-your-ground laws and simultaneously protect rights to carry weapons, we have in effect changed the terms of our civil, or social compact: some measure of public, "civic violence" is now fully permitted that was fully criminal a very short time ago. When we embrace broad defenses that shrink the sphere of criminal lethal violence, we not only expand the scope of permissible individual self-help in altercations; we also shrink the sphere of the pacific civility that is expected of us in our public as well as private spaces. If a combatant is permitted to carry a gun, start a fight, and then "stand his ground," regardless of what he did to trigger the assault, virtually every fistfight, regardless of how it began, becomes, potentially, a justified homicide. The sphere of peaceful coexistence—of community—is gravely reduced.

It seems to me that on Paine's understanding, this entire body of newly made law, with state statutory and U.S. constitutional underpinnings both, far more clearly than the jury verdict acquitting his killer, is a massive violation of Trayvon Martin's civil rights. By virtue of its enactment, Martin's civil right to the enjoyment of his physical security and his equally civil right to the state's protection of his physical security are what was not protected that night on his walk back from the store to his father's apartment. The core civil right, Paine urged, is the right to the state's protection of one's physical security. That protection, to which we have a right, is and must be provided by the state; it is the paradigmatic right that we cannot perfect on our own. The authors of the 1871 Ku Klux Klan Act[73] realized this. The authors of the Equal Protection Clause of the Fourteenth Amendment recognized this. The authors of the late twentieth century's Violence Against Women Act recognized this. The authors of our various Criminal Codes recognize this. Yet somehow, we have lost track of the civil rights underpinning of our right to be protected by the state against private violence. Instead, we shrink the scope of the right to be protected while constitutionalizing various rights to kill each other. I am not urging a massive enlargement of our overly punitive criminal justice system. But it hardly follows from the sad fact that our criminal justice system is unjust that what we should do is return the streets to the armed. The result of the abandonment of the civil right to protection against violence, and the civil duty of the state to provide it, whether through the defunding of police forces or the expanding of "self-defense" principles, is and will continue to be carnage—in homes, schools, and on public streets.

That carnage, no less than discriminatory law enforcement, is a central civil rights issue of our age. It should not need to rear its head only in the aftermath of spectacularly tragic public killings of innocents. There is now no question but that this breach of our civil rights—the failure of the state to protect all of us against private violence—affects blacks more than whites, and black youth far more than white youth. It is young black men and boys, more than white men, who are targeted not only by ordinary crime but also by vigilante neighborhood watch groups staffed by white men carrying guns and whose death-dealing acts of killing can then be tallied as justifiable homicide. The "civil right," then, of which young black men are deprived, is not only the right to be free of discriminatory policing, discriminatory profiling, and discriminatory sentencing policies, but it is also the civil right to live out their lives without fear of intimate and neighborly—and, as it turns out, fully legal—violence every time they walk from their homes to their neighborhood stores. Both they and all the rest of us are deprived of that right by virtue of neutral-sounding expansions of our self-defense laws, stand-your-ground laws, open carry laws, and constitutionally grounded gun rights, all of which, collectively, have a horrifically adverse impact on minority communities. But the existence of the civil right these laws offend does not depend on such a showing. The thoroughly positive right to thoroughly positive, state-provided protection against thoroughly private violence is a—maybe the—quintessential civil right: it is a right that can only be realized through the enactment of positive law and its fair enforcement. It is the civil right to the protection of the state against the private violence occasioned upon him by George Zimmerman, as accomplished here through the state of Florida's quite intentional shrinkage of their criminal law of homicide, which was denied Trayvon Martin.

A civil right, again, is a civil right *to* law—in this case, to laws criminalizing private violence. That civil right cannot be realized through negative rights to be free *of* law, nor can it be realized by rights to be free of state or private discrimination. It cannot even be seen, in fact, as a civil right as long as we remain besotted by our negative constitutional rights to be free of the state, leavened only by our insistence that the state not irrationally discriminate between us. Neither of the two dominant understandings of rights that circulate in our contemporary legal culture—our understanding of our beloved negative constitutional rights that shrink the role of the state in our lives or our limited understanding of our equally cherished civil rights to nondiscrimination—no matter how seriously we regard them, will be much help on this one. All the constitutional rights and antidiscrimination rights in the world would not have helped Trayvon Martin against George Zimmerman's fully legal lethal force. For that, we need to regenerate interest in and commitment to the rights to civil society, including Martin's vital civil rights to physical security and mobility, envisioned by early and forgotten architects of our classical civil rights tradition.

About the Author

Frederick Haas Professor of Law and Philosophy, faculty director, Georgetown Center for Law and Humanities. Many thanks for comments and criticisms to Nan Hunter, Chai Feldblum, Allegra McLeod, Heidi Feldman, and participants at the Georgetown Law Center Faculty Workshop and at the Michigan Law School conference commemorating the fiftieth anniversary of the Civil Rights Act.

Notes

1. Civil Rights Act of 1964, 42 U.S.C. §§ 2000e–2000e-17 (2013).

2. The identification of civil rights with the antidiscrimination norm is ubiquitous in contemporary scholarship on the Civil Rights Act. *See, e.g.*, Bruce Ackerman, *The Living Constitution*, 120 HARV. L. REV. 1737, 1779–80 (2007); William N. Eskridge Jr. & John Ferejohn, *Super-Statutes*, 50 DUKE L.J. 1215, 1237–38 (2001); Rebecca E. Zietlow, *To Secure These Rights: Congress, Courts and the 1964 Civil Rights Act*, 57 RUTGERS L. REV. 945, 946 (2005). For a historical account of how this identification became entrenched in twentieth-century legal thought and an attempt to reclaim earlier meanings, see RISA L. GOLUBOFF, THE LOST PROMISE OF CIVIL RIGHTS (2010) [hereinafter GOLUBOFF, LOST PROMISE]; Risa L. Goluboff, *The Thirteenth Amendment and the Lost Origins of Civil Rights*, 50 DUKE L.J. 1609 (2001) [hereinafter Goluboff, *Thirteenth Amendment*].

3. Labor rights in particular were identified and then fought for as "civil rights" through the first half of the twentieth century, not just in common parlance, but also by the Justice Department's Civil Rights Section lawyers charged with the duty of enforcing them. *See* Goluboff, *Thirteenth Amendment*, *supra* note 2, at 1616–18; *see generally* William E. Forbath, *Caste, Class, and Equal Citizenship*, 98 MICH. L. REV. 1, 4–6 (1999) [hereinafter Forbath, *Caste*]; William E. Forbath, *Civil Rights and Economic Citizenship: Notes on the Past and Future of the Civil Rights and Labor Movements*, 2 U. PA. J. LAB. & EMP. L. 697 (2000) [hereinafter Forbath, *Past and Future*].

4. *See* Voting Rights Act of 1965, Pub. L. No. 89-110, 79 Stat. 437 (codified as amended in scattered sections of 42 U.S.C.) (2013)) ("All citizens of the United States who are otherwise qualified by law to vote...shall be entitled and allowed to vote at all such elections, without distinction of race, color, or previous condition of servitude."); *see also* the Civil Rights Act of 1957, Pub. L. No. 85-315, 71 Stat. 634 (1957) (current version at Voting Rights Act of 1965); Civil Rights Act of 1960, Pub. L. No. 86-449, 74 Stat. 86 (1960) (current version at Voting Rights Act of 1965).

5. Civil Rights Act of 1866, ch. 31, § 1, 14 Stat. 27 (1866):

   "And such citizens, of every race and color, without regard to any previous condition of slavery or involuntary servitude, except as a punishment for crime whereof the party shall have been duly convicted, shall have the same right, in every State and Territory in the United States, to make and enforce contracts, to sue, be parties, and give evidence, to inherit, purchase, lease, sell, hold, and convey real and personal property, *and to full and equal benefit of all laws and proceedings for the security of person* [execution, imprisonment] and property, as is enjoyed by white citizens, and shall be subject to like punishment, pains, and penalties, and to none other, any law, statute, ordinance, regulation, or custom, to the contrary notwithstanding." (emphasis added)

   See also Ku Klux Klan Act of 1871, 42 U.S.C. §§ 1983, 1985, 1986 (2013), also called the Civil Rights Act of 1871 or the Force Act of 1871, which was intended to secure for African Americans the protection of the criminal law against private violence.

6. Civil Rights Act of 1866, ch. 31, § 1, 14 Stat. 27 (1866).

7. *Id.*

8. *Id.*

9. *Id.*

10. 42 U.S.C. § 2000e (2013).

11. 42 U.S.C. § 2000a (2013). *See also* Civil Rights Act of 1875, ch. 114, §§ 3–5, 18 Stat. 336, 337 (1875) (held unconstitutional in *Civil Rights Cases*, 109 U.S. 3 (1883)).

12. Title IX of the Education Amendments of 1972, 20 U.S.C. §§ 1681–88 (2013).

13. *See* United States v. Windsor, 570 U.S. , 133 S. Ct. 2675 (2013); Loving v. Virginia, 388 U.S. 1 (1967); Goodridge v. Dep't of Pub. Health, 798 N.E.2d 941 (Mass. 2003).

14. *See, e.g.*, GOLUBOFF, LOST PROMISE, *supra* note 2; KENNETH MACK, REPRESENTING THE RACE: THE CREATION OF THE CIVIL RIGHTS LAWYER (2012); Bruce Ackerman, *The Living Constitution*, 120 HARV. L. REV. 1737 (2007); Risa L. Goluboff, *Lawyers, Law and the New Civil Rights History*, 126 Harvard L. Rev. 2312 (2013); Goluboff, *Thirteenth Amendment*, *supra* note 2; Kenneth Mack, *RethinkingCivil Rights Lawyering and Politics in the Era before* Brown, 115 YALE L.J. 256 (2005) [hereinafter Mack, *Rethinking Civil Rights*]; G. Edward White, *The Origins of Civil Rights in America*, 64 CASE W. RES. L. REV. 755 (2014); Rebecca E. Zietlow, *To Secure These Rights: Congress, Courts, and the 1964 Civil Rights Act*, 57 RUTGERS L. REV. 945 (2005).

15. For example, Jack Balkin's review of Ackerman's Holmes lecture on the history and meaning of the Civil Rights Act of 1964 faults that essay for failing to account for the full meaning of the "civil rights revolution" of the 1960s, which included, according to Balkin, the rights of criminal defendants to Miranda warnings, habeas corpus, legal representation, and so forth. Jack M. Balkin, *A Review of Bruce Ackerman's Holmes Lectures, "The Living Constitution," Part One*, BALKINIZATION (May 29, 2007, 6:50 AM), http://balkin.blogspot.com/2007/05/review-of-bruce-ackermans-holmes.html; Jack M. Balkin, *A Review of Bruce Ackerman's Holmes Lectures, "The Living Constitution," Part Two*, BALKINIZATION (May 30, 2007, 6:51 AM), http://balkin.blogspot.com/2007/05/review-of-bruce-ackermans-holmes_30.html; Jack M. Balkin, *A Review of Bruce Ackerman's Holmes Lectures, "The Living Constitution," Part Three*, BALKINIZATION (May 31, 2007, 6:50 AM), http://balkin.blogspot.com/2007/05/review-of-bruce-ackermans-holmes_31.html; Jack M. Balkin, *A Review of Bruce Ackerman's Holmes Lectures, "The Living Constitution," Part Four*, BALKINIZATION (June 1, 2007, 6:50 AM), http://balkin.blogspot.com/2007/06/review-of-bruce-ackermans-holmes.html. But without some sort of jurisprudential understanding of the nature of a civil right, such that these rights of criminal defendants are core examples of such rights, it is hard not to view this critique as simply arbitrary.

16. On the nature of rights, see, e.g., RONALD DWORKIN, LAW'S EMPIRE (1986); RONALD DWORKIN, A MATTER OF PRINCIPLE (1985); RONALD DWORKIN, TAKING RIGHTS SERIOUSLY (1978); H.L.A. HART, ESSAYS ON BENTHAM: JURISPRUDENCE AND POLITICAL THEORY (1982); WESLEY NEWCOMB HOHFELD, FUNDAMENTAL LEGAL CONCEPTIONS: AS APPLIED IN JUDICIAL REASONING (Walter Wheeler Cook ed., 1964). *See generally*THEORIES OF RIGHTS (Jeremy Waldron ed., 1984). On natural rights or human rights, see, e.g., JOHN FINNIS, NATURAL LAW & NATURAL RIGHTS (2d ed. 2011); MARTHA C. NUSSBAUM, WOMEN AND HUMAN DEVELOPMENT: THE CAPABILITIES APPROACH (2001) [hereinafter NUSSBAUM, WOMEN AND HUMAN DEVELOPMENT]. On constitutional rights, see LAURENCE H. TRIBE, AMERICAN CONSTITUTIONAL LAW (3d ed. 1999). For critical treatments of our constitutional rights tradition, see MARY ANN GLENDON, RIGHTS TALK: THE IMPOVERISHMENT OF POLITICAL DISCOURSE (Free Press reprt. ed. 1993); Morton J. Horwitz, *Rights*, 23 HARV. C.R.-C.L. L. REV. 393 (1988); Mark Tushnet, *An Essay on Rights*, 62 TEX. L. REV. 1363 (1984).

17. *See, e.g.*, ROBERT D. PUTNAM, BOWLING ALONE: THE COLLAPSE AND REVIVAL OF AMERICAN COMMUNITY (2001).

18. THOMAS PAINE, RIGHTS OF MAN (Penguin Books 1984) (Part 1 first published 1791, Part 2 first published 1792).

19. *Id.* Part 1 at 464–465.

20. *Id.*

21. *Id.*

22. *Id.*

23. *Id.*

24. *See* Martha C. Nussbaum, *Nature, Functioning, and Capability: Aristotle on Political Distribution, in*OXFORD STUDIES IN ANCIENT PHILOSOPHY 145 (Supp. vol. 1988); Martha C. Nussbaum, *Human Functioning and Social Justice: In Defense of Aristotelian Essentialism,* 20 POL. THEORY 202 (1992); NUSSBAUM, WOMEN AND HUMAN DEVELOPMENT, *supra* note 16; Martha C. Nussbaum, *Capabilities as Fundamental Entitlements: Sen and Social Justice,* 9 FEMINIST ECON. 33 (2003) [hereinafter Nussbaum, *Capabilities as Fundamental Entitlements*]. *See also*AMARTYA SEN, *Rights and Capabilities, in*RESOURCES, VALUES AND DEVELOPMENT 307 (3d prtg. 1998); AMARTYA SEN, COMMODITIES AND CAPABILITIES (1999); Amartya Sen, *Well-Being, Agency and Freedom: The Dewey Lectures 1984,* 82 J. PHIL. 169 (1985); Amartya Sen, *Capability and Well-Being, in*THE QUALITY OF LIFE 30 (Martha C. Nussbaum & Amartya Sen eds., 1993).

25. Nussbaum, *Capabilities as Fundamental Entitlements, supra* note 24, at 36–42; SEN, COMMODITIES AND CAPABILITIES, *supra* note 24, at 17–21.

26. Robin L. West, *Tragic Rights: The Rights Critique in the Age of Obama,* 53 WM. & MARY L. REV. 713 (2011) [hereinafter West, *Tragic Rights*]; Robin West, *Exit Rights: Roberts' Conception of America in the ACA Decision,* JURIST-FORUM, July 26, 2012, http://jurist.org/forum/2012/07/robin-west-aca-roberts.php# [hereinafter West, *Exit Rights*].

27. PAINE, *supra* note 18, at 68.

28. *See generally* Mark Tushnet, *Civil Rights and Social Rights: The Future of the Reconstruction Amendments,* 25 LOY. L.A. L. REV. 1207 (1992).

29. PAINE, *supra* note 18, at 66.

30. *Id.* at 68.

31. *Id.*

32. *Id.*

33. Civil Rights Act of 1866, ch. 31, § 1, 14 Stat. 27 (1866).

34. *Id.*

35. Ku Klux Klan Act, now codified as 42 U.S.C. § 1985 (2013). The Act holds, in part, that when two or more persons "conspire or go in disguise on the highway or the premises of another, for the purpose of depriving...any person or class of persons of the Equal Protection of the Law," they may be sued. *See* Griffin v. Breckenridge, 403 U.S. 88 (1971).

36. Civil Rights Act of 1875, ch. 114, 18 Stat. 336 (1875) (held unconstitutional in *Civil Rights Cases,* 109 U.S. 3 (1883)).

37. GOLUBOFF, LOST PROMISE, *supra* note 2; Goluboff, *Thirteenth Amendment, supra* note 2.

38. *See e.g.,* Forbath, *Caste, supra* note 3; Forbath, *Past and Future, supra* note 3.

39. Goluboff, *Thirteenth Amendment, supra* note 2, at 1616–18.

40. *Id.*

41. Reverend Martin Luther King Jr., I Have a Dream..., Speech at the "March on Washington" (Aug. 28, 1963) (transcript available at http://www.archives.gov/press/exhibits/dream-speech.pdf).

42. 42 U.S.C. §§ 2000a, 2000e (2013); 20 U.S.C. §§ 1681–88 (2013). *See, e.g.,* Goluboff, *Thirteenth Amendment, supra* note 2, at 1619; Mack, *RethinkingCivil Rights, supra* note 14, at 331–33.

43. Obergefell v. Hodges, 135 S.Ct. 2584, 2589–90 (2015).

44. The Family Medical Leave Act (FMLA) is widely understood as a civil rights statute, as is the Violence Against Women Act (VAWA). Both laws *can* be construed as antidiscrimination rights—FMLA can be read as conferring a right not to be discriminated against in the workplace by virtue of one's status as a caregiver and VAWA as conferring a right to protection against violence, regardless of gender. Both, however, are also clear examples of civil rights statutes that convey rights to underlying substantive rights and not just rights against wrongful or irrational classification: FMLA protects the right to not lose a job by virtue of caregiving responsibilities, and VAWA protects the right to meaningful protections against intimate violence. Family Medical Leave Act (FMLA), Pub. L. No. 103-3, 107 Stat. 6 (1993) (codified as amended in scattered sections of 5 and 29 U.S.C.); Violence Against Women Act (VAWA), Pub. L. No. 103-322, tit. IV, 108 Stat. 1902 (1994) (codified as amended in scattered sections of 8, 16, 18, 28, and 42 U.S.C.). *See, e.g.,* Johanna R. Shargel, *In Defense of the Civil Rights Remedy of the Violence Against Women Act,* 106 YALE L.J. 1849 (1997).

45. Violence Against Women Act (VAWA), Pub. L. No. 103–322, tit. IV, 108 Stat. 1902 (1994) (codified as amended in scattered sections of 8, 16, 18, 28, and 42 U.S.C.).

46. No Child Left Behind Act of 2001 (NCLB), Pub. L. No. 107–110, 115 Stat. 1425 (codified as amended in scattered sections of 20 U.S.C.). *See also* Brown v. Bd. of Educ., 347 U.S. 483 (1954) (education as a civil right).

47. Education of the Handicapped Act (now Individuals with Disabilities Education Act (IDEA)), Pub. L. No. 91-230, 84 Stat. 175-188 (codified as amended in scattered sections of 20 U.S.C.).

48. Patient Protection and Affordable Care Act, Pub. L. No. 111-148, 124 Stat. 119 (codified as amended in scattered sections of 21, 25, 26, 29, and 42 U.S.C.).

49. Nussbaum presents the "capabilities approach" as an alternative to a human rights approach but also makes clear that the two are consistent and mutually supportive and that the former leaves room for the latter, where a sense of imperativism is desired. NUSSBAUM, WOMEN AND HUMAN DEVELOPMENT,*supra* note 16, at 96–98.

50. In more conventional terms, some of the capabilities are best protected by negative rights and some by positive.

51. For a related approach, see MADISON POWERS & RUTH FADEN, SOCIAL JUSTICE: THE MORAL FOUNDATIONS OF PUBLIC HEALTH AND HEALTH POLICY (2d ed. 2006); *see also* my review, Robin L. West, *Book Review: Social Justice: The Moral Foundations of Public Health and Health Policy,* 10 DEPAUL J. HEALTH CARE L. 567 (2006).

52. Patient Protection and Affordable Care Act, Pub. L. No. 111–148, 124 Stat. 119 (codified as amended in scattered sections of 21, 25, 26, 29, and 42 U.S.C.).

53. NCLB, Pub. L. No. 107-110, 115 Stat. 1425 (codified as amended in scattered sections

of 20 U.S.C.); IDEA, Pub. L. No. 91-230, 84 Stat. 175-188 (codified as amended in scattered sections of 20 U.S.C.).

54. FMLA, Pub. L. No. 103-3, 107 Stat. 6 (codified as amended in scattered sections of 5 and 29 U.S.C.).

55. VAWA, Pub. L. No. 103-322, tit. IV, 108 Stat. 1902 (codified as amended in scattered sections of 8, 16, 18, 28, and 42 U.S.C.).

56. Zietlow, *supra* note 14, at 946.

57. *Id.* at 990–91.

58. *Id.*

59. Civil Rights Act of 1866, ch. 31, § 1, 14 Stat. 27 (1866).

60. Ackerman, *supra* note 14, at 1761.

61. *See* Jonathan L. v. Superior Ct., 81 Cal. Rptr. 3d 571 (Cal. Ct. App. 2008); *seealso* Wisconsin v. Yoder, 406 U.S. 205 (1972); Michael E. Hersher, *"Home Schooling" in California*, 118 YALE L.J. 27 (pocket part 2008); Robert Reich, *Why Homeschooling Should Be Regulated*, *in*HOMESCHOOLING IN FULL VIEW: A READER 109 (Bruce S. Cooper ed., 2005); Robert Reich, *On Regulating Homeschooling: A Reply to Glanzer*, 58 EDUC. THEORY 17 (2008); Kimberly A. Yuracko, *Off the Grid: Constitutional Constraints on Homeschooling*, 96 CALIF. L. REV. 123 (2008).

62. For a defense of this right, see generally Ronald Dworkin et al., *Assisted Suicide: The Philosophers' Brief*, N.Y. REV. OF BOOKS, Mar. 27, 1997, at 41.

63. Nat'l Fed'n of Indep. Bus. v. Sebelius, 567 U.S. , 132 S. Ct. 2566, 2585–91 (2012); West, *Exit Rights*, *supra* note 26.

64. District of Columbia v. Heller, 554 U.S. 570 (2008).

65. Roe v. Wade, 410 U.S. 113 (1973).

66. Hosanna-Tabor Evangelical Lutheran Church & Sch. v. EEOC, 565 U.S. , 132 S. Ct. 694 (2012).

67. Hobby Lobby Stores, Inc. v. Sebelius, 723 F.3d 1114 (10th Cir. 2013), *petition for cert. granted*, 134 S. Ct. 678 (Nov. 26, 2013) (No. 13-354); Burwell v. Hobby Lobby Stores Inc., 134 S.Ct. 2751, 2773 (2014).

68. West, *Tragic Rights*, *supra* note 26; West, *Exit Rights*, *supra* note 26.

69. *See, e.g.*, Ralph Wedgwood, *The Meaning of Same-Sex Marriage*, N.Y. TIMES, May 24, 2012; *Sunday Dialogue: Rethinking Marriage*, N.Y. TIMES, Oct. 27, 2012.

70. Lizette Alvarez & Cara Buckley, *Zimmerman Is Acquitted in Trayvon Martin Killing*, N.Y. TIMES, July 13, 2013.

71. Over half of the states now have enacted "stand your ground" laws, at the instigation of the NRA. *See, e.g.*, ALA. CODE § 13A-3-23(b) (2013) ("A person who is justified under subsection (a) in using physical force, including deadly physical force, and who is not engaged in an unlawful activity and is in any place where he or she has the right to be has no duty to retreat and has the right to stand his or her ground."); FLA. STAT. § 776.013(3) (2013) ("A person who is not engaged in an unlawful activity and who is attacked in any other place where he or she has a right to be has no duty to retreat and has the right to stand his or her ground and meet force with force, including deadly force if he or she reasonably believes it is necessary to do so to prevent death or great bodily harm to himself or herself or another or to prevent the commission of a forcible felony."). Eric Holder has recently joined a chorus of criticisms of stand-your-ground laws for increasing

the number of killings in states that have enacted them. *See* Attorney General Eric Holder, Remarks at the 2013 NAACP Annual Convention (July 16, 2013) (transcript available at http://articles.washingtonpost.com/2013-07-16/politics/40608813_1_trayvon-martin-rights-leaders-justice-department).

72. The judge in the George Zimmerman case instructed the jury that Zimmerman was entitled to stand his ground and use lethal force if he reasonably believed his life was in danger. Prior to Florida's passage of stand-your-ground legislation, the instruction would have been that he was not so entitled if he had a reasonable way to avoid the altercation. *See generallyOutcry Unlikely to Spur Change in Stand-Your-Ground Law*, CBS NEWS, July 22, 2013, http://www.cbsnews.com/news/outcry-unlikely-to-spur-change-in-stand-your-ground-law/; FLA. STAT. § 776.013(3) (2013).

73. 42 U.S.C. §§ 1983, 1985, 1986.

5

On Class-Not-Race

Samuel R. Bagenstos

Throughout the civil rights era, strong voices have argued that policy interventions should focus on class or socioeconomic status, not race. At times, this position-taking has seemed merely tactical, opportunistic, or in bad faith. Many who have opposed race-based civil rights interventions on this basis have not turned around to support robust efforts to reduce class-based or socioeconomic inequality. That sort of opportunism is interesting and important for understanding policy debates in civil rights, but it is not my focus here. I am more interested here in the people who clearly mean it. For example, President Lyndon Baines Johnson—who can hardly be accused of failing to support robust race-based *or* class-based interventions—advised Dr. Martin Luther King after Congress passed the Voting Rights Act that the race-neutral, class-based Great Society programs had to be counted on to eliminate race inequality from that point forward.[1] William Julius Wilson famously argued that our policies should focus on "the truly disadvantaged" of all races and spelled out a rather aggressive approach to promoting economic development in American cities.[2] And Richard Kahlenberg and Richard Sander have urged that universities should get rid of race-based affirmative action in admissions but replace that policy with preferences for members of disadvantaged socioeconomic groups.[3]

Calls for class-not-race interventions are likely to grow stronger over the next few years. The Supreme Court's recent decision in *Fisher v. Uni-*

versity of Texas at Austin[4]—which did not formally change the law governing affirmative action in higher education admissions but did highlight the vulnerability of the policy with the current Supreme Court—has been read by some commentators as auguring a decisive turn toward class-based affirmative action.[5] The Supreme Court's decision upholding Michigan's state constitutional prohibition on race-based affirmative action in *Schuette v. Coalition to Defend Affirmative Action*[6] predictably led to renewed calls for class-based preferences.[7] This, then, seems an opportune time to examine the class-not-race position that underlies them.

There is a lot that can be said about the beyond-race interventions favored by class-not-race advocates. And I say a lot of it elsewhere.[8] Here, I want to focus on a single aspect of the argument. I want to develop an understanding of what sincere advocates of the class-not-race position mean and offer an initial assessment of whether that position is a sensible one.

It seems to me that sincere advocates of the class-not-race position are making one of two distinct arguments. The first argument is basically a strategic one. That argument accepts that racial inequality is a fundamental problem that we must attack. It argues, however, that for a variety of pragmatic reasons, race-targeted approaches are not likely to be the most successful ways of attacking them. There is much to this argument, but it seems to suffer a basic flaw. Problems of race inequality go well beyond problems of economic or class inequality. And there is a lot of reason to believe that efforts to respond to class inequality that do not take race into account either will not help or actually will exacerbate race inequality. I discuss those points in Part I below.

These points lead to the second distinct argument that advocates of the class-not-race position may be making. That argument is that race inequality is not in fact the fundamental problem that we should attack but is at best an example or a consequence of class or economic inequality. If we have a limited reservoir of enforcement resources, redistributive largesse, or public compassion, the argument implies, we should focus that reservoir on eliminating class-based inequality. I think some argument like this explains why many people influenced by traditional left politics support the class-not-race position. But I nonetheless believe that the argument is wrongheaded. The problem of racial inequality overlaps with, but is importantly distinct from, economic disadvantage. I discuss these points in Part II.

In Part III, I assess the prospects for getting beyond the class-not-race position. Although I find some reasons for hope on this score, I am, ultimately, pessimistic.

I. The Strategic Argument for Class-Not-Race

Many of the reasons offered for the class-not-race position are essentially strategic. These arguments assert not that class-not-race is superior as a matter of principle or first-best policy but that approaches that target class instead of race are more likely to succeed in the political or legal process than are approaches that focus directly on race. This is most apparent in the context of affirmative action. Many of the advocates of class-based affirmative action—particularly after the Supreme Court decisions making *race*-based affirmative action more difficult to defend—believe that targeting class rather than race will place the practice of affirmative action on stronger *legal* ground. The legal-doctrinal argument is certainly a key talking point for some of the most prominent advocates of class-based affirmative action.[9]

Viewed purely as a tactical gambit to shore up the legality of affirmative action, it is unclear whether a focus on class instead of race will work. Under current doctrine, it is a nice question whether admissions preferences for people of particular socioeconomic statuses are constitutional when they are motivated by a desire to achieve a particular racial outcome. The argument that they are unconstitutional involves a seemingly straightforward application of *Washington v. Davis*[10] and its progeny (which held that race-neutral practices that are motivated by race are the equivalent of racial classifications) and *Adarand Constructors v. Pena*[11] and its progeny (which held that the constitutionality of racial classifications is the same no matter which race is benefited or burdened). We know that if a school adopted a class-based preference for applicants from higher socioeconomic classes and did so with an aim of increasing the proportion of whites that are admitted, that action would violate the Fourteenth Amendment. Given *Adarand*'s holding that equal protection analysis does not depend on which race is burdened or benefited, shouldn't the result be the same when a school adopts a preference for applicants of lower socioeconomic classes, with an aim of increasing the proportion of minorities who are admitted?[12]

But the Court has never been called on to add up the *Davis* and *Adarand* lines of cases in this precise way. And there are substantial reasons to think that it will balk before ruling race-motivated but class-based affirmative action unconstitutional.[13] One is that in its cases invalidating affirmative action programs, the Court has looked carefully to ensure that race-neutral means could not achieve the same ends.[14] Although that analysis does not logically compel the conclusion that race-neutral affirmative action programs are constitutional, a contrary conclusion would stand in great tension with it. Moreover, Justice

Kennedy's pivotal concurrence in the *Parents Involved* case[15] suggests that he would vote to uphold class-based affirmative action programs. In that concurrence, Justice Kennedy explained his decision to provide the fifth vote to invalidate race-based student assignment plans in K–12 schools. He indicated that race-neutral efforts to achieve diversity and overcome racial isolation would be constitutional—and indeed probably would not even be subject to strict scrutiny.[16] As a pure predictive matter, then, it seems unlikely that five justices on this Supreme Court would invalidate class-based affirmative action.

Other strategic arguments for the class-not-race position are political rather than legal in nature. William Julius Wilson emphasizes many of these points in THE TRULY DISADVANTAGED.[17] Policies that aim overtly at protecting or advancing the interests of particular disadvantaged racial groups may be especially politically vulnerable. This may be because of implicit or overt racial bias in the political process, including the phenomenon of selective sympathy and indifference.[18] It may be because of a general support for color-blindness among the public and political leaders—a sense that race should not matter. (Query how much overlap there is between these two positions.) Or it may be because of simple majoritarianism. Policies that obviously provide benefits to a minority of the population may be politically vulnerable to efforts by the majority to get some of those benefits for itself.

As Wilson makes explicit, these arguments tie rather directly to arguments among social policy experts regarding targeted versus universal social-welfare policies.[19] Many experts argue that social-welfare policies are more politically durable when they are framed in universal terms.[20] Means-tested programs like welfare (or, perhaps now, food stamps) are understood to be more vulnerable than universal social insurance programs like Social Security. There are a couple of reasons for this. One, again, is simple majoritarianism—if everyone feels they can benefit from a program, it will be easier to persuade them to support it than if they are paying for the benefit of someone else. Another is a sense of desert. Universal programs are more easily understood in solidaristic terms as a reciprocal covenant among all citizens. As a result, solidaristic and reciprocal principles of distribution make sense—one deserves to receive benefits because one is a citizen and has contributed to the system.[21] But the public expects one to prove desert for targeted benefits more specifically—if an individual is receiving government benefits to which other individuals are not entitled, the public expects the beneficiaries to demonstrate that they really deserve them. As a result, targeted programs are administered in a much more stingy fashion than universal ones. And scandals regarding alleged waste, fraud, and abuse arise far more easily in targeted programs and are far more likely to delegitimize those programs than they are to delegitimize universal programs of social insurance.

This is a very controversial issue in the social policy world. Professors Schuck and Zeckhauser make a strong theoretical argument that targeted programs more efficiently achieve their aims and therefore are more likely to draw political support than are less efficient universalist ones.[22] Basic public choice theory also suggests that targeted programs will generate fervent support from their beneficiaries, while the broad spreading of the costs will dampen opposition from those who do not receive the benefits.[23] (This point seems more plausible when the beneficiaries are not as socially and politically disempowered as the beneficiaries of race-based interventions, however.) And the empirical evidence on targeting versus universalism is mixed. Social Security is, to be sure, far more politically stable than was welfare. But when we look at smaller programs for classes of poor people, the targeted ones (that focus on people with disabilities or children in poverty) have, on occasion, seemed more resilient than the broader universalist ones.[24]

In the race-versus-class context as well, the strategic argument for universalism is not obviously correct. For one thing, class-based interventions (like class-based affirmative action) may readily come to be understood in the public mind as really targeted toward minorities.[25] That is particularly true because in many cases, the alternative to race-based interventions is not universal social insurance; it is a policy that really is targeted at disadvantaged people, just a bit more broadly than at minorities. Think about welfare in this regard and the general axiom that programs for the poor are poor programs. One reason programs for the poor are politically vulnerable is that they are often associated in the public mind with racial minorities. Efforts to target class-based disadvantage as a way of eliminating racial disadvantage often are understood as being "really" about race and provoke political resistance accordingly—a point George Romney, U.S. Secretary of Housing and Urban Development from 1968 to 1973, learned when his efforts to achieve economic integration in housing provoked fierce resistance from white suburbanites who feared that racial integration would be the result.[26] William Julius Wilson's critique of the Great Society is apt here. Wilson argued that the Great Society's reliance on means-tested antipoverty programs associated it with minorities and made it politically vulnerable.[27] Unless efforts to focus on class rather than race take the form Wilson's effort does—by employing truly broad-scale economic development programs—they will likely remain politically vulnerable as targeted programs. And the truly universal proposals urged by Wilson and others have virtually no hope of being achieved in our current political environment, in which austerity sets the terms of economic policy debates.

Class-based policies, then, may not be especially politically strong. And there may be circumstances in which programs targeted at racial minorities are quite strong politically—precisely because they appeal to a shared commitment to equal opportunity. To the extent that race-focused programs are understood as overcoming the particular injustice of discrimination or the legacy of slavery and segregation, many people will see that disadvantage as not being the fault of the beneficiaries (unlike poverty in general). In those circumstances, candid use of race will be politically superior to the use of class as a proxy for race.

I do not doubt, however, that class-focused approaches are likely to be more defensible, legally and politically, than race-focused ones in many cases. But this brings us to the deeper problem with the strategic arguments for class-not-race. Recall that the premise of the strategic argument is that race-based injustice is a distinct and important concern that the law should address; the argument for class-not-race is that class is a more legally and politically stable way to address that concern than is targeting racial injustice directly. But that argument depends on class disadvantage being a good proxy for race disadvantage. And it is not. In other words, even if class is a more stable way of addressing the problem, it does not address the problem very well. In part, that is because there are so many more poor white people than poor minorities that any help to poor people in general dilutes what minorities get (assuming a sort of constant budget of compassion). But there is a more fundamental reason class disadvantage is not a good proxy for race disadvantage. The strategic argument assumes that racial disadvantage is a subset, a specific application, of class disadvantage—or at least that there is a large overlap between the two categories. There is certainly some overlap, but racial disadvantage is in fact quite distinct. Racial disadvantage in the United States involves economic deprivation, to be sure, but it also involves stigma and stereotypes with a variety of consequences for the day-to-day lives of even economically advantaged members of racial minority groups.[28]

And efforts to focus on class disadvantage may actually reinforce the structures that promote racial disadvantage. We know this, in part, from history. The New Deal took what was well understood as a class-not-race approach. It led to substantial economic development. But because of the lines of eligibility its programs drew—lines that were formally race-neutral—it also entrenched racial hierarchy and subordination.[29] As insightful recent work by Jessica Clarke and KT Albiston argues, these problems are not confined to history.[30] They argue that formally gender-neutral efforts to expand women's opportunities in the workplace, like the Family and Medical Leave Act, have actually entrenched gender hierarchy in workplaces. Deborah Malamud makes the same point about class-based affirmative action.[31]

I do not mean to deny that class-based approaches might be a possible second-best solution to the problem of racial disadvantage. Legal and political developments may substantially limit the prospect of relying on race-based approaches, so class-based ones might be the best available way of achieving those ends. But the same legal, and especially political, developments are likely to limit the utility of class-based approaches in achieving racial justice. If the class-not-race position is a purely strategic one, it is a deeply problematic one.

II. The Substantive Argument for Class-Not-Race

I have argued that class-based interventions are not likely to be an especially effective way of overcoming race-based disadvantage. But what if race-based disadvantage is not what we think of as the essential problem? What if the basic problem is class-based disadvantage? While race- and class-based disadvantage overlapped in the past, one might argue, there is a substantial disconnect between the two problems now, and it is class, not race, on which our policy interventions should focus. I call this the substantive argument for class-not-race. This argument is implicit or explicit in many critiques of race-based affirmative action. Numerous affirmative action critics ask why the child of the Huxtables, or of a rich African immigrant family, should get a preference over a poor white kid from Appalachia. William Julius Wilson asks why we should have policies that benefit the most advantaged blacks but do very little for the least advantaged blacks—those whom he called "the truly disadvantaged." The argument is basically that racial disadvantage may have at some point overlapped with class disadvantage but that the two have diverged. Now that they have diverged, we should identify which of these is the real problem. And, the advocates of class-not-race argue, the real problem is class. The influence of traditional left-wing thinking on this position is patent.

There is obviously something to this argument. In a nation in which economic inequality continues to grow, and our public services shrink, life chances and opportunities depend greatly on the socioeconomic circumstances in which one is born.[32] And this is true for people of all races. Policy interventions that focus on ameliorating economic inequality and class disadvantage are important tools to attack this serious problem.

But I think the substantive class-not-race argument ultimately reflects a category mistake in treating race-based policies as ultimately aimed at alleviating economic inequalities. Antidiscrimination law and affirmative action have of course provided economic advancement to some women and minority group members. And that is a significant goal of these bodies of law. Scholars tend to agree, in particular, that the first decade of enforcement of Title VII was associated with a dramatic increase in the earnings of African Americans relative to those of whites.[33]

But why must we choose which is the *real* problem? Both economic inequality and racial disadvantage are, it seems to me, real problems. We can acknowledge that members of disadvantaged socioeconomic classes face common barriers to opportunity, whatever their race. And, as I have argued, there are more poor whites than there are poor blacks and Latinos (though a much higher proportion of the black or Latino population than of the white population is poor). The problems of poor people of all races are best addressed by race-neutral programs of economic development and public assistance.

But race remains an important axis of disadvantage in America, even of its own accord. Some of this disadvantage is economic. Even middle- and upper-middle-class blacks are more likely to hold that status precariously than whites. They have less wealth on average, they are more likely to have relatives in poverty, and they are more likely to have children who are downwardly mobile economically.[34]

Some of this disadvantage relates directly to continuing discrimination. Housing discrimination keeps African Americans segregated in less desirable neighborhoods, which limits educational opportunities.[35] Employment discrimination continues to limit job opportunities.[36] Discrimination extends beyond economic opportunities: use of race by law enforcement drives home the salience of race in the day-to-day lives of members of racial minority groups, for example.[37] And racial bias in the criminal justice system has a pervasive effect on minority communities.[38] In a provocative recent paper, Betsey Stevenson and Justin Wolfers argue that "the fruits of the civil rights movement may lie" beyond economic opportunities but "in other, more difficult to document, improvements in the quality of life—improvements that have led to rising levels of happiness and life satisfaction for some blacks."[39] As they note, however, "these improvements have taken decades to be realized, and even if current rates of progress persist, it will take several more decades to fully close the black-white happiness gap."[40]

Much of this continuing race-based disadvantage results from subtle, unconscious, or implicit racial bias.[41] But the disadvantage also results from the persistence of racial stereotypes. These stereotypes and biases make it necessary for minority group members in many jobs to engage in constant impression management to demonstrate that they do not conform to the stereotypes. This impression management imposes a significant personal cost. But it also can be self-defeating, by discouraging the sort of risk-taking that leads to success in many employment settings.[42] (There is obviously a similar double-bind in the case of women in workplaces.) Even the most economically advantaged African Americans face these constraints, as the example of the fine line President Obama has had to walk in managing racialized expectations demonstrates.[43]

These problems are distinct from the problems of socioeconomic class. And we know that ameliorating economic inequality and disadvantage will not necessarily eliminate these problems of racial inequality. Rather, the most effective way we know to ameliorate problems of racial discrimination is an affirmative focus on promoting racial integration throughout society. Intergroup contact and work on common projects on terms of equality remain the best ways to break down stereotypes and bias.[44] Although there are substantial legal and political barriers to achieving that goal—something I have lamented in my earlier work[45]—policies that specifically target racial discrimination and inequality are the first-best way to respond to those problems. To say that our policy should focus on class instead of race is to say that we should not address these problems. And I can think of no good substantive, as opposed to strategic, argument for doing that.

III. Class-and-Race: The Civil Rights Act and the Great Society

I should emphasize that to be against class-not-race is not to favor the opposite policy—race-not-class. We live in a big, complex world, one with many axes of disadvantage. I do not know of any advocate for racial justice who is against ameliorating class-based injustice. Nobody seriously proposes including racial diversity as a factor in a higher-education admissions policy but refusing to consider class or economic disadvantage. Advocates of expanded antidiscrimination law typically strongly support antipoverty laws and broad-based economic development policies. Consider, in this regard, how race-oriented civil rights laws, antipoverty policies, and broad-based social insurance were all crucial pieces of the Great Society. There may be tactical questions about how and when to press different pieces of the agenda, but there is no reason we must choose to ameliorate disadvantages along only class or only race axes.

Indeed, I would argue that the most effective social justice strategies are those that, like the Great Society, combine efforts to eliminate the effects of group-targeted discrimination with broader efforts to promote social welfare. The Civil Rights Act of 1964 guaranteed nondiscrimination in employment, which helped African Americans gain access to job opportunities that had previously been closed to them. But the Elementary and Secondary Education Act, Head Start, and other Great Society Programs provided educational opportunities that made it more likely that more African Americans could take advantage of those new job opportunities. In my earlier work, I have argued that the Americans with Disabilities Act's effects on employment for people with disabilities have been significantly limited by the failure to pursue social welfare interventions (like universal health insurance and investment in accessible transportation) that would break down deep-rooted structural barriers to employment.[46] And women's workplace opportunities have been limited by both narrow interpretations of the Pregnancy Discrimination Act and the failure to provide child care and paid family leave; an effective solution to this problem would combine more robust antidiscrimination protections with more robust social provision.[47] To make further progress against racial inequality will require *both* an aggressive effort to enforce antidiscrimination provisions *and* a broader focus on economic development and providing housing and educational opportunities.[48]

So why do we have this endless fight? One reason I assumed away at the outset—bad faith. What about people who sincerely support class-oriented, but not race-oriented, interventions? The essential reason, I think, is strategic, but in a broader sense than I discussed in Part I. For many years, one of the only commitments that united both edges of the progressive movement—those influenced by social democratic politics at the left edge and mainstream centrists at the right edge—was the conviction that identity politics was bad for the movement. Each faction had a slightly different reason for, or way of articulating, its position: those on the Left believed that identity politics undermined class solidarity among the working class, while the centrists believed that identity politics made it difficult to appeal to "mainstream" Americans. But however derived, the policy agenda of both the leftists and the centrists eschewed race-oriented solutions in favor of class-oriented ones.

There is some reason to believe that political conditions now have evolved in a way that might make it possible for each of these factions newly to endorse race-focused interventions. Labor unions have achieved great success in recent years by appealing to identity politics and incorporating race- and sex-focused goals into broader class-focused ones. It appears, then, that identity politics need not undermine the class solidarity that those on the left of the progressive spectrum aim to achieve. And Barack Obama won two consecutive presidential elections by assembling a coalition of racial minorities, together with a sizeable minority of whites. So identity politics perhaps need not impede mainstream political success. In this environment, race-oriented interventions may seem less threatening to the success of progressive politics in general, and advocates of class-not-race may be persuaded to rethink the notion that there must be a choice between race- and class-based approaches.

Yet there are substantial grounds for pessimism on this score. Despite the makeup of his electoral coalition, President Obama tended to emphasize class-focused remedies at the expense of race-focused ones.[49] And the Supreme Court's evolving jurisprudence of antidiscrimination law and affirmative action are likely to make race-focused interventions less tenable, at least for the near future. Ultimately, then, the class-not-race position may be the best we can do, despite its problems.

About the Author

Frank G. Millard Professor of Law, University of Michigan Law School.

Notes

1. *See, e.g.,* JAMES T. PATTERSON: EVE OF DESTRUCTION: HOW 1965 TRANSFORMED AMERICA (2012).

2. *See* WILLIAM JULIUS WILSON, THE TRULY DISADVANTAGED: THE INNER CITY, THE UNDERCLASS, AND PUBLIC POLICY (1987).

3. *See* RICHARD D. KAHLENBERG, THE REMEDY: CLASS, RACE, AND AFFIRMATIVE ACTION (1987); Richard H. Sander, *Class in American Legal Education,* 88 DENV. U. L. REV. 631, 663, 668 (2011).

4. 570 U.S. , 133 S. Ct. 2411 (2013).

5. *See* John B. Judis, *The Unlikely Triumph of an Affirmative Action Prophet,* NEW REPUBLIC, July 18, 2013.

6. 134 S. Ct. 1623 (2004).

7. *See, e.g.,* Room for Debate: Should Affirmative Action Be Based on Income?, N.Y. TIMES, Apr. 27, 2014, *available at* http://www.nytimes.com/roomfordebate/2014/04/27/should-affirmative-action-be-based-on-income.

8. *See* Samuel R. Bagenstos, *Universalism and Civil Rights (with Notes on Voting Rights after* Shelby*),* 123 YALE L.J. 2838 (2014).

9. *See* supra note 3.

10. 426 U.S. 229 (1976).

11. 515 U.S. 200 (1995).

12. For a careful evaluation of this question, which concludes that the answer might not be the same, see Kim Forde-Mazrui, *The Constitutional Implications of Race-Neutral Affirmative Action*, 88 GEO. L.J. 2331 (2000).

13. For an extensive discussion that argues that the Supreme Court's recent decision in Texas Dept. of Community Affairs v. Inclusive Communities Project, 135 S. Ct. 2507 (2015) is best read as clarifying that class-based affirmative action, even if racially motivated, is not constitutionally problematic, see Samuel R. Bagenstos, *Disparate Impact and the Role of Classification and Motivation in Equal Protection Law After* Inclusive Communities, 101 CORNELL L. REV. ___ (forthcoming 2016).

14. *See* Fisher v. Univ. of Tex., 133 S. Ct. 2411, 2420–21 (2013); Grutter v. Bollinger, 539 U.S. 306, 339–40 (2003).

15. Parents Involved in Cmty. Sch. v. Seattle Sch. Dist. No. 1, 551 U.S. 701, 782 (2007) (Kennedy, J., concurring in part and concurring in the judgment).

16. *See id.* at 789.

17. *See* WILSON, *supra* note 2.

18. *See* Paul Brest, *The Supreme Court, 1975 Term—Foreword: In Defense of the Antidiscrimination Principle*, 90 HARV. L. REV. 1 (1976).

19. *See* WILSON, *supra* note 2, at 118.

20. *See, e.g.,* MICHAEL J. GRAETZ & JERRY L. MASHAW, TRUE SECURITY: RETHINKING AMERICAN SOCIAL INSURANCE 288–89 (1999); THEDA SKOCPOL, SOCIAL POLICY IN THE UNITED STATES: FUTURE POSSIBILITIES IN HISTORICAL PERSPECTIVE 259–72 (1995); *see also* Samuel R. Bagenstos, *Disability and the Tension between Citizenship and Social Rights* (unpublished manuscript, on file with author).

21. *See* Amy L. Wax, *Rethinking Welfare Rights: Reciprocity Norms, Reactive Attitudes, and the Political Economy of Welfare Reform*, 63 L. & CONTEMP. PROBS. 257 (2000); Bagenstos, *supra* note 20.

22. *See* PETER H. SCHUCK & RICHARD J. ZECKHAUSER, TARGETING IN SOCIAL PROGRAMS: AVOIDING BAD BETS, REMOVING BAD APPLES (2006).

23. *See* MANCUR OLSON, THE LOGIC OF COLLECTIVE ACTION: PUBLIC GOODS AND THE THEORY OF GROUPS (1965).

24. *See* CHRISTOPHER HOWARD, THE WELFARE STATE NOBODY KNOWS: DEBUNKING MYTHS ABOUT U.S. SOCIAL POLICY 92–108 (2007); PAUL PIERSON, DISMANTLING THE WELFARE STATE? REAGAN, THATCHER, AND THE POLITICS OF RETRENCHMENT 103, 128 (1994).

25. *See* RANDALL KENNEDY, FOR DISCRIMINATION: RACE, AFFIRMATIVE ACTION, AND THE LAW (2013).

26. *See* CHRISTOPHER BONASTIA, KNOCKING ON THE DOOR: THE FEDERAL GOVERNMENT'S ATTEMPT TO DESEGREGATE THE SUBURBS (2006).

27. *See* WILSON, *supra* note 2, at 125–39.

28. *See infra* Part II.

29. *See, e.g.,* IRA KATZNELSON, FEAR ITSELF: THE NEW DEAL AND THE ORIGINS OF OUR TIME (2013).

30. *See* Catherine Albiston, *Institutional Inequality*, 2009 WIS. L. REV. 1093; Jessica A.

Clarke, *Beyond Equality? Against the Universal Turn in Workplace Protections*, 86 IND. L.J. 1219 (2011).

31. *See* Deborah C. Malamud, *Class-Based Affirmative Action: Lessons and Caveats*, 74 TEX. L. REV. 1847 (1996).

32. *See, e.g.*, JOSEPH E. STIGLITZ, THE PRICE OF INEQUALITY: HOW TODAY'S DIVIDED SOCIETY ENDANGERS OUR FUTURE (2012).

33. *See* Paul Burstein & Mark Evan Edwards, *The Impact of Employment Discrimination Litigation on Racial Disparity in Earnings: Evidence and Unresolved Issues*, 28 LAW & SOC'Y REV. 79 (1994); John J. Donohue III & James Heckman, *Continuous versus Episodic Change: The Impact of Civil Rights Policy on the Economic Status of Blacks*, 29 J. ECON. LITERATURE 1603 (1991); James J. Heckman & J. Hoult Verkerke, *Racial Disparity and Employment Discrimination Law: An Economic Perspective*, 8 YALE L. & POL'Y REV. 276 (1990).

34. *See, e.g.*, MELVIN OLIVER & THOMAS SHAPIRO, BLACK WEALTH/WHITE WEALTH: A NEW PERSPECTIVE ON RACIAL INEQUALITY (1995); Annie Lowrey, *Recession Widened Wealth Gap for Races*, N.Y. TIMES, Apr. 29, 2013, at B1.

35. *See*U.S. DEP'T OF HOUSING & URBAN DEV., HOUSING DISCRIMINATION AGAINST RACIAL AND ETHNIC MINORITIES 2012 (2013).

36. *See, e.g.*, Joseph G. Altonji & Rebecca M. Blank, *Race and Gender in the Labor Market*, in 3C HANDBOOK OF LABOR ECONOMICS 3143 (Orley Ashenfelter & David Card eds., 1999).

37. *See, e.g.*, Reva B. Siegel, *From Colorblindness to Antibalkanization: An Emerging Ground of Decision in Race Equality Cases*, 120 YALE L.J. 1278, 1360–64 (2011).

38. *See, e.g.*, MICHELLE ALEXANDER, THE NEW JIM CROW: MASS INCARCERATION IN THE AGE OF COLORBLINDNESS (2010).

39. Betsey Stevenson & Justin Wolfers, *Subjective and Objective Indicators of Racial Progress*, 41 J. LEGAL STUD. 459 (2012).

40. *Id.*

41. For my own take on the evidence of implicit bias, see Samuel R. Bagenstos, *Implicit Bias, "Science," and Antidiscrimination Law*, 1 HARV. L. & POL'Y REV. 477 (2007).

42. *See*DEVON W. CARBADO & MITU GULATI, ACTING WHITE? RETHINKING RACE IN POST-RACIAL AMERICA (2013).

43. *See* RANDALL KENNEDY, THE PERSISTENCE OF THE COLOR LINE: RACIAL POLITICS AND THE OBAMA PRESIDENCY (2011); THOMAS J. SUGRUE, NOT EVEN PAST: BARACK OBAMA AND THE BURDEN OF RACE (2010); Ta-Nehisi Coates, *Fear of a Black President*, ATLANTIC, Sept. 2012.

44. *See, e.g.*, CYNTHIA ESTLUND, WORKING TOGETHER: HOW WORKPLACE BONDS STRENGTHEN A DIVERSE DEMOCRACY (2003).

45. *See* Samuel R. Bagenstos, *The Structural Turn and the Limits of Antidiscrimination Law*, 94 CALIF. L. REV. 1 (2006).

46. *See* Samuel R. Bagenstos, *The Future of Disability Law*, 114 YALE L.J. 1 (2004).

47. *See* Deborah L. Brake & Joanna L. Grossman, *Unprotected Sex: The Pregnancy Discrimination Act at 35*, 20 DUKE J. GENDER L. & POL'Y 67 (2013); Deborah A. Widiss, Gilbert *Redux: The Interaction of the Pregnancy Discrimination Act and the Amended Americans with Disabilities Act*, 46 U.C. DAVIS L. REV. 961 (2013); Ashley

Nelson, *Confessions of a Stay-at-Home Mom*, THE NATION, July 22–29, 2013. The Supreme Court's recent decision in Young v. United Parcel Service, Inc., 135 S. Ct. 1338 (2015), provides a step in the direction of the more robust antidiscrimination protections that are necessary.

48.   For a strong statement of this position, see Ronald Turner, *Thirty Years of Title VII's Regulatory Regime: Rights, Theories, and Realities*, 46 ALA. L. REV. 375 (1995).

49.   *See* SUGRUE, *supra* note 43; Coates, *supra* note 43.

6

The Diversity Feedback Loop

Patrick Shin, Devon Carbado, and Mitu Gulati

I. Introduction

By most accounts, the pursuit of racial diversity in the modern U.S. workplace is ubiquitous. The extent to which firms genuinely care about achieving it may be debatable, but assertions of commitment to a diverse workforce have become a familiar corporate refrain. But does all this routine talk of racial diversity square with the legal status of workplace diversity initiatives? Arguably, there is a tension.[1] Given recent developments,[2] it is uncertain whether Title VII permits race-conscious hiring measures that seek workplace racial diversity, especially if such measures do not fit the mold of traditional affirmative action plans designed to remedy "manifest imbalances" associated with past discrimination.[3]

This legal issue is one that the Supreme Court will eventually be called upon to resolve. In anticipation of that intervention, this chapter seeks to understand the significance of workplace affirmative action from a broader perspective that scholars have largely overlooked. We step back from the question of whether employer affirmative action can be doctrinally and theoretically justified by appeal to the value of diversity and examine, instead, the systemic role affirmative action plays in shaping workplace diversity. Significantly, our inquiry is not limited to workplace affirmative action plans. We focus our attention on university affirmative action plans as well. We do so to investigate the relation between workplace diversity and what we hypothesize to be a critical determinant: the diversity of the colleges and universities that feed the employment market. We examine, in short, the causal relation between diversity in the workplace and diversity in the student bodies of higher educational institutions. We describe this often overlooked relationship to situate race-conscious hiring by employers in the context of other important systemic factors that contribute to the production of workplace diversity. Our hope is that the framework we employ will inform the debate about the legal permissibility of employer affirmative action that is sure to come.

For purposes of the discussion, we assume that it is an open question whether employers can invoke the value of diversity to justify their affirmative action policies.[4] We assume further that, as recently restated by the Supreme Court in *Fisher v. University of Texas*,[5] the value of diversity can justify a university's consideration of race as one factor among many in deciding which applicants to admit.[6] Given the accepted value of diversity in the constitutional setting and the common goals of educational affirmative action and of Title VII in general,[7] many have argued that affirmative action is as desirable and as necessary in the workplace context as it is in the university. The thinking is that, because workplaces should be in equipoise with universities with respect to realizing the benefits of diversity, the normative justifications for diversity and the policy mechanism for implementing it—affirmative action—should be transplanted from the educational context to the employment context.[8]

Multiple scholars have endorsed some version of the "transplant" argument.[9] Some support their position with reference to the persistence of historical employment inequalities in the modern workplace. Others highlight the purposes of Title VII. Still others invoke empirical evidence showing how the presence of diversity can reduce discriminatory bias and harmful stereotyping.

We do not argue that the transplant approach is mistaken. The benefits of educational and workplace diversity may indeed be comparable. The problem is that scholars who justify affirmative action in the workplace by analogy to the educational context overlook the implications of a crucial fact: the university and the workplace are not separate and distinct institutional settings in which diversity is or is not achieved. They are part of a causally connected system.[10] This is no small thing. It means that the policies and practices surrounding diversity in each context shape and influence the diversity that emerges in the other. Scholars, policymakers, and judges have largely ignored this crucial dynamic. They continue to frame affirmative action practices in the workplace and those at colleges and universities as disaggregated diversity mechanisms. This limits our ability to understand fully what is at stake with respect to overruling *Grutter* and/or prohibiting affirmative action in the workplace. In this respect, analyses of diversity-based affirmative action in the employment context or the educational context are incomplete unless they take into account the consequences that rules permitting or restricting such action in either domain are likely to have for the system as a whole. We examine these consequences by way of a model that we call the "diversity feedback loop."

Three central features constitute our model: a *supply effect*, a *reiteration effect*, and a *demand effect*. The schematic below and accompanying texts describe how these three dynamics combine to create the diversity feedback loop.

The Diversity Feedback Loop

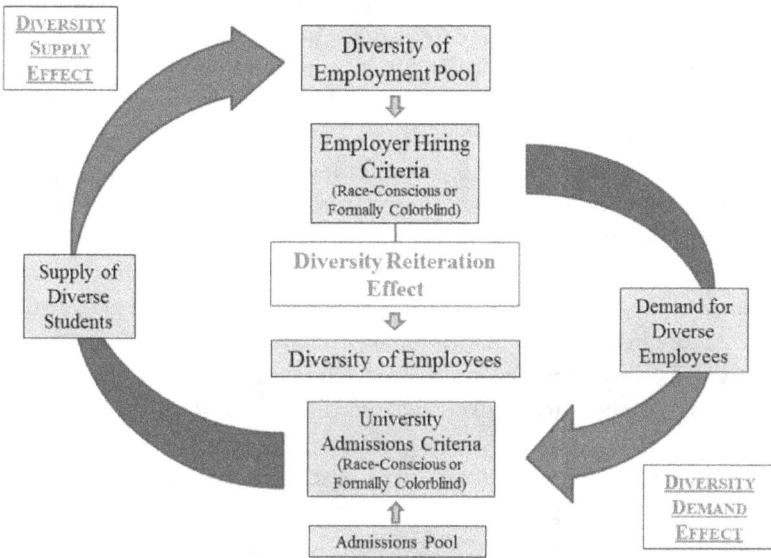

The basic dynamics are these:

- The university, through its admissions policy, assembles a diverse student body (or not) that, on graduation, becomes a key supply of labor for potential employers—*a supply effect.*

- The diversity that exists in the supply of labor is, at least to some extent relocated to or "reiterated" in the workplace through the operation of employer hiring mechanisms—*a reiteration effect.*

- The employer's diversity hiring criteria exert a demand for employees who have particular characteristics, which can influence the criteria that universities use to determine the students they admit—*a demand effect.*

The remainder of this chapter elaborates on these dynamics to demonstrate that we stand a better chance of improving the diversity of universities and workplaces if we recognize that both domains are part of the same diversity system.[11] This insight is relevant not only as a normative matter (whether it makes sense to promote affirmative action in both the workplace and the university setting) but also as a doctrinal matter (whether the legality of affirmative action in the context of the workplace should be coextensive with its legality in the context of the university).

Our argument unfolds in four parts. Part II discusses the supply and reiteration effects. These effects follow from the fact that universities are a gateway to the workplace. Today's student bodies are tomorrow's potential workforces. To the extent that employers rely on universities as a source of labor, universities function as a pathway through which diversity is supplied. The diversity of the university provides both a limit on and a template for diversity in the workplace.

Yet when employers hire from affirmative action institutions, their own diversity-enhancing selection measures might not mirror the measures implemented at the university admissions stage. When hiring, employers might seek to realize a conception of diversity that differs in significant ways from the educationally rooted ideal of a diverse student body. Actors in these two institutional contexts might therefore "screen" for diversity in distinctive ways. Part III explores the implications of the possible divergence between the employer and university diversity screens.

Part IV demonstrates how the hiring practices of employers can influence the admissions practices of universities in the educational context. Universities operate within multiple competitive markets. Among other things, they are competing to place their students with the best employers. Students, in turn, evaluate schools, at least in part, based on their placement rates. Universities with poor placement records are at a competitive disadvantage vis-à-vis those with stronger ones. This creates an incentive for universities to supply the kind of diversity employers want. Doing so maximizes the likelihood that employers will hire the graduates of those universities. To the extent that universities structure their diversity initiatives to maximize the employment opportunities available to their graduates, employer diversity preferences influence the university's admission's regime. Part IV discusses this demand effect.

II. The Supply and Reiteration Effects

A. The Basic Supply Hypothesis

The Supreme Court recognized long ago that the composition of the relevant labor market can constrain an employer's ability to eliminate patterns of racial exclusion from its workplace.[12] Of course, employers who engage in discrimination (or who practice affirmative action) can cause their workforces to be significantly less or more racially diverse than the available pool of qualified labor. But the fact remains that the makeup of that pool places certain limits on the composition of the employer's workplace. For example, if there are no Asian Americans in the labor pool, there will be no Asian Americans in the workplace, no matter what hiring preferences employers might use. Employers cannot create workplace diversity out of thin air. They need a supply.

The importance of educational diversity as a source of workplace diversity was emphasized in an amicus brief filed by Fortune 100 companies in the *Fisher* case. We quote directly from the brief:

> But amici [Fortune 100 companies] cannot reach [the] goal [of a diverse workforce] on their own...When amici make decisions about hiring and promotion, it is critical that they be able to draw from a superior pool of candidates—both minority and non-minority—who have realized the many benefits of diversity in higher education. There can be no question that "[t]he Nation's future" does indeed continue to "depend[] upon leaders"—including business leaders—"trained through wide exposure to the ideas and mores of students as diverse as this Nation of many peoples."[13]

The fact that employers rely on institutions of higher education to provide a supply of diverse labor implies that the achievement of racial diversity in the workplace will depend on not only the behavior of employers but also the behavior of educational institutions. Thus, workplace diversity is potentially affected by the use of affirmative action by universities at the admissions stage as well as by employers at the hiring stage. If this is so, understanding the conditions necessary for achieving workplace diversity requires isolating the expected effects of race-conscious selection measures at each stage. To what extent would we expect the diversity of the workplace to be affected by (1) the use of affirmative action in education and (2) the use of affirmative action by employers?

Our aim here is to provide a theoretical model that provides preliminary answers to these questions. But first, two specifications are in order. Though we believe that the model we describe below applies to employers who hire from highly selective colleges and universities generally, for simplicity, we narrow our focus to law firms who hire their associates predominantly from highly selective law schools. We will refer to the law firms that hire in this way as "elite law firms" and the selective law schools from which they hire as "elite law schools." Of course, elite law firms do hire from nonelite law schools, and nonelite law firms do hire from elite law schools as well. The principal reason we limit our analysis to the "elite" context is to simplify our analysis. We note, too, that most of the literature on racial diversity and law firms focuses on elite law firms and suggests that elite law firms are more likely to hire from elite law schools than from nonelite law schools. Indeed, there is reason to believe that elite law firms will hire very few people of color from nonelite law schools.[14] Focusing on elite law firms and elite law schools allows us to track a very real dynamic—the flow of diversity from elite law schools to elite law firms—and at the same time describe our theoretical hypothesis: namely, that the diversity of elite law school student bodies is a causal determinant of the diversity of elite law firm workplaces. This is true simply because whatever diversity exists in elite law firms has to come from somewhere, and we have stipulated that elite law firms hire from elite law schools.

The question then becomes: What affects the diversity of elite law schools? One answer is the school's admissions policy. The diversity of an elite law school student body is at least partly determined by the school's positive consideration of race as a factor in admissions—that is, its affirmative action policy. The more robust the elite law school's race-conscious affirmative action program is, the more diverse its student body will be; and the more diverse a law school's student body is, the more diverse its graduates will be. Since elite law firms, by our definition, hire from the labor pool formed by these graduates, it follows that the use of affirmative action by elite law schools is causally linked to the racial composition, and hence the diversity, of the workplace of these employers.[15]

To summarize, a law school's admissions regime affects the diversity of the student body; the diversity of the student body shapes the diversity of the labor pool; and the diversity of the labor pool influences the diversity of law firms. These observations together make up the supply effect in the university-workplace relation. With this preliminary hypothesis in place, we now model how a legal rule permitting or restricting race-conscious hiring might modulate the movement of diversity from law school student bodies to the workplace of the law firm.

B. The Reiteration Effect: Default Case

We begin by establishing what we call a reiteration effect, or the basic tendency of the level of diversity that exists in the labor supply pool to be reproduced in the relevant workplace. As a predicate, we make four additional assumptions. First, for reasons previously discussed,[16] we assume that, above some threshold of satisfactory academic performance, elite law firms are indifferent to grades.[17] Second, we assume that the diversity of the group of students who achieve this level of academic performance is the same as the diversity of the student body overall.[18] These first two assumptions imply that most graduates of elite law schools, including black and Latino students, are regarded by elite law firms as equally qualified to be hired as associates.[19] Third, we assume that the graduates of all elite law schools who are interested in working in elite law firms are equally willing to accept positions in all elite firms, but that any given firm can lure any particular graduate by expending more resources on recruiting or offering a higher salary. Fourth, we assume that the law firm's and the law school's conceptions of diversity are congruent (including judgments about whether a particular individual will contribute to diversity).[20]

With these assumptions out of the way, it is helpful to invoke a general axiom endorsed by the Supreme Court, albeit in the context of a rather different issue. According to the Court, "absent explanation, it is ordinarily to be expected that nondiscriminatory hiring practices will in time result in a work force more or less representative of the racial and ethnic composition of the population in the community from which employees are hired."[21] This axiom, as applied to our model, suggests that in the absence of employer discrimination,[22] the level of workplace diversity among elite law firms will, over time, be the same as the level of diversity that exists in law school student bodies. Whatever diversity exists in elite student bodies will be randomly supplied to all firms, with no single law firm having a higher or lower level of diversity than others, except by operation of chance.[23]

This general axiom might strike some readers as an overly simplistic assumption, one that flies in the face of empirical evidence about ongoing employment discrimination. Some might argue that any model that accepts the Court's assumption in the *Teamsters* case assumes away too much. Two responses are in order. First, if we do not assume away discrimination, that variable becomes a showstopper for our desired analysis. If employers are assumed to discriminate, then workplace diversity will be almost entirely a function of their exclusionary policies—period. Thus, we might learn more about the structural relationship between educational and workplace diversity if we think about what we would expect to happen in the absence of discrimination.

Second, and perhaps more important, imagining what we would expect to happen in the absence of discrimination is a useful exercise because a comparison of the expected consequences of that assumption with real-world observations may provide a way to test whether the assumption is true. The assumption is not an idle one. Although it would be putting the point too strongly to say that the federal courts assume that employment discrimination does not exist, it is fair to say that they have not been sympathetic to plaintiffs who bring claims of discrimination.[24] Our sense is that many people believe that employment discrimination is largely no longer a real problem and that if workplaces lack diversity, this is explained by a lack of qualified candidates, not by discrimination The assumption behind this common belief is that if there were a qualified, diverse pool of people of color, firms would hire them, and their workplaces would become diverse. Note how this view aligns with the assumptions of our model—namely, the elite law school's student body diversity will be supplied fully and uniformly into the workplace.

In any event, our claim is that in a world where our basic assumptions hold true, the racial diversity that exists in the graduating student bodies of elite law schools will be uniformly distributed among all elite law firms, such that the level of diversity in the group of students who enter the elite workplace matches the level of diversity in the elite law school student pool overall. In other words, in the default conditions of our model, workplace diversity simply reiterates student body diversity.

C. Modeling the Reiteration Effect under Four Alternative Conditions

If full and uniform reiteration is expected in our model's default conditions, what might we expect to observe if we vary both the law firm's and the law school's behavior? That is the question we now address. We will examine how the supply of diversity from the law school to the law firm might vary under four specific conditions. Condition 1 assumes that the level of law school diversity is high and that the law firm is prohibited from using affirmative action. Condition 2 imagines a low level of law school diversity; here, too, the law firm may not use affirmative action. Condition 3 permits the law firm to use affirmative action and posits a high level of law school diversity. Under Condition 4, the law firm is also permitted to use affirmative action, but the level of law school diversity is low. We discuss below how each of these conditions might affect the supply of student body diversity from the university (the law school) to the workplace (the law firm).

1. Condition 1: High Educational Diversity, Employer Affirmative Action Prohibited

Suppose that there is a high level of racial diversity in the student bodies of elite law schools, such that the presence of racial minorities in these student bodies is as high as or higher than in the general population. (We might imagine a world in which all elite law schools were permitted under applicable state and federal law to consider the race of their applicants as a positive factor in the admissions process, and all elite law schools did in fact do so.) Stipulate also that law firms are *not* legally permitted to take race into account in their hiring decisions—that is, that the law requires formally color-blind hiring. What result should be expected for law firm diversity, given the assumptions of our model?

Assuming full compliance by law firms, we should expect that, over time, all elite law firms would come to have the same high level of diversity that is present in elite law school student bodies. That is to say, the diversity of the student bodies will be fully and uniformly supplied to the workplace. To understand why, recall that we are assuming, for purposes of analysis, that there is no explicit or implicit discrimination in the labor market. Insofar as firms are not going to differentiate among elite students (per our earlier hypothesis and explanation), we should expect student body diversity to be supplied to and randomly distributed among all elite law firms. We would also expect that, over time, every elite law firm would mirror the demographic of the elite law school student bodies from which they are populated. In short, under Condition 1, workplace diversity would be established at levels matching the diversity of the student pool, even without the utilization of employer affirmative action.

2. Condition 2: Low Educational Diversity, Employer Affirmative Action Prohibited

In this condition, suppose that elite universities have low levels of racial diversity, such that the proportion of racial minorities in their student bodies is significantly lower than their proportion in the general population. This scenario could emerge in a jurisdiction (like California) that prohibits the consideration of race in university admissions; the scenario could also occur if, at some future point, the Supreme Court overruled *Grutter* and held that affirmative action was unconstitutional in the educational context. Assume, as in Condition 1, that the law prohibits race-conscious affirmative action hiring. What is the expected result?

As in Condition 1, we should expect that, under Condition 2, over time, all elite workplaces will come to share the demographic of the student bodies from which they draw. That is, all law firms will come to have an equally low level of racial diversity. A formally colorblind hiring rule, again assuming nondiscrimination, should reproduce the level of diversity present in the elite student body pool at the workplace level of the law firm. If the level of diversity in the overall pool of job candidates is low, then colorblind hiring should produce an equally low level of workplace diversity, uniformly distributed among firms.

3. Condition 3: High Educational Diversity, Employer Affirmative Action Permitted

In the third condition, stipulate that there is a high level of diversity in elite law school student bodies, as in Condition 1. But now suppose that employers are *permitted* (but not required) to consider job applicants' membership in a minority racial group as a positive factor in their hiring decisions, if doing so is reasonably necessary to create or maintain diversity in the workplace.[25] What outcomes should we expect? The short answer: roughly the same level and distribution of workplace diversity as in Condition 1, the condition with high diversity in the labor market and no affirmative action.

This might seem counterintuitive. One might think a rule permitting consideration of race for diversity purposes would lead to variances among law firms in their levels of diversity. But remember that firms are only permitted to employ affirmative action "if reasonably necessary" to ensure diversity. Since we stipulate in Condition 3 that there is a high level of diversity in the pool of available candidates, and given our overall assumption that this labor market is free of explicit or implicit forms of discrimination and biases, employers should not need to take race into account to yield meaningful diversity. A sufficiently high level of diversity in the pool of available candidates should, under formally color-blind hiring, be adequate to supply that same level of diversity uniformly across all law firms. Assuming that employers are aware of the racial demographics of the pool, it is reasonable to conclude that they would see little need to engage in affirmative action hiring and would refrain from doing so.[26] Combining the results from Conditions 1 and 3, we can conclude that in conditions of high diversity in the available pool of job candidates, we should not expect overall levels or the distribution of workplace diversity across law firms to be significantly dependent on whether or not employers are permitted to take race into account as a positive hiring factor for the sake of diversity.

4. Condition 4: Low Educational Diversity, Employer Affirmative Action Permitted

Our final condition assumes that there is a low level of racial diversity in the student bodies of elite law schools. Recall that this is also the case in Condition 1. Stipulate now that, as in Condition 3, law firms are permitted (but not required) to consider job applicants' race as a positive factor in their hiring decisions. The caveat, again, is that they may do so only if reasonably necessary to create or maintain diversity in the workplace. Under this condition, what should we expect vis-à-vis the overall supply and distribution of diversity in the workplace?

The results will depend on the extent to which law firms give positive weight to race in their hiring decisions. If law firms behave uniformly, then the results of Condition 4 should be the same as Condition 2 (the condition with low education diversity and employer affirmative action prohibited). There are two ways in which employers could act uniformly.

First, all law firms might refrain from using affirmative action. This would render Condition 4 indistinguishable from Condition 2, so the same results should follow. Second, all law firms could decide to practice affirmative action. Under the default assumptions of our model, elite law firms are all on equal footing in terms of the likely success of their diversity initiatives. Thus, a university's student body diversity would be supplied uniformly to all elite workplaces. The overall level of resultant law firm diversity will also likely be uniform.[27]

But now, let us imagine that elite firms have different views regarding the importance of establishing diversity in their workplaces. Assume that some firms give high priority to having a diverse workforce, while other firms care less about diversity as such or are committed to an ideal of formally color-blind hiring. Suppose, in other words, that only some elite firms consider race as a positive consideration (call these "prodiversity" firms), while other firms do not take race into consideration at all (call these "color-blind firms"). Under these additional assumptions, what result should we expect for workplace diversity among elite firms?

In our model, the amount of diversity in the elite law school student body pool limits the diversity that can be reiterated into the workplace, so we should expect the overall level of diversity among all elite firms to be about as low as that observed in the candidate pool. But unlike in previous conditions, we would expect the distribution of that diversity to be nonuniform across firms. Prodiversity firms, insofar as they see a greater value in establishing workforce diversity, will offer higher salaries or expend more recruiting resources to lure job candidates who would enhance or bolster the firm's diversity profile. Color-blind firms, who by definition care less about diversity or are ideologically committed to color-blindness, would have no reason to make the extra expenditures necessary to attract the diversity candidates away from prodiversity firms and so would be less likely to attract and hire them. Over time, therefore, prodiversity firms will come to have a higher level of workplace diversity than color-blind firms. As student body diversity continues to cluster in prodiversity firms from year to year, prodiversity firms will eventually achieve a level of diversity that is higher than the level of diversity available in the elite student body pool, and color-blind firms will eventually have a level of diversity that is even lower than the already-low level available in the candidate pool.

It may not seem particularly remarkable that in Condition 4, prodiversity firms will come to achieve more workplace diversity than color-blind firms, but there are two less obvious points that bear mentioning. First, Condition 4 is the only one of the four conditions in which we would expect anything other than a uniform distribution of diversity across all hiring firms. In all other conditions, including Condition 2, in which we stipulated that employers are permitted to engage in prodiversity hiring, we would expect the diversity of the workplace to be the same as the diversity of the relevant labor pool. Second, a comparison of Conditions 2 and 4 shows that where the diversity of the available candidate pool is very low, then an employment rule that permits but does not require prodiversity hiring will tend to result in a lumpy distribution of diversity among hiring firms, such that some firms will come to have high levels of diversity, while other firms will have minimal or no diversity. In contrast, an employment rule that requires color-blind hiring in conditions of low labor-market diversity will tend to produce an even, albeit low, level of diversity among all hiring firms.

D. Summary

Table 1 summarizes the results of the preceding four conditions.

Table 1

Condition	Level of Educational Diversity	Is Affirmative Action Permitted?	Level of Employment Diversity	Is Diversity Spread Uniformly Across Employer?
I	High	No	High	Yes
II	Low	No	Low	Yes
III	High	Yes	High	Yes
IV	Low	Yes	Depends on uniformity among employers:	
			Non-uniformity among employers	Uniformity among employers
			High (pro-diversity firm) Low (Colorblind firm)	Low

Six conclusions follow from these results. First, even when one takes into account the diversity practices of firms—that is, whether they engage in or refrain from using affirmative action hiring—the diversity of law school student bodies (the diversity supply) remains crucial to the analysis. Second, a similar point can be made with respect to law: whatever the governing legal regime with respect to whether employers are permitted to use affirmative action, the diversity of university student bodies will play an important role in shaping the diversity of the workplace. These two points highlight the importance of affirmative action in the educational domain. It is a significant mechanism through which diversity is supplied to the labor market.

This brings us to our third point. Our model provides only two ways to achieve high diversity in all elite workplaces. One is to ensure high diversity in elite student bodies. The other is to induce all law firms to engage in affirmative action in conditions of job scarcity (creating an amplification effect[28]).

Fourth, the results of Condition 1 might lead one to conclude that we should jettison affirmative action in the employment context if we have robust affirmative action in the educational context. The latter will necessarily be supplied to the former. That is indeed the story our theoretical model tells. But a limitation of our model is that we assume away discrimination in the marketplace. If we add discrimination back into the model—and not necessarily invidious discrimination but simply implicit bias—the results under Condition 1 would change. For example, firms whose decision making reflected implicit bias would have a lower level of diversity than firms whose decision making did not reflect this bias. For many proponents of affirmative action, this is precisely what affirmative action is designed to counteract—biases (implicit and explicit) in the labor market.

Fifth, understanding the foregoing limitation of our model is especially important in light of the Supreme Court's commitment to colorblindness and general judicial skepticism about workplace discrimination.[29] This is a point we made earlier but bears emphasizing here. Condition 1 is, for us, decidedly theoretical. However, for the conservative justices on the Court, Condition 1 might be an assumed reality. That has implications for the future of affirmative action in the context of the workplace. If a majority of the Supreme Court concludes that workplace discrimination is a thing of the past, it could conclude that, even if affirmative action is necessary in the context of university admissions to achieve student body diversity, it is unnecessary in the context of the workplace, because the diversity of the student body would be reiterated into the workplace.

Our sixth and final conclusion is this: in low educational diversity conditions, rules that permit prodiversity hiring will likely result in racial clustering, and law firms will separate themselves over time into high-diversity and low-diversity workplaces.[30] This has implications for jurisdictions like California that prohibit state universities from engaging in affirmative action. Some employees might find themselves in law firms in which there is meaningful diversity. Most will not. Still, to the extent that having meaningful diversity in some workplaces (Condition 4) is better than having low diversity across all workplaces (Condition 2), we should ensure that the prohibition of affirmative action in the context of education is not extended to the context of employment.

III. Divergent Diversity Screens: Complicating the Reiteration Dynamic

In modeling the supply of diversity from elite law schools to elite law firms in Part II of this chapter, we assumed that law firms and law schools share a common notion of "diversity." This need not be the case. A law firm might employ very different criteria than law schools. Law schools are admitting students to service multiple markets, including the public interest markets. As a general matter, these students are likely to be more racially conscious with respect to both their sense of selves and their normative commitments more generally. Moreover, as academic institutions, law schools will likely seek to admit at least some students who they think will stir things up and facilitate the robust exchange of ideas.

Law firms, on the other hand, may want very different kinds of diversity. Their corporate market context will presumably shape the kind of—and how much—diversity they pursue. For example, while law firms are prohibited from invoking customer preferences to justify screening their application pool for racially palatable African Americans, it is hard not to imagine that some firms end up (at least implicitly) doing just that.

To recognize that law schools and law firms do not necessarily employ the same diversity screens is not to say that their diversity initiatives must be regarded as autonomous. Indeed, we claim just the opposite. For one thing, law firms and law schools might actually employ precisely the same diversity criteria (e.g., looking for people who will facilitate racial cooperation and understanding), in which case we might say that their screens expressly converge. For another, even when law firms and law school diversity criteria do not expressly converge in this way, the diversity that actually arises in each context could nevertheless appear to converge on a shared conception.

Suppose, for example, that law firms care more than law schools about weeding out individuals with poor teamwork attributes. One might assume that this could cause law firm diversity to diverge from law school diversity. That is possible. But on the other hand, law firms might find that the experience of a diverse elite law school prepares students of all backgrounds to work productively and harmoniously in heterogeneous social settings. If this were true, even law firms that prioritize teamwork might be happy to accept, without much further screening, whatever type of diversity law schools produce. The general point is that if law firms perceive value in the diversity produced by law schools, they might seek to capitalize on that value by reproducing it in their workplaces.

Finally, law school and law firm diversity initiatives are not autonomous in another way: any diversity criteria the law firm utilizes at the hiring stage will necessarily piggyback on the diversity efforts of the law school at the admissions stage. As argued above, the diversity of law schools creates the diversity of the labor pool from which law firms hire.

Keeping in mind these ways in which law school and law firm diversity initiatives are connected, we turn our focus in this section to how law school and law firm initiatives can diverge. To appreciate how law firm and law school diversity screening can diverge and the implications of that divergence for the reiteration effect, let us call the set of minority individuals who are the beneficiaries of affirmative action at the law school admissions stage "Law School Diverse" or "LS-Diverse" individuals. And let us call the set of minority individuals who are beneficiaries at the law firm hiring stage "Law Firm Diverse" or "LF-Diverse" individuals. Some minorities might be both LS-Diverse and LF-Diverse, while others might be neither.

Consider the ways in which the set of LS-Diverse individuals might relate to LF-Diverse individuals. Quantitatively, the LF-Diverse group could be larger than, smaller than, or the same size as the LS-Diverse group. Qualitatively, the LF-Diverse group could overlap the LS-Diverse group in whole, in part, or not at all. These various possibilities could be combined in a number of ways. We will not attempt to march through all of the permutations, but a few comments are in order.

For various reasons, the set of people who are the beneficiaries of LF-Diversity initiatives might be different from those who previously benefited from LS-Diversity initiatives. The two sets might be quantitatively different simply because universities and employers assign different weight to racial considerations in the selection process. A heavier weighting will naturally tend to result in a larger set of individuals who benefit from the diversity initiative.

There might also be systemic reasons for this quantitative divergence between LS-Diversity and LF-Diversity. For example, if law schools engage in robust affirmative action measures and succeed in creating highly diverse student bodies, who then form the labor pool from which law firms hire, law firms might perceive that there is less of a need for them to use prodiversity affirmative action in order to achieve significant workplace diversity. They may assume, per our discussion in Part II, that the diversity in the labor market will naturally "trickle up" or be reiterated into the firm. This might be especially true of firms that conceive of themselves as nondiscriminatory. These firms would see little need to employ affirmative action as a prophylactic against the possibility of discrimination. Under this scenario, the set of people who benefit from LF-Diversity efforts may be low relative to the set of people who benefit from LS-Diversity efforts.

Law firm and law school affirmative action initiatives might also yield different sets of beneficiaries for reasons having to do with the context-dependent nature of diversity initiatives. LF-Diversity might be qualitatively different from LS-Diversity. Employers and universities might look for different characteristics in constructing their institutional diversities. For example, employers might screen candidates for compatibility with their corporate culture in ways that constrain their prodiversity hiring.[31] In some cases, what might appear to be facially neutral screening criteria could cause LF-Diversity selections to be negatively correlated with LS-Diversity selections. A silly example: a law firm might screen in favor of minority candidates who, in addition to attending elite law schools, attended prestigious private prep schools. But minority law students with prep school backgrounds might be less likely than others to have benefited from affirmative action at the law school admissions stage—that is, less likely to be LS-Diverse. If so, then law firm screening for minorities who attended prestigious private prep schools could cause LF-Diversity to be negatively correlated with LS-Diversity.

Law firm diversity and law school diversity might diverge in other ways. Elite law firms and elite law schools might have different ideas about the characteristics (in addition to simple racial phenotype) that could make one person preferable to another from the standpoint of enhancing the institution's diversity. The basic educational goals and academic principles that define the mission of elite universities (of which elite law schools are a part) do not apply to most elite employers.[32] The value of diversity in the educational context, or at least the value that has been assigned constitutional significance, encompasses a well-known mélange of goods, including enhanced educational discourse, eradication of racial stereotypes and other types of de-biasing, reduction of racial isolation, preparation for citizenry in a pluralistic society, providing good modeling for minority youth, creation of a visible path for minorities leading to leadership roles in society, and so on.[33] Against the background of these interests, a law school might make special efforts to enroll students from racial minority groups who are most likely to bring an overtly "racial perspective" to classroom discussions. This might include minority students who have the least in common with most other students with respect to their backgrounds and experiences, in order to activate *Bakke/Grutter* discourse benefits.

Law firms might also have an interest in fostering diverse perspectives in the workplace on a different basis, such as the belief that this would improve their ability to anticipate client or customer needs. But overriding concerns about workplace harmony might make employers wary of hiring individuals who will have trouble fitting into the corporate culture.[34] This does not mean that these institutions would seek individuals who dis-identify with their race or embrace a color-blind sense of self. Corporate cultures are increasingly interested in establishing so-called affinity groups—that is, groups that are organized around specific identities (such as being gay or lesbian, a person of color, or a woman). While these groups are less prevalent in the law firm context, elite law firms are still interested in hiring people of color who will perform palatable or modest forms of racial diversity work. The point is that it will be the rare elite law firm that would hire an African American applicant because that person will shake up the firm's institutional culture. This is precisely the kind of person an elite law school might admit.

More generally, the benefits that law schools as academic institutions might seek to advance will not necessarily readily map onto the priorities of a typical (nonacademic) employer's workplace. To be clear, this is not to say that law firms will perceive no value in diversity. The point, instead, is that even when they perceive positive value in a diverse workforce, they may have different reasons than law schools for pursuing diversity.

A final reason that law firm diversity screens might be different from law school diversity screens is that the employer may be hiring from a pool that has already been made diverse through affirmative action at an earlier screening stage (the admissions process). This fact may have varying implications. One possibility is that a law firm might make fine distinctions between minority individuals within the pool who may have been equal beneficiaries of prodiversity admissions criteria. It might do so, for example, in order to screen out individuals who might clash with its corporate culture.

Much of the foregoing is speculative. That should not obscure that our analysis is theoretically grounded in the fact that law firms and law schools operate under different incentive systems with respect to their pursuit of diversity. The difference in their incentive structures means that elite law firms may utilize different diversity-screening criteria than law schools.

IV. The Demand Effect

In Part III, we explored the implications of law firms and law schools employing different diversity screens. We assumed that these diversity-promoting criteria are stable over time and that they are independently fixed within each context. In this part, we relax the latter assumptions to explore the possibility that universities might adjust their admissions policies in response to observed employment patterns, including employers' revealed preferences about the kind of diversity they want.

Elite law schools operate in a competitive market. While their primary mission may be educational and academic, they compete with each other to attract exceptional students who will enrich the community, perform to the highest academic standards, and make valuable contributions to society after they graduate. One way in which law schools attract students is by trying to outperform their peer institutions in placing their graduates in the most desirable jobs. If they are unable to compete with other law schools in achieving placement of graduates in the job market, the best students will decide to matriculate elsewhere, which will erode the affected schools' prestige and academic standing, eventually making it difficult for them to maintain their status among their elite peers. The fact that placement rates figure significantly in the overall ranking of law schools makes this dynamic all the more significant.

The competition to place graduates in desirable jobs gives rise to an incentive for universities to admit more of the types of students who are sought by employers when they graduate and fewer of the types of students who are not.[35] Law schools may have multiple reasons to admit or not admit a particular type of student. In general, to the extent that employers actively seek graduates who possess some discernible set of characteristics, universities will have an added incentive to look for those characteristics in the students they admit. If law firms tend not to hire graduates with some set of characteristics, then law schools will have less reason to admit applicants fitting that type.

There is no reason that this demand effect should not apply to characteristics associated with enhancing workplace diversity. If elite law firms give priority in their hiring to elite law school graduates who possess diversity-enhancing characteristics, law schools will have an added incentive to screen in favor of those characteristics at the admissions stage. That is to say, other things equal,[36] law schools that engage in affirmative action have an incentive to craft their diversity initiatives to give preference to applicants who are likely to become LF-Diverse graduates. The demand exerted by employers for graduates meeting their diversity criteria could cause law firm and law school diversity initiatives to converge over time.[37] Whether this occurs will likely depend on the strength of the law firm's diversity demand[38] and the strength of the incentive for the law school to respond to this demand.[39]

V. Conclusion: Some Implications of Our Model

Our point of departure was the claim that the diversity of law schools and of law firms is intertwined. What happens in one setting affects the other. We then moved on to show some of the specific ways in which the two contexts interact, including a discussion of how law firm diversity initiatives might modulate the flow of diversity from law schools to law firms and how those initiatives might in turn loop back to influence the behavior of law school admissions committees. We conclude by suggesting several implications of our account for the development and promotion of workplace diversity.

First, the existence of diversity in the supply of labor that feeds into the employment market is a necessary condition of workplace diversity.

Workplace diversity cannot be created from thin air. And insofar as law school student body diversity depends on educational affirmative action, it follows that educational affirmative action is a necessary condition of workplace diversity. In other words, in addition to constituting a law school's entering class, law school admissions constitute the future law firm application pool from which law firms hire.

Second, there is a quantitative and a qualitative dimension to this supply function. Quantitatively, the more aggressively prodiversity the law school's admissions criteria are, the more diverse its contribution to the hiring pool will be. Qualitatively, the stronger the convergence between the kind of diversity in which a law firm is interested and the kind of diversity a law firm seeks to advance, the greater the likelihood that the law firm will rely on the law school's graduates as its employment pool and thus the greater the likelihood that the law school's diversity will be reiterated into the law firm.

Third, by and large, we ought not worry about law schools engaging in "too much" affirmative action. Law firm behavior in this regard will be disciplined by the competitive markets in which they operate. But the same goes for the behavior of universities. Diversity initiatives in the educational context are, after all, voluntary. Universities have no reason to engage in affirmative action beyond a level that balances educational usefulness with whatever demand for diversity actually exists in the employment market.

Finally, we should query whether the story we tell about the demand effect means that law firms may be exerting too much pressure on law schools to conform their conception of diversity to the model that happens to prevail in the workplace. Law schools might have good reasons to offer admission to the iconoclastic, overtly racialized student with a penchant for challenging hierarchy and complacency with the status quo. But law firms might be more reticent in offering that student a job—and that might affect the law school's willingness to offer admission.

Similarly, law firms and law schools might have a very different sense of how much diversity is enough. "Critical mass" from a law firm's perspective might look quite different from "critical mass" from the perspective of the law school—and the former might end up shaping the latter. To put this another way, if law firms have a diversity saturation point or a diversity ceiling, law schools have an incentive to adjust their affirmative action efforts to keep the diversity of their student bodies below that level. The concern, in short, is that the demand effect can influence both the quantitative and the qualitative supply of diversity throughout the loop. This suggests that we ought to begin a conversation about whether there are ways to effectuate a counterbalancing force so that a law school's quantitative and qualitative commitments to diversity not only are shaped by but also shape how law firms articulate their vision of a diverse workplace.

About the Authors

Faculty at Suffolk, UCLA, and Duke, respectively. For comments on or conversations regarding this article, we thank Eric Blumenson, Lee Epstein, Cheryl Harris, Sung Hui Kim, Kimberly Krawiec, Stephen Rich, Nancy Staudt, and Stephen Yeazell. We also thank participants at a conference celebrating the fiftieth anniversary of the Civil Rights Act at Michigan Law School and at the faculty colloquium at USC Law School. Special thanks to Sam Bagenstos and Ellen Katz for including us in their conference.

Notes

1. *See, e.g.*, N.Y.C. BAR ASS'N, COMM. ON LAB. & EMP. LAW, EMPLOYER DIVERSITY INITIATIVES: LEGAL CONSIDERATIONS (2012) (describing the tension), *available at* http://www2.nycbar.org/pdf/report/uploads/ 20072272-EmploymentDiversityInitiatives.pdf; JOHN SKRENTNY, AFTER CIVIL RIGHTS: RACIAL REALISM IN THE NEW AMERICAN WORKPLACE (2013) (noting the tension between the practice of diversity and the formal dictates of Title VII). For a recent study of employer practices relating to workplace diversity, see Soohan Kim, Alexandra Kalev & Frank Dobbin, *Progressive Corporations at Work: the Case of Diversity Programs*, 36 N.Y.U. REV. L. & SOC. CHANGE 171, 205–06 (2012).

2. *See especially* Ricci v. DeStefano, 557 U.S. 557 (2009) (holding that Title VII does not permit race-conscious action to alleviate racial disparities in the workforce unless employer has "strong basis in evidence" that failure to take such action would result in liability for disparate impact).

3. *See* Johnson v. Transp. Agency of Santa Clara County, 480 U.S. 616 (1987); United Steelworkers v. Weber, 443 U.S. 193 (1979). For a detailed argument that *Ricci* contravenes certain key aspects of *Johnson* and *Weber*, see Sachin S. Pandya, *Detecting the Stealth Erosion of Precedent: Affirmative Action after* Ricci, 31 BERKELEY J. EMP. & LAB. L. 285, 299 (2010).

4. *But cf.* Taxman v. Bd. of Educ. of Piscataway, 91 F.3d 1547 (3d Cir. 1996) (en banc) (rejecting the diversity rationale under Title VII as applied to facts presented), *cert. granted*, 521 U.S. 1117, *cert. dismissed*, 522 U.S. 1010 (1997).

5. Fisher v. University of Texas at Austin, 570 U.S. , 133 S. Ct. 2411 (2013).

6. *See id.* at 2421.

7. *See* Johnson v. Transp. Agency of Santa Clara County, 480 U.S. 616 (1987); United Steelworkers v. Weber, 443 U.S. 193 (1979).

8. *See* Cynthia L. Estlund, *Putting* Grutter *to Work: Diversity, Integration, and Affirmative Action in the Workplace*, 26 BERKELEY J. EMP. & LAB. L. 1 (2005). Some scholars frame this argument in terms of the basic goals of antidiscrimination law,

including Title VII—namely, to eliminate racial disparities and inequalities in the employment context. *See id.* at 37–38. This entails increasing the numbers of racial minorities in workplaces where they are underrepresented—that is, increasing racial diversity in those contexts. Affirmative action is a sensible way to do that. So if the value of diversity justifies race-conscious action in the educational context, and if we agree that racial diversity also has positive value under Title VII, it would seem to follow that race-conscious action should also be justified in the employment context.

9. *See* Michael J. Yelnosky, *The Prevention Justification for Affirmative Action*, 64 OHIO ST. L.J. 1385 (2003); Katharine T. Bartlett, *Making Good on Good Intentions: The Critical Role of Motivation in Reducing Implicit Workplace Discrimination*, 95 VA. L. REV. 1893 (2009); Kenneth R. Davis, *Wheel of Fortune: A Critique of the "Manifest Imbalance" Requirement for Race-Conscious Affirmative Action under Title VII*, 43 GA. L. REV. 993 (2009); Tristin K. Green, *Race and Sex in Organizing Work: "Diversity," Discrimination and Integration*, 59 EMORY L.J. 585 (2010); Jessica Bulman-Pozen, Note, *Grutter at Work: A Title VII Critique of Constitutional Affirmative Action*, 115 YALE L.J. 1408 (2006); Katherine M. Planer, Comment, *The Death of Diversity? Affirmative Action in the Workplace after Parents Involved*, 39 SETON HALL L. REV. 1333 (2009); Cynthia L. Estlund, *Putting Grutter to Work: Diversity, Integration, and Affirmative Action in the Workplace*, 26 BERKELEY J. EMP. & LAB. L. 1 (2005); Jared M. Mellott, Note, *The Diversity Rationale for Affirmative Action in Employment after Grutter: The Case for Containment*, 48 WM. & MARY L. REV. 1091 (2006); Anita Bernstein, *Diversity May Be Justified*, 64 HASTINGS L.J. 201 (2012); Ronald Turner, *Grutter, the Diversity Justification, and Workplace Affirmative Action*, 43 BRANDEIS L.J. 199 (2005); Corey A. Ciocchetti & John Holcomb, *The Frontier of Affirmative Action: Employment Preferences & Diversity in the Private Workplace*, 12 U. PA. J. BUS. L. 283 (2010); Jerry Kang & Mahzarin R. Banaji, *Fair Measures: A Behavioral Realist Revision of "Affirmative Action,"* 94 CALIF. L. REV. 1063 (2006).

10. Significantly, even when scholars point out potential difficulties with the transplant approach, they generally treat the educational and workplace settings as separate domains of diversity. The question these scholars then ask is whether diversity really has the same value or function in these two settings and whether it follows that these different diversity domains should be subject to the same legal constraints.

11. Justice O'Connor's argument that affirmative action helps establish a visible path to, and diversity at the level of, leadership (*see* Grutter v. Bollinger, 539 U.S. 306, 332 (2003)), is consonant with what we call the supply effect. *See also* WILLIAM G. BOWEN & DEREK BOK, THE SHAPE OF THE RIVER 128–31 (1998) (discussing reasons attendance at a selective university might enhance career opportunities). Our account goes beyond this insight by modeling how the diversity pathway functions and by showing that this linkage is just one aspect of the system that connects university and workplace diversity.

12. *See* Hazelwood Sch. Dist. v. United States, 433 U.S. 299, 308 (1977); Int'l Bhd. of Teamsters v. United States, 431 U.S. 324, 337 n.17 (1977).

13. Brief for Amici Curiae Fortune-100 and Other Leading American Businesses in Support of Respondents at 13, Fisher v. Univ. of Tex., 570 U.S. , 133 S. Ct. 2411 (2013) (quoting Regents of the Univ. of Cal. v. Bakke, 438 U.S. 265, 312–13 (1978) (internal quotation marks omitted)).

14. Although elite law firms may do some limited hiring from nonelite law schools, we suspect that for the most part, that hiring will not include black or Latino students. One explanation for this may be that, for reasons beyond the scope

of this chapter, blacks and Latinos perhaps tend to receive lower grades in law school than their white and Asian American counterparts. Because elite law firms hiring from nonelite law schools tend to limit their hiring to the very top of the graduating class, blacks and Latinos in nonelite firms might look proportionally underrepresented in the elite firm workplace were we to define the hiring pool to include nonelite firms. Such a definition might make our analysis more empirically grounded, but it would make it difficult for us to model the expected effects of racial diversity in the hiring pool alone, not confounded by the effects of employer selection for variables unrelated to race. By limiting the definition of the hiring pool to elite law schools, we can factor out this confounding variable. While elite law firms may care about the grades of black and Latino students at elite law schools, their focus tends to be on whether these—and other—elite law school students have met some threshold level of achievement, not on whether they are at the top of their class. The more "elite" the law school, the less significant the grades (again, above some threshold of academic performance). Consequently, even if blacks and Latinos at elite law firms receive lower grades than their white and Asian American counterparts, they are not outside of the elite law firm's hiring pool. Thus, by limiting our definition of the relevant hiring pool to elite law school students, we can factor out the confounding variable of class rank with a simple (albeit still idealizing) stipulation: law firms are generally indifferent to grades in their hiring of elite law school graduates.

15. Of course, there are other factors involved. We do not claim that law school affirmative action is the sole determinant of elite law firm diversity. For our purposes, suffice it to say that it is one significant factor.

16. *See supra* note 14.

17. In the interest of being thorough, let us stipulate also that elite law firms generally do not hire students who fall below that threshold.

18. This assumption probably holds true at the top five or six law schools; for law schools further down in the rankings, the assumption may be much more contestable.

19. As discussed above, the purpose of this assumption is to enable us to theorize how workplace diversity might be affected by the level of racial diversity in law school student bodies and positive consideration of race (for the sake of creating diversity) by law firms and law schools.

20. We relax this assumption in Part III below.

21. Int'l Bhd. of Teamsters v. United States, 431 U.S. 324, 339 n.20 (1977). The Court was addressing whether intentional discrimination could be proved using statistical evidence of disparities between the racial composition of the employer's workforce and the local labor market.

22. Here we use "discrimination" to refer to actions—implicitly or explicitly motivated—based on bias, prejudice, or preferences that operate to the disadvantage of racial minorities. We do not count the use of prodiversity racial preferences as discrimination. We recognize that this is a contested question in the legal context of Title VII interpretation.

23. We might add that any observed statistically significant disparities in levels of diversity between firms could presumptively be attributed to discrimination (either intentional or not) or to positive employer preferences for diversity.

24. *See* Kevin M. Clermont & Stewart J. Schwab, *Employment Discrimination Plaintiffs in Federal Court: From Bad to Worse?*, 3 Harv. L. & Pol'y Rev. 103, 115 (2009)

(arguing that empirical data on low success rates for employment discrimination plaintiffs "raises the specter that federal appellate courts have a double standard for employment discrimination cases, harshly scrutinizing employees' victories below while gazing benignly at employers' victories"); *see also* Kerri Lynn Stone, *Shortcuts in Employment Discrimination Law*, 56 St. Louis U. L.J. 111, 159–62 (2011) (summarizing recent scholarship on judicial hostility toward employment discrimination claims).

25.   The qualification in our hypothetical rule permitting consideration of race only if "reasonably necessary" is not based on current Title VII law. But if the Supreme Court were to recognize a diversity-based justification for affirmative action in hiring, we believe the Court would impose some limitation of this sort, if not an even more restrictive one.

26.   In Condition 3, if an elite firm mistakenly believes that consideration of race is necessary for workplace diversity, the firm will end up with a level of diversity that is either equal to or higher than the level of diversity in the pool of available students. If the firm's prodiversity hiring results in a level of diversity that is equal to that in the pool, then the firm's "unnecessary" consideration of race should have no effect on the overall distribution of diversity among firms. If the firm, as a result of its positive consideration of race, produces a higher level of diversity in its own workplace than is present in the overall applicant pool, this might tend to cause an increased level of diversity relative to the firms that perceive (correctly, according to our assumptions) that consideration of race is not necessary.

27.   One might think that the answer would depend on the ratio of elite students in the available labor pool to available positions. If there are at least as many employment positions available as there are elite students looking for jobs, then the uniform application of affirmative action preferences by employers should not disrupt the full and uniform propagation of the low level of diversity that exists in the elite student pool to the workplace. However, if there are fewer employment positions available than elite students in the pool, affirmative action will cause minority workers to be hired at a greater rate than nonminority workers, which will result in a level of workplace diversity that is higher than the level of diversity in the candidate pool. In this case, one might argue that the diversity of the pool would not only propagate to the workplace but also be *amplified*. While this is theoretically possible, it seems equally possible that in conditions of job scarcity, employers would either consciously or unconsciously scale back their affirmative action hiring so as not to exceed a certain "saturation" point for workplace diversity. If so, then there would be no amplification effect.

28.   See *supra* note 27.

29.   *See* Stone, *supra* note 24, at 159–62.

30.   We say this is likely—not certain—in our model because clustering would not occur if all employers act in perfect unison with respect to their permitted use of prodiversity preferences.

31.   For purposes of this discussion, we still assume, as in Part II, that employers regard all graduates of elite universities as comparably qualified for positions in their workplaces, but we introduce the possibility that employers might consider characteristics other than objective qualifications in constructing their workforce.

32.   *See* Fisher v. Univ. of Tex., 570 U.S., 133 S. Ct. 2411, 2418 (2013) (stating that "[t]he academic mission of a university is 'a special concern of the First Amendment'" (quoting Regents of the Univ. of Cal. v. Bakke, 438 U.S. 265, 312 (1978)).

33. *See generally* Devon W. Carbado, *Intraracial Diversity*, 60 UCLA L. REV. 1130 (2013).

34. Devon W. Carbado & Mitu Gulati, *The Law and Economics of Critical Race Theory*, 112 YALE L.J. 1757 (2003) (book review) (surveying the literature on the extent to which corporate workplaces are often structured to achieve homogeneity).

35. Significantly, law schools are very much aware of where their students end up. For at least the past two decades, largely because of law school rankings but also to facilitate alumni relationships and giving, schools have been keeping fairly accurate records about where their graduates end up.

36. We readily concede that other things may not be equal. For example, if LF-Diversity is insufficient to fully activate the educational benefits that might be possible with other modes of diversity, then universities might give priority to achievement of those educational benefits even at the cost of marginally lower employment of graduates. But our point is that employer demand for a particular type of diversity will exert a pull in that direction, not that the value of LF-Diversity will necessarily trump all other law school values.

37. We would not predict complete convergence because satisfying employer demand is only part of (and concededly, perhaps only a small part of) the educational benefit of a diverse student body. See discussion in Part III above.

38. At least two factors could shape the strength of this demand: the law firm's substantive commitment to diversity and the employer's symbolic commitment to diversity. With respect to the substantive commitment, an employer might be committed to diversity because it thinks (a) it is the right thing to do, (b) diversity will improve workplace efficiency and productivity, and (c) it provides access to markets. With respect to the symbolic commitment, an employer might simply want to signal ("showcase") diversity to avoid the reputational costs of not doing so.

39. The strength of this incentive would turn on (a) how important employment rankings are to the overall ranking of the institution, (b) how much attention students pay to employment rates and/or rankings, and (c) whether jobs are scarce. As to the scarcity of jobs, we note that in conditions of full employment, the demand effect will be weak unless employers actively avoid hiring students who are LS-Diverse—a possibility that is factored out by our initial assumptions of Part II. The demand effect will be most pronounced when law firms implement diversity initiatives in conditions of job scarcity. In those conditions, LF-Diverse students will be hired at a disproportionately higher rate than all other students, giving rise to an incentive for law schools to admit more students fitting that profile.

7

Is the Future of Affirmative Action Race Neutral?

Brian T. Fitzpatrick

The outlook does not appear particularly bright for affirmative action programs in the United States that grant preferences based on race to blacks, Hispanics, and others in hiring, university admissions, and bidding on government contracts. These programs continue to be unpopular with the public and face increasing hostility in courts of law.[1] In their place, courts and commentators have been promoting an alternative form of affirmative action that I will call "race-neutral affirmative action." Race-neutral affirmative action seeks to change the racial composition of those who benefit from employment, education, or government spending not by granting preferences based on race (what I will call "racially explicit affirmative action") but by granting preferences based on characteristics that are correlated with race. That is, as I will define it, the purpose of race-neutral affirmative action is the same as the purpose of racially explicit affirmative action—to increase the numbers of certain racial groups who benefit from these opportunities. But the means are different: race-neutral affirmative action uses correlates of race rather than race itself.

Perhaps the best-known race-neutral affirmative action program in the United States is the Texas Ten Percent Plan at the University of Texas, which grants automatic admission to any in-state applicant who graduated in the top 10 percent of his or her high school class.[2] For applicants admitted under this plan, the Texas legislature eschewed all other criteria in favor of high school class rank because the racial segregation that still exists in Texas high schools leads class rank to correlate with applicants who are black and Hispanic better than other traditional admissions criteria such as SAT scores.[3] For the same reason, other universities have adopted preferences for poor, bilingual, and first-generation applicants, as well as for students who have "overcome diversity" or "demonstrated cultural awareness."[4] Although many of these preferences have merits of their own, when they are motivated in whole or in part by their ability to generate racial diversity, I call them race-neutral *affirmative action*.

As I noted, courts have become increasingly hostile to racially explicit affirmative action, and many commentators have turned to promoting this sort of race-neutral affirmative action instead.[5] Indeed the United States Supreme Court recently vacated a lower court's approval of a new, racially explicit affirmative action program at the University of Texas in part because the Texas Ten Percent Plan alone had been so successful there.[6] The Court will consider the question again this coming year.

In this chapter, I examine the rise of race-neutral affirmative action in the United States and assess the costs and benefits of trying to diversify through race-neutral means. I conclude, first, that, although courts have been promoting race-neutral affirmative action, they have yet to confront serious questions about whether it is any more constitutional than racially explicit affirmative action. In my view, it is hard to square race-neutral affirmative action with the Supreme Court's cases that prohibit programs that have both the purpose and effect of racial discrimination. Second, even if the courts decide not to adhere to these past cases, it is unclear whether race-neutral affirmative action is any less problematic than racially explicit affirmative action. Although race-neutral affirmative action may be less divisive and less stigmatizing to its beneficiaries, I suspect it will be so much less efficient at bringing about racial diversity that it will require institutions to make much greater sacrifices to other aspects of their missions. Indeed, the race-neutral programs that are likely to be the least divisive and least stigmatizing are probably also those that are the least efficient at diversifying. For both of these reasons, I am not sure race-neutral affirmative action is the panacea that many seem to think it is.

I. The Rise of Race-Neutral Affirmative Action

As is well known, in the late 1960s, employers, governments, and universities began efforts to increase opportunities for racial minorities by granting preferences to blacks and Hispanics who applied for jobs, university admissions, and government contracts.[7] These efforts were highly controversial from their inception—both politically and legally[8]—but they received qualified legal blessings from the United States Supreme Court in 1978 in education,[9] in 1979 in employment,[10] and in 1980 in government contracting.[11] As the federal judiciary became more conservative in the 1980s, the legal foundation of racially explicit affirmative began to weaken,[12] but it has thus far survived, if only by the narrowest of margins.[13] Nonetheless, many observers believe it is only a matter of time before the legal foundation crumbles altogether.[14] Indeed, even jurists supportive of racially explicit affirmative action have said it should come to an end in the next several years.[15] Courts hostile to racially explicit affirmative action have cited the availability of race-neutral affirmative action as one reason for their hostility.[16]

In some ways, the political fortunes of racially explicit affirmative action have improved over time even as its legal fortunes have declined. Although the Republican Party made these programs a prominent target in the 1980s and 1990s, the party has now largely abandoned its opposition.[17] In light of the increasing racial diversity of the population of the United States, I believe the prospects for the opposition to resume are dim. Nonetheless, the programs remain unpopular with the public.[18] Consequently, antipreference activists have gone around the political parties in a number of states and directly to a plebiscite for votes to ban their governments (but not private parties) from using racial preferences.[19] These efforts have almost always succeeded and are likely to continue.[20] To date, there are now six states where state governments and state universities have been prohibited from using racially explicit affirmative action by direct democracy: California (1996),[21] Washington (1998),[22] Michigan (2006),[23] Nebraska (2008),[24] Arizona (2010),[25] and Oklahoma (2012).[26] Two other states have enacted these prohibitions through other means: Florida (1999)[27] and New Hampshire (2011).[28]

Where racially explicit affirmative action has been banned, the states faced a choice: forgo efforts to increase opportunities for racial minorities or practice race-neutral affirmative action—that is, to find correlates with race and to replace preferences for race with preferences for those correlates. In many instances, state universities chose the latter course.[29] As I explained above, one of the best-known examples is the University of Texas (which lost the ability to use race by court decision[30]), which elevated high school class rank in its admissions decisions over any other criteria because it was better correlated with black and Hispanic applicants.[31] Other states—such as California and Florida—also rely heavily on this correlate with race.[32] Class rank is better correlated with race than other traditional admissions criteria in these states because the high schools are still so racially segregated.[33] Other universities have used or considered using preferences for other correlates with race, including family income, residence in urban areas, and bilingualism.[34] There is no reason similar correlates cannot be used to replace racial preferences in employment and even government contracting (a popular example in the latter context is preferences for smaller business).[35] Although there have been periods of transition, these correlates have proven largely successful in achieving levels of racial diversity in universities similar to those achieved with racial preferences.[36] It is harder to find data on employment and government contracts, but there is some evidence that race-neutral affirmative action has been less successful at diversifying in these contexts.[37]

Many commentators believe that the trend in favor of race-neutral affirmative action will continue, compelled by the public, by the courts, or by both.[38] Indeed, many commentators believe that racially explicit affirmative action will eventually meet its demise and that the only future for affirmative action in the United States is the race-neutral variety.[39] On this point, it is interesting to note that race-neutral affirmative action apparently is now being used in other countries, even those that never had the appetite for the racially explicit variety.[40]

Some commentators have celebrated this future while others have decried it.[41] As I explain below, I am not persuaded that race-neutral affirmative action should fill the void that may be left by the demise of racially explicit affirmative action in the United States. As I explain, not only are race-neutral programs with racial purposes as legally dubious as racially explicit programs, but it also may very well be the case that race-neutral affirmative action is no less problematic than racially explicit affirmative action.

II. Is Race-Neutral Affirmative Action Constitutional?

Many commentators believe that race-neutral affirmative action can overcome the legal infirmities that still dog racially explicit affirmative action.[42] As I have written in the past and as I explain in this section, I think the legal advantages of race-neutral affirmative action have been seriously overstated.[43]

Racially explicit affirmative action is legally infirm because using racial classifications to burden or benefit individuals must pass the Supreme Court's "strict scrutiny" test in order to satisfy the Equal Protection Clause of the U.S. Constitution. Under this test, affirmative action must be supported by a "compelling government interest" and be "narrowly tailored" to support that interest.[44] Although the Supreme Court has recognized a few compelling interests in this context—for example, correcting for an institution's own past discrimination[45] and reaping the educational benefits of racial diversity[46]—the Court continues to make it hard on racially explicit affirmative action.[47] For example, in *Fisher v. University of Texas*,[48] the Court sent a racially explicit affirmative action program back for further litigation over whether the university had proven that marginal educational benefits continued to accrue at the levels of diversity it was seeking.[49] The Court will consider the question anew this coming year.

Some commentators believe that strict scrutiny can be avoided altogether with race-neutral affirmative action because it does not rely on racial classifications,[50] but I think this view is mistaken. In a number of cases, the Supreme Court has held that race-neutral classifications must satisfy the strict-scrutiny test when they have the same purpose and effect as racially explicit classifications.[51] As the Court put it in one case, "[a] racial classification...is presumptively invalid and can be upheld only upon an extraordinary justification. This rule applies as well to a classification that is ostensibly neutral but is a...pretext for racial discrimination."[52] Almost by definition, these holdings would encompass race-neutral affirmative action.[53]

Other commentators believe that the legal parity between race-neutral-but-racially-motivated classifications and racially explicit classifications should not include race-neutral classifications that are motivated to help blacks and Hispanics as opposed to hurt them.[54] But, as it has with so-called benign racially explicit classifications,[55] the Supreme Court has already applied strict scrutiny to race-neutral classifications that seek to aid blacks and Hispanics in its voting-district gerrymandering cases.[56]

In my view, there is only one way in which race-neutral affirmative action is on firmer legal footing than racially explicit affirmative action: the narrow-tailoring inquiry in the strict scrutiny test for race proxies is easier to satisfy than it is for racially explicit programs.[57] Other than that, however, race-neutral affirmative action would seem to have to overcome all the same legal barriers that racially explicit affirmative action does, including the barrier for which the Supreme Court remanded in

Fisher: to show that marginal increases in racial diversity continue to further a compelling interest.

With all this said, it should be emphasized that the Supreme Court is much like the stock market in at least one respect: past performance is no guarantee of future success. The Court's personnel changes over time, and precedents are not always followed. Moreover, Justices are free to change their minds. Constitutional law is, to a large extent, political law,[58] and, if race-neutral affirmative action maintains its popularity with the public, the Supreme Court may look for ways to facilitate it.[59] There is some reason to believe this transition is already underway.[60]

III. The Social Desirability of Race-Neutral Affirmative Action

Perhaps courts will give a green light to race-neutral affirmative action despite the precedents I marshaled in the previous part. Does that mean that race-neutral affirmative action should fill the void that many commentators believe will be left by racially explicit affirmative action's demise? I am not so sure. As I explain in this part, it may very well be that race-neutral affirmative action is just as problematic as the racially explicit variety.

A. The Advantages of Race-Neutral Affirmative Action

There are some reasons to believe that race-neutral affirmative action will be less problematic than racial preferences. Many commentators, for example, favor race-neutral affirmative action because they believe it can achieve the same amount of racial diversity as racial preferences but without as much racial divisiveness.[61] The assertion here is that the same people who find racially explicit affirmative action immoral or otherwise objectionable do not get as exercised about preferences of other sorts—even if those preferences are correlated with race and were selected for that very reason. Indeed, there does seem to be empirical support for the notion that the public favors at least some race-neutral programs more than racially explicit ones, such as the Texas Ten Percent Plan and preferences based on family income.[62] In many of these surveys, however, it may have been hard for the public to know whether the race-neutral program was or was not motivated by its racial effects as opposed to some end independent of racial diversity. Some commentators are skeptical that the public will support these programs if it is aware of the racial motivations.[63] On the other hand, the motivation behind the Texas Ten Percent Plan should have been apparent to any observer,[64] and that does not seem to have detracted from its popularity. Thus, I tend to agree that race-neutral affirmative action is probably less divisive than the racially explicit variety.

Other commentators believe that race-neutral affirmative action will not burden individuals aided by it with the same stigma that is associated with preferences based on race.[65] The notion here is that the same people who might think less of blacks or Hispanics because they may have been admitted to a university or received a government contract or job in part because of their race will not think the same way if they received the same benefits because of other criteria—even if, again, those other criteria are correlated with race and selected for that very reason. This claim is harder to prove, and I am not aware of any empirical evidence either for or against it. Nonetheless, for the same reason that race-neutral programs tend to be less divisive and more popular with the public, it may very well be that the beneficiaries of these programs are not held in lower regard.

Some people also believe that race-neutral affirmative action is a less problematic way to generate racial diversity because it avoids the messy business of figuring out who belongs in one racial group or another in order to determine who should benefit from a racial preference and who should not.[66] Although this business may have been messy at one time, in recent years, racial preferences have largely operated on the "honor system," where individuals self-declare their race.[67] Thus, it strikes me that any advantage here may be insignificant.

B. The Disadvantages of Race-Neutral Affirmative Action

Although race-neutral affirmative action may offer some advantages over racially explicit affirmative action, I believe it also comes with disadvantages. The biggest problem with race-neutral affirmative action is that it is much less efficient at generating racial diversity than racial preferences are.[68] By definition, proxies or correlates for race will sweep in individuals of all races, including those for whom greater representation is not sought, usually whites and Asians.[69] How much less efficient race-neutral affirmative action is depends on how good the correlates for race are. Some correlates—such as residence in urban areas—may be highly correlated with race. For example, Wayne State University Law School in Michigan has adopted an admissions policy that gives preferences to applicants from Detroit, which is almost 90 percent black and Hispanic, in order to maintain diversity in the face of the ban on racial preferences in Michigan.[70] But other correlates such as family income and high school class rank are very inefficient—blacks and Hispanics make up much smaller percentages of individuals from impoverished families or who graduated at the top of their high school class;[71] these correlates are not very good, but they are used because they are better than SAT scores. This loss in efficiency has a serious and negative implication: in order to achieve desired levels of diversity with race-neutral affirmative action, universities, employers, and governments may have to forgo other criteria that are important to their missions. For example, under the Texas Ten Percent Plan, in order to achieve the same racial diversity it had when it used racial preferences, huge portions of the University of Texas had to be admitted on class rank alone;[72] the state finally permitted the University to cap Ten Percent admissions at 75 percent of each freshman class.[73] All of the other characteristics that a university might think are important to assemble in a successful student body—good test scores, extracurricular activities, leadership skills, perseverance, and so on—must be relegated to the remaining 25 percent of the student body. That strikes me as an incredible sacrifice to institutional mission.

Some commentators believe another disadvantage to race-neutral affirmative action is that it undermines transparency in government because race-neutral affirmative action obscures the racial motivations behind legislation.[74] This may be one reason race-neutral affirmative action is less divisive than racially explicit affirmative action: the public simply may not realize that race-neutral affirmative action is motivated by racial diversity at all; perhaps if the public knew that, it would not support race-neutral affirmative action either. On the other hand, as I noted above, when I think it has been clear to the public that race-neutral programs were racially motivated, as it was with the Texas Ten Percent Plan, the public still supports the programs more than it does racial preferences. Of course, the Texas Ten Percent Plan is only one example, and it may be true as a general matter that it is difficult for the public to see the "affirmative action" side to race-neutral affirmative action. Certain schools of political science might see this as a cost to race-neutral affirmative action.

Some commentators also oppose race-neutral affirmative action because they think its success is a product of—rather than an antidote to—discrimination against blacks and Hispanics.[75] For example, university preferences based on class rank achieve diversity only to the extent that school segregation persists. Preferences for urban residents do so only to the extent that neighborhoods are segregated by race. Preferences for family income do so only to the extent that blacks and Hispanics are stuck in greater poverty than whites and Asians. For these commentators, race-neutral programs "lock in" racial segregation and disadvantages based on race rather than break them.[76] This argument has some rhetorical appeal, but I am unsure if race-neutral affirmative action does any less to free blacks and Hispanics from, for example, poverty and segregation than racially explicit affirmative action. If racially explicit affirmative action in education, employment, and government contracting mitigates poverty and segregation by increasing the wealth and improving the aspirations among blacks and Hispanics as many commentators suggest,[77] then why would race-neutral affirmative action not do the same so long as it places the same numbers of blacks and Hispanics into these opportunities? In other words, I am not sure this should count as a "cost" of using race-neutral affirmative action to bring about racial diversity.

C. Assessment

Although the empirical evidence is somewhat undeveloped, race-neutral affirmative action may well be able to generate the same racial diversity as racially explicit affirmative action without two serious downsides: racial divisiveness and stigmatization. At the same time, however, it may impose a cost of its own: because it is a less efficient means to achieving racial diversity, it may force institutions to sacrifice other ends important to their missions. A rigorous assessment of these costs and benefits is a difficult endeavor that certainly goes beyond the scope of this book chapter, if it is possible at all. That is, it may be impossible to discern (at least in any coherent way) which is worse: fostering racial animosity and social stigma or undermining the institutional missions of our universities and governments.

Nonetheless, there is one feature of the above discussion that leads me to suspect that it is unlikely that race-neutral affirmative action will be any less socially problematic than racially explicit affirmative action. This feature is that the advantages offered by a race-neutral affirmative action program are likely to be directly correlated with its disadvantages. In other words, the race-neutral programs that will be the *least divisive* and *least stigmatizing* are probably the same ones that rely on the *weakest correlates* for race and will pose the *greatest costs* to institutional missions. I think this might be the case for two reasons. First, weaker correlates benefit whites and Asians more frequently; thus, from simple self-interest, individuals from these groups (the groups mostly likely to find such programs divisive and to impose social stigma on others) may well prefer weaker correlates. Second, because they are so inefficient, it may be less apparent from weaker correlates that they were adopted for racial reasons. This could lead to more support from whites and Asians if racial motivations behind legislative programs are what triggers opposition to them.

Indeed, as I noted, preferences based on family income and, in the university setting, high school class rank (such as the Texas Ten Percent Plan) tend to be popular with the public, but these criteria are at the same time poorly correlated with race. In regions with segregated schools like Texas, the racial composition of individuals with top high school rankings will be little different than the racial composition of high school–aged students in the region overall; although this may make class rank a better correlate with race than other traditional university admissions criteria, it is still a weak one. Family income is a somewhat better proxy for race—the racial composition of families in poverty is more skewed toward blacks and Hispanics than is the overall population[78]—but even this correlation is not particularly strong.

If I am correct about this, and only those race-neutral programs that require institutions to make the greatest sacrifices to their missions will offer corresponding advantages over racially explicit affirmative action, then it is easy to see how race-neutral affirmative action may be no less costly to society than is racially explicit affirmative action.

IV. Conclusion

Many advocates of racial diversity have pinned their hopes on race-neutral affirmative action to take the place of racially explicit affirmative should it meet its political or legal demise. But I do not see race-neutral affirmative action as the panacea that some do. Although race-neutral programs appear to have the support of increasingly conservative courts and of many commentators, these judges and commentators have not yet wrestled with what I believe are serious constitutional questions posed by these programs. Moreover, even if these questions are pushed to the side, it is not clear to me that race-neutral programs are any less problematic: the very programs that are likely to offer the greatest advantages over racial preferences may very well pose the greatest costs. As a result, if the future of affirmative action is indeed to be race-neutral, it may not be a particularly happy one for proponents of increased opportunities for blacks and Hispanics.

About the Author

Professor of law, Vanderbilt Law School. J.D., Harvard Law School. My thanks to Suzanna Sherry and the participants at the symposium A Nation of Widening Opportunities: The Civil Rights Act at 50 (October 11, 2013) at the University of Michigan for their helpful comments and to Daniel Hay for excellent research assistance.

Notes

1. *See infra* notes 18 & 38.

2. *See generally* Brian T. Fitzpatrick, *Strict Scrutiny of Facially Race-Neutral State Action and the Texas Ten Percent Plan*, 53 BAYLOR L. REV. 289 (2001) [hereinafter Fitzpatrick, *Texas Ten Percent Plan*].

3. See id. at 325–27 ("[T]he Ten Percent Plan was selected to boost the percentage of racial minorities admitted to top universities because it could circumvent the problem of poor performance by racial minorities on standardized tests...").

4. *See infra* note 34 and accompanying text.

5. Perhaps the most prominent and ubiquitous proponent of race-neutral affirmative action has been Richard Kahlenberg, a senior fellow at the Century Foundation. *See, e.g.*, RICHARD D. KAHLENBERG, THE REMEDY: CLASS, RACE, AND AFFIRMATIVE ACTION 83–182 (1996) [hereinafter KAHLENBERG, THE REMEDY] ("Class-based affirmative action...is color-blind and yet responds to the moral desire to do something about the legacy of our nation's history."); Richard D. Kahlenberg, *Class-Based Affirmative Action*, 84 CALIF. L. REV. 1037, 1060–64 (1996) [hereinafter Kahlenberg, *Class-Based Affirmative Action*] (arguing that class-based affirmative action is morally, politically, and legally preferable to race-based affirmative action).

6. Fisher v. Univ. of Tex., 133 S. Ct. 2411, 2420–21 (2013) (holding the Court of Appeals failed to determine that adding a race-conscious component was "necessary...to achieve the educational benefits of diversity" (internal quotation marks omitted)). The plan has been successful in enrolling *total* black and Hispanic numbers; the university has argued, however, that it has not been successful in enrolling the *mix* of black and Hispanic students that the university desires. For example, the university has argued the plan enrolls too many poor students and not enough rich ones. *See* Tr. of Oral Arg. at 43-44 (Alito, J.) ("Well, I thought that the whole purpose of affirmative action was to help students who come from underprivileged backgrounds...[b]ut you say, well, [the Ten Percent Plan is] faulty because it doesn't admit enough African Americans and Hispanics who come from privileged backgrounds.").

7. For an excellent recent history of affirmative action, see RANDALL KENNEDY, FOR DISCRIMINATION: RACE, AFFIRMATIVE ACTION, AND THE LAW 39–77 (2013) (describing the development of affirmative action from the Johnson administration through the Obama administration, as well as the emergence of state ballot initiatives to ban affirmative action); *see also* TERRY H. ANDERSON, THE PURSUIT OF FAIRNESS: A HISTORY OF AFFIRMATIVE ACTION 107–09 (2004) (noting that by the end of the 1960s, "most citizens now felt that all minorities deserved political equality and equal opportunities on the job"); KAHLENBERG, THE REMEDY, *supra* note 5, at 3–15 (recounting the early history of affirmative action); RONALD TURNER, THE PAST AND FUTURE OF AFFIRMATIVE ACTION 6 (1990) (describing the efforts of the Kennedy and Johnson administrations to strengthen employment nondiscrimination policy). The term "affirmative action" first emerged as a matter of federal policy in an executive order issued by President Kennedy in 1961. Exec. Order No. 10,925, 3 C.F.R. 448 (Mar. 6, 1961). Four years later, President Johnson directed federal contractors to "take affirmative action" to end discrimination in hiring. Exec. Order No. 11,246, 3 C.F.R. 340 (Sept. 24, 1965). At the time, "affirmative action" referred to "organized efforts by government and other institutions to make sure that opportunities...were truly open to all..." RICHARD

SANDER & STUART TAYLOR, JR., MISMATCH: HOW AFFIRMATIVE ACTION HURTS STUDENTS IT'S INTENDED TO HELP, AND WHY UNIVERSITIES WON'T ADMIT IT 15 (2012). These actions paved the way for the "Zenith of Affirmative Action" in the late 1960s and 1970s. ANDERSON,*supra*, at 111–60.

8. *See*KENNEDY, *supra* note 7, at 53–54. While there is not "systemic, national polling data" from the 1960s on racial preferences, "[i]solated instances in which poll questions on affirmative action were asked in the 1960s suggest that, even in this early period, the general public was highly opposed to preferential treatment." ELAINE B. SHARP, THE SOMETIME CONNECTION: PUBLIC OPINION AND SOCIAL ORDER 74–75 (1999); *see also, e.g.*, ANDERSON, *supra* note 7, at 75–83 (describing competing notions of fairness "mired in debate" and the Goldwater-led opposition to preferences, quotas, and proportional hiring); *cf.* Richard D. Kahlenberg, *The Class-Based Future of Affirmative Action*, THE AMERICAN PROSPECT, June 25, 2013, http://prospect.org/article/class-based-future-affirmative-action [hereinafter Kahlenberg, *Class-Based Future*] ("[A]ffirmative action based on race has been politically problematic for the left from the earliest days...").

9. *See* Regents of the Univ. of Cal. v. Bakke, 438 U.S. 265, 320 (1978) ("[T]he State has a substantial interest that legitimately may be served by...the competitive consideration of race and ethnic origin.").

10. *See* United Steelworkers of Am. v. Weber, 443 U.S. 193, 208 (1979) (holding that Title VII "does not condemn all private, voluntary, race-conscious affirmative action plans").

11. *See* Fullilove v. Klutznick, 448 U.S. 448, 472 (1980) (plurality opinion) (deferring to congressional judgment that a remedial race-conscious contracting program is necessary to ensure equal protection). The Court later retreated from *Fullilove*, holding that strict scrutiny is the proper standard of review for race-conscious contracting preferences. *See* Adarand Constructors, Inc. v. Pena, 515 U.S. 200, 227 (1995).

12. *See*KENNEDY, *supra* note 7, at 54–69 (discussing the "affirmative action stalemate" that has developed since the late 1970s); ANDERSON, *supra* note 7, at 189–205 (describing the halting narrowing of affirmative action in the 1980s and general solidarity of Reagan appointees in opposing racial preferences). In a survey of federal district judges in the early 1990s, approximately 78 percent agreed with the statement, "Overall, the federal judiciary is becoming more 'conservative' than it was in the 1960s, 1970s, and early 1980s." *See*KEVIN K. LYLES, THE GATEKEEPERS: FEDERAL DISTRICT COURTS IN THE POLITICAL PROCESS 28–30 (1997). This is no doubt a residual effect of President Reagan's unprecedented opportunity to remake the federal judiciary: Reagan made more appointments to the circuit courts of appeals than any other President and is second only to President Clinton for number of district court appointments. U.S. COURTS, JUDGESHIP APPOINTMENTS BY PRESIDENT, http://www.uscourts.gov/ JudgesAndJudgeships/Viewer.aspx?doc=/uscourts/JudgesJudgeships/docs/ appointments-by-president.pdf (last visited Jan. 28, 2014); *see* David M. O'Brien, *Federal Judgeships in Retrospect, in*THE REAGAN PRESIDENCY: PRAGMATIC CONSERVATISM & ITS LEGACIES 327, 327 (W. Elliot Brownlee & Hugh Davis Graham eds., 2003) ("Reagan appointed close to half of all lower court judges, more than any other previous president."). Most of these appointees were "opposed to [racial] preferences" and laid the foundation for later Supreme Court decisions "diminish[ing] affirmative action." ANDERSON, *supra*, at 215–16. *See generally*THOMAS M. KECK, THE MOST ACTIVIST SUPREME COURT IN HISTORY: THE

ROAD TO MODERN JUDICIAL CONSERVATISM (2010) (recounting the emergence of conservative judicial activism in the late 1970s and 1980s).

13. *See, e.g.,* Grutter v. Bollinger, 539 U.S. 306 (2003) (sustaining the University of Michigan Law School's affirmative action program by 5–4 vote).

14. *E.g.,* RICHARD D. KAHLENBERG, THE CENTURY FOUNDATION, A BETTER AFFIRMATIVE ACTION: STATE UNIVERSITIES THAT CREATED ALTERNATIVES TO RACIAL PREFERENCES 1, 7–10 (2012) [hereinafter KAHLENBERG, A BETTER AFFIRMATIVE ACTION], *available at* http://tcf.org/assets/downloads/tcf-abaa.pdf ("After almost a half century, American higher education's use of racial preferences in admissions to selective colleges may well be coming to an end."); Kim Forde-Mazrui, *The Constitutional Implications of Race-Neutral Affirmative Action,* 88 GEO. L.J. 2331, 2337–51 (2000) (questioning the legal future of race-conscious affirmative action); Keith E. Sealing, *The Myth of a Color-Blind Constitution,* 54 WASH. U. J. URB. & CONTEMP. L. 157, 207 (1998) ("[A]n overly strict application of the race-neutral alternatives...[would] assure that strict scrutiny is indeed fatal in fact. There are always theoretically workable race-neutral alternatives available, and they almost always fail to work.").

15. Justice O'Connor, who joined with her more liberal colleagues to provide the critical fifth vote in *Grutter,* famously predicted: "We expect that 25 years from now, the use of racial preferences will no longer be necessary to further the interest approved today." 539 U.S. at 343.

16. *See* Fisher v. Univ. of Tex., 570 U.S. , 133 S. Ct. 2411, 2420–21 (2013) (holding the court of appeals failed to determine that adding a race-conscious component to a race-neutral affirmative action program was "necessary...to achieve the educational benefits of diversity" (internal quotation marks omitted)).

17. For example, although Ronald Reagan and George H. W. Bush waged several high-profile battles against affirmative action, George W. Bush basically abandoned the issue—if not switched sides on it. *See, e.g.,* Harry Stein, *Now the GOP Is* for *Affirmative Action?,* CITY JOURNAL (Autumn 2006), http://www.city-journal.org/html/16_4_gop_affirmative_action.html ("[T]he Republican backtracking on preferences in Michigan reflects a quiet but steady shift in the national party, too, with the Bush administration undercutting affirmative-action foes—longtime GOP supporters—by embracing the 'diversity' mantra that liberals so fervently preach."). Likewise, recent Republican presidential candidates have not emphasized the issue. *See, e.g.,* Peter Schmidt, *Texas Lawsuit Complicates Presidential Race,* CHRON. OF HIGHER EDUC., July 30, 2012, http://chronicle.com/article/U-of-Texas-Admissions-Case/133203 ("Mr. Romney's campaign has yet to make any major pronouncements on affirmative action and...[his] record on affirmative action is difficult to parse."). Similarly, while California Governor Pete Wilson made enactment of Proposition 209, a direct democracy initiative banning racial preferences by state government, a centerpiece of his administration in the 1990s, no governor in recent years has done so. *See* B. Drummond Ayres Jr., *On Affirmative Action, Wilson's Moderate Path Quickly Veered to Right,* N.Y. TIMES, Aug. 8, 1995, http://www.nytimes.com/1995/08/08/us/on-affirmative-action-wilson-s-moderate-path-veered-quickly-to-right.html?.

18. The public gives conflicting answers when it is asked whether it supports "racial preferences" (no) or "affirmative action" (yes). *See*PEW RESEARCH CTR., PUBLIC BACKS AFFIRMATIVE ACTION, BUT NOT MINORITY PREFERENCES (June 2, 2009), http://www.pewresearch.org/2009/06/02/public-backs-affirmative-action-but-not-minority-preferences/. The more meaningful surveys move beyond these vague terms and ask the public directly whether it supports using race as a factor

in decision making. Americans have consistently opposed this practice; a recent poll found opposition by a two-to-one margin (67 percent to 28 percent) even if it "result[ed] in few minority students being admitted" to colleges. Jeffrey M. Jones, *In U.S., Most Reject Considering Race in College Admissions*, GALLUP POLL NEWS SERV. (July 24, 2013), http://www.gallup.com/poll/163655/reject-considering-race-college-admissions.aspx.

19. *See*KENNEDY, *supra* note 7, at 69–76 (discussing California's Proposition 209 and subsequent ballot initiatives to ban affirmative action); DANIEL C. LEWIS, DIRECT DEMOCRACY AND MINORITY RIGHTS 42–44 (2013) (evaluating role of direct democracy in state affirmative action bans).

20. As of this writing, voters in six states have succeeded in banning affirmative action through referenda. *See infra* notes 21–26 and accompanying text. The 2008 ballot initiative in Colorado remains the only failed statewide attempt to ban racial preferences through direct democracy. *See* Reeves Wiedeman, *How Colorado Became the First State to Reject a Ban on Affirmative Action*, CHRON. OF HIGHER EDUC., Nov. 10, 2008, http://chronicle.com/article/Analysis-Why-Colorado-Failed/1317; *see also* Sam Howe Verhovek, *Referendum in Houston Shows Complexity of Preferences Issue*, N.Y. TIMES, Nov. 6, 1997, http://www.nytimes.com/1997/11/06/us/1997-elections-affirmative-action-referendum-houston-shows-complexity.html?pagewanted=all&src=pm (reporting on failed ballot initiative in Houston). For an accounting of state-based efforts to ban affirmative action, see NAT'L CONFERENCE OF STATE LEGISLATURES, AFFIRMATIVE ACTION: STATE ACTION (Nov. 2012), http://www.ncsl.org/issues-research/educ/affirmative-action-state-action.aspx.

21. CAL. CONST. art. I, § 31 (Proposition 209). *See generally*LYDIA CHÁVEZ, THE COLOR BIND: CALIFORNIA'S CAMPAIGN TO END AFFIRMATIVE ACTION (1998).

22. WASH. REV. CODE ANN. § 49.60.400 (West 2013) (Initiative 200).

23. MICH. CONST. art. I, § 26 (Proposal 2). The Michigan ban was upheld by the U.S. Supreme Court. *See* Schuette v. Coal. to Defend Affirmative Action, Integration & Immigrant Rights & Fight for Equal. By Any Means Necessary (BAMN), 134 S. Ct. 1623 (2014).

24. NEB. CONST. art. I, § 30 (Initiative 424).

25. ARIZ. CONST. art. II, § 36 (Proposition 107).

26. OKLA. CONST. art. II, § 36A (Question 759).

27. In 1999, Governor Jeb Bush banned the use of race or gender preference in college admissions by executive order. Fla. Exec. Order No. 99-281 (Nov. 9, 2009), *available at* http://www.dms.myflorida.com/content/download/705/3389/file/ExecutiveOrder99-281.pdf. This was a supplement to the state's general ban on discrimination in public education. *See*FLA. STAT. ANN. § 1000.05(2) (West 2013). In early 2000, the Florida Board of Regents adopted the governor's ban on affirmative action and his proposal for a "talented twenty" percentage plan. Karla Schuster, *Regents Approve One Florida Plan*, ORLANDO SUN SENTINEL, Feb. 18, 2000, http://articles.sun-sentinel.com/2000-02-18/news/0002180223_1_new-admissions-admissions-rules-preferences; *see also* Peter T. Kilborn, *Jeb Bush Roils Florida on Affirmative Action*, N.Y. TIMES, Feb. 4, 2000, http://www.nytimes.com/2000/02/04/us/jeb-bush-roils-florida-on-affirmative-action.html (discussing E.O. 99-281 and the "One Florida" program).

28. N.H. REV. STAT. ANN. § 21-I:52 (2013) (House Bill 623).

29. *See, e.g.*, KAHLENBERG, A BETTER AFFIRMATIVE ACTION, *supra* note 14, at 26–63

(describing states' and universities' responses to affirmative action bans); KENNEDY, *supra* note 7, at 92 ("One response is to create interventions sensitive to the racial dimensions of class stratification."); David Leonhardt, *The New Affirmative Action*, N.Y. TIMES MAG., Sept. 30, 2007, http://www.nytimes.com/2007/09/30/magazine/30affirmative-t.html (chronicling changes in the University of California System post–Prop. 209).

30. Hopwood v. Texas, 78 F.3d 932, 962 (5th Cir. 1996).

31. *Seesupra* notes 2–3 and accompanying text.

32. *See* Fitzpatrick, *Texas Ten Percent Plan, supra* note 2, at 290 (noting that California and Florida have implemented plans that guarantee admission to the top 4 and 20 percent of students, respectively).

33. *See id.* at 347 ("Members of the Texas Legislature shrewdly identified class rank as the race-neutral university admissions criterion on which blacks and Hispanics performed better than any other...").

34. *See* Brian T. Fitzpatrick, *Can Michigan Universities Use Proxies for Race after the Ban on Racial Preferences?*, 13 MICH. J. RACE & L. 277, 278–79, 292 (2007) [hereinafter Fitzpatrick, *Can Michigan Universities Use Proxies?*] ("[Michigan] universities have identified a number of criteria which would appear to correlate fairly well with African American, Hispanic, and Native American applicants: bilingualism, residency on an Indian reservation or in Detroit, and experience overcoming discrimination."); *see also*KAHLENBERG, A BETTER AFFIRMATIVE ACTION, *supra* note 14, at 52 (noting Michigan's preference for background factors such as "cultural awareness/experiences, status as first generation college student, low economic family background, and residence in an economically disadvantaged region"); UNIV. OF WASH., OFFICE OF ADMISSIONS, FRESHMAN REVIEW, http://admit.washington.edu/Admission/Freshmen/Review (last visited Jan. 31, 2014) (considering personal characteristics such as "[a]ttaining a college-preparatory education in the face of significant personal adversity, or disability...[or] economic disadvantage" and "[d]emonstrating cultural awareness").

35. The Small Business Administration, for example, has a program of technical and financial support for small, disadvantaged businesses (SDBs). 13 C.F.R. § 124.101 et seq. (2013) (establishing eligibility requirements for SDBs); *see* City of Richmond v. J.A. Croson Co., 488 U.S. 469, 507 (1989) ("[A] race-neutral program of city financing for small firms would, *a fortiori*, lead to greater minority participation."); *id.* at 526 (Scalia, J., concurring) (noting that small-business preferences "may well have racially disproportionate impact," but are nonetheless permissible); *see also* Gilbert J. Ginsburg & Janine S. Benton, *One Year Later: Affirmative Action in Federal Government Contracting after Adarand*, 45 AM. U. L. REV. 1903, 1917–45 (describing federal programs designed to benefit SDBs).

36. *See*KAHLENBERG, A BETTER AFFIRMATIVE ACTION, *supra* note 14, at 26–63 (profiling states that have banned affirmative action in college admissions).

37. *See* David G. Blanchflower & Jon S. Wainwright, *An Analysis of the Impact of Affirmative Action Programs on Self-Employment in the Construction Industry* 12–16, 24 (Nat'l Bureau of Econ. Research, Working Paper No. 11793, 2005), *available at* http://papers.ssrn.com/sol3/papers.cfm?abstract_id=851702 ("[W]hen [race-conscious] programs are removed or replaced with race-neutral programs the utilization of minorities and women in public construction declines rapidly."); MARÍA E. ENCHAUTEGUI ET AL., THE URBAN INST., DO MINORITY-OWNED BUSINESSES GET A FAIR SHARE OF GOVERNMENT CONTRACTS? 62 (1997)

("[D]isparities [in contracting] are greater in those areas in which there is no affirmative action program in place."). Isolated data also suggest that states with bans on race-conscious affirmative action have seen a decrease in minority contracting. *See, e.g.,* MICH. ROUNDTABLE FOR DIVERSITY & INCLUSION, AFFIRMATIVE ACTION DENIED: MICHIGAN IN THE WAKE OF PROPOSAL 2, at 14 (2013), *available at* http://www.miroundtable.org/assets/postproptworeport_8_30.pdf (finding "Michigan has had a very low number of minority and women-owned contracts with the state"); James Nash, *Whites Get 92% of Contracts in Post-Affirmative Action L.A.*, BLOOMBERG BUSINESS, May 9, 2013, 5:37 PM, http://www.bloomberg.com/news/2013-05-09/white-men-get-92-of-contracts-in-post-affirmative-action-l-a-.html (reporting that white men received 92 percent of all contracts with Los Angeles despite comprising just 14 percent of the city's population).

38. *See, e.g.,* KAHLENBERG, A BETTER AFFIRMATIVE ACTION, *supra* note 14, at 4–10 (explaining why racial preferences are legally and politically vulnerable); Gregory Rodriguez, *The White Anxiety Crisis*, TIME, Mar. 11, 2010, http://content.time.com/time/specials/packages/article/0,28804,1971133_1971110_1971119,00.html (predicting that demographic changes may cause whites to "develop a stronger consciousness of their political interests as a group"); Nina Totenberg, *Supreme Court Wades into Affirmative Action*, NAT'L PUB. RADIO (Feb. 21, 2012, 4:14 PM), http://www.npr.org/2012/02/21/147212858/supreme-court-wades-into-affirmative-action-issue (noting that the decisive vote in *Grutter*, Justice O'Connor, was replaced by Justice Alito, who "has quite consistently been hostile to the idea of racial preferences").

39. *See supra* note 14 and accompanying text.

40. *E.g.,* KENNEDY, *supra* note 7, at 248–49 ("French authorities have quietly sought to influence the racial demographics of college admissions...by using as criteria of eligibility for benefits the residential location and socio-economic class position of candidates—in other words, 'race neutral' affirmative action.").

41. *Compare* Kahlenberg, *Class-Based Affirmative Action*, *supra* note 5, at 1060, 1099 ("If genuine equal opportunity is the agreed-upon end, class-based preference is the obvious remedy."), *with* Richard H. Fallon Jr., *Affirmative Action Based on Economic Disadvantage*, 43 UCLA L. REV. 1913, 1951 (1996) ("[W]e should not allow proposals for economically based affirmative action to divert attention from the need for other, more effective public policies to combat both poverty and race-based disadvantage.").

42. *See, e.g.,* KAHLENBERG, A BETTER AFFIRMATIVE ACTION, *supra* note 14, at 21 ("Even opponents of using race in student assignment concede that using socioeconomic status is perfectly legal."); John Martinez, *Trivializing Diversity: The Problem of Overinclusion in Affirmative Action Programs*, 12 HARV. BLACKLETTER L.J. 49, 54 (1995) ("If we reconstruct affirmative action programs according to neutral criteria, then minimum rationality judicial review would apply instead of strict scrutiny...").

43. *See* Fitzpatrick, *Can Michigan Universities Use Proxies?*, *supra* note 34, at 281 ("[U]nder the Equal Protection Clause, not only are explicit racial classifications subjected to strict scrutiny, but so are race-neutral classifications that have the same purpose and effect as the explicit ones."); *see also* Fisher v. Univ. of Tex., 133 S. Ct. 2411, 2433 (2013) (Ginsburg, J., dissenting) ("[O]nly an ostrich could regard the supposedly neutral alternatives as race unconscious."); Ian Ayres, *Narrow Tailoring*, 43 UCLA L. REV. 1781, 1791 (1996) ("The central problem is that the race-neutral means still have a race-conscious motivation."); Chapin Cimino, Comment, *Class-Based Preferences in Affirmative Action Programs after* Miller v. Johnson*: A Race-Neutral Option, or Subterfuge?*, 64 U. CHI. L. REV. 1289, 1297 (1997)("[W]henever

the Court suspects a racial motivation behind an ostensibly neutral statute, the principle against subterfuge will prohibit the government from doing covertly what it may not do overtly."); Forde-Mazrui, *supra* note 14, at 2333 ("A serious problem facing these ostensibly race-neutral efforts to increase minority representation in higher education...is that such efforts are themselves race-conscious state action that may violate the Equal Protection Clause." (citation omitted)).

44. *See, e.g.,* City of Richmond v. J.A. Croson Co., 488 U.S. 469, 485–86 (1989) (invalidating Richmond's minority subcontracting quota because it was not "narrowly tailored to accomplish a remedial purpose").

45. United States v. Paradise, 480 U.S. 149, 167 (1987) (plurality opinion) ("The Government unquestionably has a compelling interest in remedying past and present discrimination by a state actor.").

46. *E.g.,* Grutter v. Bollinger, 539 U.S. 306, 343 (2003) ("[T]he Equal Protection Clause does not prohibit...narrowly tailored use of race in admissions decisions to further a compelling interest in obtaining the educational benefits that flow from a diverse student body.").

47. Some have argued that the Court did not faithfully apply strict scrutiny in *Grutter*. *See, e.g.,* Ian Ayres & Sydney Foster, *Don't Tell, Don't Ask: Narrow Tailoring after Grutter & Gratz,* 85 TEX. L. REV. 517, 581 n.223 (2007) ("The extreme deference that Justice O'Connor showed to state officials is deeply inconsistent with the whole idea of strict scrutiny as an attempt to smoke out unjustified governmental racial preferences.").

48. 570 U.S. , 133 S. Ct. 2411 (2013).

49. After observing that the Ten Percent Plan alone had "resulted in a more racially diverse environment," the Court remanded the case because the Fifth Circuit failed to perform the "searching examination" of whether adding a race-conscious component was "necessary...to achieve the educational benefits of diversity." *Id.* at 2414, 2416 (internal quotation marks omitted); *see also id.* at 2424 (Thomas, J., concurring) ("[D]iversity...cannot be an end pursued for its own sake."); *cf.* SANDER & TAYLOR, *supra* note 7, at 288 (noting that the racial-preferences component is "vulnerable even under *Grutter*" because the University of Texas is "one of the few elite universities that already has a facially race-neutral system").

50. *See, e.g.,* Martinez, *supra* note 42, at 54 (arguing that race-neutral criteria will bypass strict scrutiny); KENNEDY, *supra* note 7, at 176–77 (noting that many "color-blind immediatists" are willing to countenance race-neutral plans provided they "are silent as to race").

51. *See, e.g.,* Hunter v. Underwood, 471 U.S. 222, 227–28, 233 (1985) (holding that a provision in the Alabama Constitution disenfranchising citizens convicted of "crimes involving moral turpitude" violated the Equal Protection Clause because the legislature chose crimes that affected ten times as many African Americans as whites); *see also, e.g.,* Columbus Bd. of Educ. v. Penick, 443 U.S. 449, 461–62 (1979) (invalidating several race-neutral actions by the school board, including the "use of optional attendance zones, discontiguous attendance areas,...boundary changes[,] and the selection of sites for new school construction" because they "had the foreseeable and anticipated effect of maintaining the racial separation of the schools" (footnotes omitted)); Keyes v. Sch. Dist. No. 1, 413 U.S. 189, 201 (1973) (holding that "concentrating Negroes in certain schools by structuring attendance zones or designating 'feeder' schools" can violate the Equal Protection Clause). In voting-district gerrymandering cases specifically, the Court has held that race-

neutral reapportionment plans animated by race-conscious motivations violate the Equal Protection Clause. *See* Hunt v. Cromartie, 526 U.S. 541, 546–49 (1999); Miller v. Johnson, 515 U.S. 900, 916 (1995); Shaw v. Reno, 509 U.S. 630, 643 (1993).

52. Personnel Adm'r v. Feeney, 442 U.S. 256, 272 (1979) (citations omitted); *accordHunt*, 526 U.S. at 546 ("A facially neutral law...warrants strict scrutiny...if it can be proved that the law was 'motivated by a racial purpose...'").

53. *See* Fitzpatrick, *Texas Ten Percent Plan, supra* note 2, at 314–20, 334–35; Fitzpatrick, *Can Michigan Universities Use Proxies?, supra* note 34, at 284. I say "almost" by definition because it is not altogether clear what constitutes a "racial effect" in this line of Supreme Court jurisprudence; it all depends on what the baseline of comparison is, and the Court has used a number of different baselines over the years. *See* Fitzpatrick, *Texas Ten Percent Plan, supra*, at 298–306 (discussing different forms of "racial effects").

54. *See* Michael C. Dorf, *Universities Adjust to State Affirmative Action Bans: Are the New Programs Legal? Are they a Good Idea?*, FINDLAW'S WRIT (Jan. 29, 2007), http://writ.news.findlaw.com/dorf/20070129.html ("I would say that the Justices would not subject [race-neutral affirmative action] to strict scrutiny.").

55. *E.g.*, Regents of the Univ. of Cal. v. Bakke, 438 U.S. 265, 289–90 (1978) ("The guarantee of equal protection cannot mean one thing when applied to one individual and something else when applied to a person of another color. If both are not accorded the same protection, then it is not equal."); *accord* Parents Involved in Cmty. Sch. v. Seattle Sch. Dist. No. 1, 551 U.S. 701, 742 (2007) ("Th[e] argument that different rules should govern racial classifications designed to include rather than exclude is not new; it has been repeatedly pressed in the past, and has been repeatedly rejected." (internal citations omitted)); City of Richmond v. J.A. Croson Co., 488 U.S. 469, 494 (1989) ("We thus reaffirm the view...that the standard of review under the Equal Protection Clause is not dependent on the race of those burdened or benefited by a particular classification."). *But seeParents Involved*, 551 U.S. at 830–38 (Breyer, J., dissenting) (disputing that the Court has ever "repudiated this constitutional asymmetry between that which seeks to *exclude* and that which seeks to *include* members of minority races" (citation omitted)).

56. *See, e.g., Hunt*, 526 U.S. at 546 (applying strict scrutiny to facially neutral law that is "'motivated by a racial purpose or object,' or if it is 'unexplainable on grounds other than race'" (internal citations omitted)); *Miller*, 515 U.S. at 911–13 (holding that Georgia's redistrict plan fails strict scrutiny notwithstanding the fact that the plan was "race neutral on [its] face"); *Shaw*, 509 U.S. at 653 (instructing the district court to apply strict scrutiny if petitioners' allegation of racial gerrymandering is not contradicted).

57. *See* Fitzpatrick, *Can Michigan Universities Use Proxies?, supra* note 34, at 291–92.

58. For a general treatment, see BARRY FRIEDMAN, THE WILL OF THE PEOPLE: HOW PUBLIC OPINION HAS INFLUENCED THE SUPREME COURT AND SHAPED THE MEANING OF THE CONSTITUTION (2009).

59. *Seesupra* notes 18, 50, & 54 and *infra* note 62.

60. In *Parents Involved*, Justice Kennedy leaves doubt whether he would continue to subject race-neutral affirmative action to strict scrutiny: "[Facially neutral] mechanisms are race conscious but do not lead to different treatment based on a classification that tells each student he or she is to be defined by race, so it is unlikely any of them would demand strict scrutiny to be found permissible." 551

U.S. 701, 789 (2007) (Kennedy, J., concurring in part and concurring in judgment). I have explained elsewhere why I do not think Justice Kennedy's opinion should be understood to cast doubt on his adherence to precedents in this area, but it is admittedly far from clear what he meant here. *See* Fitzpatrick, *Can Michigan Universities Use Proxies?*, *supra* note 34, at 289–91 ("Although I think one could read Justice Kennedy's further dicta here to suggest that he no longer thinks that the Constitution is as concerned with racial gerrymandering as it is with explicit racial discrimination,...in my view, the meaning Justice Kennedy most likely intended was one suggesting that, if the Court adopts the 'predominant' motivation standard..., then it will be harder for plaintiffs to make the necessary showing to invoke strict scrutiny.").

61.   *See, e.g.*, Ayres, *supra* note 43, at 1790 ("[R]ace-neutral classifications seem less likely to provoke the kind of racial enmity that would itself undermine the remedial purpose of the legislative action."); Forde-Mazrui, *supra* note 14, at 2371–75 ("Race-neutral classifications are significantly less likely than racial classifications to perpetuate racial stereotypes or racial hostility..."); Don Munro, Note, *The Continuing Evolution of Affirmative Action under Title VII: New Directions after the Civil Rights Act of 1991*, 81 VA. L. REV. 565, 606–07 (1995) ("[C]lass-based preferences would provide a less controversial means of achieving minority gains in employment.").

62.   Kahlenberg surveys the public's preference for economic affirmative action vis-à-vis racial preferences:

> In 2003, for example, a *Los Angeles Times* survey found that Americans opposed (56 percent to 26 percent) the University of Michigan's racial preference policy, but those same Americans supported preferences for low-income students (59 percent to 31 percent). A *Newsweek* poll around that same time likewise found that Americans opposed preferences for blacks in university admissions (68 percent to 26 percent) but supported preferences for economically disadvantaged students (65 percent to 28 percent). A third poll, by EPIC/MRA, also found that voters opposed the University of Michigan's affirmative action plan (63 percent to 27 percent) but supported preferences for economically disadvantaged students (57 percent to 36 percent). A subsequent 2005 *New York Times* poll put support for socioeconomic preferences at nearly 85 percent.

KAHLENBERG, A BETTER AFFIRMATIVE ACTION, *supra* note 14, at 6 (footnotes omitted). In addition, a 2005 poll found that 82 percent of Texans supported the Ten Percent Plan. *See* Katie Shepherd & Dominique Cambou, *Top 10 Percent Law Vital For UT*, THE DAILY TEXAN, Mar. 28, 2005, *available at* http://www.texastop10.princeton.edu/publicity/general/DailyTexan033005.pdf; *see also supra* note 18.

63.   *See* KENNEDY, *supra* note 7, at 92–94 ("Eligibility rules that say nothing explicitly about race but are wealth sensitive will still draw fire from detractors who will claim that the rules camouflage a racial Trojan horse...").

64.   *See* Fitzpatrick, *Texas Ten Percent Plan*, *supra* note 2, at 323–34 (reviewing the legislative history of the Ten Percent Plan and motivation of its proponents).

65.   *See, e.g.*, Forde-Mazrui, *supra* note 14, at 2376 ("[R]ace-neutral classifications...are less likely than racial classifications to reinforce stigmatic racial stereotypes..."); Munro, *supra* note 61, at 608 ("[T]he traditional arguments about 'stigma' lose much of their force when applied to class-based affirmative action."); THEDA SKOCPOL, SOCIAL POLICY IN THE UNITED STATES: FUTURE POSSIBILITIES IN HISTORICAL PERSPECTIVE 253 (1995) ("[S]tereotyping of the poor helps to explain why cross-national research on social expenditures has found that universal

programs are more sustainable in democracies, even if they are more expensive than policies targeted solely on the poor or other 'marginal' groups.").

66. *See, e.g.*, Forde-Mazrui, *supra* note 14, at 2374 ("[R]ace-neutral classifications avoid the necessity of choosing which racial groups to include in a preferential program..."). *But see* Deborah C. Malamud, *Class-Based Affirmative Action: Lessons and Caveats*, 74 Tex. L. Rev. 1847, 1894–98 (1996) (describing the potentially prohibitive challenge of developing a reliable and robust index of socioeconomic inequality).

67. *See* Tseming Yang, *Choice and Fraud in Racial Identification: The Dilemma of Policing Race in Affirmative Action, the Census, and a Color-Blind Society*, 11 Mich. J. Race & L. 367, 407 (2006) ("Anecdotal evidence suggests that many race remedial and race-conscious programs operate on the basis of self-identification.").

68. *See, e.g.*, Marvin Lim, *Percent Plans:A "Workable, Race-Neutral Alternative" to Affirmative Action?*, 39 J.C. & U.L. 127, 149–57 (2013) (predicting that percentage plans can only guarantee geographic diversity); H. Lee Sarokin et al., *Has Affirmative Action Been Negated? A Closer Look at Public Employment*, 37 San Diego L. Rev. 575, 619 (2000) ("[R]ace-neutral means...may not work fast enough to significantly impact the lingering effects of discrimination."); Tung Yin, *A Carbolic Smoke Ball for the Nineties: Class-Based Affirmative Action*, 31 Loy. L.A. L. Rev. 213, 215, 229–36 (1997) (reviewing Richard R. Kahlenberg, The Remedy: Class, Race, and Affirmative Action (1996)) (arguing that "class-based affirmative action will not benefit racial minorities to any significant degree" because whites outnumber and outperform blacks at every income level); Roland G. Fryer Jr. et al., *Color-Blind Affirmative Action* 16 (Nat'l Bureau of Econ. Research, Working Paper No. 10103, 2003), *available at* http://papers.ssrn.com/sol3/papers.cfm?abstract_id=468790 ("The short-run efficiency losses...from using race-neutral policies to pursue race-conscious goals are four to five times greater than the losses incurred when the same goals are pursued via explicitly race-sighted policies.").

69. *See, e.g.*, Ayres, *supra* note 43, at 1784 ("Extending affirmative action subsidies to non-victim whites produces less-tailored, overinclusive programs.").

70. *See* Fitzpatrick, *Can Michigan Universities Use Proxies?*, *supra* note 34, at 279–80 (surveying Michigan's universities' responses to the affirmative action ban). According to the Census Bureau, Detroit is 89.5 percent black or Hispanic. *See Detroit Quick Facts*, U.S. Census Bureau (Jan. 7, 2014), http://quickfacts.census.gov/qfd/states/26/2622000.html.

71. *See, e.g.,* Caroline Hoxby & Christopher Avery, Brookings Inst., The Missing "One-Offs": The Hidden Supply of High-Achieving, Low-Income Students, at 18 (2013) (finding that only 15.4 percent of low-income high achievers are underrepresented minorities), *available at* http://www.brookings.edu/~/media/projects/bpea/spring%202013/2013a_hoxby.pdf; *cf.* Angel L. Harris & Marta Tienda, *Hispanics in Higher Education and the Texas Top 10% Law*, 4 Race & Soc. Probs. 57, 58–59 (2012) (concluding that the Texas Ten Percent Plan helps white students more than Hispanic students).

72. *See* Fitzpatrick, *Texas Ten Percent Plan*, *supra* note 2, at 336 ("The Ten Percent Plan subordinated [traditional admissions criteria] to high school class rank by admitting roughly half of each freshman class to the University of Texas at Austin solely on the basis of class rank.").

73. *See* Tex. Educ. Code Ann. § 51.803(a-1).

74. *See* Ayres, *supra* note 43, at 1793–96 ("Preferring race-neutral subsidies because the racial motivation is less visible violates Kant's publicity principle that '[a]ll actions relating to the right of other human beings are wrong if their maxim is incompatible with publicity.'"); Ilya Somin, *Why* Fisher v. Texas *Might Turn Out to Be a Pyrrhic Victory for Opponents of Racial Preferences*, VOLOKH CONSPIRACY, Feb. 29, 2012, 3:16 PM, http://www.volokh.com/2012/02/29/ why-fisher-v-texas-might-turn-out-to-be-a-pyrrhic-victory-for-opponents-of-racial-preferences/ ("If the Supreme Court strikes down explicit race-based affirmative action but endorses the ten percent plan...[r]acial preferences [would] become less transparent and more costly to society...").

75. *See, e.g.*, Gratz v. Bollinger, 539 U.S. 244, 303 n.10 (2003) (Ginsburg, J., dissenting) ("Percentage plans depend for their effectiveness on continued racial segregation at the secondary school level..."); Michelle Adams, *The Last Wave of Affirmative Action*, 1998 WIS. L. REV. 1395, 1411–12 (1998) (arguing that race-neutral affirmative action "discount[s]...that minorities have less access to the 'opportunity structure'"); Jennifer L. Shea, *Percentage Plans: An Inadequate Substitute for Affirmative Action in Higher Education Admissions*, 78 IND. L.J. 587, 614–15 (2003) ("[P]ercentage plans further exploit these inequities by relying upon them to ensure diversity on college campuses while doing nothing to improve the quality of secondary education."); Girardeau A. Spann, *Doctrinal Dilemma*, 158 U. PA. L. REV. PENNUMBRA 129, 137–38 (2009) ("[R]ace neutrality...is simply a technique for freezing an unequal baseline in the distribution of societal resources that was produced by a long history of discrimination."); Girardeau A. Spann, *The Dark Side of* Grutter, 21 CONST. COMMENT. 221, 222 (2004) (positing that the "aspirational baseline of race neutrality...is a hopelessly artificial concept in a Nation like ours"). *See generally* Marta Tienda & Sunny Xinchun Niu, *Capitalizing on Segregation, Pretending Neutrality: College Admissions and the Texas Top 10% Law*, 8 AM. L. & ECON. REV. 312 (2006).

76. *See* Daria Roithmayr, *Barriers to Entry: A Market Lock-in Model of Discrimination*, 86 VA. L. REV. 727, 734 (2000) (arguing that the current distribution in educational achievement is "the product of earlier anticompetitive behavior by whites" and that race-neutral measures are insufficient to overcome this locked-in racial preference).

77. *See, e.g.*, BRUCE P. LAPENSON, AFFIRMATIVE ACTION AND THE MEANINGS OF MERIT 42–44 (2009) (reviewing literature showing that affirmative action dispels stereotypes and provides minority role models without corresponding damage to "blacks' self-respect and self-worth"); Erwin Chemerinsky, *Making Sense of the Affirmative Action Debate*, 22 OHIO N.U. L. REV. 1159, 1160–67 (1996) (explaining the goals of affirmative action to include remedying past discrimination, increasing minority political power, providing role models, and enhancing wealth and services provided in minority communities). *See generally* WILLIAM G. BOWEN & DEREK BOK, THE SHAPE OF THE RIVER: LONG-TERM CONSEQUENCES OF CONSIDERING RACE IN COLLEGE AND UNIVERSITY ADMISSIONS (2000).

78. In 2012, more than half of all Americans living below the poverty line were black (27.2 percent) or Hispanic (25.6 percent), whereas these groups comprised less than a third of the general population (12.9 percent and 17.1 percent, respectively). CARMEN DENAVAS-WALT ET AL., U.S. CENSUS BUREAU, DEPARTMENT OF COMMERCE, INCOME, POVERTY, AND HEALTH INSURANCE IN THE UNITED STATES: 2012, at 14 (Sept. 2013), *available at* http://www.census.gov/prod/2013pubs/p60-245.pdf.

8

The Judicial Repeal of the Johnson/ Kennedy Administration's "Signature" Achievement

Judge Nancy Gertner (Ret.)

The Civil Rights Act of 1964,[1] which has been called "one of the most significant legislative achievements in American history,"[2] has been gutted. Responsibility lies not with Congress or an executive agency. For the most part, it lies with the third branch—the judges of the United States courts. Federal judges, from the trial courts to the Supreme Court, from one end of the country to the other, of all political affiliations, have interpreted the Act virtually, although not entirely, out of existence.

Many scholars have identified the pattern: plaintiffs in discrimination cases tend to lose on summary judgment, more so than any other party in any other type of case.[3] If they manage to get to trial and, significantly, if they convince a jury of their claims, their damage verdicts run a substantial risk of being reduced by trial judges and their counsel's fees slashed—again more than the verdicts or fees of plaintiffs and plaintiffs' counsel in any other category of case.[4] On appeal, the story is even more striking: while summary judgment dismissals are overwhelmingly affirmed by appellate courts, even successful plaintiffs' verdicts are reversed more than jury verdicts in other types of cases. One has to pause at that statistic: it is one thing to reject a claim without giving plaintiffs the benefit of a jury determination. That result is troubling enough since discrimination cases involve the quintessential jury question—namely, "What is the defendant's *motive* in dismissing the plaintiff?" "Was the plaintiff denied a promotion 'because of' discriminatory animus?" But it is even more troubling to reject a jury's determination of damages, or worse, overturn its verdicts in a system that ostensibly values that decision maker above all.

It is not simply *that* plaintiffs lose but *how* they lose—in decision after decision that effectively legitimize discriminatory practices and behavior that would have been abhorrent when the Civil Rights Act was passed.[5] In 1976, Fourteenth Amendment equal protection analysis was narrowed when the Supreme Court restricted it to intentional discrimination in *Washington v. Davis*.[6] More recent cases suggest the willingness of the Court to apply the same or similar analysis to statutory discrimination claims.[7] But even as limited to intentional discrimination, current case law is extraordinary. It appears to restrict or even reject a range of entirely competent evidence from which discriminatory intent may be inferred. It is ironic: just as the social-psychological literature identifies implicit race and gender bias—in organizational settings, in apparently neutral evaluative processes, and among decision makers of different races or gender—federal discrimination law moves in the opposite direction, trivializing even evidence of explicit bias.[8]

I want to understand why. First, is it a matter of ideology, in the sense of a system of beliefs fueled more and more by a more conservative Supreme Court and adopted by judges across the country? Do they simply accept the view that we are in a postracial, postgendered society? As others and I have described elsewhere, it is as if the bench is saying in its opinions: "Discrimination is over. The market is bias-free. The law's job is to find the truly aberrant actor who just didn't get the memo."[9] The phenomenon that is discrimination can be reduced to a simple paradigm—explicitly discriminatory policies and rogue individuals. If a case does not precisely reflect those facts—and few do in the twenty-first century—they are without merit. Surely some judges, if pressed, would agree with this position, but does it adequately explain the antidiscrimination plaintiff bias across the country, at all levels—not just the *fact* of dismissal but the content of the decisions?

Second, is that ideological perspective in fact *true*? Are most federal cases frivolous, with dismissals roughly commensurate with the numbers of insubstantial cases? According to this view, employment discrimination law has worked. The market is bias-free, leaving litigation only for the extreme, the explicit, the aberrant cases. Judges are appropriately reflecting the progress that discrimination law has reaped. Statistics about wage disparity as between women and men, blacks and whites, about the persistence of the "glass ceiling" for women, about maternal discrimination, to name a few, however, suggest otherwise.[10]

Or, third, is it simply selection bias in the federal courts? Have decades of narrowing discrimination law, rightly or wrongly, led plaintiffs' counsel to choose state court over federal court, thereby skewing the federal pool. Recent studies suggest that federal discrimination filings have declined; plaintiffs are literally voting with their feet to more responsive state courts.[11] The cases remaining in federal court, according to this view, are the least substantial ones. And even among the cases in federal court, so the argument goes, the better cases are settled, leaving the weak ones at the mercy of summary judgment motions and vulnerable verdicts.[12] Does selection bias fully account for the numbers of cases dismissed, verdicts slashed or overturned, or the reasoning of the decisions in these cases? The substantive law of discrimination—the fact patterns described in the case law and then rejected by the courts as not amounting to discrimination even on a forgiving summary judgment standard—suggest that something else is afoot. At least as described in opinions, many of these cases are not insubstantial for summary judgment purposes. They include, for example, narratives of the use of the N-word, of sexual harassment, and even of stalking the plaintiff, which a jury might accept or reject or might consider pervasive or minor—yet they are rejected by the courts.

Fourth, or is it, as some federal judges have insisted, that the national patterns reflect nothing more than their fealty to the law? They maintain that the Supreme Court law has set a high bar for discrimination cases and that they are just following that lead. With respect to procedural rules, like the standards governing statutes of limitations[13] or perfecting a claim of sexual harassment—that is, whether the plaintiff complained to her supervisor about coworker sexual harassment,[14] they have no discretion. But the procedural rules that bar the plaintiff's claims do not fully account for the national trends—for courts making subjective judgments rejecting sexual harassment claims because they are not sufficiently "severe and pervasive" to be actionable[15] or dismissing racist or sexist remarks as merely "stray remarks," not reflecting bias. No binding precedent obliges a court to minimize such testimony, to "slice and dice" evidence of discrimination, and reject it out of hand.[16]

Finally, are there pressures (or implicit biases) that cut across political affiliation and ideology to affect judges in their subjective judgments about what is or is not discrimination? One pressure is what Professor Judith Resnik has called the pressure to be a managerial judge,[17] which has created a culture in which judges are encouraged to resolve cases without trials, in which formal opinions are to be avoided, and in which the high transaction costs associated with civil litigation may well be seen as more important than redressing inequality.[18] Put otherwise, under this approach to judging, courts are more concerned with false positives, the wrongful accusation of bias, and the litigation costs accompanying it than false negatives, an unredressed claim of discrimination. They are bound to err on the side of rejecting discrimination claims in making the judgments the law encourages them to make.

These patterns are then reflected in, and exacerbated by, a phenomenon I have described recently as "Losers' Rules":

> Asymmetric decisionmaking—where judges are encouraged to write detailed decisions when *granting* summary judgment and not to write when *denying* it—fundamentally changes the lens through which employment cases are viewed, in two respects. First, it encourages judges to see employment discrimination cases as trivial or frivolous, as decision after decision details why the plaintiff loses. And second, it leads to the development of decision heuristics—the Losers' Rules—that serve to justify prodefendant outcomes over and over again, exacerbating the one-sided development of the law.[19]

The law of discrimination becomes more and more skewed now not only with procedural rules defining when to sue or to whom to complain but also with substantive standards that judges simply choose to apply in ways that disadvantage plaintiffs—doctrines like "stray remarks" that excuse explicitly biased statements, "honest belief" in which the court characterizes the employer as being in good faith, or judicial determinations of when harassment is "severe and pervasive."[20] Make no mistake: the law does not mandate any particular outcome in these cases; no judge is required by law to trivialize a racist or sexist remark or excuse a pattern of conduct. But judges regularly do so, dismissing cases or reversing verdicts, and if they do, they are likely to be affirmed by the appellate courts.

If there are nonideological pressures that are skewing the outcomes in these cases, how can they be changed? The disclosure of discrimination patterns on a judge-by-judge basis might well make a difference. Take sentencing, for example. Federal judges strongly resisted the disclosure of the sentencing practices and patterns of individual judges for fear it would unleash a political backlash. The Sentencing Commission kept that information, but only provided it when an individual judge requested it. Indeed, so resistant were the judges to this disclosure that they specifically negotiated with the Sentencing Commission to protect their confidentiality.[21] Looking at civil rights cases, would it matter to a judge if statistics showed that he or she dismissed 100 percent of discrimination cases in a two-year period as one study in the Northern District of Atlanta has shown? Or are the discrimination enforcement system so skewed and judicial attitudes so ossified that we should entirely reconsider the private attorneys' general/private lawyer model of enforcement? Should we look again at an adjudicative agency, like the National Labor Relations Board, or an executive agency with more robust powers than the Equal Employment Opportunity Commission? All that is clear is that the current system—private lawsuits, judicial enforcement—is flawed.[22]

I first outline the data on employment discrimination cases and the decisional law. I then consider the various explanations for the patterns. And finally, I provide tentative suggestions for change.

I. The Data

A. A First Step: The Georgia Study

The Atlanta firm of Barrett and Farahany commissioned a study of the 2011 and 2012 employment summary judgment orders from the Northern District of Georgia, the results of which surely bear careful consideration.[23] Of the 181 cases (in which the plaintiff had counsel), the Court dismissed 95 percent of them at least in part and 81 percent of the cases in full. Racial hostile work environment claims were dismissed 100 percent of the time. Data broken down per judge revealed that some judges had dismissed all discrimination cases in the two-year period and that when the magistrate judge recommended dismissal, the judge followed 100 percent of the time. Data also suggested that white plaintiffs alleging reverse discrimination had a better success rate than black plaintiffs alleging discrimination.

To be sure, there are limitations to the study; it is only a starting point. The sample was restricted to a two-year period with a relatively small number of cases per judge; plainly, a longer-term view is necessary to identify meaningful trends. Researchers need to understand the entire pool of cases, which cases are settled, and why. Are the better cases appropriately resolved by competent counsel, or are they settled "in the shadow of"[24] a substantive law so skewed against the plaintiff or judicial hostility so clear that any settlement is better than nothing. The bottom line, however, is that while the numbers for dismissals in the Northern District of Georgia were higher than the national figure—namely, 80 to 100 percent dismissal rates, there is no question that it reflects that national pattern; study after study has shown high dismissal rates across the country on summary judgment.[25]

Research is presently underway to look at these issues across a number of courts. We plan to evaluate six courts as Farahany and McAdams have done in the Northern District of Georgia—namely, Alabama, other districts in Georgia, and states without analogous state discrimination laws. In addition, we will examine Florida as well as Massachusetts, Chicago, and San Francisco. We plan to ask the questions described at the outset of this chapter: Are there some district courts that, like the Northern District of Georgia, have a 100 percent dismissal rate? Is this true for just some district court judges? Are there regional differences? Do caseload differences account for these discrepancies as between district courts or regions? Does the fact that there is no analogous state discrimination law affect these numbers? What if data suggest that precisely in the regions of the country with a history of discrimination, the rate of dismissal is the highest and the language of the decisions most forgiving? What if those patterns are reinforced by decisions of the circuit courts?

B. Reversals of Trial Verdicts

Some may say that without carefully evaluating the merits of both the dismissed cases and the settled cases, there is no way of knowing if the patterns described previously are fair—whether the decisional law is appropriately weeding out the insubstantial cases and resolving the substantial ones. As I describe in the following paragraphs, an analysis of summary judgment opinions surely raises concerns that this is not so—that district court judges are drawing lines about what is or is not discrimination in a way that fundamentally changes, even skews, the substantive law of discrimination against plaintiffs and that substantive law plainly has an impact on settlement practices.

But even if one assumed that settlements and summary judgment dismissals appropriately separate the meritorious cases from those that are not, the statistics about the judicial treatment of plaintiffs' verdicts suggest a different pattern. More discrimination plaintiffs' verdicts are reduced on remittitur than verdicts in any other case.[26] And this pattern continues at the appellate level. Favorable plaintiffs' verdicts fare worse on appeal than do other litigants' verdicts, as a 2009 study by Professor Kevin Clermont and Stewart J. Schwab found.[27] The 2009 Clermont and Schwab study of reversal rates reports that "[a]ll the circuits showed...anti-plaintiff effect," and grouped the Tenth, Fourth, Second, Ninth, Eleventh, and First as having approximately the same difference between defendant and plaintiff dismissals.[28]

That jury *losses* are affirmed on appeal is not unusual since appellate courts will defer to verdicts. More stunning is the fact that appellate courts reverse plaintiffs' trial *wins* far more often than defendants' wins.[29]

C. Legitimizing Discrimination

While the rate of losses is important, more critical is the *way* plaintiffs lose. By making pronouncements about what is or is not discrimination or a hostile work environment, courts have legitimized practices that would have horrified the early supporters of the Act.[30]

Consider cases involving the N-word. In *Johnson v. Freese*, a case in the Northern District of Georgia, the Todds, African Americans, sued the Whortons, white owners of the nightclub where they worked, for creating a racially hostile environment.[31] The defendants moved for summary judgment, which the judge granted on these facts (considered in the light most favorable to the plaintiffs): at manager meetings, Mr. Whorton directed the N-word to the plaintiffs, despite their objections. He called a staff meeting to talk about his use of the N-word, explaining that he was too old to change and inviting anyone who did not like it to quit. He made comments like the following:

> What do your people want? When this was a white club, my customers used ashtrays. Ever since the n——s have been in the club, the cigarettes have been put out on the floor. The difference between blacks and n——s is that n——s put their cigarettes out on the floor.
> And, do "days like this [make] you wish you people had stayed in chains?" He asked someone wearing a shirt with a monkey on it "Are the Obama shirts in?" and complained to Mr. Todd that he could not trust African Americans.[32]

But to the Georgia federal court, this was not enough. No reasonable jury, the court held, could find a racially hostile environment. In language that the supporters of the Civil Rights Act would have found shocking, the court added that while "the facts simply show that the Whortons are racist, bigoted, and/or offensive people," not all "profane or [racist] language or conduct will constitute discrimination in the terms and conditions of employment." None of these incidents went beyond the "ordinary tribulations of the workplace." The decision, a Final Report and Recommendation of a United States Magistrate Judge, was adopted by the trial judge without comment, no objections having been filed.

To be sure, there were weaknesses in the case. The setting was a black nightclub with white owners, and although the court is not explicit, the

clear message is that the owner's language could not have been particularly shocking to the employees given the language of the patrons.
Still, the plaintiff could argue that this language coming from a white
boss had a different resonance to the African American workers than
the conversation among their peers. Or they could argue that given the
numbers of comments and their content (about slavery, about President
Obama), the boss simply went too far. Summary judgment, after all, is
not supposed to be about screening the cases that—in the judgment of
the bench—are likely to lose before a jury, making credibility determinations, weighing the evidence in the favor of one party or another. It is
a lower bar—determining that there is *no issue* of *material* fact, after considering all of the inferences in favor of the nonmoving party.[33]

Racist comments in the workplace had been "ordinary" and "com-
monplace" when the Civil Rights Act was enacted. Even if social norms
have changed in the decades since 1964 and even if language that courts
once found wholly unacceptable has become regular currency, the law
was amended in 1991 so that those judgments would be made by a jury.[34]
A representative jury was supposed to consider the facts, not a judge
whose last employment in the private sector may have been decades
ago, who—looking at the federal bench's composition—was likely to be
white, male, a former partner in a big law firm, or a former prosecutor.

In fact, in several cases in which allegations of the use of the N-word
went to a jury, juries found for the plaintiffs. For example, a Buffalo,
New York, jury awarded $25 million in damages to a steelworker whose
coworkers repeatedly called him the N-word and other slurs. The jury
heard evidence that the employer took remedial action, such as suspending offending employees without pay, installing lights in the park-
ing lot after a toy monkey was hung from a noose beside the plaintiff's
car, and assigning an escort to protect the plaintiff. Nonetheless, the
jury elected to award over $25 million in damages against the corporate
defendant, including $24 million in punitive damages.[35] In 2011, a jury
awarded $300,000 to a personal trainer who claimed that other train-
ers at a sports club had repeatedly called him the N-word.[36] The sports
club presented evidence that it dismissed the plaintiff because the plaintiff had used similar racially offensive language against Latino trainers.
Nonetheless, the jury awarded $300,000 on the hostile work environ-
ment claim. More recently, juries in hostile work environment cases
have awarded damages in the amount of $300,000 in *Bennett v Riceland
Foods, Inc.*,[37] more than $300,000 in *Weatherly v. Alabama State Univer-
sity*,[38] and $250,000 in *Johnson v. Strive East Harlem Employment Group*.[39]

By comparison, judges on summary judgment often hold that racial
epithets did not establish a hostile work environment by characterizing

these statements as "stray remarks" or concluding that even repeated use of epithets is not evident of "pervasive and severe" racial hostility. The *Whorton* decision, despite its unique facts and unique weaknesses, is not an aberration.[40] For example, in *Oladokun v. Grafton School, Inc.*,[41] the District of Maryland granted summary judgment for the defendant on claims of discrimination against African American employees at a private school for intellectually and physically disabled children. A supervisor had told the plaintiff that "I will get you n——s out of here" and had also said to a child client at the facility: "Don't slobber on me, slobber on that black n—— over there," referring to a coworker. The court held that these remarks were not "not sufficient to satisfy the hostile work environment test" because they were "not sufficiently pervasive."[42] Similarly, in *Dotson v. Gulf*,[43] a supervisor told a longshoreman employee in response to his leaving early for a lunch break: "You n——s just don't want to do right." The supervisor fired the employee immediately on the spot, though the employee was later allowed to return to work. The court held that these "incidents of a patently offensive slur, while rude and upsetting, are insufficient to affect the terms or condition of Dotson's employment."[44]

It is not just racist speech that is acceptable; so is sexist speech. The "stray remarks" doctrine trivializes sexist (and racist) comments. They are "not evidence of discrimination" at all. Or they are the speaker's "personal opinion"—as if that eliminates their poisonous impact on the work environment. Or they were not so "severe and pervasive" as to create a hostile environment. What kinds of sexist remarks are dismissed in this fashion? Where plaintiff's supervisor repeatedly referred to her as, among other things, a "dumb sh-t," "whore," "stupid bitch," and "hooker," the district court dismissed the case because the conduct was a type of "general vulgarity that [the law] does not regulate."[45] No hostile work environment was found in the case of a female deputy sheriff even though, over a four-year period, the supervisor made inappropriate comments, invited her to sit on his lap, and kissed her on the buttocks (which the court describes as "allegedly kissing her on her clothed backside").[46] Nor did an employee whose manager "touched her inappropriately on two occasions by putting his hand on her crotch" confront "an objectively or subjectively hostile work environment" because there was evidence that she herself had "used vulgar, profane language, told dirty jokes, graphically discussed her sex life and engaged in sexual banter."[47] Nor was it a hostile environment in the case of a male coworker who called the plaintiff "a *perra*, a Mexican expletive that translates to 'bitch,' 'whore,' or 'person paid for sex,' called her stupid, grabbed his crotch, made an offensive hand gesture that signified the 'f word,' and spit on the floor."[48]

II. Tentative Conclusions

What is the reason for these patterns? First, as others have written, is the problem ideological, the overarching sense that we are at the dawn of the postracial, postsexist society? The 1964 Civil Rights Act, while once important, is seen as unnecessary today.[49] Surely, this is the message communicated by the Supreme Court. Have explicit cues from a more conservative Supreme Court (*Ledbetter*, etc.) percolated down to the lower federal courts?[50]

Second, is it true that the law has done its job? The market works and only needs to be tweaked at the margins, as the case law suggests. The data are otherwise: "Every measure of economic success reveals significant racial inequality in the U.S. labor market."[51] Data from 2009 show that people of color make up 34 percent of the private sector workforce but hold only 11 percent of senior or executive positions.[52] In 2010, the median weekly earnings for full-time employees varied significantly by race and gender: for white men, the average was $850 a week, while for black men, that number dropped to $633 and Hispanic men still lower, at $560 per week.[53] Social psychologists, organizational behavioralists, and labor economists suggest that the reason for these patterns is that racial and gender bias—implicit or explicit—continues to play a significant role in the allocation of jobs.

Is it selection bias—not merely the impact of the settled cases on the pool of federal cases but also the impact of a more welcoming state court on federal filings?[54] This would mean that the cases in federal court are in fact the less substantial ones, brought by counsel who did not realize how inhospitable the federal courts were. Whatever the validity of state law, it would not apply to the Northern District of Georgia, for example, or in Alabama, the other state that does not have a parallel state statute prohibiting discrimination by race.[55] Second, it does not necessarily account for the facts as reflected in the decisional law—allegations of explicit bias rejected by the courts or minimized in the outcome.

Is it simply a reflection of more unforgiving rules from the Supreme Court—quite apart from the ideology these rules reflect? When the Northern District of Georgia article was published, one reaction was that these cases are dismissed because judges are simply "following the law."[56] That may well be true, when certain of the Supreme Court's procedural rules are considered—rules on statutes of limitations in employment cases and rules requiring reporting harassment to a supervisor before an employer can be held accountable for coworker harassment.[57] If there are no allegations within the limitations period or the appropriate person did not receive the complaint, the judge has no discretion but to dismiss the case.[58] During a yearly panel held by the United States District Court, a lawyer asked the judges: "Why are the federal courts so hostile to discrimination claims?" The judges insisted there was no hostility and that they were just obliged to follow the law.

But the "law" does not compel the granting of summary judgment in many of the reported cases involving "stray remarks" or the standard for "severe and pervasive" harassment. Employment discrimination cases are factually complex, deal with state-of-mind issues to be proved circumstantially, and are rarely uncontested. The summary judgment legal standards are general, rarely mandating a certain result, as would a claim involving a statute of limitations issue or the failure to exhaust administrative remedies. Judges are deciding these cases not because they are forced to do so by precedent but because they choose to do so.

Is the explanation in the pressures on the bench that cross ideological lines, pressures that have fundamentally changed the federal bench and have had a singular impact on employment cases? Professor Judith Resnik has described the problem of managerial justice.[59] Judges are encouraged to resolve cases without trials, to use alternative dispute resolution, or to mediate the cases themselves. Formal written opinions are to be avoided; the author was told during a judicial training session that "if you wrote an opinion," you failed. If you could not settle the case, write your decision as a margin note on the pleading or announce it in open court—more efficient but hardly creating a meaningful precedent.

These pressures are mirrored in, and exacerbated by, a phenomenon I have described recently as "Losers' Rules." When the defendant successfully moves for summary judgment in a discrimination case, the case is over, and under Rule 56 of the Federal Rules of Civil Procedure, the judge must "state on the record the reasons for granting or denying the motion," which means writing a decision. But when the plaintiff wins on summary judgment, the judge writes a single word of endorsement—"denied"—and the case moves on to trial. At the same time, plaintiffs rarely move for summary judgment. They bear the burden of proving all elements of the claim, particularly intent. Thus, to avoid summary judgment, a defendant need only show favorable contested facts in one element of a plaintiff's claim.

The result of this practice—written decisions only when plaintiffs lose—is the evolution of a one-sided body of law. Decision after decision grants summary judgment to the defendant or, more recently, on the heels of the Supreme Court's decisions in *Bell Atlantic Corp. v. Twombly*[60] and *Ashcroft v. Iqbal*,[61] dismisses the complaint.[62] After the district court has described why the plaintiff loses, the case may or may not be appealed.

The structure of summary judgment opinions distorts the precedents further. Precedents are necessarily created in the decisional law when judges make rules "mappings from the facts of the case...to outcomes."[63] In writing summary judgment decisions, the court is obliged to summarize the record and, in particular, to highlight the plaintiff's allegations and grant inferences in favor of the plaintiff. As a result, when the court characterizes these facts as insubstantial stray remarks or not part of a "severe and pervasive" pattern of discrimination, as an example, it affects more than the outcome in the case. The decision communicates an atmosphere of impunity. Discriminatory behavior will be tolerated and will not expose the employer to risk. Over and over, the opinions suggest, we will give the benefit of the doubt to the perpetrator, excusing his conduct while subjecting the victim's perceptions to a higher standard.[64]

The effects of Losers' Rules are exacerbated on appeal. While the standard of review of summary judgment orders is de novo, appellate courts rarely reverse district courts' decisions. Employers prevailed in 86 percent of published appellate opinions.[65] Indeed, they are even more affected by the pool of cases they see—the selection effects of reviewing appeal after appeal of plaintiffs' losses. They do not see the strong cases that settle. They may see appeals from successful plaintiffs' verdicts, but those appeals are few and far between. In fact, their approach to appeals from successful verdicts may well reflect skewing I have described. A higher percentage of plaintiffs' verdicts are set aside, as Clermont and Schwab found.

To be sure, what this analysis does not include are the cases that are settled. Arguably, the better cases are removed from the pool by lawyers who have effected settlements for their clients. Marc Galanter has argued that because employers are "repeat players" while individual plaintiffs are not, the repeat players have every incentive to settle the strong cases and litigate the weak ones.[66] But settlements take place in the "shadow of the law."[67] It is not unreasonable to assume that the evolving case law figures into the settlement practices.

Losers' Rules explain not simply outcomes but also the reasoning of the cases. If case after case recites the facts that do not amount to discrimination, decision makers have a hard time imagining the facts that comprise discrimination. And they believe most of the claims are trivial. That attitude further distorts the evolution of substantive legal standards. Decision heuristics evolve, the kind of decision heuristics described above. As I described, "[c]ourts create decision heuristics to enable them to quickly dispose of complex cases. They then write decisions employing the heuristics and publish their opinions. In short order, other courts rely on the heuristics, which become precedent, and the process is repeated over and over again."[68] Obviously, discrimination heuristics, like all heuristic devices, run the risk of false positives and false negatives.

When courts believe that most employment claims are meritless, as the judges do over time, they will be much more concerned with false positives—the wrongful accusation of discrimination—than false negatives, when discrimination is unredressed. Indeed, that concern—wrongful accusations of discrimination and the transaction costs associated with it—has come to dominate the decisional law of civil procedure.[69]

III. Conclusion

Judges have created decisional rules that have gutted Title VII, rules not required by the statute (which, after all, says very little), its legislative history, or the purposes of the Act. The patterns have garnered little attention from the popular media, and, as a consequence, there is little or no pressure for legislative change. Since Title VII was the very model of civil rights law reform legislation, it is critical to show how has this has happened and, more important, why? How should these patterns be addressed? Should Title VII be amended yet again, creating a more explicit statute—more code-like than a statement of principles—that would cabin judicial discretion? Or would regular monitoring of judicial decisions—like the Northern District of Georgia study—make a difference, letting the judge know the patterns—if not overt the hostility—their decisions reflect? Or should we consider a new enforcement structure beyond the private attorneys' general model of Title VII? For example, would a more robust EEOC, with the power to adjudicate disputes and not just the power to investigate, make a difference, staffed by hearing officers who can envision what discrimination looks like, in contrast to judges who plainly do not? One thing is clear: these patterns and the attitudes they reflect should not be ignored.

About the Author

United States District Court Judge, District of Massachusetts (retired); senior lecturer on law, Harvard Law School.

Notes

1. 42 U.S.C. § 2000e (2006). I deal here only with Title VII of the Civil Rights Act of 1964, which prohibits discrimination based on race, sex, religion, and national origin.

2. U.S. SENATE, LANDMARK LEGISLATION: THE CIVIL RIGHTS ACT OF 1964, http://www.senate.gov/artandhistory/history/common/generic/ CivilRightsAct1964.htm (last visited Feb. 21, 2014).

3. *See* Kevin M. Clermont & Stewart J. Schwab, *Employment Discrimination Plaintiffs in Federal Court: From Bad to Worse?*, 3 HARV. L. & POL'Y REV. 103, 108–14 (2009).

4. Alan David Freeman, *Legitimizing Racial Discrimination through Antidiscrimination Law: A Critical Review of Supreme Court Doctrine*, 62 MINN. L. REV. 1049 (1978) [hereinafter Freeman, *Legitimizing Racial Discrimination*].

5. *Id.* at 1054–56 (1978) (identifying the extent to which discrimination law, by focusing only on the individual perpetrator, legitimized all other discrimination and failed to focus on discrimination's root causes).

6. 426 U.S. 229 (1976).

7. *See, e.g.*, Ricci v. DeStefano, 557 U.S. 557 (2009) (curtailing disparate impact in Title VII litigation).

8. *See, e.g.*, John T. Jost et al., *The Existence of Implicit Bias is Beyond Reasonable Doubt: A Refutation of Ideological and Methodological Objections and Executive Summary of Ten Studies that No Manager Should Ignore*, 29 RES. ORGANIZATIONAL BEHAV. 39 (2009) (discussing ten recent studies demonstrating implicit bias with respect to race, ethnicity gender, and social class). For discussions of the failure of the courts to address these issues, see Samuel R. Bagenstos, *Implicit Bias, "Science," and Antidiscrimination Law*, 1 HARV. L. & POL'Y REV. 477 (2007); Samuel R. Bagenstos, *The Structural Turn and the Limits of Antidiscrimination Law*, 94 CALIF. L. REV. 1 (2006); and Linda Hamilton Krieger & Susan T. Fiske, *Behavioral Realism in Employment Discrimination Law: Implicit Bias and Disparate Treatment*, 94 CALIF. L. REV. 997 (2006).

9. Nancy Gertner, *Losers' Rules*, 122 YALE L. J. ONLINE 109, 111 (2012), http://yalelawjournal.org/images/pdfs/1111.pdf.

10. MAJORITY STAFF OF JOINT ECON. COMM., 111TH CONG., WOMEN AND THE ECONOMY 2010: 25 YEARS OF PROGRESS BUT CHALLENGES REMAIN 1 (2010) (noting that in 2009 the weekly wage for a woman was, on average, 80 percent of a comparable man's wages); Nathan Berg & Donald Lien, *Measuring the Effect of Sexual Orientation on Income: Evidence of Discrimination?*, 20 CONTEMP. ECON. POL'Y 394, 394 (2002) (examining wages from 1991 to 1996 and finding that nonheterosexual men earn 22 percent less than heterosexual men, while nonheterosexual women earn 30 percent more than heterosexual women); Marianne Bertrand & Sendhil Mullainathan, *Are Emily and Greg More Employable Than Lakisha and Jamal? A Field Experiment on Labor Market Discrimination*, 94 AM. ECON. REV. 991, 1006–07 (2004); Catherine Rampell, *Older Workers without Jobs Face Longest Time out of Work*, N.Y. TIMES: ECONOMIX (May 6, 2011, 6:27 PM), http://economix.blogs.nytimes.com/ 2011/05/06/older-workers-without-jobs-face-longest-time-out-of-work (observing that the typical duration of unemployment increases with age and is at an all-time high for those over 55).

11. Clermont & Schwab, *supra* note 3, at 104.

12. Mark Galanter, *Why the "Haves" Come Out Ahead: Speculations on the Limits of Legal Change*, 9 LAW & SOC'Y REV. 95, 101 (1974) (describing selection bias in general with respect to settled cases).

13. *See, e.g.*, Ledbetter v. Goodyear Tire & Rubber Co., Inc., 550 U.S. 618, 642–43 (2007) (holding that the statute of limitations for disparate pay claims extends expires 180 days after the moment of a discriminatory pay decision, even if the disparate pay continues beyond the limitations period), *superseded by statute*, Ledbetter Fair Pay Act, Pub. L. No. 111-2, 123 Stat. 5 (2009).

14. *See* Burlington Indus., Inc. v. Ellerth, 524 U.S. 742, 765 (1998) (holding that an employer could avoid liability for workplace sexual harassment if "the plaintiff employee unreasonably failed to take advantage of any preventive or corrective opportunities provided by the employer").

15. *See* Harris v. Forklift Sys., Inc., 510 U.S. 17, 21 (1993) ("Conduct that is not severe or pervasive enough to create an objectively hostile or abusive work environment—an environment that a reasonable person would find hostile or abusive—is beyond Title VII's purview.").

16. Michael J. Zimmer, *Slicing & Dicing of Individual Disparate Treatment Law*, 61 LA. L. REV. 577 (2001) (discussing the different ways that a judge will "slice and dice" the evidence to fit into the existing summary judgment standards).

17. Judith Resnik, *Managerial Judges*, 96 HARV. L. REV. 376, 379, 407 (1982).

18. Elizabeth M. Schneider & Hon. Nancy Gertner, *"Only Procedural": Thoughts on the Substantive Law Dimensions of Preliminary Procedural Decisions in Employment Discrimination Cases*, 57 N.Y.L. SCH. L. REV. 767, 777–78 (2013).

19. Gertner, *supra* note 9, at 110.

20. For example, in *Shorter v. ICG Holdings, Inc.*, 188 F.3d 1204 (10th Cir. 1999), the court held that a supervisor calling the plaintiff an "incompetent nigger" was not actionable because this derogatory slur was a "personal opinion" and therefore not "directly" related to the supervisor's motive for firing the plaintiff. *Id.* at 1206–08. The court approvingly cited *Heim v. Utah*, 8 F.3d 1541, 1546–47 (10th Cir. 1993), in which the defendant had remarked, "I hate having fucking women in the office," and the court concluded that this comment was not direct evidence of discriminatory intent. To be sure, both cases predated *Desert Palace, Inc. v. Costa*, 539 U.S. 90, 92 (2003), which held that the plaintiff need not provide direct evidence of discrimination to shift the burden of proof to the employer in mixed-motive cases. But the conclusions that these statements did not directly reflect discriminatory animus are still extraordinary. Similarly, courts rely on the doctrine of "honest belief" to dismiss discrimination claims when an employer claims that a wrong discriminatory belief was "honest" or "honestly described," even if this explanation appears pretextual or baseless. *See* Gustovich v. AT&T Commc'ns, Inc., 972 F.2d 845, 848–49 (7th Cir. 1992); *see also* Kariotis v. Navistar Int'l Transp. Corp., 131 F.3d 672, 677 (7th Cir. 1997) (stating that the issue is not whether "the employer's reasons for a decision [were] '*right*' but whether the employer's description of its reasons [was] *honest*'" (quoting *Gustovich*, 972 F.2d at 848)); Fischbach v. D.C. Dep't of Corr., 86 F.3d 1180, 1183 (D.C. Cir. 1996) (stating that courts review not "'the correctness or desirability of [the] reasons offered...[but] whether the employer honestly believes in the reasons it offers.'" (alterations in original) (quoting McCoy v. WGN Cont'l Broad. Co., 957 F.2d 368, 373 (7th Cir. 1992)).

21. Hon. Nancy Gertner, *Judge Identifiers, TRAC, and a Perfect World*, 25 FED. SENT'G REP. 46, 47 (2012).

22. There of course may be other explanations for these skews in the case law, such as uneven access to quality representation, which in turn prevents judges from citing and expanding on good case law. *See* Scott A. Moss, *Bad Briefs, Bad Law, Bad Markets: Documenting the Poor Quality of Plaintiffs' Briefs, Its Impact on the Law, and the Market Failure It Reflects*, 63 EMORY L.J. 59 (2013).

23. Amanda Farahany & Tanya McAdams, *Analysis of Employment Discrimination Claims for Cases in Which an Order Was Issued on Defendant's Motion for Summary Judgment in 2011 and 2012 in the U.S. District Court for the Northern District of Georgia*, BENCHMARK LITIGATION (Sept. 16, 2013), http://ssrn.com/abstract=2326697.

24. Catherine Albiston, *The Rule of Law and the Litigation Process: The Paradox of Losing by Winning*, 33 LAW & SOC'Y REV. 869, 872 (1999).

25. For example, a 2007 report by the Federal Judicial Center noted that 74 to 77 percent of all summary judgment motions ruled on in employment discrimination cases in 2006 were granted in whole or in part—more than for any other type of case studied. *See* Memorandum from Joe Cecil & George Cort, Fed. Judicial Ctr., to Judge Michael Baylson, U.S. Dist. Court for the E. Dist. of Pa. 7 tbl.4 (Nov. 2, 2007), https://bulk.resource.org/courts.gov/fjc/insumjre.pdf.

26. *See* Suja A. Thomas, *Re-Examining the Constitutionality of Remittitur under the Seventh Amendment*, 64 OHIO ST. L.J. 731, 746 (2003).

27. Clermont & Schwab, *supra* note 3, at 108–14.

28. *Id.* at 119 n.47.

29. Between 1988 and 2004, appellate courts reversed over 40 percent of trial judgments for plaintiffs in employment discrimination cases, compared to under 9 percent of defendant wins. *Id.* at 110 tbl.2 (2009)

30. Freeman, *Legitimizing Racial Discrimination, supra* note 4, at 1054–55.

31. *See* Final Report and Recommendation, Johnson v. Freese, No. 1:10-CV-481 (N.D. Ga. June 17, 2011), *available at* http://media.cmgdigital.com/shared/news/documents/2013/10/17/Johnson_v._Freese.pdf.

32. *Id.* at 7.

33. Celotex Corp. v. Catrett, 477 U.S. 317, 322 (1986) (quoting FED. R. CIV. P. 56(c)).

34. Civil Rights Act of 1991, Pub. L. No. 102-166.

35. Turley v. ISG Lackawanna, Inc., 06-CV-794S, 2013 WL 150382 (W.D.N.Y. Jan. 14, 2013). The district court upheld the $1 million compensatory damages award but ordered a new trial on punitive damages unless the plaintiff accepted reduced punitive damages of $5 million.

36. Abel v. Town Sports Int'l, LLC, 09 Civ. 10388(DF), 2012 WL 6720919 (S.D.N.Y. Dec. 18, 2012).

37. 721 F.3d 546, 551 (8th Cir. 2013).

38. 728 F.3d 1263, 1269 (11th Cir. 2013). Significantly, the same judge who had adopted the magistrate's finding in the *Todd v. Freese* case (when no objections had been filed) was also on the panel in the *Alabama State* case, affirming a jury verdict in the plaintiffs' favor.

39. No. 12-4460 (S.D.N.Y. Jan. 15, 2014) (order on defendant motion for new trial). The trial court later ordered a new trial unless the plaintiff agreed to a reduced

compensatory award of $128,109.59, *see id.* at *1, but also awarded $173,252.73 in attorneys' fees and costs. *See* Johnson v. Strive East Harlem Employment Group, No. 12-4460 (S.D.N.Y. Jan. 28, 2014) (order on attorneys' fees and costs).

40. *See, e.g.,* Nicholson v. City of Clarksville, Tenn., 530 F. App'x 434 (6th Cir. 2013) ("isolated incidents of general profanity" and a "few incidents involving racial slurs" are not sufficient to amount to the kind of "extreme" conduct that changes the terms and conditions of employment). *Cf.* Ayissi-Etoh v. Fannie Mae, 712 F.3d 572 (D.C. Cir. 2013) (majority reverses summary judgment on claims including use of the N-word).

41. 182 F. Supp. 2d 483 (D. Md. 2002).

42. *Id.* at 493–94.

43. Civ. A. H-05-0106, 2006 WL 44071, at *13 (S.D. Tex. Jan. 9, 2006).

44. *Id.* at *13. *See also* Alexander v. Opelika City Sch., 352 F. App'x 390 (11th Cir. 2009) (affirming lower court grant of summary judgment as not sufficiently "severe and pervasive," where African American employee could "only" recall eight instances over the course of two years where he was called "boy" by his supervisor); Ash v. Tyson Foods, Inc., 190 F. App'x 924, 926 (11th Cir. 2006) (plant manager's use of the word "boy" to refer to African American employees not sufficient to provide a basis for a jury to determine pretext where they were, in part, "stray remarks"); White v. Geico, 457 F. App'x 374 (5th Cir. 2012) (no hostile work environment despite references to a client as "n word," characterizing one of the offices as a "ghetto" or "FEMA trailer," and reference to another African American worker as someone who "always wanted to be a white female"); Williams v. CSX Transp. Co., 643 F.3d 502 (6th Cir. 2011) (affirming the dismissal on summary judgment where plaintiff, the only African American and the only woman in a four-person office, was told by two supervisors "that she was a Democrat only because she was a black woman," that this country should get rid of Al Sharpton and Jesse Jackson because without those two "monkeys," this country would be "a whole lot better," that she should return to school because she would not have to pay for her education as a single black mother, and that an unmarried woman cannot "have the love of God in their heart[s]").

45. Shorter v. ICG Holdings, Inc., 188 F.3d 1204 (10th Cir. 1999) (addressing the question of whether derogatory comments were direct evidence of discrimination rather than circumstantial evidence), *abrogated by* Desert Palace, Inc. v. Costa, 539 U.S. 90, 98–102 (2003).

46. Final Report and Recommendation at 27–30, Lindquist v. Fulton County, No. 1:09-cv-01102-RWS (N.D. Ga. Nov. 23, 2010) (No. 88).

47. Derrico v. Pinkerton's, Inc., No. 97 C 5851, 1999 WL 311757, at *4 (N.D. Ill. May 12, 1999).

48. Colon v. Envtl. Tech., Inc., 184 F. Supp. 2d 1210, 1214 (M.D. Fla. 2001).

49. *See generally* Trina Jones, *Anti-Discrimination Law in Peril?*, 75 Mo. L. Rev. 423 (2010); *see also* Helen Norton, *The Supreme Court's Post-Racial Turn Towards a Zero-Sum Understanding of Equality*, 52 Wm. & Mary L. Rev. 197, 223–28 (2010).

50. *See* Simon Lazarus, *Stripping the Gears of National Government: Justice Stevens's Stand Against Judicial Subversion of Progressive Laws and Lawmaking*, 106 Nw. U. L. Rev. 769, 771 (2012) (describing the techniques employed by the Supreme Court to dismantle progressive laws since Justice Rehnquist in 1986).

51. Bertrand & Mullainathan, *supra* note 10.

52. EQUAL EMPLOYMENT OPPORTUNITY COMM'N, 2009 JOB PATTERNS FOR MINORITIES AND WOMEN IN PRIVATE INDUSTRY, *available at* http://www1.eeoc.gov/eeoc/statistics/employment/jobpat-eeo1/2009/ (last visited Feb. 21, 2014).

53. U.S. DEP'T OF LABOR, MEDIAN WEEKLY EARNINGS OF FULL-TIME WAGE AND SALARY WORKERS BY SEX, RACE, AND HISPANIC OR LATINO ETHNICITY, 1979–2010 ANNUAL AVERAGES 41 (2011), *available at* http://www.bls.gov/cps/cpsrace2010.pdf.

54. Clermont & Schwab, *supra* note 3, at 107–08.

55. *SeeState Laws on Employment-Related Discrimination*, NATIONAL CONFERENCE OF STATE LEGISLATURES, (Jan. 2014), http://www.ncsl.org/research/labor-and-employment/discrimination-employment.aspx. Although all fifty states have some laws prohibiting employment-related discrimination, the Alabama statute does not cover discrimination based on race, and the Georgia statute only covers discrimination based on race in state employment.

56. *See* Richard Kopf, *Kopf's Additional Response to Ms. Farahany*, HERCULES AND THE UMPIRE (Nov. 1, 2013), http://herculesandtheumpire.com/2013/11/01/kopfs-additional-response-to-ms-farahany/ ("The fact is that the law on summary judgment motions in employment cases favors the granting of summary judgment motions in a high percentage of the cases and, not surprisingly, that is what you see happening in the Northern District of Georgia and with 'yours truly' too.").

57. *See supra* note 14.

58. Of course, these restrictions could be equitably waived when a plaintiff shows that there is a "continuing violation," a doctrine that judges have chosen to apply using the same approaches as their approaches to the merits. *See, e.g.*, Cordero-Suarez v. Rodriguez, 689 F.3d 77, 83 (1st Cir. 2012) (The court finds no continuing violation because there is no "anchoring" violation in the limitations period, discounting evidence that after the plaintiff was transferred because of harassment, the harasser continued to visit her new officer, that she continued to complain of the harassment, and that he threatened her by saying that he "would not rest until [she] was permanently dismissed from the Treasury Department.").

59. Resnik, *supra* note 17, at 379, 407.

60. 550 U.S. 544 (2007).

61. 556 U.S. 662 (2009).

62. While the full effect of *Iqbal* and *Twombly* is not yet clear, it has increased the numbers of dismissals in general and likely will do so with respect to discrimination cases. Kiel Robert Brennan-Marquez, *The Epistemology of* Twombly *and* Iqbal, 26 REGENT U. L. REV. 167, 169 n.9 (2013).

63. Gillian K. Hadfield, *Bias in the Evolution of Legal Rules*, 80 GEO. L.J. 583, 587 (1992).

64. Freeman, *Legitimizing Racial Discrimination*, *supra* note 4, at 1056.

65. Albiston, *supra* note 24, at 885.

66. Galanter, *supra* note 12, at 101. Indeed, Galanter concluded that strategic settlement practices produce judicial interpretation of rights that favor the repeat players' interests, an effect that is exacerbated by Losers' Rules. *Id.* at 102.

67. Robert H. Mnookin & Lewis Kornhauser, *Bargaining in the Shadow of the Law: The Case of Divorce*, 88 YALE L.J. 950 (1979).

68. Gertner, *supra* note 9, at 116.

69. In *Twombly*, the Supreme Court concluded that a deficient complaint should "be exposed at the point of minimum expenditure of time and money by the parties and the court." Bell Atlantic Corp. v. Twombly, 550 U.S. 544, 558 (2007) (citation omitted) (internal quotation marks omitted). The Court in *Iqbal* reiterated this theme that "[l]itigation...exacts heavy costs in terms of efficiency and expenditure of valuable time and resources" and reasoned that a higher pleading standard was necessary to prevent groundless claims from imposing costs on defendants. *See* 556 U.S. 662, 685 (2009).

9

Taking Seriously Title VII's "Floor, Not a Ceiling" Invitation

Craig Gurian

Introduction

For more than twenty-five years, it has been the practice of federal and state judges around the country to throw victims of workplace sexual harassment out of court because they have not been harassed "enough." The practice is a function of the judicially created doctrine that only "severe or pervasive" harassment is actionable under Title VII.[1] In New York City, however, the "severe or pervasive" requirement has been rejected by virtue of case law[2] that developed in the wake of the 2005 Local Civil Rights Restoration Act,[3] a law designed to "underscore that the provisions of New York City's Human Rights Law are to be construed independently from similar or identical provisions of New York state or federal statutes"[4] in a manner to accomplish the City Human Rights Law's "uniquely broad and remedial purposes."[5]

This sea change in harassment doctrine is but one of several ways in which the Restoration Act has brought new strength to local antidiscrimination provisions. Some of the Act's changes sought to vindicate provisions in the comprehensive 1991 amendments to the City Human Rights Law[6] that judges had long ignored; others responded to Supreme Court decisions hostile to civil rights enforcement that were issued subsequent

to the 1991 Amendments. All reflected an intent to develop a distinct —
and distinctly plaintiff-friendly — jurisprudence.

While the animating perspective of the Restoration Act is a striking
departure from the norm, the authority of New York City (or any other
jurisdiction) to forge protections stronger than those provided by federal
law was not new. From the beginning, Title VII disclaimed preemption,
stating that:

> Nothing in this subchapter shall be deemed to exempt or relieve any person
> from any liability, duty, penalty, or punishment provided by any present *or
> future* law of any State or political subdivision of a State, other than any such
> law which purports to require or permit the doing of any act which would
> be an unlawful employment practice under this subchapter.[7]

Title VII was designed to act as a floor below which civil rights protections could not fall, not a ceiling above which those protections could
not rise. Over the decades, this invitation has been used most commonly
in states and cities around the country to extend employment discrimination protection to workplaces with fewer than the fifteen-employee
minimum required by Title VII. It has also been used to provide compensatory damages beyond those available under Title VII and to prohibit on a state level additional types of discrimination (such as discrimination on the basis of sexual orientation) beyond that proscribed by Title
VII.

It is less common, however, for a state or local law to be designed
specifically to fight back against the narrowing contours of Title VII,
especially by means of directing state and federal judges to modify their
approach to statutory interpretation. Under the Restoration Act, judges
are required to probe critically the question of whether interpretations
of federal or state civil rights law provisions genuinely further the purposes of their local counterpart.[8]

This chapter identifies the approach and architecture of the Restoration Act and explains the ways in which the local law's attempt both to
protect the New York City Human Rights Law against erosion and to
expand the law's reach still further has begun to have an impact. It then
illustrates several additional barriers to strong coverage and enforcement that could be tackled if civil rights advocates focused more of
their efforts on the state and local level. Finally, it offers some observations about what is needed to deepen the Restoration Act's early success
locally and to spur efforts like the Restoration Act in jurisdictions across
the country.

I. Why Was a Restoration Act Needed?

The short answer to the question "Why was the Restoration Act needed?" is that courts were not paying heed to either the language of the 1991 Amendments or the City Council's intention in passing them.[9]

Every change made by the 1991 Amendments — whether dealing with protected classes, vicarious liability, theories of discrimination, or damages — had been aimed at augmenting coverage, limiting evasion, or otherwise strengthening enforcement. And the City Council's intentions had been unmistakable. As then-Mayor David Dinkins stated when he signed the bill, the intention was that "judges interpreting the City's Human Rights Law...take seriously the requirement that this law be liberally and independently construed."[10] Nevertheless, prior to the Restoration Act, courts were almost universally refusing to do more than engage in what I have elsewhere dubbed "rote parallelism,"[11] simply assuming that the result under the City Human Rights Law would be identical to that under federal civil rights law or New York State human rights law.[12]

A year before the enactment of the Restoration Act, New York's highest court made plain just how completely it was prepared to ignore the plea for independent interpretation that underlay the 1991 Amendments and the liberal construction requirement of the City Human Rights Law as it existed in 2004.

The case before the court related to the private right of action that had been created by the 1991 Amendments — one that provided for uncapped compensatory damages, uncapped punitive damages, and attorneys' fees.[13] Only that kind of regime allows for the possibility of making a victim whole, punishing a wrongdoer sufficiently to create an actual deterrent, and providing a sufficient incentive for private counsel to undertake representation. At the time that the 1991 Amendments were enacted, the Supreme Court had not yet cut back on the availability of fees in cases that resulted in the award of only nominal damages, and prevailing doctrine in the Second Circuit was that attorney's fees were available in such cases.[14] The federal limitation on those fees occurred a year later, in 1992, when the Supreme Court issued its 5–4 decision in *Farrar v. Hobby* and concluded that, where nominal damages are awarded, "the only reasonable fee is usually no fee at all."[15]

In *McGrath v. Toys "R" Us, Inc.*,[16] New York's court of appeals acknowledged that the City Council, in passing the 1991 Amendments, could not have had the intention to apply the yet-to-be-decided *Farrar* doctrine but the court imported *Farrar* nonetheless because of the court's "general practice of interpreting comparable civil rights statutes consistently," asserting that policies underlying the City Human Rights Law were "identical" to those underlying federal civil rights statutes.[17] In importing *Farrar*, *McGrath* engaged in no analysis of whether *Farrar* had actually been consistent with either federal or local civil rights policy.

Perhaps most important, *McGrath* stated that the City Council's failure to take affirmative action to rebut *Farrar* represented the Council's implicit ratification of the importation of *Farrar*.[18] As such, the protections of the City Human Rights Law would be subject to being automatically ratcheted down every time federal or state law was narrowed by judicial construction.

Along with this sort of refusal to construe the City Human Rights Law liberally, the period between 1991 and 2005 was characterized by the wholesale failure of courts to recognize even basic modifications in statutory text. For example, it had already been illegal under the City Human Rights Law "to retaliate...against any person," but the 1991 Amendments modified that language so that it became illegal "to retaliate *in any manner*...against any person."[19] Surely, the addition of the phrase "in any manner" was intended to mean and do *something*. Year after year, however, judges failed to appreciate that the legislative change had any meaning at all.

In a particularly acute example of judicial lawlessness in 2003, a state appellate court, in the case of *Priore v. New York Yankees*,[20] conjured up an entirely imaginary legislative history to get around the fact that the 1991 Amendments had made individuals liable for their own discriminatory workplace conduct. The City Council had taken the phrase common to Title VII and many state employment discrimination statutes that it was unlawful for "an employer" to engage in certain actions and broadened that to make it unlawful for an employer "or an employee or agent thereof" to engage in those actions.[21] Mayor Dinkins had explained that the 1991 Amendments had taken "the fundamental step of making all people legally responsible for their own discriminatory conduct."[22]

Several courts had started to abide by the plain language (and plain import) of this change.[23] All of this, however, was of no moment to an intermediate appeals court panel that simply did not want to believe that anyone would (or should) want to impose individual liability. To achieve its ends, the *Priore* court claimed that the added language ("or an employee or agent thereof") was simply reflecting language that had been in a New York State Human Rights Law provision dealing with licensing agencies. This was a complete fabrication. The section of the City Human Rights Law at issue did not have anything to do with licensing agencies (a different section was created for that), and the added language about employees or agents was language *not* found in the State Human Rights Law.[24] But the *Priore* court needed to create a "context."

Priore rejected the idea that the change in statutory language "automatically open[s] the door to an entirely new category of defendants"stating that the new language had to be read "in context" (that is, the context it had invented) and asserted that there was "no indication in the local ordinance, explicit or implicit, that it was intended to offer a separate right of action against any and all fellow employees based on their independent and unsanctioned contribution to a hostile environment."[25] For the First Department of the Appellate Division (covering cases arising in Manhattan and the Bronx), individual liability was dead.[26]

For civil rights advocates, City Human Rights Law development since 1991 — or, more precisely, the *lack* of independent development since 1991 — meant that the City Council had to send a message to the judiciary that could not be ignored.

II. A Hybrid Approach

In some respects, the Restoration Act proceeded conventionally, making specific changes to specific provisions. Thus, for example, protection against discrimination based on domestic partner status was added to the City Human Rights Law's proscriptions against discrimination in employment, housing, and public accommodations,[27] and the maximum civil penalty available in a case brought administratively was raised to $250,000.[28]

The Restoration Act also went back to try to give force to the City Council's intent to have a broad antiretaliation provision (the "in any manner" language having been insufficient to do the job). It explicitly set forth in the antiretaliation provision the proviso that retaliation complained of need not result in either an "ultimate action" or a "materially adverse change" in terms and conditions in order to be actionable.[29]

In a direct rejection of the Supreme Court's dramatic narrowing of the circumstances in which attorney's fees would be available in cases where the litigation had acted as a catalyst for a change in policy on the part of the defendant,[30] the Restoration Act explicitly declared that fees would be available in such cases.[31]

But the most important contribution of the Restoration Act was the undoing of rote parallelism. Section 1 of the Restoration Act stated that the "sense of the Council that New York City's Human Rights Law has been construed too narrowly to ensure protection of the civil rights of all persons covered by the law."[32] It went on to "underscore" that the law's provisions "are to be construed independently from similar or identical provisions of New York state or federal statutes."[33] And, in contrast to *McGrath's* downward ratchet effect, it created an upward ratchet effect: interpretations of the provisions of counterpart federal and state statutes could be viewed "as a floor below which the City's Human Rights law cannot fall, rather than a ceiling above which the local law cannot rise."[34]

Section 1 of the Restoration Act set forth its purpose; section 7 did the work of amending the construction section of the law. Rather than requiring liberal construction to accomplish the "purposes" of the law, the Council now required such construction to accomplish the "uniquely broad and remedial" purposes.[35] Any decision that asserted that the purposes of the City Human Rights Law were equivalent to the purposes of counterpart statutes simply could not be harmonized with this language.

For good measure, the Council added additional language making clear that the liberal construction was required "regardless of whether federal or New York State civil and human rights laws, including those laws with provisions comparably-worded to provisions of this title, have been so construed."[36]

Each element of the Restoration Act's legislative history focused on the importance of independent construction[37] and included this statement made on the floor of the City Council at the meeting at which it voted on the Restoration Act:

> Insisting that our local law be interpreted broadly and independently will safeguard New Yorkers at a time when federal and state civil rights protections are in jeopardy.
>
> There are many illustrations of cases, like *Levin* on marital status, *Priore*[,] *McGrath* and *Forrest* that have either failed to interpret the City Human Rights Law to fulfill its uniquely broad purposes, ignore the text of specific provisions of the law, or both.
>
> With [the Restoration Act], these cases and others like them will no longer hinder the vindication of our civil rights.[38]

The question, of course, was whether the courts would heed what the Council had done.

III. The Courts Take Notice

In civil rights, as in other areas of life, victory can be fleeting. Nevertheless, the tentative judgment to be made ten years after the passage of the Restoration Act is that an independent City Human Rights Law jurisprudence has indeed begun to take shape, despite some continuing resistance in the judiciary. Much work remains for the law to fulfill its intended potential. Ironically, the greatest need is for civil rights advocates to be willing to take up more wholeheartedly what the Restoration

Act has offered through its enhanced liberal construction provision and articulate in specific cases the specific reasoning that demands specific departures from existing legal doctrine.

Williams v. New York City Housing Authority,[39] decided early in 2009, was not the first case to take account of the passage of the Restoration Act, but it represented the most thorough and important exposition by any court, let alone an appellate court, of the Act's intent, and demonstrated how the process of independent construction should proceed. The overview from *Williams*:

> [T]he Restoration Act notified courts that (a) they had to be aware that some provisions of the City HRL were textually distinct from its State and federal counterparts, (b) *all* provisions of the City HRL required independent construction to accomplish the law's uniquely broad purposes, and (c) cases that had failed to respect these differences were being legislatively overruled.[40]

Reiterating that the Restoration Act had legislatively overruled *McGrath*, the court was careful to point out that the City Council envisioned the enhancement of the liberal construction provision as "obviating the need for wholesale textual revision of the myriad specific substantive provisions of the law."[41] The court continued:

> While the specific *topical* provisions changed by the Restoration Act give unmistakable *illustrations* of the Council's focus on broadening coverage, § 8-130's specific *construction* provision required a "process of reflection and reconsideration" that was intended to allow independent development of the local law "in all its dimensions..."[42]

The legislative history provided guidance from multiple sources as to how courts should proceed to perform the task of deciding how provisions of the City Human Rights Law should be interpreted. *All* of the legislative history pointed in the direction of choosing an interpretation that maximized coverage;[43] a related lesson was that it would be a mistake to imagine that, for City Human Rights Law purposes, the upper bound of coverage was in any way a "settled" question. Every provision of the law had to be examined in light of the direction to courts to interpret to fulfill the law's uniquely broad and remedial purpose. Consistent with this, the court cited with approval the argument I had made in *Return to Eyes on the Prize*:

> [A]reas of law that have been settled by virtue of interpretations of federal or State law "will now be reopened for argument and analysis...As such, advocates will be able to argue afresh (or for the first time) a wide range of issues under the City's Human Rights Law..."[44]

One of the specific issues before the *Williams* court was the scope of protection against sexual harassment, and the court demonstrated how the process of "reflection and reconsideration" was supposed to be handled. In the first instance, the court, true to the language of the statute before it, treated sexual harassment as one type of gender-based discrimination in terms and conditions of employment. It then asked "what constitutes inferior terms and conditions based on gender."[45]

Rather than taking the Supreme Court's approach as the necessary answer for City Human Rights Law purposes, *Williams* stated that the "severe or pervasive" doctrine — characterized by the Supreme Court as a "middle path"[46]— hindered those local objectives: "Experience has shown," the court stated, "that there is a wide spectrum of harassment cases falling between 'severe or pervasive' on the one hand and a 'merely' offensive utterance on the other."[47] Keeping with its focus on whether conduct created inferior terms and conditions, the court got to the heart of workplace reality: "It would be difficult to find a worker who viewed a job where she knew she would have to cope with unwanted gender-based conduct (except what is severe or pervasive) as equivalent to one free of unwanted gender-based conduct."[48]

Williams concluded that the purposes of the City Human Rights Law could best be achieved by allowing severity and pervasiveness to go only to the question of damages, not to the question of underlying liability. In the ordinary case, therefore, liability is established when there is evidence of an employee being treated less well than others because of gender.[49] To "narrowly target" concerns about "truly insubstantial" cases, the court recognized an affirmative defense "whereby defendants can still avoid liability if they provide that the conduct complained of consists of nothing more than what a reasonable victim of discrimination would consider 'petty slights and trivial inconveniences.'"[50]

Critically, *Williams* illuminated how to tie an enhanced liberal construction analysis to each of the guideposts for interpretation set out in the Committee Report that accompanied the Restoration Act:

1. "Traditional methods and principles of law enforcement ought to be applied in the civil rights context."[51] Determining liability by the existence of differential treatment without regard to severity or pervasiveness creates a greater incentive for employers to "create workplaces that have zero tolerance," and, the court ruled, maximizing deterrence is a traditional method and principle of law enforcement.[52]

2. "Discrimination should not play a role in decisions made by employers, landlords, and providers of public accommodation."

The court stated that the "severe or pervasive" rule was inconsistent with the "play no role" principle because it means that "discrimination is allowed to play *some significant role* in the workplace."[53]

3. "Victims of discrimination suffer serious injuries for which they ought to receive full compensation." The court stated that "severe or pervasiveness" contradicts the principle that discrimination injuries, without limitation, are serious injuries.[54] It should be immediately apparent that this kind of analysis is transferable to virtually any issue that would arise in the antidiscrimination law context.

New York's Court of Appeals has grappled with the Restoration Act in two important cases. The first was principally a matter of accepting that the City Human Rights Law meant what it appeared to say. In *Zakrzewska v. New School*,[55] the court took up the question of whether the *Faragher-Ellerth* affirmative defense to employer liability[56] applied to employment discrimination claims in the City Human Rights Law context.[57]

The court concluded it did not: section 8-107(13) of the City Human Rights Law "creates an interrelated set of provisions to govern an employer's liability for an employee's discriminatory conduct in the workplace" that "simply doesn't match up with the *Faragher-Ellerth* defense."[58] For acts of those employees or agents who exercised managerial or supervisory authority, the section provides for strict liability,[59] and the existence of antidiscrimination policies and procedures can only go to the question of whether civil penalties (administratively) or punitive damages (in a civil action) should be mitigated.[60] The court ruled that the statutory text made clear that the provision, contrary to the employer's position, applied to *all* supervisors and managers,[61] a very different result from the Supreme Court's decision finding that an employee is a "supervisor" for Title VII vicarious liability purposes only if he or she is empowered by the employer to take tangible employment actions against the victim.[62] It is only in the context of actions of nonsupervisory coworkers that the existence of antidiscrimination policies and procedures can be considered in determining liability (and only where the conduct is *not known* to managers or supervisors but *should have been*).[63]

Beyond the implications of confirming strict liability, the case represented a belated recognition that the 1991 Amendments (of which the addition of section 8-107(13) was part) constituted a "major overhaul" of the City Human Rights Law.[64]

New School, of course, represented a circumstance where all the court needed to do was resist the *Priore*-like urge to say, "The statute just *can't* mean what it says." An even more important pronouncement from the New York Court of Appeals came the following year (2011) in a retaliation case brought against the New York City Police Department.[65] The question at issue was the meaning of the term "oppose"—that is, whether action was taken against the plaintiff for having opposed discrimination. One can say with absolute certainty that, in the pre–Restoration Act, *McGrath* era, the court would simply have looked at how Title VII and the State Human Rights Law had interpreted the term.

Now, however, a unanimous court recognized that the enhanced liberal construction provision introduced by the Restoration Act required it to construe the language of the retaliation provision, *"like other provisions of the City's Human Rights law,* broadly in favor of discrimination plaintiffs, to the extent that such a construction is reasonably possible."[66]

This holding could not be more significant. First, the requirement of enhanced liberal construction analysis is applicable not only to the term "oppose" but also to *every* term found in the law.[67] Second, it captures the intent of the Restoration Act to require judges to weigh alternative interpretations, not to pick the road that has previously been most frequently selected. Third, it dispenses with the prominent notion in Title VII jurisprudence that Congress wanted Title VII tailored to "balance" the interests of employers. Fourth, courts are *not* asked to indulge their own policy preferences in rendering interpretations but rather to adhere to a policy decision already made by the City Council to take the most pro-plaintiff position that is reasonably possible.

In the case at hand, the only evidence that the plaintiff had opposed discrimination was that, at a meeting, she reacted to her supervisor's criticism of her recommendation to transfer a third party into the unit in which she worked by telling the supervisor that the person she had recommended "'was the better candidate for the job'" and that "'[i]f I had to do it all again, I would have recommended [the same person] again.'"[68] This is not the usual basis for a finding that discrimination has been opposed. But the court found: "While [plaintiff] did not say in so many words" that her preferred candidate "was a discrimination victim" on the basis of perceived sexual orientation, "a jury could find that both [the supervisor and plaintiff] knew that he was, and that [plaintiff] made clear her disapproval of that discrimination by communicating to [her supervisor], in substance, that she thought [the supervisor's] treatment of [her candidate] was wrong."[69]

By the time *Albunio* was decided, the Second Circuit Court of Appeals had also, separately, provided direction on the Restoration Act. In *Loef-*

fler v. Staten Island University Hospital,[70] a public accommodations case, the Second Circuit ruled that the Restoration Act "confirm[ed] the legislative intent to abolish 'parallelism' between the City HRL and federal and state anti-discrimination law...."[71] The court aptly described the City Human Rights Law as having a "one-way ratchet" where state and federal enactments serve only as a floor for coverage, not the ceiling.[72] *Weiss v. JPMorgan Chase* is an example of a district court following *Loeffler*'s command.[73] *Weiss* declined to apply the Supreme Court's decision in *Gross v. FBL Financial Services*,[74] the case that had required a showing of but-for causation in age discrimination cases (rejecting what, at least in some circuits, had been the use of mixed-motive analysis). Noting that the City Human Rights Law does not differentiate between age and other types of discrimination claims, the court reasoned that application of *Gross* in an age case would mean that mixed-motive analysis would not be available in any employment discrimination claims, including those involving protected classes where Title VII provides for mixed-motive analysis.[75] Reducing the City Human Rights Law below that Title VII floor was impermissible, the court ruled, also finding that an independent interpretation of the City Human Rights Law allowing liability where protected class basis was "a motivating factor" was consistent with the law's text.[76]

In sum, the application of the Restoration Act has generated a strong body of basic case law on which to build.

IV. Unfinished Business and Attempts at Sabotage

In many respects, though, the Restoration Act's work has just begun. I am not aware, for example, of any case that has specifically recognized that *Priore*'s excision-by-fiat of individual liability has been legislatively overruled.[77] And another element of *Williams*, that which rejected the Supreme Court's limitations on continuing violation doctrine for City Human Rights Law purposes,[78] has only, to my knowledge, been applied by one federal court.[79] More broadly, large areas of the law simply have not been subject to any reexamination yet.

The most troubling developments in the last few years are circumstances where courts have not very subtly attempted to evade the requirements of the Restoration Act. Two areas have stood out: the treatment of sexual harassment claims and the attempt to wall off "procedural" matters from enhanced liberal construction analysis.

Wilson v. N.Y.P. Holdings, Inc.[80] is a 2009 case out of the Southern District of New York that came to be cited repeatedly.[81] What did the court treat as no more than "petty slights and trivial inconveniences" (the

Williams affirmative defense)? Comments that included "training females is like 'training dogs'" and "women need to be horsewhipped."[82] Among the cases citing *Wilson* is *Mihalik v. Credit Agricole Cheuvreaux North America, Inc.*,[83] another case where the conduct complained of — which included evidence that the chief executive officer "explicitly told [plaintiff] that male employees should be respected because they were 'male' and thus 'more powerful' than women"[84]— was found to fit the "petty slights and trivial inconveniences" exception.[85] The district court's decision in *Mihalik*, too, was then cited again and again by other judges in the Southern District Court of New York.[86]

That these cases contravene *Williams* (and the intent of the Restoration Act) was first pointed out in a remarkably critical footnote reference in a subsequent case decided by the appellate court that had decided *Williams*. The principal focus of 2011's *Bennett v. Health Management Systems, Inc.*[87] will become clear later in this section, but the court was also concerned that the *Williams* affirmative defense should be treated as the "narrowly drawn affirmative defense" it was intended to be, that it was important for "borderline" fact patterns to be allowed to be heard by a jury, and that it should be understood that one could "easily imagine a single comment that objectifies women being made in circumstances where [the] comment would, for example, signal views about the role of women in the workplace and be actionable."[88] The court skewered *Wilson* and *Mihalik* for, among other things, "ignoring the *Williams* holding," relying on cases that "nominally acknowledge *Williams* but ignore its teaching."[89]

Two years later, the Second Circuit vacated and remanded *Mihalik* and taught many of the lessons of the Restoration Act again. Specifically in the context of sexual harassment, the circuit rejected the district court's analysis for placing "too much emphasis on *Williams*'s recognition that the NYCHRL should not 'operate as a "general civility code,"' and too little emphasis on its exhortation that even 'a single comment' may be actionable in appropriate circumstances."[90] The question remains whether lower courts will take the guidance provided (and the rebukes) seriously.

Another area of resistance or confusion is found in connection with what are sometimes called procedural matters. Is the manner in which the *McDonnell Douglas* framework is or is not used a matter beyond enhanced liberal construction analysis? *Bennett* found that it was not: "the identification of the framework for evaluating the sufficiency of evidence in discrimination cases does not in any way constitute an exception to the Section 8-130 rule that all aspects of the City HRL must be interpreted to accomplish the uniquely broad and remedial purposes of the law," and for the court to "create an exemption from the sweep of the Restoration Act for the most basic provision of the City HRL — that it is unlawful 'to discriminate' — would impermissibly invade the legislative province."[91]

Yet a divided panel of the same appellate court later issued a ruling in *Melman v. Montefiore Medical Center* that states that neither the Restoration Act nor the Committee Report "set forth a new framework for consideration of the sufficiency of proof of claims under the [City Human Rights Law] or indicates that the *McDonnell Douglas* framework is to be discarded."[92] The statement of the *Melman* majority is a non sequitur: that the Restoration Act did not set forth specific modifications to *McDonnell Douglas* does nothing to limit a court's obligation to interpret the term "to discriminate" as it must interpret all other terms of the law: pursuant to the direction of the enhanced liberal construction provision. It is as though that majority could not (or did not wish to) appreciate that *McDonnell Douglas* is not an immutable principle of the physical universe that predates all legislation but rather is a judicial creation designed to give one of many possible answers to how to give shape to identifying what constitutes discrimination.[93]

As a practical matter, *Melman* adhered to *Bennett*. It was, for example, confirmatory of the principle that the City Human Rights Law insists that discrimination "play no role" and that mixed-motive analysis is applicable to every case. *Melman* accepted *Bennett's* direction that summary judgment of City Human Rights Law claims should only be granted if "no jury could find defendant liable under any of the evidentiary routes — *McDonnell Douglas*, mixed motive, 'direct' evidence, or some combination thereof...."[94]

The Second Circuit in *Mihalik* also confirmed that the "no evidentiary route" principle was to be applied in all City Human Rights Law cases,[95] but observed in a footnote that, comparing *Bennett* with *Melman*, "[i]t is unclear whether, and to what extent, the *McDonnell Douglas* burden-shifting analysis has been modified for NYCHRL claims."[96] In fact, however, apart from its opening statement about what the Restoration Act had not explicitly done, *Melman* did not speak to or rebut some of *Bennett's* other conclusions.

For example, *Bennett* had rejected the *Reeves* standard for failing to take sufficiently into account:

(a) The traditional power to be accorded to the inference of wrongdoing that arises from evidence of consciousness of guilt; (b) the importance of deterring a defendant's proffer of false reasons for its conduct; and (c) the impropriety of a court weighing the strength of evidence in the context of a summary judgment motion.[97]

Picking up themes sounded by the dissent in *Hicks*,[98] *Bennett* had ruled that:

> Once there is some evidence that at least one of the reasons proffered by defendant is false, misleading, or incomplete, a host of determinations properly made only by a jury come into play, such as whether a false explanation constitutes evidence of consciousness of guilt, an attempt to cover up the alleged discriminatory conduct, or an improper discriminatory motive co-existing with other legitimate reasons.[99]

Melman simply did not attempt to articulate a substantive objection to *Bennett*'s reasoning or conclusion.

In light of the dictates of *Albunio*, it is difficult to imagine that "to discriminate" will be walled off from enhanced liberal construction analysis. Likewise, it is hard to believe that *Bennett*'s interpretation (picking up on what was, after all, a four-Justice dissent in *Hicks*) will be found not to fall within a "reasonably possible" pro-plaintiff construction of "discrimination," but the ultimate willingness of judges to follow *Albunio* faithfully remains to be determined.

V. How Might Other Jurisdictions Proceed?

I do not suggest that a push for state and local legislation would represent a cure-all for the problems and limitations in federal antidiscrimination law doctrine. First, and most obviously, there are many jurisdictions that would not be politically congenial to such an effort. Second, states and localities are not empowered to undo congressional or Supreme Court efforts to stymie state-based remedies. The Class Action Fairness Act of 2005 (CAFA) is a particularly notable example of the former;[100] the Supreme Court's repeated expansions of the Federal Arbitration Act are examples of the latter.[101]

Nevertheless, the list of nonpreempted problems or limitations in antidiscrimination law doctrine is very long indeed; hence, the list of ways that state or local legislation can be helpful is very long, too. Some are suggested by the kinds of changes made either by the Restoration Act directly or by the 1991 Amendments before them,[102] but there are many more.

From the point of view of the restoration of rights, an examination of closely divided Supreme Court decisions on civil rights is the obvious place to begin. *Bennett* went back to 1993 to draw on the dissent in *St. Mary's Honor Center v. Hicks*,[103] but one could just as easily turn to the Supreme Court's 2013 decisions in which the term "supervisor" was defined extraordinarily narrowly for the purpose of the determination of vicarious liability under Title VII,[104] and plaintiffs were stripped of the ability to use mixed-motive analysis in Title VII retaliation cases.[105]

Another source for potential state or local legislative activity is legislation that has been stymied on the federal level. The Paycheck Fairness Act,[106] for example, has not been able to get through Congress. It would prohibit retaliation against employees for discussing salary information and would require the defense to a claim under the Fair Labor Standards Act that women were being paid less than men to be a bona fide factor other than sex that the employer proves is job related, consistent with business necessity, and "not based upon or derived from a sex-based differential in compensation."[107]

Disparate impact liability is another obvious area for state and local legislating. Although national civil rights organizations have, surprisingly, failed to take advantage of it, the City Human Rights Law's provision is a useful model of a disparate impact scheme more robust than provided by Title VII.[108] First, it applies to all protected classes and to all contexts of discrimination. This avoids (and fixes) the problem that arose in *Smith v. City of Jackson*;[109] it also provides a basis for the building of a broader coalition than is offered when legislation extends protection for a single protected class group.

Second, unlike Title VII (even as amended by the Civil Rights Act of 1991), the City Human Rights Law's disparate impact provision permits a plaintiff to identify a *group* of practices that cause a disparate impact without demonstrating "which specific policies or practices within the group results in such disparate impact" (something that can be devilishly difficult for a plaintiff).[110]

The City Human Rights Law also gives the concept of less discriminatory alternative an important tweak: where the plaintiff "produces substantial evidence that an alternative policy or practice with less disparate impact is available to the covered entity," the burden is on the covered entity to "prove that such alternative policy or practice would not serve the covered entity as well."[111] There is no limitation on compensatory or punitive damages set forth in the City Human Rights Law, either in the context of a civil action generally or for disparate impact claims in particular.[112]

Robust state and local legislation proscribing conduct that causes disparate impact based on protected class status might also help reduce the impact of *Ricci v. DeStefano*,[113] the 2009 case in which the Supreme Court, treating the desire to *avoid* race-based disparate impact to be a species of intentionally discriminatory action, held that an employer's decision not to certify the results of a job examination that it believed had a racially disparate impact was "impermissible under Title VII unless the employer can demonstrate a strong basis in evidence that, had it not taken the action, it would have been liable under the disparate-impact statute."[114] According to *Ricci*, "a threshold showing of a significant statistical disparity...and nothing more" is "far from a strong basis in evidence that the [employer] would have been liable under Title VII had it certified the results."[115]

A state or local law that makes disparate impact claims easier to prove would likewise make it easier for an employer to have the requisite "strong basis in evidence." Such a case would place Title VII's floor-not-a-ceiling provision under a rare highlight: those in favor of broader disparate impact provisions would argue that § 2000e-7 blessed such extensions of civil rights protections; those seeking to limit disparate impact would argue that disparate impact proscription beyond that provided by Title VII represented intentional discrimination that § 2000e-7 does *not* permit a jurisdiction to sanction on the basis that such legislation "purports to require or permit the doing of any act which would be an unlawful employment practice."[116]

One set of important questions that each state or locality has to answer concerns who is proscribed from committing discriminatory conduct, who is responsible for such conduct, and what relationship a person needs to have with a discriminatory actor to be protected. At the most basic level, there is the question of the size at which an employer becomes covered. For example, those working at the smallest employers, while not a large part of the labor force, are not a trivial part, either. In California alone, there are more than 1.2 million people working in firms with fewer than five employees.[117] Should those people not have protection against discrimination? Though California has extended protection against discriminatory harassment to employees of employers of all sizes,[118] employers with fewer than five employees are exempt from the other employment discrimination provisions (like discriminatory hiring and firing).[119]

Decisions as to who is covered are no less subject to political compromise than other legislative matters (perhaps more so, given the hold that the idea of not "burdening" small businesses has on the American imagination). But as a matter of what discrimination law seeks to provide baseline protection against, size should not matter. Another context of discrimination — that which occurs in public accommodations — provides interesting perspective on this question. The value sought to be upheld in state statutes that commonly have a list of places — bowling alleys, ice cream parlors, and so forth — where discrimination shall not be allowed is that *public life* shall not be polluted by bias, regardless of how transitory an interaction might be.[120] One's employment — even at the smallest employer — is no less a matter of public life and should not be polluted by discrimination.

Similarly, a person victimized by bias in connection with work is harmed regardless of whether the victimizer is an "employer" or the victim is an "employee" or "independent contractor." California has taken some steps here, as well, although only in the harassment context. Harassers are individually liable, persons "providing services pursuant to a contract" are protected, and extensive vicarious liability is set forth.[121] Other states have the opportunity to expand coverage as much or more, including, for example, considering whether to protect one business entity from discrimination by another business entity because of the protected class status of the first entity's employers, agents, or associates.[122]

I would be remiss if I did not touch on one additional prospective addition to state and local antidiscrimination statutes. Ever since 1982, standing for fair housing organizations and their testers has existed to the furthest limits of Article III of the Constitution (there are no prudential limitations that may be imposed on standing in this context); if a tester has been deprived of accurate information about housing availabilities, that is one injury; if an organization has "diverted resources" from nontesting activities, that is another injury.[123] Testing is a crucial technique: discrimination often will not announce itself to an individual victim of a practice. Someone looking for a home, for example, knows the listings that he has been shown but very well may not know (even in the Internet age) of listings that he has not been shown.

The utility of testing to ferret out employment discrimination should be obvious. An individual is not going to be able to get a picture of hiring patterns that exist; with the exception of government entities,[124] only an organization that engages in testing can decipher the patterns (whether based on using names on resumes as proxies for race or otherwise).

There has not been very much employment testing, however, subsequent to *Fair Employment Council of Greater Washington, Inc. v. BMC Marketing Corporation* in 1994.[125] There, the D.C. Circuit denied the testers standing altogether, holding that neither Title VII nor § 1981 contemplated such standing.[126] As for the Fair Employment Council, the court reached the same result with respect to § 1981 and only allowed Title VII organizational standing as the organization may have proven injuries (a) flowing from actions taken against bona fide job applicants (not testers); and (b) only insofar as there was "perceptible injury" to the Council's nontesting programs (beyond the decision to shift funding from nontesting to testing activities).[127] The hurdles apparent from the preceding description make it difficult as a practical matter for an organization to achieve standing with respect to its employment discrimination test-ing.[128]

As I have argued elsewhere, fair housing injuries are easily concep-tualized as injuries to the government that warrant the construction of a "private attorney general" provision.[129] Employment discrimina-tion injuries should be accorded the same importance. A straightforward approach would be to specifically grant organizations standing when they are deprived of accurate information about employment openings because of the protected status of their agents (testers) or when they have expended funds that result in the discovery of discrimination (avoiding collateral litigation over whether they have "diverted resources").[130]

All of the foregoing discussion in this section has identified various substantive goals, but there are important strategic and tactical decisions that have to be made when mounting a state or local legislative effort. One is the importance of creating as robust a legislative history as possi-ble.[131] The problem of judge incredulity at efforts to maximize coverage is not going to disappear, and that legislative history can be an important tool to persuade judges that "we really meant it."

The question that will need to be addressed on a case-by-case basis is the extent to which an effort should rely on the adoption of an enhanced liberal construction provision and how much on specific changes to a law's substantive and procedural coverage. To me, an enhanced liberal construction provision that emphasizes independent construction is essential to prevent retrogression. Beyond that, a legislative direction to reexamine how a statute should be interpreted can empower civil rights advocates who are seeking to explain to courts the reasons a variety of provisions deserve a broader reading than they have gotten. This can be especially important in connection with matters that may seem techni-cal to legislators — the ability to inspire a layperson to focus on who bears the burden of persuasion, for example, is not unlimited[132]– but have tremendous practical importance on the ability of victims of dis-crimination to achieve redress.

If specific changes are made, it is crucial that the legislation state explicitly that the changes are *not* intended to ratify prior judicial con-struction of provisions not modified (again highlighting the importance of having an enhanced liberal construction provision to reference).

VI. Closing Observations

The promise of expanding civil rights at the state and local level — or, one might say, the expedience of doing so given the political and judicial environments that currently exist in Washington — is unmistakable.[133]

But efforts to make this sort of change have been sporadic. An informal survey of the websites of several major national civil rights organizations reveals relatively little attention being paid to this area (legislative advocacy with respect to marriage equality is an important exception to the rule). Why isn't more being made of the political space that is available? Especially given the trajectory of marriage equality, why wouldn't the model of seeding an effort in the most congenial jurisdictions first be more generally appealing?

I am acutely aware that civil rights organizations and their allies do not have limitless funds, but my own experience over the last twenty-seven years as a civil rights lawyer tells me that limited funding is only a small part of the problem.

Many of the issues discussed in this chapter — the nuts and bolts of employment discrimination litigation over the decades — are not among the areas seen as either new or exciting (in the academy, among civil rights organizations, and elsewhere) and thus are not ranked as high priorities. Some of the problem comes from a habitual distaste among some civil rights lawyers to have to be litigating in state court instead of federal court. Another element of the problem is the failure to take the time to study and appreciate how much stronger nonfederal causes of action can be.

Many civil rights organizations and advocates focus attention on only one protected class and, sometimes, on one context of discrimination. It should not be difficult to appreciate that a coalition seeking to make changes across the lines of protected class (e.g., those affecting age, gender, race, and disability) and across the lines of discrimination context (e.g., changes affecting both employment and housing) will generally be able to bring more pressure on a legislative body than a single-issue group acting alone. But despite frequent invocations of the importance of coalition, its practice—both in developing multi-issue legislation and in terms of coordinating advocacy—has remained more the exception than the rule.

In my own judgment, the single most important factor is that most attorneys have not considered, or are uncomfortable with, the idea that it is still possible to write on a clean slate. I have seen this reticence hinder the development of the City Human Rights Law as broadly as it otherwise could be,[134] and I think the same reticence does a lot to explain the paucity of similar efforts elsewhere.

It is surely more difficult to accomplish one's goals when judges have to be directed to take an active role in developing a statute to its full potential than when there are judges already inclined to do so. But it is worth thinking about state and local legislation as in many ways being at the earliest stage of development, comparable to where Title VII was immediately after its passage more than fifty years ago. Neither *McDonnell Douglas*, nor *Griggs*, nor any other case came packaged with the law; advocates had to see the potential, imagine the doctrines needed, and marshal evidence and reason to get those doctrines established as best they could. Those kinds of efforts are needed at the state and local levels today.

About the Author

Executive director, Anti-Discrimination Center. Mr. Gurian was the principal drafter of the 2005 New York City Local Civil Rights Restoration Act and a principal drafter of the comprehensive 1991 revisions to the New York City Human Rights Law.

Notes

1. Meritor Sav. Bank, FSB v. Vinson, 477 U.S. 57, 67 (1986). In many cases, judges are more hostile to these claims than the originally articulated doctrine required. *See, e.g.*, Judith J. Johnson, *License to Harass Women: Requiring Hostile Environment Sexual Harassment to Be "Severe or Pervasive" Discriminates Among "Terms and Conditions" of Employment*, 62 MD. L. REV. 85, 87 (2003).

2. Williams v. New York City Hous. Auth., 872 N.Y.S.2d 27 (N.Y. App. Div. 2009).

3. New York City, Local Law No. 85 Int. (2005) [hereinafter Restoration Act]. The Restoration Act is found in N.Y.C. Legislative Annual, at 528–35 (2005), *available at* http://www.antibiaslaw.com/RestorationAct.pdf.

4. Restoration Act § 1.

5. Restoration Act § 7, *amending* N.Y.C. Admin. Code tit. 8, § 8-130. The "City Human Rights Law" composes the entirety of Title 8 of the N.Y.C. Administrative Code.

6. N.Y.C., Local Law No. 39 (1991) [hereinafter 1991 Amendments]. The 1991 Amendments are found in N.Y.C. Legislative Annual 145–81 (1991), *available at* http://www.antibiaslaw.com/LL39.pdf.

7. 42 U.S.C. § 2000e-7 (2013) (emphasis added) (originally enacted as § 708 of the Civil Rights Act of 1964, Pub. L. No. 88-352, 78 Stat. 241 (July 2, 1964)).

8. *Cf.* William J. Brennan Jr., *State Constitutions and the Protection of Individual Rights*, 90 HARV. L. REV. 489, 502 (1977) (warning against the practice of reflexively importing federal constitutional decisions when interpreting counterpart state constitutional guarantees, instead of making sure that the relied-upon decisions are "logically persuasive and well-reasoned" and pay due regard to "the policies underlying specific constitutional guarantees").

9. The long answer, a comprehensive examination of the intent and intended consequences of the Restoration Act written in the immediate aftermath of the passage of the legislation, is found in Craig Gurian, *A Return to Eyes on the Prize:*

Litigating Under the Restored New York City Human Rights Law, 33 FORDHAM URB. L.J. 255 (2006).

10. Remarks by Mayor David N. Dinkins at Public Hearing on Local Laws 2 (June 18, 1991) (on file with the New York City Council's Committee on General Welfare), *available at* http://www.antibiaslaw.com/MayorsRemarks061891.pdf [hereinafter Dinkins' Remarks]. The requirement referred to by the mayor was set forth in section 8-130 of the City Human Rights Law (textually unchanged by the 1991 Amendments).

11. *See* Gurian, *supra* note 9, at 262.

12. Prior to the 1991 Amendments, those complaining of discrimination had no private right of action and were forced to proceed administratively. After the 1991 Amendments established a private right of action, many cases were filed. Before the passage of the Restoration Act, literally hundreds of cases were disposed of on the basis that a City Human Rights Law claim must fail where a federal or state civil rights claim had not been made out, often in nothing more than a footnote that asserted the (unanalyzed) proposition of equivalence and citing other courts that had habitually made the same error.

13. New York City, N.Y., Admin. Code § 8-502(a) [hereinafter N.Y.C. Admin. Code § 8-502(a)].

14. *See, e.g.*, Ruggiero v. Krzeminski, 928 F.2d 558, 564 (2d Cir. 1991).

15. 506 U.S. 103, 115 (1992).

16. 821 N.E.2d 519 (N.Y. 2004).

17. *Id.* at 525.

18. *Id.* at 525–26.

19. 1991 Amendments § 1; N.Y.C. Legislative Annual 160 (1991) (emphasis added).

20. 761 N.Y.S.2d 608 (N.Y. App. Div. 2003).

21. 1991 Amendments § 1; N.Y.C. Legislative Annual 152–53 (1991).

22. Dinkins' Remarks, *supra* note 10, at 4. The statement was consistent with the committee report that had accompanied the legislation. *See*COMM. ON GEN. WELFARE, REPORT ON PROP. INT. NO. 465-A AND PROP. INT. NO 536-A, at 9–10 (1991) [hereinafter 1991 COMMITTEE REPORT], *available at* http://www.antibiaslaw.com/LL39CommitteeReport.pdf (noting that the employment discrimination provisions had been "silent" as to individual liability of employees and agents but that the "amendment would make explicit such individual liability").

23. *See, e.g.*, Murphy v. ERA United Realty, 674 N.Y.S.2d 415, 417 (N.Y. App. Div. 1998) (Section 8-107(1)(a) of the New York City Human Rights Law "expressly provides that it is unlawful for 'an employer or an employee or agent thereof' to engage in discriminatory employment practices. Accordingly, the plaintiff has a cause of action under this provision against the employer as well as her co-employees"); Harrison v. Indosuez, 6 F. Supp. 2d 224, 233–34 (S.D.N.Y. 1998) ("As the [City law] specifically allows for employee liability, there is no question that the law is applicable against [the defendant] in his individual capacity."); Alvarez v. J.C. Penney Co., No. 96 CV 5165, 1997 WL 104772, at *2 (E.D.N.Y. Feb. 14, 1997) ("[T]he plain language of the Code provides for liability against individual employees.").

24. *Priore* is discussed in more detail in Gurian, *supra* note 9, at 272–75.

25. Priore v. N.Y. Yankees, 761 N.Y.S.2d at 614.

26. The decision did not purport to remove liability for aiding and abetting an act of discrimination, proscribed separately by N.Y.C. Admin. Code § 8-107(6). But the idea that the added language would add nothing to that aiding and abetting proscription violated elementary rules of statutory construction.

27. Restoration Act (amending N.Y.C. Admin. Code §§ 8-107(1), (2), (4), (5), (9), and (18)).

28. *Id.* (amending N.Y.C. Admin. Code § 8-126(a)).

29. *Id.* (amending N.Y.C. Admin. Code § 8-107(7)).

30. Buckhannon Bd. & Care Home, Inc. v. W. Va. Dep't of Health & Human Res., 532 U.S. 598 (2001).

31. Restoration Act (amending N.Y.C. Admin. Code § 8-502(f)). The Committee Report that accompanied the Restoration Act specifically adopted the analysis set forth in Justice Ginsburg's dissent in *Buckhannon.See* COMM. ON GEN. WELFARE, REPORT ON PROP. INT. 22-A (2005) [hereinafter 2005 COMMITTEE REPORT]; N.Y.C. Legislative Annual 536–39 n.9 (2005), *available at* http://www.antibiaslaw.com/2005CommitteeReport.

32. Restoration Act § 1.

33. *Id.*

34. *Id.*

35. Restoration Act § 7 (amending N.Y.C. Admin. Code § 8-130).

36. *Id.*

37. The sources of construction are discussed in detail in Gurian, *supra* note 9, at 260–62.

38. Annabel Palma, Statement at the Meeting of the New York City Council 41–42 (Sept. 15, 2005) (transcript on file with the office of the New York City Clerk).

39. 872 N.Y.S.2d 27 (N.Y. App. Div. 2009).

40. *Id.* at 32.

41. *Id.* at 36–37.

42. *Id.* (quoting Gurian, *supra* note 9, at 280).

43. *Id.* at 37 n.20.

44. *Id.* at 39 n.24.

45. *Id.* at 37.

46. Harris v. Forklift Sys., Inc., 510 U.S. 17, 21 (1993).

47. *Williams*, 872 N.Y.S.2d at 38 (citation omitted).

48. *Id.* at 38 n.22.

49. The holding of *Williams* as to sexual harassment, and its approach more broadly, was adopted by New York's Appellate Division, Second Departmentthe intermediate-level appeals court with jurisdiction over the boroughs of New York City not covered by the First Departmentin *Nelson v. HSBC Bank USA*, 929 N.Y.S.2d 259 (N.Y. App. Div. 2011). *Nelson* deployed the liberal construction requirement of the City Human Rights Law as enhanced by the Restoration Act to find as well that the Restoration Act had retroactive effect. *Id.* at 262–63.

50. *Williams*, 872 N.Y.S.2d at 41 (internal citation omitted).

51. This and the following two guideposts are found in the 2005 Committee Report, *supra* note 31.

52. *Williams*, 872 N.Y.S.2d at 38.

53. *Id.*

54. *Id.* (internal citation omitted).

55. 928 N.E.2d 1035 (N.Y. 2010).

56. *See* Faragher v. Boca Raton, 524 U.S. 775, 777–78 (1998) and Burlington Indus., Inc. v. Ellerth, 524 U.S. 742, 765 (1998) (the two cases, decided on the same day, hold that an affirmative defense to a harassment claim, available where the bad actor is a supervisor or manager, "comprises two necessary elements: (a) that the employer exercised reasonable care to prevent and correct promptly any sexually harassing behavior, and (b) that the plaintiff employee unreasonably failed to take advantage of any preventive or corrective opportunities provided by the employer or to avoid harm otherwise").

57. *New School*, 928 N.E.2d at 1038–39.

58. *Id.* at 1039.

59. *Id.* at 1039–40.

60. *Id.* at 1039 (discussing paras. (b)(1) and (e) of N.Y.C. Admin. Code § 8-107(13)). Strict liability also exists where the acts of a nonsupervisory employee were known to someone exercising managerial or supervisory responsibility and the employee failed to take "immediate and appropriate corrective action." *Id.*

61. *Id.* at 1040.

62. Vance v. Ball State Univ., 570 U.S. , 133 S. Ct. 2434 (2013).

63. *New School*, 928 N.E.2d at 1039.

64. *Id.*

65. Albunio v. City of New York, 947 N.E.2d 135 (N.Y. 2005).

66. *Id.* at 137 (emphasis added).

67. The continuing desire to exempt "to discriminate"the most basic term in the lawfrom this analysis (a desire that may stem from conceptual confusion or ideological resistance) is discussed *infra* Section IV.

68. *Albunio*, 947 N.E.2d at 136.

69. *Id.* at 138.

70. 582 F.3d 268 (2d Cir. 2009).

71. *Id.* at 278.

72. *Id.*

73. No. 06 Civ. 4402 (DLC), 2010 WL 114248 (S.D.N.Y. Jan. 13, 2010).

74. 557 U.S. 167 (2009).

75. *Weiss*, 2010 WL 114248, at *3.

76. *Id.* at *4.

77. Although when a judge simply looks at the text of the statute without reference to *Priore*, he or she has no problem concluding that individual liability is provided for. *See, e.g.*, Malena v. Victoria's Secret Direct, LLC, 886 F. Supp. 2d 349, 366 (S.D.N.Y. 2012).

78. In *Williams*, the court noted that, both before the 1991 Amendments and until such time as the Supreme Court decided *National Railroad Passenger Corp. v.*

Morgan, 536 U.S. 101 (2002), "discrete acts" of discrimination otherwise outside the limitations period had been actionable in the Second Circuit as continuing violations if they were part of a continuing pattern. *Williams,* 872 N.Y.S.2d at 35. *Williams* rejected the *Morgan* limitation for City Human Rights Law purposes: "the Restoration Act's uniquely remedial provisions are consistent with a rule that neither penalizes workers who hesitate to bring an action at the first sign of what they suspect could be discriminatory trouble, nor rewards covered entities that discriminate by insulating them from challenges to their unlawful conduct that continues into the limitations period." *Id.*

79. In *Sotomayor v. City of New York,* 862 F. Supp. 2d 226, 250–51 (E.D.N.Y. 2012), the federal district court followed this analysis.

80. No. 05 Civ. 10355, 2009 WL 873206 (S.D.N.Y. Mar. 31, 2009).

81. *See, e.g.,* Bermudez v. City of New York, 783 F. Supp. 2d 560, 593 (S.D.N.Y. 2011); Fullwood v. Ass'n for the Help of Retarded Children, Inc., No. 08-CV-6739, 2010 WL 3910429 (S.D.N.Y. Sept. 28, 2010).

82. *Wilson,* 2009 WL 873206, at *28 (internal citation omitted).

83. 09 Civ. 1251, 2011 WL 3586060 (S.D.N.Y. July 21, 2011), *vacated and remanded,* 715 F.3d 102 (2d Cir. 2013).

84. This fact was not adverted to in the district court's opinion but was cited in the Second Circuit remand. *See* Mihalik v. Credit Agricole Cheuvreaux N. Am., Inc., 715 F.3d 102, 113 (2d Cir. 2013).

85. *Mihalik,* 2011 WL 3586060, at *9–10.

86. *See, e.g.,* Ardigo v. J. Christopher Capital, LLC, No. 12 Civ. 3627, 2013 WL 1195117 (S.D.N.Y. Mar. 25, 2013); Clarke v. Pacifica Found., No. 07-CV-4605, 2011 WL 4356085 (S.D.N.Y. Sept. 16, 2011).

87. 936 N.Y.S.2d 112 (N.Y. App. Div. 2011).

88. *Id.* at 123 n.16.

89. *Id.*

90. *Mihalik,* 715 F.3d at 114 (citations omitted). There was also a retaliation claim in the case. In vacating the district court's grant of summary judgment on this claim, the circuit built on both *Albunio* and the retaliation holding of *Williams* (not previously discussed in this article). A court needs to make the assessment of whether complained-of conduct was "'reasonably likely to deter a person from engaging in protected activity[]'" with "a keen sense of workplace realities, of the fact that the 'chilling effect' of particular conduct is context-dependent, and of the fact that a jury is generally best suited to evaluate the impact of retaliatory conduct." *Id.* at 112 (internal quotation marks omitted) (quoting *Williams,* 872 N.Y.S.2d at 34).

91. *Bennett,* 936 N.Y.S.2d at 116–17 (citation omitted).

92. Melman v. Montefiore Med. Ctr., 946 N.Y.S.2d 27, 30 (N.Y. App. Div. 2012).

93. *Cf.* Albunio v. City of New York, 947 N.E.2d 135, 137 (N.Y. 2005) (requiring the selection of the broadest, most plaintiff-friendly interpretation reasonably possible).

94. *Melman,* 946 N.Y.S.2d at 30 (internal quotation marks omitted) (quoting *Bennett,* 936 N.Y.S.2d at 124).

95. *Mihalik,* 715 F.3d at 113.

96.   *Id.* at 110 n.8. New York's Appellate Division, Second Department has also issued a *Melman*-like decision. Brightman v. Prison Health Serv., Inc., 970 N.Y.S.2d 789 (N.Y. App. Div. 2013). As in *Melman*, the court asserts that the Restoration Act's enhanced liberal construction provision did not "alter the procedural framework" applicable to City Human Rights Law claims, but neither addresses the reasoning in *Bennett* nor engages in its own liberal construction analysis. *Id.* at 791. Likewise, it fails to cite its decision in *Nelson* (which accepted the need for broad construction in all respects), and its decision in *Furfero v. St. John's University*, 941 N.Y.S.2d 639, 642 (N.Y. App. Div. 2012), by which it adopted *Bennett*.

97.   *Bennett*, 936 N.Y.S.2d at 122.

98.   Hicks v. St. Mary's Honor Ctr., 509 U.S. 502, 525 (1993) (Souter, J., dissenting).

99.   *Bennett*, 936 N.Y.S.2d at 123.

100. Pub. L. No. 109-2, 119 Stat. 4 (2005) (codified in various sections of 28 U.S.C.). CAFA provides for the removal of most class actions initiated in state court under state law regardless of the absence of complete diversity between and among the parties. *See* 28 U.S.C. § 1332(d). This is not to say that potential workarounds might not exist (perhaps, for example, creating a state-based pattern-and-practice declaratory judgment action with the availability of attorneys' fees). One such workaround was attempted by a panel of the Ninth Circuit Court of Appeals in *Romo v. Teva Pharmaceuticals USA, Inc.*, 731 F.3d 918 (9th Cir. 2013), *cert. denied* ___ U.S. ___, 124 S.Ct 2872 (2014) . The court rejected removal to federal court under CAFA's mass action provision, 28 U.S.C. § 1332(d)(11)(B)(i), because a request to "coordinate" proceedings in state court did not explicitly state that the coordination would involve a joint triala joint trial being the trigger for removal). *Id.* at 920–25. After the Circuit decided to rehear the matter *en banc*, 742 F.3d 909 (9th Cir. 2014), it concluded that the cases had to be removed to federal court after all. *Corber v. Xanodyne Pharaceuticals, Inc.*, 771 F.3d 1218 (9th Cir. 2014) *Cf.* Standard Fire Ins. Co. v. Knowles, 568 U.S. , 133 S. Ct. 1345 (2013) (holding unanimously that a voluntary stipulation by a representative of a putative class not to seek damages in excess of the CAFA threshold for removal does not remove the case from CAFA's scope because the representative cannot bind members of the class).

101. *See, e.g.*, Circuit City Stores, Inc. v. Adams, 532 U.S. 105 (2001) (mandatory arbitration applies to all employment contracts other than those of transportation workers); AT&T Mobility LLC v. Concepcion, 563 U.S. 333 (2011) (preempting a California Supreme Court doctrine that had defined some class arbitration waivers in consumer arbitration agreements as unconscionable and hence unenforceable).

102. *See* Gurian, *supra* note 9, at 284–87 for a discussion of many of the issues tackled by the 1991 Amendments.

103. *Hicks*, 509 U.S. at 525–43.

104. Vance v. Ball State Univ., 570 U.S. , 133 S. Ct. 2434 (2013).

105. Univ. of Tex. Sw. Med. Ctr. v. Nassar, 570 U.S. , 133 S. Ct. 2517 (2013).

106. Most recently introduced as Paycheck Fairness Act, S. 862, 114th Cong. (2015).

107. *Id.* §§ 3(a) and (b). The defense would not apply where the employee proves that there is a less discriminatory alternative available that the employer refuses to adopt despite the alternative's ability to meet the employee's business need. *Id.* § 3(a).

108. N.Y.C. Admin. Code § 8-107(17).

109. 544 U.S. 228, 240 (2005) ("The scope of disparate-impact liability under [the] ADEA is narrower than under Title VII.").

110. N.Y.C. Admin. Code § 8-107(17)(a)(2).

111. *Id.*

112. N.Y.C. Admin. Code § 8-502(a) (providing that a civil action shall allow a plaintiff to seek "damages, including punitive damages, and...injunctive relief and such other remedies as may be appropriate"); *see also* N.Y.C. Admin. Code § 8-107(17) (setting forth disparate impact claims contains no damage limitation).

113. 557 U.S. 557 (2009).

114. *Id.* at 563.

115. *Id.* at 587 (citation omitted).

116. 28 U.S.C. § 2000e-7.

117. Data on number of employees by size of employer for 2014 is available at the website of California's Employment Development Department, http://www.calmis.ca.gov/file/indsize/chart_sob2014_3.pdf (last accessed on Aug. 20, 2015).

118. Cal. Gov. Code §§ 12940(j)(1), (j)(4)(A) (West 2013).

119. *Id.* §§ 12940(4)(A), 12926(d).

120. It was this recognition that led to a provision in the 1991 Amendments that changed the focus on the public accommodations provisions of the City Human Rights Law from one focused on "place" to one that covered "providers, whether licensed or unlicensed, of goods, services, facilities, accommodations, advantages or privileges of any kind." N.Y.C. Admin. Code § 8-102(9).

121. Cal. Gov. Code § 12940(j); *see* Roby v. McKesson Corp., 219 P.3d 749 (Cal. 2010) (confirming individual liability and discussing statutory provision generally). The state, however, is still stuck with the "severe or pervasive" standard. *See, e.g.,* Miller v. Dep't of Corr., 115 P.3d 77, 89–92 (Cal. 2005).

122. Minnesota has made it unlawful for a person who engages in a trade or business or in the provision of a service "to intentionally refuse to do business with, to refuse to contract with, or to discriminate in the basic terms, conditions, or performance of the contract because of a person's race, national origin, color, sex, sexual orientation, or disability, unless the alleged refusal or discrimination is because of a legitimate business purpose." Minn. Stat. Ann. § 363A.17 (West 2013). The Minnesota Supreme Court gave effect to the language insofar as permitting an injured business to sue but excluded the individual discriminated against (who was not a party to a contract) from being able to sue. Krueger v. Zeman Constr. Co., 781 N.W.2d 858 (Minn. 2010). The court majority asserted that the statutory language unambiguously did not provide for such liability but noted in the alternative its fear: under the plaintiff's theory, every person affected by the defendant's conduct could have an individual cause of action, and "[t]here is no indication that the legislature intended such an expansive reading of the statute." *Id.* at 864.

123. *See generally* Havens Realty Corp. v. Coleman, 455 U.S. 363 (1982).

124. Nothing stops a governmental entity from engaging in employment testing except the lack of political will.

125. 28 F.3d 1268 (D.C. Cir. 1994).

126. *Id.* at 1271–72.

127. *Id.* at 1276–79.

128. In the fair housing context, it is not at all clear that *Havens* would survive if the standing issue arose before the current Supreme Court. Even if it would, "diversion of resources" claims require an organization to engage in complicated choreography (or hope that a defendant does not probe too hard). A more direct statement of standing would be preferable but is not currently politically feasible on the federal level.

129. *See* Craig Gurian, *Using Local and State Legislation to Preserve and Expand the Ability of Fair Housing Organizations to Prosecute the Discrimination They Uncover*, HARV. L. & POL'Y REV. ONLINE (Oct. 2007), *available at* http://www.antibiaslaw.com/sites/default/files/all/Private_Attorney_General.pdf (last visited Aug. 30, 2015). The concept of a private attorney general provision is best known through its use in the False Claims Act, 31 U.S.C. § 3729 et seq.

130. Nassau County, N.Y., incorporated such a provision in 2006. Nassau Cty. Local Law 9-2006, *available at* http://www.nassaucountyny.gov/DocumentCenter/View/1686 (last visited Aug. 30, 2015). That law added, *inter alia*, section 21-9.7(d)(3)(vi). This private attorney general provision, which, to my knowledge, has not yet been the subject of a court decision, did not contain a definition that limited the cause of action to certain organizations but allowed any person to proceed who had made the substantive showing required. A way to delimit the class of persons eligible would be to provide standing for an "eligible civil rights organization," defined as "any not-for-profit organization that is recognized as exempt from taxation pursuant to section 501(c) of the Internal Revenue Code and whose primary mission is fighting discriminatory practices made unlawful under local, state, or federal anti-discrimination law."

131. In the case of the Restoration Act, the Committee Report served a useful function, but the fact that a councilmember was able to incorporate into the record the testimony of the Anti-Discrimination Center and the statements of the Brennan Center and the Association of the Bar (now the New York City Bar Association) turned out to be helpful as well.

132. The broad support created for the restorative Civil Rights Act of 1991, Pub. L. No. 102-166, 105 Stat. 1071 (1991), does provide an important counterexample.

133. Certainly, the American Legislative Exchange Council (ALEC), an organization devoted to "limited government," "free markets," and "federalism" has understood the importance of state-level advocacy for many years and has achieved significant success in having its agenda adopted.

134. Unfortunately, I have seen many occasions where a practitioner, having taken on a weak case, develops an argument that is really no more than "the Restoration Act says I win anyway." Especially because judicial obedience to legislative command can never be taken for granted, those pursuing cases under the City Human Rights Law, therefore, have an obligation to make that obedience as easy as possible. At the core of that obligation is making sure that, when relying on the enhanced liberal construction provision, the practitioner develop for the judge an interpretation that is grounded in the purposes of the City Human Rights Law, fully explaining how that interpretation, as compared with others, best serves the law's purposes.

10

Leveraging Antidiscrimination

Olatunde Johnson

On turning fifty, a friend of mine said: "You can't pretend you are young anymore."

I. Introduction

As the Civil Rights Act turns fifty, antidiscrimination law has become unfashionable. For those commentators and reformers who concern themselves with addressing racial, ethnic, and gender disparities, antidiscrimination law occupies a less central role than it did fifty years ago, perhaps even a marginal one. The core problem, it seems, is that discrimination is a limited explanation for current forms of contemporary inequality. Discussing race, economist Glenn Loury has argued that discrimination should be "demoted, dislodged from its current prominent place in the conceptual discourse on racial inequality in American life." Richard Ford and Richard Banks offer a similar assessment, arguing that if "we are legitimately concerned about substantive disparities," then the "goal of eliminating discrimination is too modest, not ambitious enough."[1] It is not uncommon to speak of remedying discrimination as separate from a larger goal of addressing inequality. And civil rights strategies are posited as not up to the serious task of improving mobility for low-wage workers or providing access to entry-level employment. The antidiscrimination approach, it is said, is "based on the principle of freedom of individual opportunity," which necessarily helps the more advantaged and better trained, and is thus inadequate for reducing substantive inequality in our society.[2] If one is seeking innovations to address poverty and inequality or to promote economic and social opportunity, much commentary suggests that antidiscrimination law is not the place to find them.

It is not hard to harness reasons to demote "discrimination" in contemporary inequality discourse. Discrimination remains prevalent in our society and continues to explain extant disparities between groups.[3] However, there is much to suggest that addressing contemporary inequities requires confronting the full range of mechanisms that disparately affect racial and ethnic minorities and women, including improving education and training of minority workers,[4] the decreasing fortune of less-skilled workers,[5] the effects of immigration status on social mobility, and how geography and place structures opportunity.[6] Given the complex reasons for contemporary inequality, social reform is less likely to center merely on questions of individualized bias, but on social welfare and education programs, interventions to improve the economic status of unskilled and semiskilled workers, and strategies to diminish spatial segregation and improve the conditions facing communities of concentrated poverty. Contemporary advocates might now organize their work around narratives of social inclusion,[7] or addressing spatial inequities in the distribution of opportunity.[8]

Yet there is a danger in casting aside the Civil Rights Act as one charts this new course. For one, as I discuss in Part I, such a move misunderstands the force of the antidiscrimination directive that undergirded the Act, one that is not limited to formal discrimination or bias and that drew on a broad set of private and public implementation tools to respond to evolving problems of exclusion. Reminding ourselves of the implementation strategies that emerged in the first decade after the Act produces a richer account of what we mean by "discrimination" and attunes us to a broader set of implementation tools than is conventionally associated with antidiscrimination law. Second, as I show in Part II, the Civil Rights Act continues to sustain an important set of strategies to promote inclusion. In that Part I, discuss the emergence of strategies to address contemporary disparities under Title VI of the Civil Rights Act, as well as emerging efforts under Title VII—reminiscent of Title VII's early years—to make Title VII more responsive to contemporary forces shaping exclusion in labor markets.

Part III concludes with the value of retaining hold of this civil rights infrastructure, even as reformers develop other tools and strategies for promoting equity and inclusion. My argument here is that the Act provides an important regulatory framework for addressing problems of exclusion facing a broad range of groups (including women and racial and ethnic minorities), across a range of domains (education, employment, transportation, environment, agriculture, and more) and using a range of potentially powerful public and private enforcement strategies. Transformative statutes do not come to us every day. For pragmatic as well as expressive reasons, it is worth continuing to consider what one might wrest from the Act's great aspirations and powerful design.

I. Revisiting Ambition

Antidiscrimination is at the core of the Civil Rights Act of 1964. While the Act uses a range of terms—Title VI of the Act provides that "[n]o person in the United States shall, on the ground of race, color, or national origin, be excluded from participation in, be denied the benefits of, or be subjected to discrimination under any program or activity receiving Federal financial assistance"[9] and Title VII prohibits discrimination as well as segregation and classification in ways that deprive employees of opportunities[10]—our collective shorthand for the Act is that it prohibits "discrimination."

Among those concerned with addressing contemporary race, ethnic, or gender disparities or with promoting economic inclusion, the antidiscrimination approach typified by the Act is often framed as inadequate.[11] In part, this assessment stems from a determination that discrimination is either in significant decline or a fairly marginal explanation of contemporary disparities.[12] In part, this assessment also represents a critique of the strategies underlying civil rights law: the antidiscrimination approach is seen as intertwined with an emphasis on litigation at the expense of other approaches.[13] The thrust of these critiques is that the antidiscrimination idea centers on formal, market discrimination and bias, and is thus not sufficiently robust to be relevant today.

However, I urge caution in characterizing the 1964 Act as centered on formal or explicit discrimination. Rather, one can fairly characterize the Act's regime as seeking to address a range of institutional practices that disadvantaged blacks (the main target at the Act's inception). By "regime," I mean to emphasize both the Act as apparently contemplated by its initial drafters and legislative and executive proponents but even more by the private and public enforcement structure that emerged in the years after its enactment.

The statutory history—which has been much pored over in the half a century following passage of the Act—shows the breadth of the Act's goals. In finally announcing support for civil rights legislation in employment and education, President John F. Kennedy promoted such efforts as necessary to ensure full equality in American society and participation in economic life.[14] In his address on the floor of the U.S. House of Representatives introducing the legislation, Kennedy cast fair employment laws as part of a quest to end racial disparities in unemployment, en route to the larger goal of assuring full employment for all workers.[15] Introducing Title VI, which prohibited discrimination in federally funded programs, Kennedy expansively defined the antidiscrimination idea underlying the legislation, declaring that: "[S]imple justice requires that public funds, to which all taxpayers of all races contribute, not be spent in any fashion which encourages, entrenches, subsidizes, or results in racial discrimination."[16] "Indirect discrimination" through subsidization, Kennedy emphasized, is "invidious" discrimination.[17]

Legislative history from the House and Senate speaks to the goals of this new legislation.[18] The House Report to one of the bills that would culminate in the Civil Rights Act declared that discrimination is an "urgent and most serious national problem" requiring extensive action to eradicate exclusion in voting, public accommodation, federal financial assistance, and employment.[19] Recognizing that states had initiated important civil rights legislation, the House Report nevertheless recognized the need for national action: "in the last decade it has become increasingly clear that progress has been too slow and that national legislation is required to meet a national need."[20][21] In addition, the legislature identified goals that went beyond market discrimination, emphasizing that discrimination was not limited to explicit exclusionary actions but "ranges in degrees from patent absolute rejection to more subtle forms of invidious distinctions."[21] As an example, this House Report alluded to the effect of seemingly racially neutral practices such as "last hired, first fired" and to the relegation of minorities "to 'traditional' positions and through discriminatory promotion practices."[22] Occupational segregation was achieved through "traditional expectations" as well as the segregation of minorities in "involuntary part-time work."[23] Discrimination could be subtle: the House Report noted that while employment agencies often engaged in "outright refusal to deal with minority group applications," as prevalent was the refusal to refer minorities due to "expressed agreements, tacit understandings, and assumptions based on traditional practices."[24] In this congressional history, labor and entry-level jobs emerge as a particular point of focus. The House Report refers to efforts to improve opportunities in construction unions and ensure access to apprenticeship training programs often run by labor unions because of the crucial role these pathways played in "improving the skills, knowledge and capability of" workers.[25]

To be sure, key portions of the legislative history of the Act reveal legislative concerns about avoiding race-conscious action or intrusions into the "prerogatives" of management (prefiguring subsequent debates in Title VII over the extent to which the Act should be interpreted to allow disparate impact or affirmative action).[26] And forces aligned against the Act sought to minimize administrative power to implement Title VII, most notably succeeding in diminishing the powers of the Equal Employment Opportunity Commission.[27] Yet this journey into the statutory history is meant to check modern characterizations of the antidiscrimination goal as aimed at simply removing explicit or blatant barriers or as disconnected from the goal of economic opportunity. Instead, the legislative history offers a more richly conceived notion of the degree to which discrimination was embedded in employment and credentialing institutions such as unions, the range of explicit and implicit barriers to inclusion, and the connection between the antidiscrimination method and achieving fuller economic participation.

The ambition of the Act is further revealed when we consider the Act's implementation context—the strategies that public and private actors undertook to implement and enforce the Act. Implementation would come to include strategies (1) defining the Act broadly to reach more than intentional discrimination; (2) leveraging administrative and private resources for systemic enforcement; and (3) requiring regulated actors to take affirmative inclusionary steps.

The move beyond intentional discrimination is seen most sharply in the public and private implementation of the Act to reach actions with an unjustified disparate impact. Within a year after passage of the Act, federal agencies charged with implementing Title VI of the Act interpreted the provision to reach not just actions by funding recipients that were intentional but also those that had the "*effect* of subjecting individuals to discrimination."[28] (Notably, these regulations were drafted by the agencies, with the involvement of private actors and the White House, and formally approved by the president.) What we now understand as the disparate impact standard in employment grew in part out of the guidelines issued by the EEOC on employment tests, in response to the adoption by Southern employers of formally race-neutral practices that operated to discriminate.[29] Two years after passage of the Act, the EEOC issued guidance instructing employers to administer an occupational test only where it "fairly measures the knowledge or skills required by the particular job or class of job."[30] A few years later, the EEOC issued additional guidelines requiring that employers using tests have "available 'data demonstrating that the test is predictive of or significantly correlated with important elements of work behavior which comprise or are relevant to the job or jobs for which candidates are being evaluated."[31] It was in giving "substantial deference" to the EEOC in *Griggs v. Duke Power* that the Supreme Court allowed that the Act prohibited in some cases employers' facially neutral practices that in fact are "discriminatory in operation."[32]

Commentators have debated whether the EEOC's move interpreting the Act to reach disparate impact claims was distorting the meaning of a statute centered on disparate treatment and color-blindness, or whether this move was supported by the language and prevailing understandings of "discrimination."[33] Regardless of the position one takes on fidelity to the language or the original legislative deal, the point here is that these early moves by the EEOC implement the Act in ways that reached beyond thin notions of formal discrimination. Instead, the meaning of antidiscrimination emerges in response to the efforts to address the evolving barriers facing workers.

Second, public and private enforcement strategies focused on opening up large-scale institutions to black workers by targeting salient industries and leveraging systemic tools such as regulatory guidance, investigations, and hearings, and using litigation mechanisms such as the class action device and pattern and practice authority. As other commentators have shown, the EEOC adopted structurally oriented strategies––interpreting language in Title VII to permit it to collect data on the racial composition of employers[34] and using this data to systemically publicize and investigate problems of labor market discrimination in particular regions, sectors, and industries.[35] Private enforcement also followed a systemic approach that targeted particular industries,[36] employed the class action device,[37] and sought to take aim at a range of exclusionary practices, in particular the use of non-job-related occupational tests[38] and exclusionary seniority practices.[39] As former NAACP Legal Defense Fund (LDF) attorney Robert Belton has explained: "by 1965 overt discrimination on the basis of race was not fashionable."[40] Instead, LDF harnessed an approach to challenge "superficially neutral practices, such as testing and educational devices or seniority systems that appeared facially neutral or color-blind but operated to perpetuate the effects of past discrimination"[41] and "systemic discrimination imbedded in basic personnel policies or organizational structures of companies and unions."[42]

Third, the enforcement agency used its regulatory power to promote goals apart from the litigation context. Although the EEOC (designed to be a weak enforcement agency) lacked (and still lacks) power to issue binding substantive regulations to enforce Title VII,[43] the agency developed guidelines on how to avoid discriminatory practices such as seniority systems and, most famously, on the use of occupational tests. Robert Lieberman has described these guidelines as emerging out of the EEOC's investigation and conciliation power—an attempt by the EEOC to provide a guide for "employers and employees about what practices the commission would find acceptable and unacceptable in probable cause determinations."[44]

This implementation context reveals a robust conception of the antidiscrimination directive at the core of the Act—one that reaches beyond explicit practices to attain subtle, embedded mechanisms that excluded or inhibited opportunities for black workers. In addition, this review of the implementation context makes clear that reformers employed a range of strategies to move the Act beyond the redress of individual claims. This is manifest in the leveraging of federal contracting and spending power, the requirement of affirmative inclusionary strategies, the reliance on administrative investigations and regulatory guidance, the use of the class action device, and the attempt to connect the work of private litigators and community-based organizations. Finally, this context reveals that antidiscrimination strategies would be cognizant of the realities of the industrial economy at that time and connected to core questions of social and economic equality. For instance, the paradigm beneficiary of Title VII was the blue collar worker, evident in reformers' focus on manufacturing and construction industries and on organized labor. In its goals and implementation, the Act centered on opening up access to jobs with training and career ladders and on providing avenues for the acquisition of skills.

By some key accounts, this enforcement approach contributed significantly to improving the social and economic status of blacks in the late 1960s and early 1970s[45] and to substantial progress in the desegregation of schools.[46] However, I do not want to overstate the success or ambition of these public-private strategies[47] or to ignore the possibility of even more transformative paths that might have been pursued, particularly with regard to reform of labor institutions.[48] What I propose is in the spirit of correcting how we often regard "antidiscrimination" today—a useful check on our modern tendency to characterize the antidiscrimination idea at the center of the Act as limited to a concern about individual bias, as too court-centered, insufficiently structural, or attenuated from core questions of access to opportunity.

II. Claiming Relevance

Today, much of how commentators understand the relevance and capacity of antidiscrimination law is shaped by regimes of court enforcement and by Title VII litigation in particular. Title VII generates more litigation than any other portion of the Act. Title VII cases are more frequently heard at the Supreme Court than litigation involving other provisions of the Act (or other civil rights statutes).[49] And Title VII commands the greatest share of commentary about the Act in the legal academic literature. Title VII's rise and prominence has coincided with a move away from the earlier more systemic or "structural" focus of the Act. For instance, while individual Title VII cases have continued to rise since the Act's inception, pattern and practice and class action litigation has fallen.[50] And, even as the overall volume of litigation has increased, litigation has shifted away from the hiring discrimination cases that prevailed in Title VII's earlier years, which sought to open up opportunity for previously excluded workers in economically salient industries toward more individual claims of termination. This is a trend that researchers identified in the early 1990s before passage of the Civil Rights Act of 1991 (which, through damages and other mechanisms, increased incentives to bring Title VII claims),[51] and that has continued in the subsequent years.[52] Attorneys on the ground have noted the irony of this interplay between the Civil Rights Act of 1991's strengthening of Title VII through a damage regime and the decline of systemic reform litigation.[53] Some of these changes in the shape of litigation no doubt reflect Title VII's success in creating incentives for fairer employment practices and the provision's salience.[54] Still, with the individual Title VII case in mind, one might come to understand the Act as centered on individual bias; one might have reason to question the Act's broader relevance to contemporary forces and patterns of exclusion.

Yet focusing on Title VII's enforcement in individual cases pays insufficient heed to other provisions of the Act, such as Title VI, which do not operate primarily in courts or as a tool for redress of individualized bias claims. In addition, emphasizing court enforcement in individual cases overlooks the broader regulatory tools of the Act—in both Title VI and Title VII—that can reach beyond *ex post* court enforcement in individual cases and that can operate to promote or encourage inclusion and disrupt patterns of exclusion.

To begin with Title VII, as the story of the 1964 Act's early history shows, effective implementation of Title VII depended not just on litigation in individual cases but also on use of a broad set of tools, including private class action and agency pattern and practice litigation, regulatory guidance, industry targeting, data analysis, and investigations. Furthermore, implementation of Title VII depended not only on narrow conceptions of discrimination centered on market bias or prejudice but also on the use of these hybrid enforcement tools to address a set of on-the-ground, evolving practices that inhibited opportunity for workers and to open up key institutions and industries.

At the outset, it is worth noting even as Title VII litigation today is hobbled by significant doctrinal constraints,[55] such litigation has continued capacity to address patterns of group exclusion and reform organizational practices. Class actions, pattern and practice, and hiring cases may have declined relative to the early years of Title VII enforcement, but they are not extinct. In recent years, privately initiated Title VII litigation has sought to address exclusionary employment practices by public agencies that exclude minority workers[56] and practices such as steering and downward channeling that perpetuate occupational segregation in lower-skilled, service sector employment.[57] Litigation in this vein maintains relevance by taking aim at systemic practices and targeting pathways, training institutions like public employment and unions—a traditional focus of Title VII—as well the service sector in which large numbers of women and workers of color are employed (though often in the lowest ranks).

Moreover, innovative litigation stems from important collaborations between antidiscrimination lawyers and groups that organize not around questions of discrimination but toward the goals of improving the condition of workers within particular industries. One group that has received some attention in the academic literature in recent years is the Restaurant Opportunities Center of New York (ROC-NY), which seeks to improve the working conditions and pay of restaurant workers in fine dining establishments in New York City. The group organizes restaurant workers to address wage and hour violations by employers and improve benefits like sick or parenting-related leave.[58] Yet central to the group's mission is addressing what the group sees as pervasive discrimination and occupational segregation in the restaurant industry. Much as public and private implementers used the data collected by the EEOC to highlight the exclusion of black workers by Southern manufacturers, ROC-NY also publicizes practices in the restaurant industry that limit opportunity for women, immigrant workers, and workers of color.[59] ROC-NY relies on audit testing—that classic tool of antidiscrimination enforcement used most extensively in the fair housing context[60]—to document discrimination in hiring for particular restaurant positions.[61] In addition, although the group's strategies center on organizing and policy reform, ROC-NY partners with private attorneys to litigate discrimination cases, securing remedies in individual and group litigation. Significantly, ROC-NY leverages its investigations into discriminatory practices, its deep knowledge of the industry, its representation of workers, and its litigation successes to publicize exclusionary practices (such as the lack of formal and transparent practices for hiring, training, and promotion). It advocates for specific reform interventions and celebrates and involves employers that perpetuate best practices in the industry.[62]

There is evidence, too, of revitalization of the type of public systemic enforcement that gave Title VII its salience in the early years of the Civil Rights Act. The EEOC has long been seen as a broken enforcement agency. Historically overtaxed and underresourced, the increase in Title VII and other employment discrimination cases in the 1990s created additional pressures on the EEOC since Title VII and most other employment claims must first be filed with the agency.[63] And there are serious questions about whether the agency has adapted to accommodate this crush of complaints. Indeed, if the early EEOC sought to move away from the volume of individual complaints by focusing on systemic remedies and investigations, accounts of the EEOC in the 1990s and 2000s suggest an agency paralyzed by processing individual complaints.[64] The EEOC, too, has recognized its need to enhance its systemic litigation program.[65]

But rather than wholly abandon the prospect of wresting more from this flawed public enforcement mechanism, it seems worth devoting creative attention to strategies for strengthening the regime. After all, the EEOC has formal tools and capacity unavailable to private litigants. Unlike private litigants, the EEOC can maintain systemic litigation without meeting the requirements of class action Rule 23[66] (the difficulties in meeting the rule's requirements have hampered private class actions in recent years[67]). The EEOC can also pursue investigations without an actual complainant by filing a commissioner's charge.[68] More, the EEOC can pursue conciliations, hold hearings to investigate patterns of discrimination, collect data, and issue regulatory guidance.

To reverse its slide away from systemic litigation, the EEOC has recently announced a renewed focus on systemic discrimination, developing a plan for doing so after extensive consultation with experts and advocates.[69] Indeed, in the last few years, the EEOC has begun to bring more pattern and practice litigation; in 2012, it significantly increased its recoveries against employers in systemic discrimination cases over prior years.[70] The EEOC has announced an increased emphasis on preventing employment discrimination through education and outreach, including by partnering with community groups to focus on the most disadvantaged workers and underserved communities.[71] And the EEOC has instituted important regulatory guidance on current barriers facing workers, notably revising its prior guidance on best practices in considering an applicant's criminal history.[72] Further, the EEOC could utilize its existing powers more effectively. For instance, the EEOC might increase its ability to identify industries with discriminatory employment practices and to analyze the EEO-1 and other data that it collects on private employers.[73] The EEOC could use data to hold hearings on problematic industry practices, disseminate information and best practices, generate regulatory guidance, and pursue litigation. Another tool the EEOC might deploy, perhaps in conjunction with nongovernmental organizations and nonprofits, is the use of audit studies to identify hiring discrimination. Although courts are not settled on the ability of employment testers to recover damages and injunctive relief,[74] the results of audit studies might still prove useful for conducting investigations and providing insight into industry practices.[75] But the agency's current emphasis recaptures the focus on systemic discrimination—it attunes us to the possibilities that might still remain in a Title VII that moves beyond a focus on individual litigation.

The other key provision of the Act—Title VI—has also served as an important location in recent years for addressing contemporary problems of exclusion. Title VI differs from Title VII in that its central enforcement target is not private industry but federal agencies and grantees. Its key mode of enforcement is not litigation but administrative regulation, backed by the threat of funding withdrawal. In recent years, regulatory enforcement of Title VI has yielded an important array of regulations that place affirmative requirements of inclusion on grantees. Implementing Title VI, the Department of Agriculture requires federal agencies administering agriculture, forestry, food, and nutrition programs to undertake ongoing analyses to ensure that minorities benefit from these federally funded programs.[76] Federally funded public transit and highway programs must take affirmative steps to assess the impacts of their programs on minorities and persons with limited English proficiency, adopt mitigating alternatives, and include minority groups in their planning.[77] In an account of these directives in mass transit, I showed how they required grantees to incorporate impact assessments in their planning, engage in best practices for ensuring participation of covered groups, and design inclusionary alternatives.[78]

These Title VI directives bear on the debate about the relevance of discrimination law today: they extend beyond individual bias, and their implementation depends not on *ex post* enforcement by courts (although litigation may sometimes play a role in enforcement) but on implementation by regulated actors. In addition, these directives intervene in regulatory domains that are linchpins for determining inclusion and opportunity distribution today. For instance, mass transportation policy and design have strong effects on economic mobility—high minority and poor communities are often disconnected from important job centers—and access to transportation is a key determinant of the distribution of resources and patterns of racial segregation and concentrated poverty across a metropolitan region.[79] By encouraging inclusion of the needs of minority communities in design decisions, promoting ongoing equity assessments, and mitigation, Title VI mass transit directives seek to interrupt the reproduction of existing, unequal patterns of transportation access and the attendant spatial inequalities. In addition, as in the employment example described above, these Title VI directives are harnessed by groups that do not centrally organize around questions of antidiscrimination—but who instead organize their advocacy around the problems of particular geographic communities or on a specific policy problem (such as transit equity).[80]

Perhaps even more than Title VII, Title VI makes plain the risk of leaving the Act behind as reformers focus on questions of mobility, opportunity, and spatial equality. Because Title VI commands attention to race and ethnicity in a vast number of federal programs involving billions of dollars, its regulatory infrastructure is too powerful not to employ as a tool for advancing reform.

III. Antidiscrimination's Place

As a way of defining a problem, and as a legal intervention, antidiscrimination is no doubt less central than it once was. In education, discriminatory discipline, racialized tracking, and discriminatory student assignment, policies may remain problems, but reformers' attention is understandably attuned to addressing disparities through reforms to improve the quality of educational interventions. In employment, important concerns about discrimination and occupational segregation in labor markets might be overtaken by the fate of workers in an economy that leaves little room for less-skilled and semiskilled workers.[81] Those interested in inclusion and particularly in reducing racial and ethnic disparities would be gravely wrong to frame their claims solely in terms of discrimination (whether a thin or robust account) without engaging a broader set of reform strategies.

Still, the Civil Rights Act has an important role to play in these domains. Understanding the Act's place requires recovering the Act's central ambition as well as innovating to make the Act responsive to contemporary problems. Some may argue that the Act in its current formulation is not worth such sustained attention. After all, much innovation might be accomplished through new regulation and new statutes at the federal, state, and local levels. Such innovation is reflected in statutes requiring targeted attention to the progress of racial and ethnic minorities in education[82] or by requirements that state actors address racial disparities in their juvenile justice systems.[83] Innovation is evident, too, in efforts to intervene to address practices that may have a particular impact on minorities or women but that address the declining fates of all lower-wage workers, such as skills training, the expansion of school-to-work and apprenticeship programs, wage reform, reentry programs, the creation of new collective bargaining regimes for low-wage workers,[84] child care and sick leave policy[85] or reform of the inappropriate uses of employment background checks.[86]

The reasons for continuing nevertheless to ask how the Civil Rights Act can bear on contemporary questions are both pragmatic and expressive. The pragmatic argument is that it is hard to make progress on inequality without attention to questions of how status—race, ethnicity, and gender—structure opportunity in distinct ways. The Civil Rights Act contains one of the few places in American law that directs attention to these categories, and that provides mechanisms for disrupting long-standing patterns of exclusion. More, it provides an expansive, if imperfect, public and private regulatory infrastructure for advancing these goals. The second perhaps more expressive reason is that the Act was never simply about antidiscrimination in the narrowest sense. Even if so conceived by some of its drafters, it has absorbed a meaning through implementation and cultural salience that gestures toward broader claims of citizenship and inclusion.

IV. Conclusion

As the Civil Rights Act of 1964 turns fifty, I am sympathetic to the idea that we should demote discrimination. Recognizing this, social reformers increasingly organize their equality claims around questions of opportunity, economic mobility, and diminishing disparities based on geography and place. Yet the meaning of the 1964 Civil Rights Act is not limited to narrow notions of discrimination; it still has a role to play in structuring claims and advancing reforms in these new domains. As reformers design new strategies, the Act's initial structural reform ambitions are worth remembering.

About the Author

Professor of law, Columbia Law School. For helpful research, I am grateful to Lane Feler and Hannah Lepow. Many thanks to Samuel Bagenstos and Ellen Katz for organizing the important symposium that provided the foundation for this book. Glenn C. Loury, The Anatomy of Racial Inequality 92–93 (2002).

Notes

1. Ralph Richard Banks & Richard Thompson Ford, *(How) Does Unconscious Bias Matter?: Law, Politics, and Racial Inequality*, 58 EMORY L.J. 1053, 1120 (2009).

2. WILLIAM JULIUS WILSON, WHEN WORK DISAPPEARS: THE WORLD OF THE NEW URBAN POOR 196 (1996).

3. *See, e.g.*, Roland G. Fryer et al., *Racial Disparities in Job Finding and Offered Wages*, 56 J.L. & ECON, 633, 635–36 (2011) (finding that racial discrimination in offered wages accounted for at least one third of the black-white wage gap); Devah Pager et al., *Discrimination in a Low-Wage Labor Market: A Field Experiment*, 74 AM. SOC. REV. 777. 792–93 (2009) (study of white, black, and Latino applicants seeking entry-level jobs in the low-wage labor market in New York City finding that blacks were half as likely to receive callbacks or job offers as were equally qualified whites, and that black and Latino applicants without a criminal record were treated no better than a white applicant just released from prison). *See also* KEVIN STAINBACK & DONALD TOMASKOVIC-DEVEY, DOCUMENTING DESEGREGATION: RACIAL AND GENDER SEGREGATION IN PRIVATE-SECTOR EMPLOYMENT SINCE THE CIVIL RIGHTS ACT (2013).

4. *See* Roland Fryer, *The Declining Significance of Discrimination* 30–31 (Nat'l Bureau of Econ. Research, Working Paper No. 16256, 2010), *available at* http://scholar.harvard.edu/files/fryer/files/racial_inequality_in_the_21st_century_the_declining_significance_of_discrimination.pdf (urging educational intervention to address the skills gap).

5. *See, e.g.*, WILSON,*supra* note 3.

6. *See* PATRICK SHARKEY, STUCK IN PLACE: URBAN NEIGHBORHOODS AND THE END OF PROGRESS TOWARD RACIAL EQUALITY 67 (2013).

7. *See, e.g.*, CTR. FOR SOCIAL INCLUSION, http://www.centerforsocialinclusion.org/ (last visited Jan. 29, 2014).

8. *See, e.g.*, INST. FOR METRO. OPPORTUNITY, http://www.law.umn.edu/metro/index.html (last visited Jan. 29, 2014); POVERTY & RACE RESEARCH ACTION COUNCIL, http://www.prrac.org (last visited Jan. 29, 2014); KIRWAN INST., OPPORTUNITY MAPPING INITIATIVE AND PROJECT LISTING, http://kirwaninstitute.osu.edu/initiatives/opportunity-communities/mapping/; THE OPPORTUNITY AGENDA, http://www.opportunityagenda.org.

9. 42 U.S.C. § 2000d.

10. Title VII makes it unlawful for an employer "to fail or refuse to hire or to discharge an individual, or otherwise to discriminate against any individual with respect to his compensation, terms, conditions, or privileges of employment, because of such individual's race, color, religion, sex, or national origin..." 42 U.S.C. §2000e-2(a). The Act also makes it an unlawful employment practice for an employer "to limit, segregate, or classify his employees or applicants for employment in any way which would deprive or tend to deprive any individual of employment opportunities or otherwise adversely affect his status as an employee, because of such individual's race, color, religion, sex, or national origin." *Id.*

11. *See* Banks & Ford, *supra* note 2, at 1113–14 (contending that "many decisions and practices that adversely affect racial minorities do not fit neatly within the conventional antidiscrimination framework"); Glenn C. Loury, *Discrimination in*

the Post-Civil Rights Era: Beyond Market Interactions, 12 J. ECON. PERSP. 117 (1998) (arguing that "market discrimination is only one small part of" contemporary racial disparities). And this argument is not new. When the Civil Rights Act was not yet twenty-five years old, Derek Bell decried the insufficiency of antidiscrimination law in addressing ongoing "race-related disadvantages," noting that "[t]he harvest is past, the summer is ended, and we are not saved." DERRICK BELL, AND WE ARE NOT SAVED: THE ELUSIVE QUEST FOR RACIAL JUSTICE 5 (1987).

12. *See, e.g.*, Banks & Ford, *supra* note 2, at 1113 (doubting that racial bias "explains all or even most of the racial injustices that plague our society"); LOURY, *supra* note 1, at 160 (arguing in the context of racial inequality that thinking simply in terms of "discrimination" obscures the "causal feedback loops that can perpetuate racial inequality from one generation to the next").

13. *See, e.g.*, RICHARD THOMPSON FORD, RIGHTS GONE WRONG: HOW LAW CORRUPTS THE STRUGGLE FOR EQUALITY 11–14 (2011).

14. *See Civil Rights and Job Opportunities*, 109 CONG. REC. 11,175 (1963) (statement of John F. Kennedy, President of the United States).

15. *Id.* at 11,178.

16. *Id.*

17. *Id.*

18. *See* H.R. REP. NO. 570 (1963). This report accompanies the Equal Employment Opportunity Act of 1963, the "nominal" ancestor to Title VII. H.R. 405, 88th Cong., 1st Sess. (1963). *See* Francis J. Vaas, *Title VII: Legislative History*, 7 B.C. INDUS. & COM. L. REV. 431, 433 n.10 (1966).

19. H.R. No. 814 (to accompany H.R. 7152, 88th Cong. (1st Sess. 1963)), at 2 (citing evidence from hearing making it "abundantly clear that job opportunity discrimination permeates the national social fabric-North, South, East and West").

20. *Id.*

21. *Id.*

22. *Id.* at 3

23. *Id.*

24. *Id.*

25. *Id.*

26. *See, e.g.*, United Steelworkers of Am. v. Weber, 443 U.S. 193 (1979) (holding that Title VII permitted voluntary race-conscious affirmative action plan over dissent's claim that the language and legislative history of the Act did not permit "quotas" or racial "preference[s]"); Johnson v. Transp. Agency of Santa Clara County, 480 U.S. 616, 670 (1987) (extending *Weber* to gender-based affirmative action and rejecting dissent's argument that *Weber* "rewrote the statute it purported to construe").

27. Civil rights reformers had advocated for a strong fair employment agency akin to the National Labor Relations Board (NLRB) with power to enforce antidiscrimination laws through cease-and-desist action. Instead, legislative compromises meant an EEOC with limited power—charged only with the power to investigate claims and mediate disputes. *See* Francis J. Vaas, *Title VII: Legislative History*, 7 B.C. INDUS. & COM. L. REV. 431, 453 (1966) (detailing Title VII legislative proposals for strong enforcement agency); Robert C. Lieberman, *Private Power and American Bureaucracy: The EEOC and Civil Rights Enforcement* 1–2 (Colum.

Univ. Dep't of Political Science, Working Paper, 2010) *available at* http://web1.millercenter.org/apd/colloquia/pdf/col_2005_0318_lieberman.pdf ("As originally conceived by civil rights advocates, the EEOC was to have full regulatory powers, particularly the power to issue binding cease-and-desist orders to employers."). Until 1972, the EEOC even lacked power to sue private employers in its own name. *See* Equal Employment Opportunity Act, Pub. L. No. 92-261, 86 Stat. 103 (1972).

28.   45 C.F.R. § 80.3(b)(2) (1965) ("A recipient...may not directly or through contractual or other arrangements, utilize criteria or methods of administration which have the *effect* of subjecting individuals to discrimination because of their race, color, or national origin, or have the effect of defeating or substantially impairing accomplishment of the objectives of the program as respect individuals race, color, or national origin.") (emphasis added). These regulations were created by a task force consisting of the White House, the Civil Rights Commission, the Justice Department, and the Bureau of the Budget. *See* Comment, *Title VI of the Civil Rights Act of 1964—Implementation and Impact*, 36 GEO. WASH. L. REV. 824 (1968). Each agency drafted a rule and submitted it to the Department of Justice, which then participated in the task force to draft these rules. *Id.* The task force first developed regulations for the Department of Health, Education, and Welfare, which then became the model for other federal agencies. *Id.*

29.   *See* HUGH DAVIS GRAHAM, THE CIVIL RIGHTS ERA: ORIGINS AND DEVELOPMENT OF NATIONAL POLICY, 1960–1972 (1991); Alfred W. Blumrosen, *Strangers in Paradise*: Griggs v. Duke Power Co. *and the Concept of Employment Discrimination*, 71 MICH. L. REV. 59 (1972) (stating that during the one-year delay in enforcing the 1964 Civil Rights Act instead of pursuing voluntary compliance with the Act, many Southern employers "adopted seemingly neutral personnel policies, which, in fact, perpetuated the subordinate position of black workers" including tests and educational requirements) (footnote omitted).

30.   Griggs v. Duke Power Co., 401 U.S. 424, 433 n.9 (1971) (quoting and construing Equal Opportunity Commission (EOC) Guidelines on Employment Testing Procedures (Aug. 24, 1966)).

31.   Guidelines on Employee Selection Procedures, 29 C.F.R. § 1607 (1970); *Griggs*, 401 U.S. at 433 n.9 (relying on 1970 guidelines).

32.   *Griggs*, 401 U.S. at 431.

33.   *Compare* PAUL D. MORENO, FROM DIRECT ACTION TO AFFIRMATIVE ACTION: FAIR EMPLOYMENT LAW AND POLICY IN AMERICA 1933–1972, at 1–2 (1999) (introducing "disparate impact" as a deviation from the "unequal treatment" colorblindness mandate that undergirded civil rights laws) *and* JOHN DAVID SKRENTNY, THE IRONIES OF AFFIRMATIVE ACTION: POLITICS, CULTURE & JUSTICE IN AMERICA 120–21, 127–131(1996) (describing developments such as racial reporting and disparate impact as moving away from the "color-blind approach" of Title VII, which focused on the intent of the discriminator), *with* Susan D. Carle, *A Social Movement History of Title VII Disparate Impact Analysis*, 63 FLA. L. REV. 251, 294–97 (2011) (describing how disparate impact standards drew on existing theories of discrimination evident in the practices of state fair employment commissions) *and* George Rutherglen, *Disparate Impact under Title VII: An Objective Theory of Discrimination*, 73 VA. L. REV. 1297, 1306–07 (1987) (describing disparate impact as an appropriate common law gap-filling given the absence of a definition of "discrimination" in the statute).

34.   *See* 42 U.S.C. §2000e-8(c); 29 C.F.R. §§ 1602.7–1602.14. The EEOC developed what

is now known as the EEO-1 form (the Employer Information Report form), which requires certain employers to collect and report data on their employees' race, ethnicity, and sex.

35. *See* Alfred W. Blumrosen, *Administrative Creativity: The First Year of the Equal Employment Opportunity Commission,* 38 GEO. WASH. L. REV. 694, 711–20 (1970). As sociologist John Sktrentny has observed, the EEO-1 forms allowed EEOC administrators to move beyond an individual approach: "the administrators could sit back and look at entire industries or geographic areas, and see racial differences not just freely contracting, abstract individuals." SKRENTNY, *supra* note 34, at 131. The EEOC used this data to develop "conciliation" plans that required employers to adopt particular hiring practices and affirmative remedies and to hold forums that brought public attention to the employment practices of major industries. *See* Robert C. Lieberman, *Private Power and American Bureaucracy: The EEOC and Civil Rights Enforcement* 27–28 (Colum. Univ. Dep't of Political Science, Working Paper, 2010) (relying on EEOC research report outlining potential use of EEO-1 data to file "commissioner charges" of discrimination—which did not require a specific plaintiff's coming forward—and to develop "technical assistance" programs to work with employers with discriminatory practices); *see* SKRENTNY, *supra* note 34, at 132 (describing forum on hiring practices for the textile industry in the Carolinas, which included forty witnesses representing management, labor, government, and private industries); *see id.* (noting forums on white collar employment and the pharmaceutical industry).

36. The NAACP Legal Defense Fund (LDF) and other civil rights and labor activists early on targeted particular industries in the South, including the textile industry, the paper industry, and the steel industry that were large sources of non-farm employment and provided more lucrative wages than many blacks were then earning. *See id. See also* NANCY MACLEAN, FREEDOM IS NOT ENOUGH: THE OPENING OF THE AMERICAN WORKPLACE 79 (2008) (detailing that the NAACP and the EEOC targeted textile mills because they were the largest non-farm employer of workers with limited education and supplied "more than half of all industrial jobs in the Carolinas and Georgia" and explaining that these jobs, though hard, paid higher wages than what was available to most black men and women at the time).

37. *See* Robert Belton, *A Comparative Review of Public and Private Enforcement of Title VII of the Civil Rights Act of 1964,* 31 VAND. L. REV. 905, 930 (1978). The late Professor Robert Belton served as an attorney at the NAACP LDF during this period. *Id.*

38. *See id.* at 936–38 (detailing LDF's litigation efforts in *Griggs*).

39. *See id.* at 945–46 (describing litigation culminating in *Robinson v. Lorillard Corp.,* 444 F.2d 791 (4th Cir. 1971)).

40. Belton, *A Comparative Review*, supra note 38, at 927.

41. *Id.*

42. *See id.* at 928.

43. *See* 42 U.S.C. §2000e-1 (directing EEOC to issue "suitable procedural regulations to carry out the provisions of this subchapter").

44. Lieberman, *supra* note 36, at 28.

45. *See* John J. Donohue III & James Heckman, *Continuous versus Episodic Change: The Impact of Civil Rights Policy on the Economic Status of Blacks,* 29 J. ECON. LITERATURE 1603, 1641 (1991) (providing evidence that enforcement of federal civil rights law, including Title VII, "was the major contributor to the sustained improvement in black economic status that began in 1965"); *id.* at 1637–38 ("much of the black

improvement in the decade following enactment of Title VII of the 1964 Civil Rights Act came in the South"); *id.* (detailing the role of federal promotion of school integration and enforcement of Title VII). *See also* MACLEAN, *supra* note 37, at 80 (quoting labor organizers in the 1960s who credited federal executive order on nondiscrimination in government contractors with opening up positions for blacks in Southern textile mills); *id.* at 88 (detailing increased hiring of black workers by Southern textile workers and the contribution manufacturing employment made to the economic status of blacks in the South); Jonathan S. Leonard, *The Impact of Affirmative Action Regulation & Equal Employment Law on Black Employment*, 4 J. OF ECON. PERSP. 47 (1990).

46. In the area of education, key researchers have credited Title VI and its implementing guidelines with "provid[ing] the standard operating principles" that enabled key advances in school integration. GARY ORFIELD, THE RECONSTRUCTION OF SOUTHERN EDUCATION: THE SCHOOLS AND THE 1964 CIVIL RIGHTS ACT 101 (1969).

47. *See, e.g.*, Paul Frymer, *Acting When Elected Officials Won't: Federal Courts and Civil Rights Enforcement in U.S Labor Unions 1935–85*, 97 AM. POL. SCI. REV. 483, 483–99; Lieberman, *supra* note 36 (providing account of the EEOC's backlog in processing individual complaints in the late 1960s and early 1970s).

48. *See* RISA L. GOLUBOFF, THE LOST PROMISE OF CIVIL RIGHTS (2010).

49. For recent Title VII cases, see *University of Texas Southwest Medical Center v. Nassar*, 570 U.S. , 133 S. Ct. 2517 (2013) (requiring a showing of "but for" causation to recover for claims of retaliation); *Vance v. Ball State Univ.*, 570 U.S. , 133 S. Ct. 2434, 2439 (2013) (defining "supervisor" for the purposes of Title VII as one "empowered by the employer to take tangible employment actions against the victim"); *Lewis v. City of Chicago*, 560 U.S. 205 (2010) (holding that a plaintiff who fails to file a timely charge when a disparate impact practice is adopted may challenge the later application of that practice in a disparate impact suit); *Ricci v. DeStefano*, 557 U.S. 557 (2009) (holding that employers may take race-conscious steps to avoid disparate impact liability under the Act only where there is a "strong basis in evidence" of such liability).

50. After 1991, the volume of charges filed with the EEOC involving Title VII claims of gender, race, national origin, and religion discrimination increased over the prior years. *See* Sean Farhang, *Congressional Mobilization of Private Litigants: Evidence from the Civil Rights Act of 1991*, 6 J. EMP. LEGAL STUD. 1 (2009). Farhang's data consist of charges with the EEOC, which, though they are a precondition to court filing, do not in all cases lead to court filing. Since at least the 1980s, commentators have identified patterns of declining class action. *See* J. LeVonne Chambers & Barry Goldstein, *Title VII at Twenty: The Continuing Challenge*, 1 LAB. LAW. 235, 238 (1985).

51. *See* John J. Donohue III & Peter Siegelman, *The Changing Nature of Employment Discrimination Litigation*, 43 STAN. L. REV. 983, 1015–17 (1991) (While hiring cases dominated EEOC and court dockets in 1966, by 1985, wrongful termination charges significantly outnumbered hiring cases.).

52. *See* EEOC, STATUTE BY ISSUE, FY 2010–FY 2012, http://www.eeoc.gov/eeoc/statistics/enforcement/statutes_by_issue.cfm (last visited Feb. 3, 2013) (EEOC charge data from fiscal years 2010, 2011, and 2012 showing that discharge complaints outnumbered hiring complaints by nine to one).

53. As two legal services' attorneys noted several years ago: "the volume of employment discrimination litigation has produced more aggressive gatekeeping by the courts, even as the lawsuits that offer the most hope for long term

economic security for our clients—by opening jobs and pathways to advancement—become increasingly rare." Sharon M. Dietrich & Noah Zatz, *A Practical Legal Services Approach to Addressing Racial Discrimination in Employment*, 36 CLEARINGHOUSE REV. 39, 42 (2002).

54. *See* SEAN FARHANG, THE LITIGATION STATE: PUBLIC REGULATION AND PRIVATE LAWSUITS IN THE UNITED STATES 29–31 (2010) (reviewing available empirical evidence and concluding that the threat of private enforcement litigation in particular regions led employers to adopt equal opportunity practices that improved the employment status of women and minorities). Laws, private enforcement, and regulatory action can also lead to the creation of rules and organizational structures within organizations to promote diversity and equal opportunity. *See, e.g.*, John R. Sutton & Frank Dobbin, *The Two Faces of Governance: Responses to Legal Uncertainty in U.S. Firms, 1955 to 1985*, 61 AM. SOC. REV. 794 (1996); Lauren B. Edelman, *Legal Ambiguity and Symbolic Structures: Organizational Mediation of Civil Rights Law*, 97 AM. J. SOC. 1531 (1992). (At the same time, this literature also questions whether this organizational compliance leads to substantive change.)

55. *See* Susan Sturm, *Second Generation Employment Discrimination: A Structural Approach*, 101 COLUM. L. REV. 458, 467–68 (2001) (describing limitations of Title VII law in addressing contemporary, second-generation discrimination that involves "patterns of interaction among groups within the workplace that, over time, exclude nondominant groups").

56. *See, e.g.*, Lewis v. City of Chicago, 560 U.S. 205 (2010) (litigation successfully brought against the Chicago Fire Department for the use of written tests with a unjustified disparate impact on black applicants); United States v. City of New York, 717 F.3d 72 (2d Cir. 2013) (finding selection practices of the Fire Department of New York to have an unjustified disparate impact on Latino and black applicants).

57. *See, e.g.*, Wright v. Stern, 553 F. Supp. 2d 337 (S.D.N.Y. 2008) (settling claims of systemic discrimination against the New York City Park departments for racially segregated job assignments and discrimination in pay and promotion); Settlement Agreement and Joint Stipulation, Cogdell v. Wet Seal, Inc., No. SACV 12-01138 AG (C.D. Cal. June 11, 2013), ECF No. 78-1 (settling claims of systemic discrimination in hiring and promotion by large retailer).

58. *See, e.g.*, REST. OPPORTUNITIES CTR. OF N.Y. UNITED & N.Y.C. REST. INDUS. COAL., THE THIRD SHIFT: CHILD CARE NEEDS AND ACCESS FOR WORKING MOTHERS IN RESTAURANTS (2013), http://rocunited.org/wp-content/uploads/2013/11/reports_third-shift-final-mm.pdf (last visited Sep. 11, 2015) [hereinafter THE THIRD SHIFT].

59. *See* REST. OPPORTUNITIES CTR. OF N.Y. UNITED & N.Y.C. REST. INDUS. COAL., THE GREAT SERVICE DIVIDE: OCCUPATIONAL SEGREGATION AND INEQUALITY IN THE RESTAURANT INDUSTRY (2009) (reporting findings on discrimination in hiring, pay, promotion and training opportunities) [hereinafter THE GREAT SERVICE DIVIDE].

60. Testers have been used most prominently to address housing discrimination, and the Supreme Court has held that the Fair Housing Act provides standing for fair housing testers. *See* Havens Realty Corp. v. Coleman, 455 U.S. 363 (1982) (holding that § 804(d) of the Fair Housing Act's language making it illegal to "'represent to *any person*...that any dwelling is not available for inspection, sale, or rental when such dwelling is in fact so available'" provides a sufficient basis for standing) (citation omitted); Olatunde Johnson, *The Last Plank: Rethinking Public and Private*

Power to Advance FairHousing, 13 U. PA. J. CONST. L. 1191, 1198–99 (2011) (describing use of audit testing to document and address discrimination in housing).

61. Researcher Mark Bendick conducted the matched pair audits of 138 fine dining restaurants and found pervasive discrimination in hiring for server positions. *See* THE GREAT SERVICE DIVIDE, *supra* note 60, at 2, 24. Specifically, the study found that testers of color were only 54 percent as likely as white testers to be offered server positions and were less likely to receive a job interview. *See id.* at 54 (81.4 percent of white testers were granted an interview, compared to 60.5 percent for testers of color). White testers who received a job interview were more likely to be offered a job than testers of color.

62. *See id.* (offering recommendations for industry changes); REST. OPPORTUNITIES CTR. OF N.Y. UNITED & N.Y.C. REST. INDUS. COAL., http://rocunited.org/wp-content/uploads/2012/01/ROCGuide_Report_F4.pdf (listing restaurants that take the "high road" by providing safe working conditions, complying with wage and hour law, and providing formal and transparent policies for employment opportunities and grievances).

63. *See* 42 U.S.C. § 2000e-5(b), (e), (f) (2006) (detailing the procedures for filing a Title VII charge with the EEOC and for bringing claims in court).

64. *See* Michael Selmi, *The Value of the EEOC: Reexamining the Agency's Role in Employment Discrimination Law*, 57 OHIO ST. L.J. 1, 7–10, 21–22 (1996) (concluding that the agency has capacity to investigate only a few cases and in the end it determines that most claims have no merit). In the words of one commentator, the "EEOC has been forced to focus on handling charges instead of pursuing enforcement initiatives." Michael Z. Green, *Proposing a New Paradigm for EEOC Enforcement after 35 Years: Outsourcing Charge Processing by Mandatory Mediation*, 105 DICK L. REV. 305, 309–10 (2001).

65. *See* LESLIE E. SILVERMAN, SYSTEMIC TASK FORCE REPORT TO THE CHAIR OF THE EQUAL EMPLOYMENT OPPORTUNITY COMMISSION 4–5, *available at* http://www.eeoc.gov/eeoc/task_reports/upload/systemic.pdf (listing deficiencies of current EEOC systems for tackling systemic discrimination).

66. *See id.* at 2 (noting that the EEOC was well positioned to tackle systemic discrimination because "unlike private litigants, EEOC need not meet the stringent requirements of Rule 23 of the Federal Rules of Civil Procedure in order to maintain a class suit in federal court").

67. *See, e.g.*, Wal-Mart Stores, Inc. v. Dukes, 564 U.S. , 131 S. Ct. 2541 (2011) (holding 5–4 that plaintiffs lacked the "commonality" of factual and legal claims required to satisfy Federal Rule of Civil Procedure 23(a)); *id.* (holding unanimously that plaintiffs' claims for back pay could not be certified pursuant to Rule 23(b)(2)); *see also* Melissa Hart, *Will Employment Discrimination Class Actions Survive?*, 37 AKRON L. REV. 813, 820–27 (2004) (describing pre-*Wal-Mart* lower courts' constraints on the use of Rule 23(b)(2) certification—the traditional route for class certification in employment discrimination class actions—in cases involving compensatory and punitive damages).

68. *See* 42 U.S.C. § 2000e-5(b) (outlining EEOC's commissioner's charges procedure).

69. *See* EEOC, STRATEGIC PLAN, FISCAL YEARS 2012–2016 (2012) (outlining renewed focused on systemic and pattern and practice litigation), *available at* http://www.eeoc.gov/eeoc/plan/upload/sep.pdf.

70. *Id.* (noting fourfold increase in the amount of damages recovered from employers in systemic discrimination cases between FY 2012 and FY 2011). *See* EEOC,

STRATEGIC PLAN FOR FISCAL YEARS 2007–2012 (2006), *available at* http://www.eeoc.gov/eeoc/plan/upload/strategic_plan_07to12_mod.pdf.

71. *See* EEOC, *supra* note 69; EEOC, Performance and Accountability Report, FY 2012, *available at* http://www.Eeoc.gov/eeoc/plan/2012par_performance.cfm (last visited Feb. 3, 2014).

72. *See* EEOC ENFORCEMENT GUIDANCE NO. 915.002, ENFORCEMENT GUIDANCE ON THE CONSIDERATION OF ARREST AND CONVICTION RECORDS IN EMPLOYMENT DECISIONS UNDER TITLE VII OF THE CIVIL RIGHTS ACT OF 1963 (2012), *available at* http://www.eeoc.gov/laws/guidance/upload/arrest_conviction.pdf   (issuing guidance on how employers might avoid disparate impact discrimination in the consideration of arrest and conviction records in employment decisions). I offer these examples not to deem them successes—success remains to be fully seen. The EEOC has had prominent setbacks in its recent systemic disparate impact litigation.[footnote]*See* EEOC v. Kaplan Higher Educ. Corp., No. 01:10 CV 2882, 2013 WL 322116 (N.D. Ohio, Jan. 28, 2013) (dismissing EEOC's suit against an employer for screening applicants based on credit histories, holding that expert's evidence of disparate impact was inadmissible); EEOC v. Freeman, No. RWT-09-CV-2573, 2013 WL 4464553 (D. Md. Aug. 9, 2013) (granting summary judgment to employer in case involving claims of discriminatory impact of criminal and credit history background checks on minority applicants, holding that expert testimony was unreliable and that disparate impact was not caused by a specific employment practice).

73. *See* Alfred W. Blumrosen, Intentional Job Discrimination in Metropolitan America 4 (2002) (unpublished paper) (on file with author) (describing the EEOC's failure to make consistent use of EEO-1 data over the period from 1965 to the late 1990s). Even when the EEOC has displayed the political will to utilize this data, it has not been able to make good use of this data because it lacked internal resources (staff and technological systems) for adequate data analysis. *See* STAINBACK & TOMASKOVIC-DEVEY, *supra* note 4. Also, the EEOC has failed to organize collect, organize, and tabulate the data in effective ways. *See* EEOC, SYSTEMATIC TASK FORCE REPORT (2006), n. 37, *available at* http://www.eeoc.gov/eeoc/task_reports/upload/systemic.pdf (recommending that the EEOC organize data to allow for automatic generation of reports on firms and their subsidiaries and comparative analysis between firms within an industry or relevant labor market).

74. The Supreme Court has not ruled on the question of whether Title VII grants standing for employment testers (Title VII has different language from the FHA), and lower courts are split on the question. *Compare* Fair Emp't Council of Greater Wash., Inc. v. BMC Mktg. Corp., 28 F.3d 1268 (D.C. Cir. 1994) (finding that employment testers lacked standing to sue because they did not actually intend to form an employment contract with the employer, though allowing organizational standing for group that sponsored the testers), *with* Kyles v. J.K. Guardian Sec. Servs., Inc., 222 F.3d 289, 297 (7th Cir. 2000) (finding that employment testers had standing to sue under Title VII, reasoning that FHA and Title VII both take "broad aim at discrimination in their respective sectors and in that sense are the functional equivalents of one another"). In regulatory guidance, the EEOC has taken the position that testers can file charges and litigate claims of employment discrimination. *See* EEOC ENFORCEMENT GUIDANCE NO. 915.002, WHETHER "TESTERS" CAN FILE CHARGES AND LITIGATE CLAIMS OF EMPLOYMENT DISCRIMINATION (1996), *available at* http://www.eeoc.gov/policy/docs/testers.html.

75. The EEOC has in recent years indicated that it will "explore the use of matched-pair testing," *see* EEOC, THE E-RACE INITIATIVE: ERADICATING RACISM & COLORISM

FROM EMPLOYMENT, www.eeoc.gov/eeoc/initiatives/e-race/index.cfm (last visited Feb. 3, 2014), but currently operates no testing program. The EEOC has tried to initiate matched-pair testing over the past several decades but has abandoned the project in the face of opposition from some members of Congress. *See* Michael Yelnosky, *Testers Revisited* (Roger Williams Law Sch. Legal Stud. Working Paper, Research Paper No. 74, 2009) (describing how in 1998, Congress conditioned a budgetary increase for the EEOC on the agency's abandoning its request for funding for testers). The EEOC has directed funding to private groups to conduct such testing. *See id.* at 5 (noting that after Congress blocked the EEOC's testing program, the agency provided $200,000 to private groups to carry out a testing program).

76. *See* U.S. Dep't Agric., Office of Civil Rights, DR 4300-4, Civil Rights Impact Analysis 1 (2003), *available at* http://www.ocio.usda.gov/sites/default/files/docs/2012/DR4300-004%5B1%5D.htm (requiring that agency grantees conduct a "civil rights impact analysis").

77. *See* 49 C.F.R. pt. 21 (2011) (imposing duties of nondiscrimination, assessment of impacts, and inclusion on federal grantees). U.S. Dep't of Transp., Fed. Transit Admin., Circular FTA C 4702.1A, Title VI and Title VI-Dependent Guidelines for Federal Transit Administration Recipients 11-1 (2007) (listing goals of regulation as preventing disparities, promoting participation, and ensuring access to transportation by all groups); U.S. Dep't of Transp., Fed. Highway Admin., No. 6640.23A, FHWA Actions to Address Environmental Justice In Minority Populations and Low-Income Populations (cancelled June 14, 2012), *available at* http://www.fhwa.dot.gov/legsregs/directives/orders/6640_23.htm.

78. Olatunde C. A. Johnson, *Beyond the Private Attorney General: Equality Directives in American Law*, 87 N.Y.U. L. Rev. 1339, 1384–86 (2012).

79. *See, e.g.*, Thomas W. Sanchez, *The Impact of Public Transportation on U.S. Metropolitan Wage Inequality*, 39 Urb. Stud. 423, 434 (2002) (showing links between the availability of public transportation and wage inequality in large metropolitan areas). The effect of transportation on segregation is well documented. *See generally* Kenneth T. Jackson, Crabgrass Frontier: The Suburbanization of the United States (1985) (detailing the contribution of highway development to suburbanization, sprawl, and racial segregation).

80. For instance, groups that have been key in implementing and leveraging Title VI's transportation directives including environmental justice groups, public transit advocacy groups, civil rights organizations, and regionalism groups. *See* Johnson, *supra* note 80, at 1406 n.303; *id.* at 1409 n.314; *id.* at 1411 n.321.

81. *See, e.g.*, Wilson, *supra* note 3, at 26–27 (detailing the effect of the decline of mass production on low-skilled workers). On the weakening of labor unions, see, e.g., Dorian T. Warren, *The American Labor Movement in the Age of Obama: The Challenges and Opportunities of a Racialized Political Economy*, 8 Persp. on Pol. 847, 848 (2010) (noting steep decline of labor unions' share of the American workforce—from over 30 percent of all workers in the 1940s to just 12.3 percent of all workers in 2009). On the decline of living wage jobs with career ladders, see Wilson, *supra* note 3, at 25.

82. *See* American Recovery and Reinvestment Act of 2009 § 14006, 123 Stat. at 284-84; U.S. Dep't of Education, Race to the Top Executive Summary (2009), *available at* http://www2.ed.gov/programs/racetothetop/executive-summary.pdf; No Child Left Behind, Pub. L. No. 107-110, 115 Stat. 1425 (codified as amended at 20 U.S.C. § 6301 note (Supp. II 2002)).

83. *See, e.g.,* Disproportionate Minority Contact, Act of Nov. 4, 1992, Pub. L. No. 102-586, § 2(f)(3)(a)(ii), 106 Stat. 4982, 4993–94 (codified as amended at 42 U.S.C. § 5633 (Supp. III 2005)).

84. *See* WILSON, *supra* note 3, at 216–17 (proposing improvement in school to work transition programs, skills training and other interventions). For an account of this statute, see Olatunde C. A. Johnson, *Disparity Rules,* 107 COLUM. L. REV. 374 (2007).

85. *See, e.g.,* THE THIRD SHIFT, *supra* note 59.>

86. *See* NAT'L EMP'T LAW PROJECT, BAN THE BOX: U.S. CITIES,COUNTIES AND STATES ADOPT FAIR HIRING POLICIES TO REDUCE BARRIERS TO EMPLOYMENT OF PEOPLE WITH CONVICTION RECORDS (2015), *available at* http://www.nelp.org/content/uploads/Ban-the-Box-Fair-Chance-State-and-Local-Guide.pdf (listing more than one hundred cities and counties that have "banned the box"); Amy Traub, *Ending Unjust Employment Credit Checks, Demos,* DEMOS, Feb. 7, 2012, http://www.demos.org/publication/ending-unjust-employment-credit-checks (reporting that seven states—Washington, Connecticut, Hawaii, Illinois, California, Maryland, and Oregon—have passed laws prohibiting credit checks in employment).

11

A Signal or a Silo? Title VII's Unexpected Hegemony

Sophia Z. Lee

In February 1976, the National Labor Relations Board (NLRB or Board) held hearings on whether to continue denying its services to unions that discriminated on the basis of race or sex.[1] Board members, like administrators at a number of the major federal regulatory agencies, had understood the 1964 enactment of Title VII to empower them to adopt its equal employment mission as their own. The Board's greatest champion of this effort, Member Howard Jenkins Jr., believed the Board was uniquely situated to provide "meaningful answers to the interrelated problems of race relations and industrial relations."[2] But after twelve years of expanding the scope of the Board's antidiscrimination policies, its members had doubts. Rather than harmonizing civil and labor rights as Jenkins had hoped, these policies, members feared, were undermining the right to collective action that the Board was designed to protect.[3] The Board's 1976 hearing only exacerbated these concerns. Attorneys for the AFL-CIO warned that employers "seek to defeat organization through any weapon put at hand," and the Board's policies were a weapon whose "one cutting edge directed at the 'right to self-organization.'"[4] That employers were the only parties urging the Board to more fully import Title VII standards confirmed the labor lawyers' concern.[5]

For scholars attuned to labor and civil rights, as for the Board members convening that 1976 hearing, Title VII has had a mixed legacy. On the one hand, as historian Nancy MacLean has demonstrated, Title VII transformed the workplace, not only opening jobs but also empowering workers and forging new political coalitions among women and communities of color.[6] Labor scholar Benjamin Sachs has noted ways that Title VII facilitates collective action today at a time when traditional labor law is "ossified."[7] Others have sought to revitalize the labor movement by reframing labor rights as civil rights and amending Title VII to prohibit discrimination against union organizing.[8]

Yet Title VII's triumphs have come, other scholars note, at a steep cost to unions. To some, Title VII was based on an individual rights regime that was fundamentally adverse to the collective rights on which New Deal labor laws such as the Wagner Act were premised.[9] To others, the early EEOC staff and plaintiff-side lawyers were insensitive to how unions worked and unreasonably destructive in their demands.[10] In BLACK AND BLUE: AFRICAN AMERICANS, THE LABOR MOVEMENT, AND THE DECLINE OF THE DEMOCRATIC PARTY, political scientist Paul Frymer argues that decades of inaction (or insufficient action) by Congress, the executive branch, and the labor movement led to a bifurcated legal regime in which the NLRB protected labor rights while the federal courts implemented Title VII. The courts ended up being much more effective at integrating unions than anyone had anticipated. But this approach left union discrimination in the hands of officials, attorneys, and judges who were neither familiar with unions nor motivated to accommodate civil and labor rights. The unfortunate result, Frymer argues, was a court-based civil rights regime that gravely weakened labor policy and the labor movement.[11]

I have suggested elsewhere that a more unified legal regime was both more vigorously sought and more complicated to achieve than existing scholarship recognizes.[12] I explain my skepticism at far greater length in my book, THE WORKPLACE CONSTITUTION FROM THE NEW DEAL TO THE NEW RIGHT, by demonstrating that efforts to fuse labor and civil rights faced daunting political and legal hurdles from the inception of the New Deal labor regime.[13] For this fiftieth anniversary of Title VII, however, I focus on that law's relationship to the National Labor Relations Act (NLRA) during Title VII's first fifteen years. As the opening vignette suggests, efforts to charge the NLRB with Title VII's implementation as a means to strengthen employment discrimination law while better harmonizing it with labor rights turned out to be as, if not more, detrimental to unions than Title VII's enforcement by the courts. Court enforcement of Title VII dominates employment discrimination today partly as a result of efforts to protect workers' right to collective action.

Below I trace an impulse I call "Title VII as signal," showing how Title VII was initially understood to instantiate a broader constitutional obligation to ensure workplace equality and to simultaneously heighten the federal government's duty to fulfill that obligation. This penumbra emanating from Title VII encouraged the NLRB during the 1960s and 1970s to expand its antidiscrimination policies. In the latter half of the 1970s, however, Title VII was reconceived as a silo in which antidiscrimination efforts should be consolidated. This was in part because of concerns that the NLRB's antidiscrimination policies came at too great a cost to its primary mission of ensuring workers' right to self-organization. By 1979, employment discrimination enforcement was concentrated in the agency Title VII created, the Equal Employment Opportunity Commission (EEOC), and Title VII litigation in the courts had achieved preeminence within that enforcement regime. This history casts doubt on the viability of a more harmonized labor and civil rights regime, then, and offers a cautionary tale to those eager to fuse the two regimes today.

I. Title VII as Signal

When Title VII was enacted in 1964, about one in four nonfarm American workers belonged to a union.[14] While this represented a drop-off from the midcentury peak of one in three workers, unions were still powerful actors—so powerful, in fact, that their support was pivotal to Title VII's passage.[15] Similarly, the NLRB, although a political punching bag for business interests and anti-New Deal conservatives, was a powerful, closely watched regulatory agency. Indeed regulatory agencies generally loomed much larger then, presiding over major monopolized industries—gas and electric utilities, airlines, telecommunications—that have since been broken up and deregulated. These agencies were seen as potential agents of reform: when consumer advocate Ralph Nader sent armies of law student interns out to change the world in the late 1960s and early 1970s, they wrote carefully researched manifestos about agencies like the Interstate Commerce Commission.[16] There was one prominent exception to this era of regulatory prowess: the EEOC. Indeed, so weak was the EEOC and the statute it was created to implement that civil rights advocates sought to strengthen the employment discrimination regime by disseminating Title VII's enforcement throughout the federal government.

A. Title VII's Formal Weakness

For the thirty years prior to Title VII's enactment, moderate and conservative Republicans, to the extent that they supported a federal fair employment law, favored one that relied on voluntary compliance or at most would be enforced by the judiciary.[17] Civil rights advocates' experience with unions' duty of fair representation under the federal labor laws, a court-enforced protection that African American workers won in 1944, made them leery of this approach.[18] As they frequently told Congress, litigation had proved "expensive and cumbersome" as well as "inadequate."[19] Instead, civil rights and labor advocates as well as their congressional allies countered that any federal fair employment law should be enforced by an agency like the NLRB that had the power to adjudicate and remedy discrimination claims.[20] Title VII, however, had required moderate and conservative Republicans' support and thus adopted their preferred court-enforced approach. In the opinion of the law's civil rights supporters, this was a significant compromise.[21]

Title VII's first years only aggravated civil rights advocates' concerns. The EEOC quickly earned a reputation for ineffectiveness. Demand outstripped the agency's resources. The EEOC's tiny staff received nearly nine thousand complaints in its first year alone, developing a backlog that neared two thousand. Furthermore, at first, the EEOC made only limited use of the resources and power it had, its efforts stymied by internal strife and rapid staff turnover.[22] And even after the EEOC got around to investigating and conciliating a complaint, the wait was not necessarily over. If this approach failed, complainants had to find an attorney to file a private lawsuit and then engage in just the kind of drawn-out litigation that had proved so "inadequate" in duty of fair representation cases. In 1967, two years after filing a complaint with the EEOC, workers at the El Dorado, Arkansas, Monsanto plant reported having gained only "a feeling of depression, real low down."[23]

The federal courts surprised everyone with their robust enforcement of Title VII, but civil rights advocates still worried about the law's weaknesses.[24] In some industries, most employers were too small to be covered by Title VII, for instance.[25] Even where Title VII applied, advocates lamented aspects of the law's approach. There were "major limitations upon relying on law suits as the sole or even principal instrument of implementing fair employment policy," advocates insisted in 1972.[26] They contended that courts lacked expertise in industries' business practices, hampering their ability to determine whether employment qualifications that tended to exclude African Americans were justified. Lawsuits also affected only a single employer, while industry-wide consent decrees required copious time, effort, and expense. Advocates sought a means to instead "induce a great deal of voluntary compliance."[27]

B. Title VII's Penumbral Strength

For those who thought lawsuits were not the best, or at least should not be the exclusive, way to counter workplace discrimination, Title VII nonetheless held promise. Even before Title VII's passage, some government officials acknowledged a national policy against employment discrimination that derived from the Constitution.[28] Although Congress technically relied on the Commerce Clause to authorize Title VII, the law was believed by many to also codify this constitutionally grounded antidiscrimination requirement.[29] Officials argued that Title VII strengthened this national policy against discrimination and indicated that all government officials should implement its aims.[30] At the same time, Title VII's constitutional roots meant that government actors were not bound by the law's formal limits.[31] Title VII, the Justice Department advised, did not "circumscribe the authority of Federal agencies...to regulate employment practices."[32] Agencies were instead free to regulate in Title VII's name, even if they exceeded its formal provisions.

C. Title VII's Dissemination

Federal officials made use of Title VII's penumbra. In the late 1960s and early 1970s, the Federal Communications Commission (FCC) adopted rules requiring all broadcasters and common carriers to adopt equal employment policies. Broadcasters had argued that Congress in Title VII delegated "regulatory power over civil rights" to the EEOC, not the FCC.[33] The FCC disagreed, reasoning that the "national policy against discrimination in employment" was "particularly embodied" in Title VII but was not limited to its provisions.[34] The agency therefore imposed equal employment requirements, including on broadcasters too small to trigger Title VII coverage.[35] At the Federal Power Commission (FPC), attorneys likewise argued that the agency's duty to regulate in the public interest obligated it to consider the national policy against discrimination when licensing or certificating utilities. As at the FCC, they reasoned that because Title VII embodied but did not delimit this policy, the FPC could demand equal employment even from utilities that were not technically violating Title VII.[36] Similar arguments were made by officials from numerous federal agencies.[37]

Other than the FCC, the agency that made the most use of Title VII's penumbra was the NLRB. The Board had long policed some types of racism in the workplace, prohibiting unions from designating the group of workers it would represent (called a "bargaining unit") based solely on those workers' race and regulating the use of racially charged speech during union election campaigns.[38] If a union demonstrated sufficient worker support, the NLRB would "certify" it as the exclusive representative of all workers in the bargaining unit. In the 1940s, the NLRB promised to rescind the certification of any union that failed to fairly represent the African Americans in its bargaining unit, but the Board defined fair representation narrowly. As the NAACP's Labor Secretary quipped in 1949, under the Board's policy, "[u]nions may exclude colored people from membership, they may segregate them into separate locals and they may refuse to let them share in the full benefits of the union, but no union may discriminate against them because of race."[39] In the 1950s, spurred in part by *Brown v. Board of Education*, the Board put more teeth in its existing antidiscrimination policies.[40] In the early 1960s, even before Title VII was enacted, it further strengthened them, including by finally decertifying a union for segregating its membership by race—a decision it symbolically released the same day President Johnson signed Title VII into law.[41]

Title VII's enactment did not dampen the Board's policy innovations. One member contended that the law had affirmed the Board's obligation to police racial discrimination.[42] Others, faced with charges that Title VII, once enacted, became the exclusive basis for policing workplace discrimination, insisted that it "had not...limit[ed] the Board's duty or authority in this area."[43] Over the next ten years, the Board found repeatedly that unions' racially discriminatory practices violated their duty of fair representation and constituted an "unfair labor practice" under all three of the possible statutory provisions.[44] The latter legal tools were the most union-friendly because they allowed the Board to order a union to remedy its discriminatory practices without threatening its status as the bargaining unit's representative. The Board also extended its antidiscrimination policies to reach employers who were complicit in unions' discrimination or who failed to bargain in good faith about their own discriminatory policies.[45] In 1974, the Board, after much internal deliberation and dissensus, established its most aggressive antidiscrimination policy yet. In *Bekins Moving & Storage Co.*, the Board refused to certify a union that had won an election on the grounds that it had *in the past* demonstrated a "propensity" to discriminate.[46]

II. Title VII as Silo

Even as Title VII fed equal employment policy innovation in federal agencies, some officials pushed back against the trend. The FPC, for instance, recognized in 1970 the "national policy that discrimination in employment is to be eliminated by all elements of our society, public and private."[47] But it contended that it was not authorized to require equal employment from the utilities it regulated because employment discrimination was not sufficiently related to any of its regulatory purposes.[48] Several years later, its lawyers asked the Supreme Court to "set the fences" between the nation's antidiscrimination and economic regulatory statutes.[49] Agency oversight of utilities' employment practices, they argued, would draw the FPC into a "hopeless morass...of litigation" it was ill equipped to handle.[50] The FPC declined to adopt equal employment policies because its leadership's politics changed after Richard Nixon's election in 1968. Nixon appointees to the NLRB, in contrast, embraced their agency's antidiscrimination duties. Yet they too began to see the need to set some fences between the NLRA and Title VII.

A. Title VII and Mission Preservation

Edward Miller, Nixon's choice for NLRB chairman, was enthusiastic about the Board's antidiscrimination responsibilities. In the early 1970s, Miller undertook an ambitious effort to develop a comprehensive policy for handling claims of union discrimination[51] and gave speeches touting the Board's antidiscrimination responsibilities.[52] He insisted that Title VII "had not...limit[ed] the Board's duty or authority in this area."[53] But he worried about making the Board, which already suffered from an infamous backlog, too attractive an alternative to Title VII.

During the latter half of the 1960s, when the Board innovated and Title VII disappointed, commentators praised the Board's policies and argued that they were superior to Title VII.[54] One author lauded the NLRB's well-established administrative machinery, experienced staff, and swifter, more economical approach.[55] The Board had "sharper enforcement teeth than Congress has provided minority workers in recent civil-rights legislation," another observed.[56] The free legal services the General Counsel's office provided and the public hearings the Board held could also draw complaints to the NLRB and away from the EEOC.[57] Indeed, African Americans were reportedly "claim[ing that] their demands for equal job opportunities have been frustrated under both the law [Title VII] and agency [EEOC] specifically created by Congress to deal with race bias."[58] After a federal appeals court ruled that the Board could sanction employer discrimination even in nonunion workplaces, one government official predicted that the Board "could put the [EEOC]...out of business."[59]

This was an outcome Miller wanted to avoid. He worried that if the Board's policies were coextensive with Title VII, it would be "so inundated with cases that its procedures would bog down in a hopeless morass."[60] As a result, he implemented more narrow antidiscrimination policies than Title VII required. In 1968, a federal court remanded a case to the Board to determine whether an employer engaged in a "pattern or practice" of racial discrimination (a term lifted straight from Title VII) and therefore should be subject to an unfair labor practice order for "interfer[ing] with, restrain[ing] or coerc[ing] employees in the exercise of their rights" to self-organization under the NLRA.[61] Such a policy could empower the NLRB to remedy employer discrimination at the vast majority of nonunionized workplaces. Miller rejected the court's premise that *any* pattern or practice of discrimination would be grounds for an unfair labor practice order. Instead, the Board would issue such orders only where there was a "direct relationship between the alleged discrimination" and workers' exercise of their rights under the NLRA.[62] He also rejected the disparate impact standard the Supreme Court adopted under Title VII, finding that racial imbalance or disparate effects alone were insufficient to prove union and employer discrimination.[63]

B. Title VII and Employer Pretext

In addition to bureaucratic overload, Board members worried that their antidiscrimination policies were facilitating employer intransigence. In the 1960s and 1970s, resisting unionization at all costs became a mainstream business position. A new "union avoidance" industry of lawyers and consultants advised employers to delay elections and, if unsuccessful, put off signing a contract as long as possible.[64] An employer could accomplish both aims by charging the union with discrimination, either to prevent its certification as representative or as grounds for the Board to deny the union an order requiring the employer to bargain in good faith. Chairman Miller's replacement, Betty Southard Murphy, was the Board's first female member, the only woman at the helm of a major regulatory agency, and a strong proponent of "civil rights and equal employment opportunity for workers."[65] Worried about "employer[s] raising for pretextual reasons...that a union discriminated racially," however, she called the 1976 Board hearings to reconsider her agency's antidiscrimination policies.[66]

The employers who appeared at the hearing underscored the problem. Bell & Howell claimed a union's *sex* discrimination barred it from representing the company's *all-male* stationary engineers. Trumbull Asphalt Company, Inc. accused a Teamsters local organizing its all-*white*, all-*male* truck drivers of *race* and *sex* discrimination.[67] At the time of the hearings, these unions' petitions were already two to three years old. "[I]t is just outrageous for an employer who was the discriminator" to be bringing these charges, the Teamsters' lawyer charged at the Board's 1976 hearing.[68]

Meanwhile, civil rights advocates had abandoned these claims. From the 1940s to the 1960s, the NAACP waged a decades-long fight to convince the Board to police discrimination more aggressively. Although it greeted enthusiastically the Board's early 1960s decision to do so, by the 1970s, it had all but ceased bringing discrimination charges before the Board. When the NLRB issued an open call to participate in its 1976 hearings, no one from the NAACP responded. The most obvious explanation would seem to be that the NAACP had decided Title VII litigation in the courts was a more fruitful avenue. Yet the NAACP continued to pursue equal employment policies before other regulatory agencies.[69] With its labor allies concerned that the Board's antidiscrimination policies would give union opponents "an opportunity to destroy collective bargaining in this country," the NAACP likely decided that the NLRB remedies were not worth defending.[70]

C. The Three Branches Disentangle Title VII

During the second half of the 1970s, the Supreme Court, Congress, and the president enclosed Title VII—and employment discrimination policy more generally—in a legal and institutional silo. The Court was first to act. In the mid-1970s, the Supreme Court disentangled Title VII from the Constitution and federal regulatory statutes such as the NLRA. In its 1975 *Emporium Capwell v. Western Addition Community Organization* decision, a nearly unanimous Court ruled that the NLRB did not have to protect employees discharged for protesting employer discrimination after they rejected working through their union to redress it.[71] Employees' right to be free from discrimination "cannot be pursued at the expense of the orderly collective-bargaining process contemplated by the NLRA," the Court held.[72] The fact that Title VII's antiretaliation provisions may have protected the employees did not mean that the NLRA had to. Read most broadly, the Board appeared under no duty to counter discrimination if doing so would frustrate its core statutory mission.[73]

The next year, the Court further disentangled Title VII. *NAACP v. Federal Power Commission* reaffirmed and refined the principle the Court had laid down in *Emporium Capwell*. Again, a unanimous Court rejected the premise that regulatory agencies had a broad mandate to implement the national policy against discrimination. "Setting the fences" just as the FPC had asked, the Court ruled that agencies need only implement antidiscrimination if it was related to their primary statutory mission.[74] Further undermining agencies' authority to diffuse Title VII's antidiscrimination mandate throughout the federal bureaucracy, the Court erected a similar boundary between the Constitution and Title VII in *Washington v. Davis*.[75] Contrary to the assumption of federal courts and government officials, the Court declined to hold that the "constitutional standard for adjudicating claims of invidious racial discrimination is identical to the standards applicable under Title VII."[76] Henceforward, only Title VII would protect against nonintentional discrimination.

During 1977 and 1978, the executive branch and Congress similarly disentangled employment discrimination policy from the federal bureaucracy and consolidated it under the EEOC. In February 1977, President Carter announced that he intended to concentrate implementation of federal employment discrimination policies.[77] One year later, he sent a plan to Congress that centralized enforcement of nearly forty different equal employment requirements handled by nearly twenty different agencies under the EEOC.[78] "Fragmentation of authority among a number of federal agencies," Carter contended "has meant confusion and ineffective enforcement for employees, regulatory duplication and needless expense for employers."[79] That summer, Congress allowed the plan to go into effect.[80] With "[v]irtually all the groups protected by Title VII of the Civil Rights Act...support[ing]" the plan, the era of policy dissemination was over.[81]

D. The NLRB Reverses Course

With pressure to incorporate employment discrimination into Board policy removed, the Board rejected the policies it found most likely to hurt its primary statutory mission. In 1977, the Board decided the cases that had been the subject of its hearings. Denying certification or bargaining orders to discriminatory unions, the Board held, gave employers "an incentive to inject charges of union racial discrimination into Board...proceedings as a delaying tactic...rather than to attack racial discrimination."[82] These policies thus "significantly impair[ed] the national labor policy of facilitating collective bargaining, the enforcement of which is our primary function," the Board concluded, and denied workers' right to a representative of their choosing.[83]

The Board noted that the Supreme Court's fence-laying decisions supported its decision. When enforcing the challenged policies, a federal appellate court had previously required the Board to assess discrimination using the same statistical methods that courts used when they were applying Title VII. The appellate court had done so, however, because it held that the NLRB was constitutionally obligated to police discrimination and assumed that Title VII established the standard for this constitutional duty. The appellate court's approach, the Board now found, had not survived *Washington v. Davis*, which, the Board observed, had separated the two. The Board was thus free to reject the Title VII evidentiary standards the appellate court preferred. The Board also reasoned that *Emporium Capwell* had recognized that the Board must interpret the NLRA in light of "the national labor policy" but had rejected the proposition that the NLRA "should give way to the paramount value of combating racial discrimination." *NAACP* had further clarified that when implementing national antidiscrimination policy, "consideration must be given to whether such action promotes or runs counter to the [NLRA's] basic policies and purposes." Because the certification and bargaining policies the Board was reconsidering impeded its "primary function" of "facilitating collective bargaining," the Board found that it was justified in rejecting them.[84]

The NLRB faced no resistance for this turnaround. Congress's approval of Carter's reorganization plan in 1978 ratified the spirit of the NLRB's approach. In 1979, the D.C. Circuit Court of Appeals put the judiciary's more specific stamp of approval on the Board's decision to carefully limit its antidiscrimination policies. In *Bell & Howell Co. v. NLRB*, the court found that the Board's statutory purpose gave it a role in countering discrimination. The court nonetheless found this obligation better satisfied by the postcertification remedies the Board developed in the 1960s, such as issuing unfair labor practice orders against unions that violated their duty of fair representation or possibly decertifying them. These, the court held, were more "consistent with the other policies of the" NLRA.[85] Henceforth, the NLRB would police discrimination only in unionized workplaces and only according to its more narrowly defined notion of discrimination. The days of it serving as a serious competitor to the EEOC were over for good.

III. Conclusion: Title VII's Unexpected Hegemony

Scholars today write wistfully of an alternate legal regime that could have better harmonized antidiscrimination with labor law's recognition of workers' right to organize and bargain collectively. During Title VII's uncertain first fifteen years, advocates, legislators, administrators, and workers sought to disseminate enforcement of Title VII's mandate throughout administrative agencies, pursuing a more powerful Title VII and one more harmonized with labor rights. But empowering Title VII via dissemination proved less effective than its proponents expected, while achieving a more harmonious regime was more complicated than is currently thought. Title VII litigation's domination of employment discrimination law today was not inevitable, immediate, or particularly desired at the law's inception. Fifteen years on, however, it had become the consensus position across government, as well as among civil rights *and* labor advocates.

While only speculative, this history should give pause to those who advocate incorporating labor rights under Title VII. Just as incorporating antidiscrimination into labor law threatened workers' right to organize in the 1970s, incorporating labor rights into Title VII in the twenty-first century might threaten what is left of antidiscrimination law today. The EEOC is already overloaded—perhaps even more than the NLRB was in the 1970s—while the courts have steadily weakened Title VII.[86] Yet employers have gutted labor law with greater vigor and coordination than they have employment discrimination law.[87] Indeed, as this history shows, employer hostility to unions has at times fostered *support* for antidiscrimination laws.[88] Given the challenges already facing employment discrimination law today, it might be best to keep the two regimes separate, especially if Title VII is currently proving a useful tool in organizing campaigns.[89]

About the Author

Assistant professor, University of Pennsylvania Law School. This was prepared for the University of Michigan Law School conference, A Nation of Widening Opportunities: The Civil Rights Act at 50. *Thank you to the conference participants and especially its conveners, Ellen Katz and Samuel Bagenstos, as well as their editors. What follows draws on research and conversations made possible by the generosity of too many individuals and institutions to thank here individually, but I hope they will all still accept my hearty thanks. Errors are my own.*

Notes

1. As will be explained at greater length below, the specific Board policies at issue were denying certification and bargaining orders to discriminatory unions.

2. NLRB, "Howard Jenkins Sworn in for Second Term on NLRB" (Aug. 1, 1968) (RG 25, NLRB Records [hereinafter NLRB Records], Committee Management Files, 1934–1974: Former Chairman Miller, 1953–1973, Box 16, "Board Member: Howard Jenkins" Folder, National Archives and Record Administration, College Park, Md. [hereinafter NARA]) (all archival sources are on file with author).

3. News Release, NLRB, NLRB to Hear Race and Sex Arguments (Jan. 29, 1976), *available at* http://apps.nlrb.gov/link/document.aspx/09031d4580ca52f7.

4. Brief for the AFL-CIO as Amicus Curiae, Trumbull et al. v. NLRB, Feb. 13, 1976 [hereafter 1976 Board Hearing Brief—AFL-CIO] (NLRB Records, Selected Taft-Hartley Cases, 1978 [hereinafter NLRB Records-STHC-78], FRC Boxes 54–55), 3–4.

5. Official Report of Proceedings, Murcel Mfg. Corp., 231 N.L.R.B. 623 (Feb. 2, 1976), No. 10-CA-10122 et al., [hereinafter 1976 Board Hearing Transcript] (NLRB Records-STHC-78, FRC Boxes 54–55), 58–59, 99–100.

6. NANCY MACLEAN, FREEDOM IS NOT ENOUGH: THE OPENING OF THE AMERICAN WORKPLACE (2008). MacLean, while not overlooking the law's limits, argues that it worked a "veritable revolution in thinking about race and gender at work." *Id.* at 2. Although scholars are right to critique the law's limits, it is equally important that we not lose sight of its accomplishments.

7. Benjamin Sachs, *Employment Law as Labor Law*, 29 CARDOZO L. REV. 2685 (2008). *See also* Cynthia L. Estlund, *The Ossification of American Labor Law*, 102 COLUM. L. REV. 1527 (2002).

8. RICHARD D. KAHLENBERG & MOSHE MARVIT, WHY LABOR ORGANIZING SHOULD BE A CIVIL RIGHT: REBUILDING A MIDDLE-CLASS DEMOCRACY BY ENHANCING WORKER VOICE (2012).

9. JEFFERSON COWIE, STAYIN' ALIVE: THE 1970S AND THE LAST DAYS OF THE WORKING CLASS (2010); NELSON LICHTENSTEIN, STATE OF THE UNION: A CENTURY OF AMERICAN LABOR (2002); Reuel E. Schiller, *The Emporium Capwell Case: Race, Labor Law, and Crisis of Post-War Liberalism*, 25 BERKELEY J. EMP. & LAB. L. 129 (2004); Reuel E. Schiller, *From Group Rights to Individual Liberties: Post-War Labor Law, Liberalism, and the Waning of Union Status*, 20 BERKELEY J. EMP. & LAB. L. 1 (1999).

10. JUDITH STEIN, RUNNING STEEL, RUNNING AMERICA: RACE, ECONOMIC POLICY AND THE DECLINE OF LIBERALISM (1998).

11. PAUL FRYMER, BLACK AND BLUE: AFRICAN AMERICANS, THE LABOR MOVEMENT, AND THE DECLINE OF THE DEMOCRATIC PARTY (2007).

12. Sophia Z. Lee, Book Review, 28 LAW & HIST. REV. 554 (2010) (reviewing FRYMER, *supra* note 11); Sophia Z. Lee, Untitled Paper at the Am. Ass'n of Law Sch. Panel, "Solidarity: The New Antidiscrimination Law?" (Jan. 5, 2012); Sophia Z. Lee, *Hotspots in a Cold War: The NAACP's Postwar Workplace Constitutionalism, 1948–1964*, 26 LAW & HIST. REV. 327 (2008).

13. SOPHIA Z. LEE, THE WORKPLACE CONSTITUTION FROM THE NEW DEAL TO THE NEW RIGHT (2014).

14. Leo Troy, *Trade Union Membership, 1897–1962*, 47 REV. ECON. & STAT. 93, 94 (1965).

15. NELSON LICHTENSTEIN, THE MOST DANGEROUS MAN IN DETROIT: WALTER REUTHER AND THE FATE OF AMERICAN LABOR 384–88 (1995).

16. ROBERT C. FELLMETH, RALPH NADER, & CENTER FOR STUDY OF RESPONSIVE LAW, SURFACE TRANSPORTATION, THE PUBLIC INTEREST AND THE ICC (1970).

17. he most comprehensive treatment of the partisan and political forces shaping federal fair employment law is ANTHONY S. CHEN, THE FIFTH FREEDOM: JOBS, POLITICS, AND CIVIL RIGHTS IN THE UNITED STATES, 1941–1972 (2009). For a more specialized treatment of Republicans, see Anthony S. Chen, *The Party of Lincoln and the Politics of State Fair Employment Practices Legislation in the North, 1945–1964,* 112 AM. J. SOC. 1713 (2007). *See also* David Freeman Engstrom, *The Lost Origins of American Fair Employment Law: Regulatory Choice and the Making of Modern Civil Rights, 1943–1972,* 63 STAN. L. REV. 1071 (2011).

18. Steele v. Louisville & Nashville R.R. Co., 323 U.S. 192 (1944); Tunstall v. Bhd. of Locomotive Firemen & Enginemen, 323 U.S. 210 (1944).

19. *See, e.g., H. Comm. on Interstate and Foreign Commerce,* 81st Cong., 2d Sess. 278, 282 (1950) (testimony of Theodore E. Brown); *S. Subcomm. of the Comm. on Labor and Pub. Welfare,* 81st Cong., 2d Sess. S. 3295, at 30 (1950) (testimony of Joseph Waddy).

20. *See* CHEN, *supra* note 17, at 51–55; Engstrom, *supra* note 17.

21. SEAN FARHANG, THE LITIGATION STATE: PUBLIC REGULATION AND PRIVATE LAWSUITS IN THE UNITED STATES 106–19 (2010); 3 BRUCE ACKERMAN, WE THE PEOPLE: THE CIVIL RIGHTS REVOLUTION (2014).

22. James P. Gannon, *Negro Hopes Wane as '64 Civil Rights Law Founders,* WALL ST. J., Jan. 13, 1967, at 10. MACLEAN, *supra* note 6, at 111; JOHN DAVID SKRENTNY, THE IRONIES OF AFFIRMATIVE ACTION: POLITICS, CULTURE AND JUSTICE IN AMERICA 120–25 (1996).

23. Gannon, *supra* note 22.

24. FARHANG, *supra* note 21, at 132–47; FRYMER, *supra* note 11, at 70–94.

25. *See, e.g.,* BROADCASTING, 1967 BROADCASTING YEARBOOK A-170 (1967). Even after Congress expanded Title VII in 1972 to cover smaller employers, 76 percent of AM stations and 86 percent of FM stations still fell outside the law's reach. *Id.* The 1972 amendments had a much greater impact on television broadcasters—the proportion that fell outside the law's coverage dropped from 85 percent to 12 percent. *Id.*

26. William L. Taylor, Problems in Developing and Enforcing Fair Employment Law in the United States, Speech to the Villa Sebelloni Conference at Lake Como, Italy 18–19 (Oct. 2–6, 1972) (transcript available in the University of Notre Dame Archives, Howard A Glickstein Papers, MGLI 20.2539).

27. *Id.* Taylor was very involved in the Leadership Conference for Civil Rights, an umbrella group of liberal organizations, many of which were pursuing the strategy Taylor advocated. *See* LEE, *supra* note 13, at ch. 10.

28. Memorandum from N. Thompson Powers to Norbert A. Schlei 3 (July 8, 1963) (Dep't of Justice Records, John F. Kennedy Library, microcopy NK-2, roll 91, "Employment," NARA) (enclosing FCC memo).

29. *See, e.g.,* 33 Fed. Reg. 9960, 9964 (July 11, 1968). *See also* 118 CONG. REC. 3959, 3960–61, 3965 (1972). This was reflected in federal courts' assumption that Title VII violations were coextensive with violations of the Equal Protection Clause. *See* Davis v. Washington, 512 F.2d 956, 958 n.2 (D.C. Cir. 1975) (collecting cases), *rev'd,*

426 U.S. 229 (1976). *See generally*SERENA MAYERI, REASONING FROM RACE: FEMINISM, LAW, AND THE CIVIL RIGHTS REVOLUTION 106–10, 132–36 (2011).

30. Nondiscrimination in Employment Practices of Broadcast Licensees, 33 Fed. Reg. 9960, 9960–62 (July 11, 1968).

31. *Hearing on Responsibilities of the Federal Power Commission in the Area of Civil Rights, before the Subcomm. on Civil Rights Oversight of the H. Comm. on the Judiciary,* 92d Cong. 90 (1972) (letter from David J. Bardin to Lee C. White) [hereinafter *Responsibilities*]. *See, e.g.,* 16 U.S.C. §§ 797, 824, 824d (2006); *Responsibilities, supra,* at 99–109, 104 n.10, 106, 109 (letter from Robert A. Jablon to David J. Bardin); Nondiscrimination in Employment Practices of Broadcast Licensees, 33 Fed. Reg. at 9960–62.

32. Nondiscrimination in Employment Practices of Broadcast Licensees, 33 Fed. Reg. at 9960–62 (statement of Stephen J. Pollak to Rosel H. Hyde).

33. *Id.*

34. *Id.* at 9961–62.

35. *See*BROADCASTING, *supra* note 25.

36. *Responsibilities, supra* note 31, at 90, 99–109, 104 n.10, 106, 109.

37. For more on agencies' equal employment debates, see LEE, *supra* note 13, at ch. 8, 10; Sophia Z. Lee, *Race, Sex, and Rulemaking: Administrative Constitutionalism and the Workplace, 1960 to the Present,* 96 VA. L. REV. 799 (2010).

38. *See, e.g.,* U.S. Bedding Co., 52 N.L.R.B. 382 (1943). For an excellent treatment of the Board's election speech regulations, see FRYMER, *supra* note 11, ch. 5.

39. Speech of Clarence A. Mitchell on the Fair Employment Practices Commission (Jul. 14, 1949), *in* PAPERS OF THE NAACP, PART 1: MEETINGS OF THE BOARD OF DIRECTORS, RECORDS OF ANNUAL CONFERENCES, MAJOR SPEECHES, AND SPECIAL REPORTS, 1909–1950, (Randolph Boehm and August Meier, eds. 1982), reel 12.

40. LEE, *supra* note 13, at ch. 5.

41. *Id.* at ch. 7.

42. Jubilee Mfg. Co., 202 N.L.R.B 272, 275–76, 278 (1973) (Jenkins, Member, dissenting).

43. Edward B. Miller, A View from the NLRB, Speech at the Kansas City Bar Association Seminar 8, 12, 20 (Apr. 11, 1974) (transcript available in UAW Washington Office: Steve Schlossberg Collection, Box 23, Folder 6, Archive of Labor and Urban Affairs, Walter P. Reuther Library, Wayne State University, Detroit, Mich.). *See generally*LEE, *supra* note 13, at ch. 9.

44. Galveston Mar. Ass'n, Inc., 148 N.L.R.B. 897, 898 (1964); Rubber Workers (AFL-CIO) Local 12 (Business League of Gadsden), 150 N.L.R.B. 312, 314–15 (1964); Houston Mar. Ass'n, Inc., 168 N.L.R.B. 615 (1967); Astrove Plumbing & Heating Corp., 152 N.L.R.B. 1093 (1965).

45. Houston Mar. Ass'n, Inc., 168 N.L.R.B. 615 (1967); Farmers' Coop. Compress, 169 N.L.R.B. 290 (1968).

46. Bekins Moving & Storage Co., 211 N.L.R.B. 138 (1974), *overruled by* Handy Andy, 211 N.L.R.B. 138 (1974).

47. Pac. Gas & Elec. Co., 44 F.P.C. 1365, 1366–68 (1970).

48. *Id. See generally*LEE, *supra* note 13, at ch. 10.

49. Transcript of Oral Argument at 1–2, 9, NAACP v. FPC, 425 U.S. 662 (1976) (Nos. 74-1619, 74-1608), 1–2, 9 (available in the Records of the Center for National Policy Review, Box 126, Folder 3, Library of Congress Manuscript Division, Washington, D.C.).

50. *Id.* at 9.

51. See generally the documents collected in RG 25, N.L.R.B., Program Correspondence Files, 1934–79: Group II Former Chairmen, 1935–74 [hereafter NLRB Papers—GFC], Box 5, "Rules Revision: Revocation of Certification and/or Withholding of Certification" Folder, NARA.

52. Miller, *supra* note 43. The Board members saw this duty as deriving from the Constitution rather than Title VII. *See* LEE, *supra* note 13, at ch. 9.

53. Miller, *supra* note 43, at 8, 12, 20. Jenkins went further, contending that Title VII had in fact *affirmed* the Board's obligation to police racial discrimination. Jubilee Mfg. Co., 202 N.L.R.B. at 275–76, 278 (Jenkins, Member, dissenting).

54. *See, e.g.,* Robert L. Molinar, *The National Labor Relations Act and Racial Discrimination*, 7 B.C. INDUS. & COM. L. REV. 601, 602 (1965); Herbert Hill, *The Role of Law in Securing Equal Employment Opportunity: Legal Powers and Social Change*, 7 B.C. INDUS. & COM. L. REV. 625, 648 (1965); Sanford Jay Rosen, *The Law and Racial Discrimination in Employment*, 53 CALIF. L. REV. 729, 795 (1965).

55. Sam Barone, *The Impact of Recent Developments in Civil Rights on Employers and Unions*, 17 LAB. L.J. 413 (1966). *See also* William B. Gould, *The Negro Revolution and the Law of Collective Bargaining*, 34 FORDHAM L. REV. 207, 246–49 (1965).

56. Louis M. Kohlmeier, *NLRB's Role in Job Bias Disputes Is Enhanced by the Supreme Court*, WALL ST. J., Nov. 11, 1969, at 3.

57. Murray Seeger, *NLRB May Be Forced to Rule on Bias Cases*, L.A. TIMES, Mar. 16, 1969, 14. *See also Hail Court's Bias Case Ruling as Legal Landmark for Labor*, CHICAGO DEFENDER, Dec. 6, 1969, at 36.

58. Kohlmeier, *supra* note 56.

59. Seeger, *supra* note 57.

60. Miller, *supra* note 43, at 16. How much Miller needed to fear this outcome by the early 1970s is unclear; counter to predictions, the Board had not received a large number of discrimination charges. Interview of Frank McCulloch by Barbara Stoyle Mulhallen, in Charlottesville, Va., at 90 (Sept. 5, 1989) (available at the Kheel Center for Labor-Management Documentation and Archives, M.P. Catherwood Library at Cornell University, Collection 5843, Box 1, Folder 1159).

61. United Packinghouse, Food, & Allied Workers Int'l v. NLRB, 416 F.2d 1126, 1130, 1135 (D.C. Cir. 1969).

62. Jubilee Mfg. Co., 202 N.L.R.B. at 272–73.

63. Mansion House Ctr. Mgmt. Corp., 190 N.L.R.B. 437, 437 n.3 (1971); Farmers' Coop. Compress, 194 N.L.R.B. at 86–87, 89. In *Griggs v. Duke Power Co.*, 401 U.S. 424 (1971), the Supreme Court recognized disparate impact claims under Title VII.

64. For more on the union avoidance industry, see LEE, *supra* note 13, at ch. 11.

65. "Biography," Aug. 14, 1974 (RG 6891, WHCF Name Files, Box 2268, "Murphy, Betty Southard" Folder, Gerald R. Ford Library and Archive, Ann Arbor, Mich.).

66. NLRB, NLRB to Hear Race and Sex Arguments, (Jan. 29, 1976) (on file with author).

67. 1976 Board Hearing Transcript, 44, 67.

68. *Id.* at 53.

69. LEE, *supra* note 13, at ch. 10, 11.

70. Letter from Plato E. Papps to Edward B. Miller (Aug. 6, 1973) (NLRB Papers—GFC, Box 5, "Rules Revision: Revocation of Certification and/or Withholding of Certification" Folder).

71. 420 U.S. 50 (1975).

72. *Id.* at 69.

73. *Id.* at 66, 69, 71–72.

74. NAACP v. FPC, 425 U.S. 662 (1976).

75. 426 U.S. 229 (1976).

76. *Id.* at 239, 243–45.

77. Editorial, *The Equal Employment Mess*, N.Y. TIMES, Feb. 12, 1977, at 15.

78. *One Voice for Equal Employment*, PHILADELPHIA TRIB., Jan. 31, 1978, at 6; *President Sends Congress Master Plan on Job Rights*, L.A. TIMES, Feb. 23, 1978, at A2.

79. *President Sends Congress Master Plan on Job Rights, supra* note 78, at A2.

80. *Carter's First Big Push for Reorganizing Government Is Seen Taking Effect Today*, WALL ST. J., May 5, 1978, at 10; Martin Tolchin, *Grappling with the Monster of Bureaucracy*, N.Y. TIMES, July 23, 1978, at E2.

81. *One Voice for Equal Employment, supra* note 78, at 6. The final plan left some enforcement with the Office of Federal Contract Compliance (OFCC) at the Department of Labor after Carter was unable to overcome congressional resistance. Even this exception proved the centralizing rule, however, as the plan similarly withdrew contract enforcement authority from contracting agencies and concentrated it in OFCC.

82. Handy Andy, Inc., 228 N.L.R.B. 447, 452–53, 456 (1977). The other decisions were *Bell & Howell Co.*, 230 N.L.R.B. 420 (1977); *Murcel Manufacturing Co.*, 231 N.L.R.B. 623 (1977); and *Trumbull Asphalt Co.*, 230 N.L.R.B. 646 (1977).

83. Handy Andy, Inc., 228 N.L.R.B. at 452–53,456.

84. Bell & Howell Co., 230 N.L.R.B. at 421–23; Handy Andy, Inc., 228 N.L.R.B. at 451.

85. Bell & Howell Co. v. N.L.R.B., 598 F.2d 136, 147, (D.C. Cir. 1979).

86. See, e.g., the other chapters in this volume.

87. For instance, Title VII's antiretaliation provisions remain one area in which the courts still robustly interpret the law. *See* Thompson v. North Am. Stainless, LP, 562 U.S. , 131 S. Ct. 863 (2011). *But see* Univ. of Tex. Sw. Med. Ctr. v. Nassar, 570 U.S. ,133 S. Ct. 2517 (2013). Title VII's superior antiretaliation provision is precisely why Benjamin Sachs has advocated using Title VII as a way around deficiencies in labor law protections for worker organizing. Sachs, *supra* note 7, at 2690.

88. *See also*JENNIFER DELTON, RACIAL INTEGRATION IN CORPORATE AMERICA, 1940–1990 (2009); LEE, *supra* note 13, at ch. 8, 9, 11.

89. Sachs, *supra* note 7.

12

Labor Unions and Title VII: A Bit Player at the Creation Looks Back

Theodore J. St. Antoine

During the debates over what became Title VII (Equal Employment Opportunity) of the Civil Rights Act of 1964,[1] I was the junior partner of the then General Counsel of the AFL-CIO, J. Albert Woll. There were only three of us in the firm. The middle partner, Robert C. Mayer, handled the business affairs of the Federation and our other union clients. Bob was also the son-in-law of George Meany, president of the AFL-CIO, which gave us a unique access to Meany's thinking. The Federation had only one in-house lawyer, Associate General Counsel Thomas Everett Harris. Tom was an aristocratic Southerner and a brilliant lawyer who had clerked for Justice Harlan Fiske Stone on the U.S. Supreme Court. He and I were the labor law technicians, and we briefed and occasionally argued the court and administrative cases in which the Federation became involved, usually in an amicus capacity.

The often-fraught relationship of organized labor and the civil rights movement is a well-known story.[2] Before Title VII, African Americans were openly excluded from membership in most railroad unions, and their numbers were sharply limited in the skilled construction trades, even though all those unions eventually had the legal obligation to provide "fair representation" of any minorities who did manage to get jobs within the unions' jurisdiction.[3] Given the mores and culture of that time, it was probably inevitable that many if not most rank-and-file union workers placed their perceived economic self-interest above any concerns about promoting racial equality. Yet the story is more complicated than that of white workers simply taking advantage of discrimination against black workers, and the other side of the story needs to be remembered. Union leadership took a more principled position, and ultimately the official policy of the AFL-CIO was to support passage of the Civil Rights Act, including the prohibition of discrimination in employment by both employers and unions.

The initial bill proposed by the Kennedy administration would have concentrated on voting rights, access to public accommodations, and public school desegregation.[4] A fair employment practices (FEP) provision was considered too controversial and likely to doom the entire package. Two very different men, Walter Reuther and George Meany, played the key roles in shaping organized labor's response and helping to secure the addition of the Title VII that was finally adopted. Reuther, president of the United Automobile Workers and head of the AFL-CIO's Industrial Union Department (largely the former CIO unions before the merger), had long been a champion of black workers' civil rights, including equal job rights, and was a member of the NAACP's board of directors. He was an eloquent speaker and a charismatic, sometimes imperious leader who on occasion could strain the patience even of his natural allies. On June 13, 1963, he and other labor leaders met with President Kennedy, and Reuther made an "impassioned plea" for the inclusion of an FEP title in the administration's civil rights bill.[5] About a week later, Reuther joined a group of top civil rights leaders to see the president at the White House to reiterate the demand.[6] Reuther also participated in the March on Washington in August 1963, becoming the sole white union speaker when Martin Luther King delivered his famous "I Have a Dream" oration.[7]

In personality, AFL-CIO President George Meany and Walter Reuther were almost polar opposites. Reuther resonated to abstract principles and noble causes. Meany, who hailed from the Plumbers Union in New York City, was a cautious, crafty politician, struggling to hold together a highly divergent coalition of labor adherents. In contrast to Reuther's vaulting, evangelical speaking style, Meany's oral presentations were clear, methodical, down-to-earth. Yet Meany could also be moved by the plight of black workers. Although he would not have the AFL-CIO endorse the March on Washington, he set out on his own to convey the message to the White House that an FEP provision was essential, including coverage of labor unions. As reported through my partner,

Bob Mayer, President Kennedy responded: "George, I didn't think we needed one. I thought you could keep your troops in line." At this point Reuther might have delivered a sermon on the evils of racial discrimination. Meany's riposte was characteristically hard-nosed and lacking in self-righteousness: "Mr. President, that's exactly the problem. I *can't* keep the troops in line. I need a law I can *blame!*" More formally, Meany told the Senate Labor and Public Welfare Committee in July 1963: "We need the power of the federal government to do what we are not fully able to do [by ourselves]."[8]

It can be argued whether the Meany or Reuther style was ultimately more effective. It is certainly true that at least for some significant listeners, Reuther's moralistic hectoring could wear thin over time. When the March on Washington leaders met afterward with president Kennedy, Martin Luther King modestly sought to divert attention from his own great speech by asking the president whether he had heard Reuther's excellent address. Kennedy replied dryly, "Oh, I've heard him plenty of times."[9] Numerous persons who found Reuther more congenial philosophically wound up fonder of Meany personally. How might that affect persuasiveness? What is most important in the long run, however, is that these two men, Meany and Reuther, in their diverse ways, united in getting the labor movement officially to back the cause of an equal employment opportunity title. It is still debatable just how critical union support was. At least one reasonably disinterested observer, Professor Nelson Lichtenstein, then at the University of Virginia, declared flatly: "The trade union movement, both the AFL-CIO and the UAW, was primarily responsible for the addition of FEPC, now rechristened the Equal Employment Opportunity Commission (EEOC), to the original Kennedy bill."[10] But Herbert Hill, former labor secretary of the NAACP, has bitterly attacked this view, insisting that it exaggerated the position of organized labor as a progressive social force and overlooked massive union efforts to marginalize the effects of Title VII as finally enacted.[11]

The AFL-CIO's leadership endorsement of an FEP or EEO provision did not end the matter, however, in the eyes of much of the rank-and-file. Senator Lister Hill of Alabama was an ardent segregationist but an economic populist. He somehow obtained the addresses of about seventy thousand local unions affiliated with nationals belonging to the AFL-CIO. He wrote them, warning that passage of the civil rights bill would destroy one of their most prized possessions, seniority. Seniority reflects time with a particular employer or in a particular job or department. It can determine priority in layoffs, recalls, promotions, and fringe benefits like vacations. In many locations, especially in the South, black workers were deprived of access to the better job lines and the seniority attached to them. As a result of Hill's intervention, AFL-CIO headquarters was inundated with outraged cries from local memberships, protesting this threat to their precious seniority rights. I was assigned to draft the Federation's response.

My thoughts were as follows, although the exact wording was the result of refinement by several hands:

> Title VII would have no effect on established seniority rights. Its effect is prospective and not retrospective. Thus, for example, if a business has been discriminating in the past and as a result has an all-white working force, when the title comes into effect the employer's obligation would be simply to fill future vacancies on a nondiscriminatory basis. He would not be obliged—or indeed, permitted—to fire whites in order to hire Negroes or to prefer Negroes for future vacancies, or, once Negroes are hired to give them special seniority rights at the expense of the white workers hired earlier.

That language was later adopted, after extensive negotiations by AFL-CIO representatives and the legislation's sponsors, by Senators Joseph S. Clark (Democrat of Pennsylvania) and Clifford P. Case (Republican of New Jersey), in an "Interpretive Memorandum" on Title VII, for which they were the "bipartisan captains" in the Senate.[12] The Justice Department submitted a rebuttal to the arguments of Senator Lister Hill to the same effect.[13]

Once the 1964 Civil Rights Act was safely passed and Title VII became law, civil rights groups understandably downplayed this particular legislative history and insisted that the "current perpetuation" of past discrimination in seniority constituted a *present* violation of the statute. As one African American lawyer friend put it to me: "Ted, *I* was not part of whatever compromise may have been struck in getting Title VII enacted, and as a good advocate I am going to push the statutory language as far as I think it should go." As it turned out, that was quite a way. Until the U.S. Supreme Court resolved the issue, six courts of appeals in more than thirty cases held that seniority systems that perpetuated the effects of pre-Act discrimination did violate Title VII.[14] Two other courts of appeals were in accord in dicta.[15] In *International Brotherhood of Teamsters v. United States*,[16] however, a 7–2 Supreme Court majority ruled that § 703(h) of Title VII (and the legislative history previously cited) immunized bona fide seniority systems from liability under the CRA. Naturally, I believe the majority got it right. Section 703(h) provides in pertinent part:

> Notwithstanding any other provision of this subchapter, it shall not be an unlawful employment practice for an employer to apply different standards of compensation, or different terms, conditions, or privileges of employment pursuant to a bona fide seniority or merit system, or a system which

measures earnings by quantity or quality of production or to employees who work in different locations, provided that such differences are not the result of an intention to discriminate because of race, color, religion, sex, or national origin...[17]

Civil rights proponents protested, not unreasonably, that the inevitable tendency of the seniority cases was to lock a whole generation of African American workers into the less desirable jobs to which pre–Title VII discrimination had confined them. Even if they somehow managed to move into the higher-level jobs that were now theoretically available to them, they would wind up at the very bottom of the seniority ladder for those positions or departments. They would thus risk being the first laid off and the last recalled in the event of any economic downturn, as well as losing other benefit priorities. Those were indeed the regrettable facts.

But labor leaders wishing to support Title VII also faced some harsh realities. The rank-and-file were up in arms over what they perceived (correctly, as it first developed) to be a serious threat to their valuable seniority. Union officials must face elections, and the 1960s were a time of flux, when numerous incumbents were voted out of office. The Kennedy administration was initially opposed to an FEP or EEO title, with the Justice Department calling labor-liberal efforts to add one "a disaster."[18] Under all those circumstances, it seems entirely sensible for Title VII supporters among the labor leadership to feel they had to mollify their memberships by preserving seniority rights as they did. In effect, postponing for a generation the full promise of Title VII's nondiscrimination strictures may well have been the price that had to be paid to get an EEO title. By its very nature, of course, a bona fide seniority plan can hold back only about one generation when it is set in the context of a law prohibiting discrimination in hiring, promotions, and other terms and conditions of employment.

Retired federal District Judge Nancy Gertner has asserted: "Federal judges from the trial court to the Supreme Court have interpreted the [Civil Rights] Act virtually, although not entirely, out of existence."[19] Judge Gertner places much emphasis on the actual experience of discrimination plaintiffs compared to other plaintiffs in the litigation process, from summary judgment through trial through appeal. In what is surely the single most important judicial gloss on Title VII, however, the Supreme Court came out most favorably for alleged victims of discrimination. In *Griggs v. Duke Power Co.*,[20] Chief Justice Burger spoke for a unanimous Court in holding that the statute was violated not only by *intentional* discrimination but also by the *use* of any job qualification—such as a high school education or passing a general intelligence test—that disproportionately disqualifies a particular protected group and is not shown to be significantly related to successful job performance.

Griggs thus introduced the now famous "disparate impact" theory of discrimination, as distinguished from the more conventional "disparate treatment" or intentional theory. Subsequently, the Court acknowledged: "Undoubtedly disparate treatment was the most obvious evil Congress had in mind when it enacted Title VII."[21] The Court went on to state that disparate impact claims "involve employment practices that are facially neutral in their treatment of different groups, but that in fact fall more harshly on one group than another, and cannot be justified by business necessity....Proof of discriminatory motive...is not required under a disparate-impact theory."[22]

For someone like me, who was concededly only a bit player in this great undertaking but who nonetheless had a ringside seat at it, it is significant that I cannot ever recall during the endless discussions of Title VII any explicit reference to something like the "disparate impact" theory. Moreover, despite the *Griggs* Court's tussle with the legislative history, I find nothing there that clearly and positively supports disparate impact.[23] Chief Justice Burger invoked a striking image when he said: "Congress has now provided that tests or criteria for employment or promotion may not provide equality of opportunity merely in the sense of the fabled offer of milk to the stork and the fox."[24] But the artistry cannot conceal the conclusory, unproven nature of the proposition. Section 703(h), the one provision expressly dealing with testing, states in pertinent part:

> [N]or shall it be an unlawful employment practice for an employer to give and to act upon the results of any professionally developed ability test provided that such test, its administration or action upon the results is not designed, intended or used to discriminate because of race, color, religion, sex or national origin.[25]

Chief Justice Burger found comfort in the word "used" in the sentence dealing with ability tests; it does not appear in the part of the same section dealing with seniority and merit systems. That can be scored as a good debater's point. But in the absence of any further explanation of its significance in the legislative history, one has to wonder about how much weight to attach to that single generalized word. Would Congress have been that indirect or circumspect in promulgating a whole new theory of discrimination?

How necessary was the disparate impact theory, anyway? Section 8(a)(3) of the National Labor Relations Act prohibits "discrimination...to encourage or discourage membership in any labor organization."[26] In

NLRB v. Brown, the Supreme Court concluded that "Congress clearly intended the employer's purpose in discriminating to be controlling."[27] But then the Court immediately added:

> [W]hen an employer practice is inherently destructive of employee rights and is not justified by the service of important business ends, no specific evidence of intent to discourage union membership is necessary to establish a violation of § 8(a)(3). This principle, we have said, is "but an application of the common-law rule that a man is held to intend the foreseeable consequences of his conduct."[28]

As I see it, most if not all of what the Court accomplished in *Griggs* through enunciating the new disparate impact theory under Title VII could have been achieved less controversially by an application of the commonsense principle that persons may be held to have intended the natural consequences of their actions.[29] Does anyone have any serious doubts about what Duke Power was up to when it instituted new job qualifications on the very day Title VII went into effect? At most, disparate treatment analysis would seem to permit a challenged party one free pass on a claim of business necessity as a defense. Once that defense was overcome and the consequences known, any *continuation* of the practice could appropriately be regarded as an intentional violation.

One can safely say that even the present conservative Supreme Court would be reluctant to back away from the unanimous decision in *Griggs*. Moreover, in the Civil Rights Act of 1991, Congress confirmed the existence of disparate-impact violations by spelling out their manner of proof in a new § 703(k).[30] Nonetheless, in a concurring opinion in *Ricci v. DeStefano*, Justice Scalia warned that the Court's disposition of that case "merely postpones the evil day on which the Court will have to confront the question: Whether, or to what extent, are the disparate-impact provisions of Title VII...consistent with the Constitution's guarantee of equal protection?"[31] Justice Scalia elaborated his position:

> [T]itle VII's disparate-impact provisions place a racial thumb on the scales, often requiring employers to evaluate the racial outcomes of their policies, and to make decisions based on (because of) those racial outcomes. That type of racial decisionmaking is, as the Court explains, discriminatory.[32]

Professor Richard Primus suggests a means of defending disparate impact analysis.[33] He starts by spelling out what he calls the *Ricci* premise: the City of New Haven's suspension of a written job test because of its disproportionately adverse effect on African American firefighters "would constitute disparate treatment under Title VII unless suspending the test were justified by Title VII's provisions regarding disparate impact."[34] Primus concedes that if the emphasis is placed on the race conscious action of a *public* employer (subject to constitutional limitations) in implementing a disparate impact remedy, which is how Justice Scalia sees it, disparate impact doctrine is likely to be in "fatal" conflict with equal protection's requirement of racial neutrality.[35]

Primus insists, however, that there are two other ways of viewing the situation. First, there is an *institutional* difference between the roles of public employers and courts.[36] Courts are authorized to remedy racial discrimination and they cannot assess any kind of discrimination claim without knowing the race of the parties. Public employers are precluded from such race-conscious decision making. Second, the attention may focus on the *visible victims*.[37] In *Ricci*, Primus points out, New Haven's decision "disadvantaged determinate and visible innocent third parties—that is, the white firefighters," while "[m]ost disparate impact remedies avoid creating such victims."[38] Primus concludes that the constitutionality of disparate impact doctrine may turn on the particular lens through which the Court subsequently views such equal protection claims—and the skill of advocates in bringing the right case before the Court.[39] My own conclusion is that the *Griggs* Court could have avoided these problems by a more generous and realistic reading of Congress's actual design—to prohibit intentional discrimination in all its manifestations.

The problem of disparate impact pales by comparison with the problem of "affirmative action"—conceptually, ethically, and sociologically. Affirmative action—racial or other preferences among human groups—to achieve some seemingly desirable or compelling public interest is well covered by other contributors to this volume.[40] I will therefore limit myself to a few brief personal observations. The first and most obvious is that the primary, abiding theme of both the text and the legislative history of Title VII is color-blindness (or equivalent blindness regarding gender and other protected categories). The Clark-Case Memorandum filed by the senators who were in effect floor managers for the EEO provision is replete with such references. It is a model of the "plain meaning" approach to language:

> It has been suggested that the concept of discrimination is vague. In fact it is clear and simple and has no hidden meanings. To discriminate is to make a distinction, to make a difference in treatment or favor, and those distinctions or differences in treatment or favor which are prohibited by section 704 [now 703] are those which are based on any five of forbidden criteria: race, color, religion, sex, and national origin.[41]

Congress, like the rest of us promoting equal employment opportunity, was very naïve—or else we all affected naïveté. It was as if the magic wand of one federal statute could erase three hundred years of bondage, degradation, and exclusion. At least by hindsight, we know it did not work.

Justice Brennan showed more sophistication when he wrote for the Court in the *Weber* case:

> It would be ironic indeed if a law triggered by a Nation's concern over centuries of racial injustice and intended to improve the lot of those who had "been excluded from the American dream for so long," constituted the first legislative prohibition of all voluntary, private, race-conscious efforts to abolish traditional patterns of racial segregation and hierarchy.[42]

In *Weber*, a 5–2 Court upheld the legality of a union-employer affirmative action plan that reserved 50 percent of the openings in a plant's craft training program until the percentage of black craft workers in the plant was commensurate with the percentage of blacks in the local labor force.[43] Yet however much one might wish to applaud the result in *Weber* on the basis of policy, it contained a very serious analytical flaw. Justice Brennan never came to grips with the meaning of the critical word, "discriminate."

The Clark-Case Memorandum equated "discriminate" with "distinguish" on certain specified grounds. That reading, if straightforwardly applied, would have been fatal to the *Weber* approach. But there is another way to interpret "discriminate." One of the great federal judges, Henry Friendly, had this to say: "Although '[i]n common parlance, the word (to discriminate) means to distinguish or differentiate,'...it more often means, both in common and particularly in legal parlance, to distinguish or differentiate *without sufficient reason*."[44] That could have opened the door to a more capacious interpretation than a strictly literal reading. Once Justice Brennan had accomplished that, his reliance on the spirit rather than the letter of the law, and his use of somewhat strained but favorable portions of legislative history, would have seemed more acceptable.

Another aspect of *Weber* has always seemed anomalous to me as someone who is not a constitutional specialist. Justice Brennan emphasized it right at the outset of his analysis: "Since the Kaiser-USWA plan does not involve state action, this case does not present an alleged violation of the Equal Protection Clause of the Fourteenth Amendment."[45] The implication is that equal protection would have been a more stringent standard for a valid affirmative action plan. Indeed, subsequent decisions invalidating the plans of governmental bodies appear to bear that out.[46] Yet it is Title VII that defines the prohibited conduct so explicitly as "to discriminate...because of...race."[47] Section 1 of the Fourteenth Amendment does not even mention race and speaks very broadly: "[N]or shall any State...deny to any person within its jurisdiction the equal protection of the laws."[48] If one emphasizes the text, "equal protection" is surely the more flexible test. And a philosopher whose mind was uncluttered by vacillating judicial pronouncements might well conclude that a state is not denying equal protection when it treats differently—and preferentially—groups of persons who are in fact differently—and unequally—situated.[49] Those unequal situations could be the result of hurricanes, earthquakes, plagues, or physical or mental disabilities. Why not generations of racial discrimination?

I hardly expect a return to such a pristine concept at this relatively advanced stage in the development of equal protection theory. But the more we recognize that the equal treatment of *unequals* may *not* be the best way to ensure the "equal protection of the laws," the more we may be ready to extend such established doctrines as "compelling state interest" as a qualification on the prohibition of racial distinctions.

A half-century ago, many of us, those in the civil rights movement and union supporters alike, shared Martin Luther King's "dream." The "dream" was a dream of genuine integration—the existence of all races in our society on a plane of equality. We felt Title VII was our vehicle. Yet fifty years after the passage of Title VII, the median household income of blacks is $33,321 while that of whites is $57,009, or 71 percent more.[50] The unemployment rate of blacks is 12.5 percent, or double that of whites at 6.2 percent.[51] We may have come a long way in certain respects since 1964. But to fulfill that dream, we still have a very long way to go.

About the Author

James E. & Sarah A. Degan Professor Emeritus of Law, University of Michigan.

Notes

1. Pub. L. No. 88-352, 78 Stat. 253 (1964) (codified as amended at 42 U.S.C. §§ 2000e–2000e-17 (2012)).

2. *See generally* WILLIAM B. GOULD, BLACK WORKERS IN WHITE UNIONS: JOB DISCRIMINATION IN THE UNITED STATES 281–430 (1977); Herbert Hill, *Black Workers, Organized Labor, and Title VII of the 1964 Civil Rights Act: Legislative History and Litigation Record, in*RACE IN AMERICA: THE STRUGGLE FOR EQUALITY 263 (Herbert Hill & James E. Jones Jr. eds., 1993); Bayard Rustin, *The Blacks and the Unions*, HARPER'S MAG., May 1971, at 73.

3. *See, e.g.*, Steele v. Louisville & Nashville R.R. Co., 323 U.S. 192 (1944) (under Railway Labor Act); Syres v. Oil Workers Int'l Union, Local No. 23, 223 F.2d 739 (5th Cir. 1955) (under National Labor Relations Act), *rev'd per curiam*, 350 U.S. 892 (1955);

cf. Oliphant v. Bhd. of Locomotive Firemen and Enginemen, 262 F.2d 359 (6th Cir. 1958) (denial of union membership not prohibited), *cert. denied,* 359 U.S. 935 (1959).

4. H.R. 7152, 88th Cong. (1963); CHARLES & BARBARA WHALEN, THE LONGEST DEBATE: A LEGISLATIVE HISTORY OF THE 1964 CIVIL RIGHTS ACT 1–2 (1985); BUR. NAT'L AFF., THE CIVIL RIGHTS ACT OF 1964: TEXT, ANALYSIS, LEGISLATIVE HISTORY (1964).

5. NELSON LICHTENSTEIN, THE MOST DANGEROUS MAN IN DETROIT: WALTER REUTHER AND THE FATE OF AMERICAN LABOR 382 (1995). *See also* HUGH DAVIS GRAHAM, THE CIVIL RIGHTS ERA: ORIGINS AND DEVELOPMENT OF NATIONAL POLICY, 1960–1972, at 82–83 (1990).

6. LICHTENSTEIN, *supra* note 5, at 382.

7. *Id.* at 386–87.

8. GRAHAM, *supra* note 5, at 83. *See also*Hearings before Subcomm. No. 5 of the House Comm. on the Judiciary on Miscellaneous Proposals Regarding the Civil Rights of Persons within the Jurisdiction of the United States, 88th Cong. 1791 (1963) (statement of George Meany, President, AFL-CIO) ("[W]e need a Federal law to help us do what we want to do—mop up those areas of discrimination which still persist in our own ranks.").

9. LICHTENSTEIN, *supra* note 5, at 387.

10. *Id.* at 387–88.

11. *Compare* Herbert Hill, *Lichtenstein's Fictions: Meany, Reuther and the 1964 Civil Rights Act,* 7 NEW POLITICS 82–107 (Summer 1998), *and* Herbert Hill, *Lichtenstein's Fictions Revisited: Race and the New Labor History,* 7 NEW POLITICS 148 (Winter 1999), *with* Nelson Lichtenstein, *Walter Reuther in Black and White: A Rejoinder to Herbert Hill,* 7 NEW POLITICS 133 (Winter 1999). *See also* Rustin, *supra* note 2, at 76.

12. 110 CONG. REC. 7212, 7213 (1964). *See also id.* at 7217 (Sen. Clark remarking, "Seniority rights are in no way affected by the bill.").

13. *Id.* at 7207 (1964) ("Title VII would have no effect on seniority rights existing at the time it takes effect."). *See also id.* at 5423, 6549 (remarks of Sen. Humphrey).

14. Int'l Bhd. of Teamsters v. United States, 431 U.S. 324, 378–79 (1977) (Marshall, J., dissenting).

15. *Id.* at 379.

16. 431 U.S. 324 (1977). *See also* American Tobacco Co. v. Patterson, 456 U.S. 63 (1982), where a 5–4 Court held that § 703(h) applied to post–Title VII seniority plans as well as pre–Title VII plans. The dissenters argued that § 703(h) was designed only to protect seniority rights vested at the time Title VII was passed. They would have distinguished between the subsequent application of a preexisting seniority plan and the post-Act adoption of a new plan. The majority declared that § 703(h) evinces no such distinction and that the key is always whether there is an "intention to discriminate" in establishing a seniority plan.

17. 42 U.S.C. § 2000e-2(h) (2012).

18. ARTHUR M. SCHLESINGER, JR., ROBERT KENNEDY AND HIS TIMES 365 (1978).

19. Nancy Gertner, *The Court's Repeal of Johnson/Kennedy Administration's "Signature" Achievement,* in A NATION OF WIDENING OPPORTUNITIES? THE CIVIL RIGHTS ACT AT 50 (2014).

20. 401 U.S. 424 (1971). Disparate impact theory also applies to gender discrimination. Dothard v. Rawlinson, 433 U.S. 321 (1977).

21. Int'l Bhd. of Teamsters v. United States, 431 U.S. 324, 335 n.15 (1977).

22. *Id.*

23. For contrasting scholarly analyses, see Michael Evan Gold, Griggs' *Folly: An Essay on the Theory, Problems, and Origin of the Adverse Impact Definition of Employment Discrimination and a Recommendation for Reform*, 7 INDUS. REL. L.J. 429, 497–503, 588–98 (1985) (Congress meant to prohibit only intentional discrimination, but a person can be held to intend the natural consequences of one's actions); George Rutherglen, *Disparate Impact under Title VII: An Objective Theory of Discrimination*, 73 VA. L. REV. 1297, 1303–11 (1987) (Congress recognized the problem of "pretextual discrimination" but left its solution to the federal courts).

24. *Griggs*, 401 U.S. at 431.

25. 42 U.S.C. § 2000e-2(h) (2012).

26. 29 U.S.C. § 158(a)(3) (2012).

27. 380 U.S. 278, 287 (1965).

28. *Id.* (quoting Radio Officers' Union v. NLRB, 347 U.S. 17, 45 (1954)). *See also* NLRB v. Great Dane Trailers, Inc., 388 U.S. 26, 33–34 (1967); NLRB v. Erie Resistor Corp., 373 U.S. 221, 227 (1963).

29. I can think of at least one possible exception. Nepotism was rampant in the skilled construction trades in pre–Title VII days. Jobs were often passed down from father to son. In certain instances, this was truly not a pretextual situation; the actual intent was not to discriminate "because of race" but to discriminate against *everybody* outside the family. Such activity lends itself much more readily to a disparate impact analysis than to a disparate treatment analysis.

30. 42 U.S.C. § 2000e-2(k) (2012).

31. 557 U.S. 557, 594 (2009) (Scalia, J., concurring).

32. *Id.*

33. Richard Primus, *The Future of Disparate Impact*, 108 MICH. L. REV. 1341 (2010).

34. *Id.* at 1343–44 (citing *Ricci*, 557 U.S. at 580).

35. *Id.* at 1344.

36. *Id.* at 1344–45, 1364–69.

37. *Id.* at 1345, 1369–74.

38. *Id.* at 1345.

39. *Id.* at 1385–87.

40. *See, e.g.,* Samuel Bagenstos, *On Class-Not-Race, in*A NATION OF WIDENING OPPORTUNITIES?; Vicki Schultz, *Reimagining Affirmative Action, in* A NATION OF WIDENING OPPORTUNITIES?, *supra*; Patrick Shin, Devon Carbado & Mitu Gulati, *The Diversity Feedback Loop, in*A NATION OF WIDENING OPPORTUNITIES?, *supra*.

41. 110 CONG. REC. 7213 (1964). Even an employer who had discriminated in the past could not "prefer Negroes for future vacancies." *Id.*

42. United Steelworkers v. Weber, 443 U.S. 193, 204 (1979) (citation omitted).

43. *Id.* at 197.

44. NLRB v. Miranda Fuel Co., 326 F.2d 172, 181 (2d Cir. 1963) (Friendly, J., dissenting) (emphasis added).

45. *Weber*, 443 U.S. at 200.

46. *See, e.g.*, Wygant v. Jackson Bd. of Educ., 476 U.S. 267 (1986); City of Richmond v. J.A. Croson Co., 488 U.S. 469 (1989); Parents Involved in Cmty. Schs. v. Seattle Sch. Dist. No. 1, 551 U.S. 701 (2007). *But cf.* Grutter v. Bollinger, 539 U.S. 306 (2003) (5–4 decision upholding consideration of race and other factors to ensure diversity in higher education as a compelling state interest). Nonetheless, purpose or intent is required for an equal protection violation, while Title VII may also be violated without intent under a disparate impact analysis. Washington v. Davis, 426 U.S. 229 (1976).

47. 42 U.S.C. § 2000e-2(a)(1).

48. U.S. Const. amend. XIV, § 1. *See also* the Slaughter-House Cases, 83 U.S. 36, 81 (1873) (expressing "doubt" that the provision would ever apply beyond state action dealing with race).

49. *See, e.g.*, Ronald Dworkin, *Bakke's Case: Are Quotas Unfair?*, *in* A Matter of Principle 293 (1985); Thomas Nagel, *John Rawls and Affirmative Action*, 39 J. Blacks in Higher Educ. 82 (2003).

50. Carmen DeNavas-Walt et al., U.S. Census Bureau, Income, Poverty, and Health Insurance Coverage in the United States: 2012, at 5 (2013), *available at* http://www.census.gov/prod/2013pubs/p60-245.pdf.

51. News Release, U.S. Dep't of Labor, The Employment Situation—November 2013, USDL-13-2315, at Table A-2 (Dec. 6, 2013), *available at* http://www.bls.gov/news.release/archives/empsit_12062013.pdf.

13

Justice Ginsburg's Umbrella

Ellen D. Katz

I. Introduction

Near the end of her dissent in *Shelby County v. Holder*,[1] Justice Ginsburg suggested a simple analogy to illustrate why the regional protections of the Voting Rights Act (VRA) were still necessary. She wrote that "[t]hrowing out preclearance when it has worked and is continuing to work to stop discriminatory changes is like throwing away your umbrella in a rainstorm because you are not getting wet."[2]

The image went viral in the aftermath of the decision. It appeared in media accounts, academic commentary, fundraising appeals, and sundry blogs. And for good cause. The image crisply captured why the VRA's supporters[3] believed the preclearance regime remained necessary and why they thought scrapping it would be so damaging. It is still raining, they had been urging, and the umbrella the VRA offers continues to provide critical protection. Throw out that umbrella, the argument went, and lots of people are sure to get soaked.[4]

Curiously, the *Shelby County* majority seemed to agree. Chief Justice Roberts's opinion for the Court held § 4(b) of the VRA unconstitutional and thereby rendered the preclearance regime inoperative.[5] But while the Chief Justice discarded the umbrella Justice Ginsburg deemed so important, he never disputed the consequences she said would follow from doing so. Indeed, the reasons he provided for shutting down the preclearance regime suggested that he, too, expected that many people would get wet as a result of the decision.

It turns out that Chief Justice Roberts and Justice Ginsburg disagreed about a different point entirely. To belabor the analogy—something, be warned, this chapter will do repeatedly—the Justices disagreed about whether getting wet was worse than carrying an umbrella. For the Chief Justice, carrying an umbrella, at least one like the VRA's preclearance regime, is an extremely costly and damaging activity. By contrast, Justice Ginsburg viewed getting wet as the more damaging experience. She recognized that carrying an umbrella may be inconvenient and even costly but, in her view, well worth the bother. Keeping dry should be the priority.

The "umbrella" at issue in *Shelby County* was, without doubt, an unusual one. With its regionally applicable, burden-shifting requirements, the VRA's preclearance regime has long been understood to be an "exceptional" and "extraordinary" statute.[6] Disagreement among the Justices about its continued use might accordingly be minimized or even dismissed as a regime-specific dispute. And yet, I will argue that the different ways in which the majority and dissent in *Shelby County* valued getting wet and staying dry exposes a more foundational and far-reaching disagreement.

Specifically, this chapter presses the idea that Chief Justice Roberts's willingness to discard Justice Ginsburg's umbrella reveals a distinct conception of federal antidiscrimination law. It is a conception that sees the existing regime to be a source of unjust enrichment to its beneficiaries. Under this view, the regime does not simply make victims of undeniable discrimination whole but instead places a host of interested parties, victims included, in a decidedly better position than they would have been had the discrimination never occurred. For this reason, the regime is viewed to be a costly and damaging enterprise that should be limited at every opportunity.

Notably, this conception of federal antidiscrimination law does not deny the persistence of discrimination, and indeed, discrimination of the old-school, unconstitutional variety. To be sure, adherents of this view continue to be concerned that the linkage between challenged conduct and invidious intent has become too attenuated in some, and perhaps most, cases.[7] But their more pressing worry is that the regime today does more harm than the discrimination it presently addresses, even when that discrimination is indisputably unconstitutional or otherwise invidious in nature.

Put differently, the issue disputed in *Shelby County*, and in a host of other contemporary civil rights cases, is not about whether people are still getting wet but whether it is worth it to keep them dry. And for a majority of the present Court—and a majority for some time now—keeping dry is no longer cost-justified.

* * *

This chapter proceeds as follows. Part I explores why the *Shelby County* majority discarded Justice Ginsburg's umbrella. Specifically, it argues that Chief Justice Roberts did not mistake dry conditions for a problem solved but instead implemented a considered preference for getting wet. Part II situates this preference in a larger jurisprudence, in which a majority of the Court has limited the use of the umbrella provided by federal antidiscrimination law even as it acknowledged the rain to be ongoing. Part III argues that these cases represent a distinct strand in the Court's long-standing antipathy to federal antidiscrimination law, one that seeks to limit the regime based on the belief that it is more costly than the discrimination it presently addresses.

II. Was It Raining in Shelby County?

Much of the debate preceding the Court's decision in *Shelby County* focused on the conditions for political participation in covered jurisdictions. No one disputed that these conditions had improved markedly since Congress first crafted the statute and that the VRA itself was largely responsible for these improvements.[8] What was disputed was the extent to which these improvements were dependent on the VRA's continued operation and the degree of backsliding that would occur if the regime were scrapped. In other words, the dispute concerned whether or not the rain had stopped.

Justice Ginsburg's umbrella analogy captured what supporters of the VRA had been arguing—namely, that the improved conditions in covered jurisdictions existed only because the preclearance regime actively blocked misconduct where it applied. Under this view, the VRA was not only responsible for improved conditions in covered jurisdictions, but its continued operation was essential to maintaining those conditions. As Justice Ginsburg explained, do not mistake dry conditions under the umbrella for a sunny day.[9]

The regime's critics countered that conditions in covered jurisdictions looked better because they were better and that preclearance no longer had much to do with it.[10] After all, some rainy days turn into sunny ones, and when they do, putting away the umbrella makes a lot of sense. It was, notably, this view that animated Chief Justice Roberts's suggestion in 2009 that the preclearance regime might be nothing more than an elephant whistle, shooing away a nonexistent threat.[11]

And yet, the Chief Justice's opinion in *Shelby County* did not pursue this line of argument. True, it dismissed a defense based on deterrence as analytically flawed, explaining that deterrence could always be invoked to justify the regime even if evidence on the ground suggested the risk of backsliding was negligible.[12] What the opinion did not do, however, was take issue with Justice Ginsburg's argument that severe backsliding would occur absent the preclearance regime. Indeed, Chief Justice Roberts declined to dispute Justice Ginsburg's characterization of the evidence. He did not question the scope of unconstitutional conduct she described or the consequences she said would follow from the Court's ruling in *Shelby County*.

Justice Ginsburg described that evidence in detail, and her description made clear that she thought the evidence left no doubt that it was still raining in places like Shelby County, Alabama. She cited numerous examples in which covered jurisdictions violated both the VRA and the Constitution.[13] She observed, moreover, that contemporary unconstitutional conduct in covered jurisdictions remained remarkably widespread even as the evidence showed that the preclearance regime worked to deter and block a good deal of misconduct in covered jurisdictions.[14] Put differently, the evidence showed how preclearance, much like a real umbrella, operated imperfectly as a shield against the rain and that this imperfect protection provided a good indication of what would follow should the umbrella be discarded.

The *Shelby County* majority likely viewed the evidence Justice Ginsburg cited more equivocally. Much of it involved dilution claims stemming from redistricting disputes of the sort that once prompted the Chief Justice to lament this "sordid business, this divvying us up by race."[15] More broadly, the *Shelby County* majority no doubt suspected that many of the examples cited by Justice Ginsburg and collected in the congressional record sounded more in discriminatory effect than intent or simply tracked a jurisdiction's inability to disprove animus rather than its affirmative existence.

But insofar as the Justices in the majority held these suspicions, Chief Justice Roberts opted not to voice them.[16] Rather than take issue with Justice Ginsburg's characterization of the evidence, the Chief Justice concluded that the discrimination she described *as she described it* was legally insufficient to justify the statute's continued regional application.[17] As explanation, he observed that this discrimination was not as severe as it was when Congress first crafted the regime in 1965; that it had not led Congress to alter the statute's preexisting coverage formula; and that it encompassed subjects different from the ones that Congress listed in the coverage formula when it first subjected places to the regime's requirements.[18]

I have explained elsewhere why these observations, all of which are true, should have been insufficient to render preclearance obsolete—and indeed should have been irrelevant—under applicable doctrine that the *Shelby County* majority did not purport to displace.[19] For present purposes, however, the doctrinal inadequacy of these observations matters less than what they expose about the Court's toleration for unremedied or inadequately remedied discrimination, including, notably, discrimination that violates the Constitution. And it turns out that the Court is willing to tolerate quite a bit.

For example, Chief Justice Roberts observed that the discrimination documented in the 2006 record was not as severe as the discrimination that first led Congress to enact the VRA. As he noted, the record evidence did not "show[] anything approaching the 'pervasive,' 'flagrant,' 'widespread,' and 'rampant' discrimination that faced Congress in 1965, and that clearly distinguished the covered jurisdictions from the rest of the Nation at that time."[20]

The Chief Justice was certainty correct about this. The 2006 record documented a host of ugly incidents but nothing that rose to a level equivalent to the systemic, brazen defiance of constitutional norms that defined the pre-VRA South. Even with the aggressive backsliding now under way in places like Texas and North Carolina, no one expects conditions to deteriorate to the level that prompted Congress to enact the statute in the first place.

That's good news, as far as it goes, but it does not explain why contemporary, persistent, and prevalent unconstitutional discrimination in covered jurisdictions should not be remedied in the manner in the manner Congress had selected. The Warren Court had recognized Congress to possess close to plenary authority when crafting remedies for unconstitutional racial discrimination in voting.[21] And even when the Rehnquist Court pulled back, requiring a tight connection between remedies and unconstitutional conduct, it never suggested that some constitutional violations were more worthy of remedy than others.[22] That Court's concern was with remedies that targeted conduct that was not itself unconstitutional rather than with gradations among constitutional injuries.

Shelby County, by contrast, appears to stake out a distinction between discrimination of the extreme Jim Crow variety, and the more contained type of unconstitutional conduct we see today. And it suggests that Congress may not select what it reasonably believes is the most effective way to remedy unconstitutional racial discrimination when that discrimination falls short of the type that defined Alabama in 1965.

Chief Justice Roberts, however, makes clear that the discrimination Justice Ginsburg described was insufficient not simply because Jim Crow–era discrimination was worse. He explained that it was also flawed because it involved problems that were different in kind from those that first prompted Congress to enact the regime. He wrote, "The dissent relies on 'second-generation barriers,' which are not impediments to the casting of ballots, but rather electoral arrangements that affect the weight of minority votes."[23] In other words, the discrimination that Justice Ginsburg described differed from the type of discrimination captured by the original coverage formula, which was "based on voting tests and access to the ballot, not vote dilution."[24] This difference, apparently, renders contemporary discrimination legally insufficient to justify Congress's decision to retain the original coverage formula.[25]

Much like the observation that contemporary discrimination is not as rough as the Jim Crow variety, the Chief Justice's suggestion that second-generation barriers are off-point demands more explanation than he provided. It is true, of course, that the coverage formula invalidated by *Shelby County* made no mention of so-called second-generation problems, such as the practice of manipulating district lines to inhibit minority influence, and was based instead on the use of tests and devices and low voter participation.[26] But that fact hardly means that the practices grouped as "second-generation" are unrelated to the concerns Congress meant to target when it crafted the coverage formula. In fact, just the opposite is true.

So-called second-generation practices predate the VRA by decades and stand with the white primary, the literacy test, the poll tax, and other tactics that were used concurrently in the Jim Crow South to ensure that African American citizens lacked the ability to cast "meaningful"[27] ballots and to "strip" them "of every vestige of influence" in selecting public officials.[28] True, Congress relied on the use of tests and devices as the "trigger" for the original coverage formula, but it did so not in order to limit the statute's reach. Instead, it selected the specified trigger because it captured with remarkable accuracy the places that engaged in the broader range of conduct (including "second-generation" conduct) that had rendered the Fifteenth Amendment a nullity throughout the pre-VRA South.[29] The statutory trigger linked tests and devices to low participation, but the statute's target was never so limited.[30]

The Supreme Court itself recognized as much in 1969.[31] Justice Harlan disagreed at the time,[32] and Justices Thomas and Scalia would do so later.[33] But a majority of the Court has repeatedly recognized congressional intent for the VRA to apply to these practices and confirmed Congress's power to deploy the VRA in this way. Chief Justice Roberts's opinion in *Shelby County* nevertheless suggested otherwise but did not explain why.

What is clear, however, is what the opinion as written accomplished. It brought the preclearance regime to an immediate and, perhaps permanent,[34] halt, even as it countenanced evidence of widespread and ongoing discrimination. This discrimination, to be sure, fell short of the Jim Crow norm and did not directly involve those "tests or devices" listed in the original coverage formula. It was discrimination, nevertheless, and a good deal of it ran afoul of the Constitution. Critically, Chief Justice Roberts never suggested otherwise. Indeed, he seemed to agree with Justice Ginsburg when she wrote that it was still raining in covered jurisdictions and that it would continue to rain, predictably, for some time to come. At a minimum, the Chief Justice said nothing that called her forecast into question.

Therein lies *Shelby County*'s significance. The decision displays the Court's willingness to discard an umbrella on a rainy day with full knowledge that rain will continue. It may have been raining harder in the past, and the present rainstorm may (or may not) differ in other ways from what came before. Regardless, the *Shelby County* majority opted to toss out an umbrella in the middle of a rainstorm, fully aware of what it was doing.

The umbrella at issue in *Shelby County* was an unusual one, and it is certainly arguable that the Court's willingness to discard it rested on its distinctive features. Long considered strong medicine, the VRA's preclearance requirement reversed the presumption of validity that typically attaches to legislative and administrative action, and presumed instead that public officials in places subject to the requirement were engaged in discrimination unless and until they could convince a federal official otherwise.[35]

It turned out, however, that this defining aspect of the preclearance regime was less controversial in *Shelby County* than the regime's limited geographic reach. The fact that the preclearance obligation existed in some places but not others has always bristled,[36] but it had also been thought to contribute to the regime's legitimacy. Far from a blanket obligation, preclearance had long been seen as a targeted remedy, applying only in places where the need for it was most acute. Indeed, geography was one reason Justice Kennedy once cited the VRA as the paradigmatic example of congruent and proportional legislation.[37]

That, of course, was nearly two decades ago, and times change, as the Chief Justice has reminded us.[38] Ultimately, it was the regime's limited geographic application that contributed more directly to its downfall in *Shelby County* than its burden-shifting requirements.[39] A majority of the

Justices found themselves unconvinced that places subject to the statute were sufficiently different from other places to justify their being subjected to the statute's distinct requirements. And it was this skepticism that may best explain the Court's willingness to scrap the regime.

If so, the *Shelby County* majority's willingness to discard preclearance in the face of persistent, documented discrimination might be dismissed as a regime-specific move to secure a desired end. Whether the Court was more troubled by the regime's geographic selectivity or the burden-shifting obligations it imposed, it was convinced that preclearance had to go. Under this view, the holding is consequential, to be sure, but only because the specific statute the decision incapacitated was itself a consequential one, in terms of both its real world effect and the salient place it occupied in the public's imagination.

And yet, this reading of *Shelby County* is not, in my view, the best reading of the decision. Rather than simply charting a one-time path to a desired destination, the Court's willingness to discard an umbrella in the rain is better understood within a broader jurisprudence, described below.

III. Is It Raining Elsewhere?

Far from unique, *Shelby County*'s tolerance for ongoing discrimination represents a common stance in modern civil rights law. In numerous cases, the Court has limited federal antidiscrimination measures such as the VRA, Title VII, and the Age Discrimination in Employment Act (ADEA) in the face of uncontested evidence of discrimination of the sort the statutes at issue were designed to address. These cases, moreover, all generated dissenting opinions, often written by Justice Ginsburg, which disputed both the holdings and the analytical moves used to reach them. Situated within Justice Ginsburg's *Shelby County* construct, these dissenting opinions all argued that an umbrella should be used in the rain, while a majority, time and again, sided with getting wet.

Consider a few eclectic but representative examples.

Nassar and *Gross*: Two days before the Court handed down *Shelby County*, it held that an employee alleging retaliation under Title VII needed to show that the complaints he lodged about status-based discrimination not only contributed to his being denied a coveted transfer but also were the but-for cause of that denial. *University of Texas Southwestern Medical Center v. Nassar*[40] relied heavily on the Court's 2009 ruling in *Gross v. FBL Financial Services, Inc.*, which applied the same rule to an employee alleging age discrimination under the ADEA.[41] Both decisions deemed the employees involved to be ineligible for the more forgiving "motivating factor" analysis Congress set forth in § 703m of the Civil Rights Act of 1991.[42] The Court split 5–4 in both cases, with dissenting opinions by Justices Ginsburg and Stevens challenging the way the majority understood relevant precedent, the purpose and structure of the 1991 CRA, and applicable agency action.[43]

Amid this disagreement, however, all of the Justices seemed to agree—or, at least, no one denied—that the plaintiff-employees who brought both cases had been subjected to intentional discrimination of the sort the statutes at issue targeted[44]—namely, that Naiel Nassar's complaints about disparate treatment based on his Middle Eastern descent contributed to his being denied a transfer,[45] and that Jack Gross's age contributed to the restructuring of job responsibilities he challenged.[46] In both cases, then, the Justices seemed well aware and willing to accept that intent-based discrimination had occurred. They split over whether the employees should be entitled to relief given this discrimination.

Put differently, no one doubted that the employees who brought these cases had been caught in the rain. What they disagreed about was whether they were entitled to the umbrella provided by Title VII and the ADEA. And a majority held they were not.

Coleman: A year before *Nassar*, the Court struck down a provision of the Family Medical Leave Act (FMLA) that guaranteed twelve weeks of unpaid medical leave to eligible employees suffering from serious medical conditions.[47] Justice Ginsburg's dissenting opinion in *Coleman v. Court of Appeals of Maryland* argued that the sex-neutral "self-care" provision constituted an essential part of a comprehensive statutory regime that included the family care provisions that the Court had already upheld.[48] She explained that Congress crafted this regime to address the pervasive discrimination women confronted in the workplace stemming from pregnancy-related issues and more general sex stereotypes about family care responsibilities.[49]

Justice Ginsburg did not invoke umbrella imagery in *Coleman*, but she might easily have employed it. Her argument, at bottom, was that the umbrella provided by the FMLA would have a gaping hole in it without the statute's self-care provision. The self-care provision, she explained, "serves to blunt the force of stereotypes of women as primary caregivers by increasing the odds that men and women will invoke the FMLA's leave provisions in near-equal numbers."[50]

A majority of the Court, however, was unmoved. Justice Kennedy's plurality opinion held that the relationship between the self-care provision and the discrimination Justice Ginsburg described was too complex and attenuated to satisfy constitutional scrutiny.[51] And yet, much like Chief Justice Roberts's opinion in *Shelby County*, Justice Kennedy's opinion in *Coleman* did not question the prevalence of the discrimination Justice Ginsburg described.[52] Like the Chief Justice, moreover, Justice Kennedy opted to discard the umbrella Congress crafted to address that discrimination.

Ledbetter: In 2007, a majority of the Court held that an employee's claim for sex-based wage discrimination was time barred because she filed suit long after the employer's initial discriminatory wage decision. Justice Alito's majority opinion in *Ledbetter v. Goodyear Tire & Rubber Co.*[53] held that the statute of limitations ran from that initial decision rather than from the issuance of subsequent paychecks, the amount of which reflected the initial discrimination.[54]

Justice Ginsburg's dissent argued that the statute was better read to allow Ledbetter's suit to proceed, an argument she might easily have bolstered by invoking the umbrella image she employed in *Shelby County*. Indeed, Justice Ginsburg's dissent made clear that Goodyear had been raining on Lilly Ledbetter for a very long time and that Title VII should be available to provide her relief. Justice Ginsburg closed her opinion calling for a statutory amendment to reverse the majority's ruling, a call Congress heeded.[55]

The majority in *Ledbetter* was not persuaded by Justice Ginsburg's argument, but it never questioned that Goodyear had intentionally discriminated against Ledbetter based on sex by paying her less than both similarly situated and less-qualified male colleagues. Justice Alito expressed no doubt about this point. But in his view, Ledbetter's failure to use the Title VII umbrella at the beginning of the storm precluded her from using it later.

Bossier Parish: Like *Ledbetter*, *Reno v. Bossier Parish School Board* was reversed by subsequent statutory amendment (albeit one that was later ruled to be unconstitutional).[56] Back in 2000, Justice Scalia's majority opinion held that the VRA permitted implementation of a districting plan in which African American voters constituted a majority in none of the plan's twelve electoral districts. It was alleged and, somewhat surprisingly, stipulated that the School Board had refused to draw a majority-minority district because it wanted to prevent an African American candidate from being elected to the board.[57]

Justice Scalia's majority opinion held that the redistricting plan could be implemented notwithstanding this discriminatory purpose. The opinion explained that § 5 of the VRA did not block implementation of electoral changes enacted with discriminatory intent. Instead, it blocked only that subset of electoral changes enacted with "retrogressive" intent—that is, the intent to make things worse for the minority group in question. Mere animus would not suffice.[58] The opinion, moreover, suggested any rule to the contrary would raise a serious constitutional question.[59]

Justice Souter's dissent argued that electoral changes enacted with a discriminatory, albeit not "retrogressive" purpose, fell within the § 5 proscription. As he put it, blocking implementation of unconstitutional conduct of this sort—the rain Justice Ginsburg subsequently described—was precisely what Congress had designed § 5 to address and what Congress, in his view, had ample power to mandate.[60]

Thirteen years later, *Shelby County* made clear that Congress lacks this power. The decision viewed Congress's 2006 decision to adopt Justice Souter's *Bossier Parish* reading as evidence of constitutional overreach. It thereby suggested Congress had no power to include within the statutory proscription conduct that was unconstitutional.[61]

Bossier Parish, Ledbetter, Coleman, Gross, and *Nassar* are, without doubt, distinguishable from one another on numerous grounds. Yet they share a defining characteristic that makes them representative examples of a more general stance in federal civil rights law. Like *Shelby County,* these decisions all circumscribe the federal regime in contexts in which the occurrence of intentional, invidious, and even unconstitutional conduct is left unquestioned. Placed within Justice Ginsburg's *Shelby County* framework, these cases all involved rain; the Court knew it, and a majority was nevertheless steadfast that an umbrella should not be used.

Admittedly, likening the discrimination observed in these cases to rain is a contestable move. My premise is that discrimination may be distinguished from liability, at least in certain contexts, and that we learn something by making this distinction. That premise accordingly rejects the idea that discrimination is necessarily or most usefully understood as a legal conclusion that is coextensive with liability. Instead, it posits that people like Naiel Nassar and Lilly Ledbetter found themselves in the rain even though the Court ruled against them. They lost despite the fact that it was raining and decidedly not because the Court thought the sky was clear.

Understanding the cases in this manner—that is, by parsing discrimination from liability—brings into focus a distinct strand of civil rights jurisprudence. To be sure, judicial skepticism toward the federal civil rights regime is nothing new, and the Court has long sought to scale back federal antidiscrimination law. Decisions that do so in the face of uncontested evidence of intentional discrimination are undoubtedly part of this effort. And yet, my claim is that they are a distinct component of it. Unlike those cases that deny relief by deeming challenged conduct to be nondiscriminatory, these decisions discard the umbrella even as the need for it persists. The suggestion is that the federal civil rights project, while hardly complete, is no longer worth pursuing. Rather than a mission accomplished, it is a mission abandoned.

Of course, not every decision circumscribing the federal civil rights regime falls decisively into one group or the other. Some deny the rain, or at least express skepticism about it, but also voice mistrust about using the available umbrella should the rain alleged actually be falling.[62] Elsewhere, however, the distinction is clear, with a growing number of decisions displaying a willingness to discard the umbrella in the rain knowing full well people will get wet as a result.

Shelby County's willingness to immobilize § 5 of the VRA without disputing the discrimination Justice Ginsburg described is part of this latter group of decisions. Far from unique, *Shelby County* stands with a host of other decisions that acknowledge discrimination persists and yet posit that core elements of the federal civil rights project are no longer worth pursuing. The next section explores why this sensibility drives so much of contemporary antidiscrimination law.

IV. On Unjust Enrichment and Harmless Error

Decisions that limit federal antidiscrimination law typically view the regime's broader application as deeply problematic. Among the concerns most often cited is the worry that an expansive approach to the regime encourages frivolous lawsuits, exposing employers and other defendants to wasteful litigation costs and spurring inefficient defensive decision making.[63] Curb the regime, it is argued, lest undeserving plaintiffs be unjustly enriched at the expense of diligent defendants and, in many circumstances, the rest of us.

Animating this concern is the suspicion that frivolous claims outnumber legitimate ones and that the discrimination federal antidiscrimination law was crafted to address is largely a thing of the past. Unsurprisingly, decisions that find challenged conduct to be nondiscriminatory highlight this sensibility, with the dispute at hand seen either to involve a frivolous claim or to suggest circumstances in which one might find expression.[64]

Less expected, decisions that deny relief in the face of uncontested discrimination also voice concern that frivolous claims are rising as genuine discrimination declines. These decisions acknowledge the rain but deem it insufficiently worrisome to warrant use of the umbrella at issue.[65] More pressing is the need to check the regime and guard against its unjustified application.

Under this view, victims of documented discrimination might be understood or even dismissed as unfortunate, but unavoidable, collateral damage sacrificed for the greater good. And yet, it is not the unpleasantness of the image that keeps it off the pages of U.S. reports but instead the belief that the victims of discrimination in these cases have not been significantly damaged at all. True, they have been caught in the rain, but these decisions suggest that getting wet may not be as damaging as some seem to think. In fact, they suggest it might not be damaging at all.

With this suggestion, *Shelby County* and cases like it shift the terrain on which civil rights disputes have long been fought. Rather than contest allegations or evidence of discrimination, they dismiss discrimination itself as inconsequential. They reject Justice Ginsburg's belief that getting caught in the rain is the source of enduring damage and, in its place, insert the idea of harmless error into civil rights jurisprudence.

That idea, in turn, has led the Court to view much of federal antidiscrimination law as providing a windfall to its beneficiaries. Far from making victims of discrimination whole, the regime is seen as leaving them in a decidedly better position than they would have been had they never gotten wet. The umbrella Justice Ginsburg thinks provides vital protection is seen instead to be a source of unjust enrichment to those it shields. The resulting project consequently becomes one dedicated to limiting use of the umbrella whenever possible, rain notwithstanding.

Hence, the recent mixed-motive decisions requiring plaintiffs to show "but-for" causation work hard to make sure that getting wet is not the vehicle for getting ahead. These decisions hold that if, absent the discrimination alleged, the plaintiff would have been denied the disputed promotion or transfer, the discrimination itself should not be the source of liability.[66] Because Title VII's "motivating" factor rule allows for liability in such circumstances,[67] *Nassar* and *Gross* rejected it, finding the plaintiff-employees ineligible for both the acknowledgment of wrongdoing a liability ruling embodies and the attorneys' fees that accompany it. Of no moment was the fact that the rejected approach barred injunctive relief when the desired transfer or promotion would have otherwise been denied.[68]

As telling, and perhaps even more so, is a little noted aspect of Chief Justice Roberts's opinion in *Shelby County*, in which he described the 2006 amendment overruling *Bossier Parish* to "prohibit laws that *could have favored* [minority voters] but did not do so because of a discriminatory purpose."[69] The words "could have favored" are revealing. Far from unartful drafting, they suggest that the Bossier Parish School Board did not injure minority voters when it adopted a districting plan avowedly designed to prevent the election of an African American representative. Instead, *Shelby County* suggests that the school board's unconstitutional conduct only blocked adoption of a plan "that could have favored" black voters. The broader suggestion is that unconstitutional discrimination does not necessarily deny minority voters an equal opportunity to participate in the political process but instead may simply deprive them of favored or preferential treatment.

That suggestion is a remarkable one, and one that documents the extent to which the locus of civil rights jurisprudence has shifted. A long-standing worry in this realm has been the concern that the prohibition on disparate impact would devolve into a mandate for affirmative action and prompt potential defendants to adopt preferential policies in order to shield themselves from liability.[70] To guard against this result (and its apparent conflict with explicit statutory language), the Court has long refused to read bans on disparate impact expansively.

But now, this concern about preferential treatment is also shaping the Court's approach to discriminatory intent. In a growing number of cases, it has read the VRA, Title VII, and other federal civil rights measures narrowly in contexts where animus was evident (or at least evidence of it went unchallenged), and it has done so because more expansive statutory readings were thought to yield unwarranted preferential treatment. Notably absent from these cases is a well-intentioned defendant laboring to comply with a statutory mandate. Instead, the Court has come to see federal antidiscrimination law itself as the source of damaging preferences. Even the prohibition on invidious intent, the core tenet of federal civil rights law, has evolved into a problem and hence a target. It is what needs to be constrained, if not eliminated, while the conduct the regime once targeted is dismissed as harmless and those once understood as victims are transformed into the unjustly enriched.

V. Conclusion

The Court has long sought to scale back the federal civil rights regime and has typically done so by characterizing challenged conduct as nondiscriminatory. This chapter tracks a distinct line of cases that are undeniably part of the larger effort but that limit the regime while recognizing discrimination rather than denying it. These decisions throw out an umbrella in a rainstorm, knowing full well it is raining and that the rain will continue. They accordingly posit that the rain does less damage than the umbrella, at least in certain circumstances, and that the Court is institutionally able to figure out the circumstances in which the umbrella should be discarded.

About the Author

Ralph W. Aigler Professor of Law, University of Michigan Law School. Many thanks to Cali Cope-Kasten for excellent research assistance.

Notes

1. Shelby Cty. v. Holder, 570 U.S. , 133 S. Ct. 2612 (2013).

2. *Id.* at 2650 (Ginsburg, J., dissenting).

3. This includes me. *See* Brief of Amici Curiae Ellen D. Katz and the Voting Rights Initiative in Support of Respondents, Shelby Cty. v. Holder, 133 S. Ct. 2612, 2013 WL 457386 (2013).

4. *See, e.g.*, Brief for the Federal Respondent, Shelby Cty. v. Holder, 133 S. Ct. 2612, 2013 WL 315242 (2013); Brief for Respondent-Intervenors Earl Cunningham et al., Shelby Cty. v. Holder, 2013 WL 315241, 133 S. Ct. 2612 (2013); Brief for Respondent-Intervenors Bobby Pierson et al., Shelby Cty. v. Holder, 133 S. Ct. 2612, 2013 WL 325379 (2013).

5. Section 4(b) of the VRA "covered" jurisdictions if they utilized a "test or device" as a prerequisite to voting and had low levels of voter participation on specified dates between 1964 and 1972. *See* 42 U.S.C. § 1973b(b) (2006), transferred to 52 U.S.C. § 10303 [hereinafter "§ 4(b)"]. Once covered, jurisdictions could no longer use their test or device and could not implement any electoral changes without first showing that the proposed change would be nondiscriminatory. *See* 42 U.S.C. § 1973c (2006), transferred to 52 U.S.C. § 10303, [hereinafter "§ 5"]. This preclearance obligation applied only to jurisdictions covered by Section 4(b). *See id.* As a result, eliminating § 4(b) dissolved all existing obligations to seek preclearance.

6. *See, e.g.*, South Carolina v. Katzenbach, 383 U.S. 301, 334 (1966) ("[Section 5] may have been an uncommon exercise of congressional power…but the Court has recognized that exceptional conditions can justify legislative measures not otherwise appropriate."); Reno v. Bossier Parish Sch. Bd., 520 U.S. 471, 501 (1997) ("Section 5…was highly controversial because it imposed novel, extraordinary remedies in certain areas where discrimination had been most flagrant.").

7. *See, e.g.*, Nw. Austin Mun. Util. Dist. No. One [NAMUDNO] v. Holder, 557 U.S. 193, 226–29 (2009) (Thomas, J., concurring).

8. *See, e.g.*, *Shelby Cty.*, 133 S. Ct. at 2625–26; Brief for Petitioner at 9–12, *Shelby Cty.*, 133 S. Ct. 2612 (2013).

9. *SeeShelby Cty.*, 133 S. Ct. at 2650–51 (Ginsburg, J., dissenting); Brief for the Hon. Congressman John Lewis as Amicus Curiae in Support of Respondents and Intervenor-Respondents at 24–38, Shelby Cty. v. Holder, 2013 WL 476051, 133 S. Ct. 2612 (2013) (describing the importance of § 5).

10. Transcript of Oral Argument at 30–35, 65–68, Shelby Cty. v. Holder, 133 S. Ct. 2612 (2013).

11. Transcript of Oral Argument at 28, NAMUDNO, 557 U.S. 193 (2009).

12. *SeeShelby Cty.*, 133 S. Ct. at 2627.

13. *See id.* at 2639–43, 2646–47 (Ginsburg, J., dissenting).

14. *Seeid.* at 2639–42 (Ginsburg, J., dissenting).

15. League of United Latin American Citizens [LULAC] v. Perry, 548 U.S. 399, 511 (2006) (Roberts, C.J., concurring). Meanwhile, Justices Thomas and Scalia think these claims are not judicially cognizable. *SeeLULAC*, 548 U.S. at 511–12 (Scalia, J., dissenting in part); Holder v. Hall, 512 U.S. 874, 891–930, 944–46 (1994) (Thomas, J., concurring).

16. Nor did Justice Thomas. His concurring opinion argued that the majority's analysis left the preclearance requirement not simply moot but unconstitutional as well. Still, he did not delve into the evidence. *Shelby Cty.*, 133 S. Ct. at 2631–32 (Thomas, J., concurring).

17. *SeeShelby Cty.*, 133 S. Ct. at 2619, 2629–31.

18. *Shelby Cty.*, 133 S. Ct. at 2629–31.

19. *See* Ellen D. Katz, *What Was Wrong with the Record?*, 12 ELECTION L.J. 329 (2013).

20. *Shelby Cty.*, 133 S. Ct. at 2629.

21. Katzenbach v. Morgan, 384 U.S. 641 (1966); South Carolina v. Katzenbach, 383 U.S. 301 (1966).

22. City of Boerne v. Flores, 521 U.S. 507 (1997).

23. *Shelby Cty.*, 133 S. Ct. at 2629.

24. *Id.*

25. *Id.* In a related objection, the majority opinion observed that when Congress opted to "reenact[]" the original coverage formula when it reauthorized the VRA in 2006, it "did not use the record it compiled to shape a coverage formula grounded in current conditions." *Id.* Part of this problem concerned the substance of the discrimination documented, discussed above. Part, however, was procedural, reflecting the Court's unhappiness with Congress's decision to preserve the coverage formula rather than revise it or craft a new one. Shelby County rejected the idea that Congress might have rationally concluded that current conditions justified preserving a formula crafted forty years earlier. It thus suggested that Congress needed to revise the coverage formula or craft a new one. Preserving the formula was not a constitutional option. Congress's decision to preserve the formula could not be "shaped" by the record; only a decision to revise it could be. *See* Katz, *supra* note 19, at 330.

26. *See* Katz, *supra* note 19, at 331.

27. Terry v. Adams, 345 U.S. 461, 476 (1953) (Frankfurter, J., concurring).

28. *Id.* at 470. *See generally* QUIET REVOLUTION IN THE SOUTH: THE IMPACT OF THE VOTING RIGHTS ACT, 1965–1990 (Chandler Davidson and Bernard Grofman eds., 1994).

29. *See* Brief for the Federal Respondent at 48–50, *Shelby Cty.*, 133 S. Ct. 2612 (2013).

30. Allen v. State Bd. of Elections, 393 U.S. 544, 566–67 (1969) (Preclearance was meant "'to be all-inclusive of any kind of practice,'" and to be given "the broadest possible scope.").

31. *Id.* at 567.

32. *Id.* at 582–91 (Harlan, J., dissenting in part).

33. *See* Holder v. Hall, 512 U.S. 874, 892–903 (Thomas, J., and Scalia, J., concurring).

34. The decision, notably, falls short of holding that Congress cannot reach practices like racial vote dilution with a remedy like preclearance. The counterfactual suggestion that Congress did not intend a statute of this breadth, theoretically, allows a legislative response. Replacements have been proposed, *see* https://www.congress.gov/bill/114th-congress/house-bill/2867; http://beta.congress.gov/bill/113th-congress/house-bill/3899, that are of more limited reach than the preclearance regime they purport to replace. Should a bill of this sort become law, the new regime will likely be challenged for the reasons Justice Thomas provides in his concurrence. *See* Shelby Cty. v. Holder, 133 S. Ct. at 2612, 2631–32 (Thomas, J., concurring).

35. *See* South Carolina v. Katzenbach, 383 U.S. 301, 327 (1966).

36. *See id.* at 358–61 (Black, J., dissenting).

37. *See* City of Boerne v. Flores, 521 U.S. 507, 532–33 (1997).

38. *See Shelby Cty.*, 133 S. Ct. at 2625–26; *NAMUDNO*, 557 U.S. at 203–04, 211.

39. *See Shelby Cty.*, 133 S. Ct. at 2623–24, 2628–31.

40. Univ. of Tex. Sw. Med. Ctr. v. Nassar, 570 U.S. , 133 S. Ct. 2517 (2013).

41. *See* Gross v. FBL Fin. Servs., Inc., 557 U.S. 167 (2009).

42. 42 U.S.C. § 2000e-2(m) ("Except as otherwise provided in this subchapter, an unlawful employment practice is established when the complaining party demonstrates that race, color, religion, sex, or national origin was a motivating factor for any employment practice, even though other factors also motivated the practice.").

43. *Nassar*, 133 S. Ct. at 2534–47 (Ginsburg, J., dissenting); *Gross*, 557 U.S. at 180–90 (Stevens, J., dissenting).

44. *See* Jackson v. Birmingham Bd. of Educ., 544 U.S. 167, 173 (2005) (describing retaliation as a "form of intentional [status-based] discrimination").

45. *Nassar*, 133 S. Ct. at 2532.

46. *Gross*, 557 U.S. at 170–72.

47. Coleman v. Ct. of Appeals of Md., 566 U.S. , 132 S. Ct. 1327 (2012) (striking down 29 U.S.C. § 2612(a)(1)(D) (2009)).

48. *Id.* at 1342 (Ginsburg, J., dissenting). *See also* Nev. Dep't of Human Res. v. Hibbs, 538 U.S. 721 (2003) (upholding provisions of the FMLA).

49. *Coleman*, 132 S. Ct. at 1340–49 (Ginsburg, J., dissenting).

50. *Id.* at 1348 (Ginsburg, J., dissenting) (internal quotations omitted) (quoting Brief for Nat'l P'ship for Women & Families et al. as Amici Curiae Supporting Petitioner 26, Coleman v. Ct. of Appeals of Md., 132 S. Ct. 1327 (2012)).

51. *Coleman*, 132 S. Ct. at 1334–37.

52. *See id.* at 1334 ("In enacting the FMLA, Congress relied upon evidence of a well-documented pattern of sex-based discrimination in family-leave policies. States had facially discriminatory leave policies that granted longer periods of leave to women than to men."); *Shelby Cty.*, 133 S. Ct. at 2619 ("[V]oting discrimination still exists; no one doubts that.").

53. 550 U.S. 618 (2007), *superseded by statute*, Lilly Ledbetter Fair Pay Act of 2009, Pub. L. No. 111-2, 123 Stat. 5 (codified in scattered sections of 29 U.S.C. and 42 U.S.C.).

54. *Ledbetter*, 550 U.S. at 639–42.

55. *Seeid.* at 661 (Ginsburg, J., dissenting). *See also* The Lilly Ledbetter Fair Pay Act of 2009, Pub. L. No. 111-2, 123 Stat. 5 (providing that the 180 statutes of limitations for filing an equal pay lawsuit regarding pay discrimination resets each time the employer issues a paycheck that reflects the pay discrimination).

56. *See* Reno v. Bossier Parish Sch. Bd. [Bossier Parish II], 528 U.S. 320 (2000), *superseded by statute*, Fannie Lou Hamer, Rosa Parks, and Coretta Scott King Voting Rights Act Reauthorization and Amendments Act of 2006, Pub. L. No. 109-246, 120 Stat. 577 § 2(b)(6) (2006) (declaring that *Bossier Parish II* "misconstrued Congress' original intent in enacting the Voting Rights Act of 1965 and narrowed the protections afforded by section 5 of such Act"); *Shelby Cty.*, 133 S. Ct. at 2626–27.

57. *See* Jurisdictional Statement at 8, *Bossier Parish II*, 528 U.S. 320 (2000) ("There was evidence that several Board members preferred the [redistricting plan with all white-majority districts] because they did not want black representation on the Board. Board member Barry Musgrove said that 'the Board was "hostile" toward the idea of a black majority district.'"). It was alleged, and assumed for purposes of the litigation, that § 2 of the VRA required the creation of such a district. *Bossier Parish I* held even if that was true, a § 2 violation was not grounds to deny preclearance under § 5. *See* Reno v. Bossier Parish Sch. Bd. [Bossier Parish I], 520 U.S. 471, 483 (1997) ("[A] violation of § 2 is not grounds in and of itself for denying preclearance under § 5.").

58. The decision meant the Bossier Parish School Board could implement its redistricting plan because the evidence did not suggest the Board had been seeking to make political participation more difficult for African American voters in the parish. Because no African American candidate had been elected to the school board, the Board members' intent to keep such a candidate from winning did not involve an intent to make things *worse* for black voters in Bossier Parish. *See Bossier Parish II*, 528 U.S. at 340–41.

59. *Bossier Parish II*, 528 U.S. at 336.

60. *Id.* at 361, 363–67 (Souter, J., dissenting).

61. *Shelby Cty.*, 133 S. Ct. at 2626–27.

62. An example is the 2009 decision in *Bartlett v. Strickland*, 556 U.S. 1 (2009), in which the Court held that § 2 of the VRA does not require the aggregation of minority voters too few in numbers to constitute a majority in a single-member district. Under certain conditions, minority voters comprising less than 50 percent of a district's electorate are able to elect candidates of choice by forming coalitions with like-minded white voters. *Bartlett*, 556 U.S. at 3, 14–15. Justice Souter's dissent in *Bartlett* argued that § 2 should be used to foster such coalitions, *id.* at 27 (Souter, J., dissenting), but Justice Kennedy's plurality opinion held that the very prospect of such coalitions meant the failure to draw districts that fostered them could not be discriminatory. That is, a refusal to draw the district alleged was not discriminatory within the meaning of § 2. *Id.* at 14–15 (plurality opinion). Justice Kennedy then went on to explain why reading § 2 to require such districts gave rise to a host of concerns that counseled against adopting that reading, regardless of how the challenged conduct might be characterized. *Id.* at 20–22. *See also* Ricci v. DeStefano, 557 U.S. 557, 579–84 (2009) (plurality opinion).

63. *See, e.g.,* St. Mary's Honor Ctr. v. Hicks, 509 U.S. 502 (1993); Wards Cove Packing Co. v. Atonio, 490 U.S. 642 (1989).

64. *See, e.g., Hicks*, 509 U.S. 502; *Wards Cove*, 490 U.S. 642.

65. *See supra* notes 40–62 and accompanying text.

66. *See supra* notes 40–46 and accompanying text.

67. 42 U.S.C. § 2000e-2(m).

68. *See* Univ. of Tex. Sw. Med. Ctr. v. Nassar, 570 U.S. , 133 S. Ct. 2517 (2013); Gross v. FBL Fin. Servs., Inc., 557 U.S. 167 (2009).

69. 133 S. Ct. at 2626–27 (emphasis added).

70. *See, e.g.,* Ricci v. DeStefano, 557 U.S. 557 (2009) (plurality opinion); Wards Cove Packing Co. v. Atonio, 490 U.S. 642 (1989); Furnco Constr. Corp. v. Waters, 438 U.S. 567 (1978). *See also* Johnson v. Transp. Agency of Santa Clara County, 480 U.S. 616, 670 (1987) (Scalia, J., dissenting).

14

Disparate Impact Abroad

Julie Suk

The Civil Rights Act of 1964 banned discrimination in various realms of social and economic life. Title VII, prohibiting discrimination in employment, gave rise to an innovative body of jurisprudence theorizing the very concept of discrimination. For the past five decades, Title VII doctrine has influenced not only the American workplace but also the growth of antidiscrimination law throughout the world. Several European jurisdictions took inspiration from Title VII to develop a body of equality law that appears more robust today than its American cousins. On the occasion of Title VII's fiftieth anniversary, this chapter reflects on this alternative trajectory of the disparate impact theory, Title VII's most ambitious and contested doctrine. European "indirect" discrimination law is a notable legacy of Title VII that raises hard questions about the future of the American Civil Rights Act.

Citations to *Griggs v. Duke Power Company*, the U.S. Supreme Court's landmark disparate impact case, can be found in the decisions of English courts, the Court of Justice of the European Union (CJEU), and the European Court of Human Rights (ECtHR) elaborating the doctrine of "indirect" discrimination. *Griggs* was transplanted into soil that had already been fertilized by similar legal reasoning in an earlier line of cases developed by the CJEU in the late 1960s and throughout the 1970s on the free movement of workers. European treaties guaranteed free movement of workers by dismantling employment practices that favored a nation's own citizens. In early cases construing free movement of workers, the CJEU understood that barriers to the shared treaty goal of a common European market could arise from existing policies that indirectly disadvantaged nonnationals of any given member state. These cases draw out aspects of disparate impact doctrine that have not been fully appreciated in the United States. The comparison highlights the significance of pursuing a substantive shared goal, such as a single, common, integrated European labor market, in giving coherence to disparate impact theory. It points to a question that must be confronted in the next fifty years of antidiscrimination law in the United States: What, if anything, does this body of law aspire to achieve?

I. The Civil Rights Act and the Rise and Fall of Disparate Impact Discrimination

Griggs v. Duke Power Company[1] was the first decision in which the Supreme Court repudiated an employer practice as a violation of Title VII. As is well known, the Duke Power Company required a high school diploma and a cutoff score on a general ability test for workers employed in any department other than its Labor Department.[2] Prior to the adoption of these requirements, which coincided with the effective date of Title VII, the Duke Power Company had segregated its workers on the basis of race: black workers could only be assigned to the Labor Department and could not be transferred or promoted to the better-paid jobs in the company's other departments.[3] In *Griggs*, the Supreme Court held that, even though the new criteria appeared racially neutral, they violated Title VII because they disproportionately disqualified blacks and were not shown to be significantly related to successful job performance. Writing for a unanimous Court, Justice Burger explained: "[G]ood intent or absence of discriminatory intent does not redeem employment procedures or testing mechanisms that operate as 'built-in headwinds' for minority groups and are unrelated to measuring job capability."[4] Justice Burger also blessed consequentialist thinking about Title VII: "Congress directed the thrust of the Act to the consequences of employment practices, not simply the motivation."[5] In a subsequent paragraph, Justice Burger generally challenged traditional indicators of accomplishment:

> The facts of this case demonstrate the inadequacy of broad and general testing devices as well as the infirmity of using diplomas or degrees as fixed measures of capability. History is filled with examples of men and women who rendered highly effective performance without the conventional badges of accomplishment in terms of certificates, diplomas, or degrees. Diplomas

and tests are useful servants, but Congress has mandated the commonsense proposition that they are not to become masters of reality.[6]

For decades, scholars have debated the theory underlying the disparate impact definition of discrimination.[7] On one end of the spectrum, the disparate impact is regarded primarily as an evidentiary dragnet for intentional discrimination. In the facts of this case, the Duke Power Company had been discriminating overtly on the basis of race until it was no longer lawful to do so, so it is perfectly plausible that the new facially neutral policy was a covert way of continuing the same racial discrimination. On the other end of the spectrum, the disparate impact theory articulates a principle that goes far beyond the elimination of intentional discrimination and its lingering effects. Individual employees are entitled, under a disparate impact theory, to consideration for jobs based on rational criteria that correspond to successful job performance and not based on arbitrary indicators of past privilege.[8]

During the years immediately following *Griggs*, as Reva Siegel has eloquently exposed, a majority of the federal courts of appeals used disparate impact frameworks to interpret equal protection, viewing a policy's racial effects as evidence of presumed purposes.[9] The Supreme Court, however, limited the disparate impact theory in at least three different phases. First, in the late 1970s, the Supreme Court declined to extend the disparate impact theory to the Equal Protection Clause, holding that the Constitution only proscribes intentional discrimination.[10] Second, in the 1980s, the Court heightened the burdens on Title VII plaintiffs seeking to establish disparate impact discrimination.[11] Third, in the past decade, the Court in *Ricci v. DeStefano* has limited the scope of employers' permissible actions to avoid racially disparate outcomes by holding such actions to be intentionally discriminatory.[12] The Obama administration has embraced the disparate impact theory as a construction of discrimination in violation of the Fair Housing Act.[13] Although the Supreme Court has recently validated the disparate impact theory under the Fair Housing Act, its decision sustained disparate impact in its modern weakened form. The Court has noted that disparate impact must be "properly limited in key respects that avoid the serious constitutional questions that might arise...if such liability were imposed based solely on a showing of a statistical disparity."[14]

Even as disparate impact continues to be used in the United States, the Supreme Court's construction of it in Title VII cases has limited its potential. The second phase—by which U.S. courts heightened the burdens of proving the prima facie case for disparate impact plaintiffs and deferred to the justifications for disparate impacts proffered by defendants—brings out the contrast between American and European courts' approaches. The U.S. Supreme Court has required plaintiffs to do more than simply point to statistical disparities between groups to shift any burden, whether it is a burden of production or persuasion, to the employer. The plaintiff must identify a specific practice or requirement and show that it causes the disparity alleged to be discriminatory.

In *Wards Cove Packing v. Atonio*, cannery workers had sought to establish a prima facie case of disparate impact discrimination by relying on statistics showing a high percentage of nonwhite workers in certain jobs and a low percentage of nonwhite workers in better jobs.[15] The Supreme Court held that a prima facie case could not be established by these facts alone, noting that "[i]f the absence of minorities holding such skilled positions is due to a dearth of qualified nonwhite applicants (for reasons that are not petitioners' fault), petitioners' selection methods or employment practices cannot be said to have had a 'disparate impact' on nonwhites."[16] In short, statistical disparities had to be accompanied by a causal theory about a practice undertaken by the employer that caused the disparity. In this decision, the robust prima facie case was purportedly necessary to avoid a world in which

> any employer who had a segment of his work force that was—for some reason—racially imbalanced, could be hauled into court and forced to engage in the expensive and time-consuming task of defending the 'business necessity' of the methods used to select the other members of his work force.[17]

In that landscape, the Court predicted, the "only practicable option for many employers would be to adopt racial quotas."[18] And since quotas were "expressly rejected" by the drafters of Title VII and would be "far from the intent of Title VII," the *Wards Cove* Court concluded that statistical disparities alone could never be enough to force an employer to articulate some explanation or justification for those disparities.[19]

After *Wards Cove* and the Civil Rights Act of 1991, courts have consistently required plaintiffs to identify the specific employment practice that caused the disparate outcomes that are being challenged.[20] In *Wal-Mart v. Dukes*, the Supreme Court rejected the class certification of plaintiffs' disparate impact claims by invoking the disparate impact plaintiff's burden of identifying a specific practice to establish the prima facie case.[21] The Court noted: "Other than the bare existence of delegated discretion, respondents have identified no 'specific employment practice'—much less one that ties all their 1.5 million claims together."[22]

And even when the plaintiff establishes a prima facie case of disparate impact discrimination, the burden that shifts to the employer is not particularly demanding. Once a prima facie case is established, the plaintiff wins unless the employer can prove that the specific practice is justified by business necessity. The employer must show a legitimate business purpose for the policy that causes a disparate impact, and the employee can then point to alternative means of achieving that purpose that have less of a disparate impact. *Wards Cove* had held that the employer merely had a burden of production, not persuasion, in response to the plaintiff's prima facie case of disparate impact discrimination.[23] Congress amended Title VII in 1991 to overrule this aspect of *Wards Cove*.[24] So, for the past two decades, employers have the burden of showing business necessity once a prima facie case of disparate impact has been made. Yet, following the 1991 Act, courts accepted reasonable legitimate nondiscriminatory reasons as meeting the "business necessity" standard required by the statute.[25] As Michael Selmi notes, "courts readily accept most proffered justifications."[26] The weakness of U.S. disparate impact doctrine comes into clearer focus when encountering the development of disparate impact doctrine abroad.

II. The Migration of *Griggs*

While the evolution from *Griggs* to *Ricci* is a story of disparate impact's decline in the United States, *Griggs* migrated and followed an alternative trajectory in Europe, by way of Britain. *Griggs* influenced the drafting of the United Kingdom's Sex Discrimination Act. Roy Jenkins, the U.K. Home Secretary, made a visit to the United States in 1974, when the government was proposing a new law on sex discrimination.[27] Jenkins was accompanied by Anthony Lester, a lawyer who had been active in litigating on behalf of discrimination plaintiffs under the Race Relations Act.[28] Shortly before their visit to the United States, the government had published a white paper, *Equality for Women*, largely drafted by Lester. The white paper had proposed that unlawful discrimination should only include intentional discrimination: "In the absence of any intention (or inferred intention) to treat one person less favourably than another on the grounds of sex or marriage, there will be no contravention of the proposed Bill."[29] However, after Jenkins's visit to the United States, the Sex Discrimination Act was redrafted to include indirect discrimination, an idea that was directly shaped by the Jenkins's and Lester's encounter with *Griggs*. Lester recounts:

> We were much influenced in determining the content of the sex and race equality laws by the U.S. civil rights law, including the crucial concept of disparate impact discrimination articulated by the American Supreme Court in Griggs v. Duke Power Co. in 1971....We learned about that concept when we

visited the United States in December 1974; but it was expressed in unnecessarily restrictive language in section 1(1)(b) of the Sex Discrimination Act.[30]

Thus, the line of influence between *Griggs* and the indirect discrimination provision of the Sex Discrimination Act was conscious and direct.

The Sex Discrimination Act, like the Race Relations Act of 1968, begins by defining discrimination as less favorable treatment:

> (1) In any circumstances relevant for the purposes of any provision of this Act...a person discriminates against a woman if—
> a. On the ground of her sex he treats her less favourably than he treats or would treat a man.[31]

But after Jenkins's and Lester's encounter with *Griggs*, the proposed statute that eventually passed also included the disparate impact provision at section 1(1)(b), which then influenced a revision of the Race Relations Act in 1976:

> b. [H]e applies to her a requirement or condition which applies or would apply equally to a man but—
> i. which is such that the proportion of women who can comply with it is considerably smaller than the proportion of men who can comply with it, and
> ii. which he cannot show to be justifiable irrespective of the sex of the person to whom it is applied, and
> iii. which is to her detriment because she cannot comply with it.[32]

Anthony Lester also invoked the indirect discrimination idea when litigating cases arising under the British Equal Pay Act. Lester's litigation strategy involved requests to English courts to refer the disparate impact construction of the Equal Pay Act to the European Court of Justice, with the aim of bringing the disparate impact theory to European Community law and then harmonizing EC law with English law.[33] Thus, *Griggs*'s disparate impact theory migrated yet again to the European level, and it is in the jurisprudence of the CJEU that the law of disparate impact, through the doctrine of indirect discrimination, has been given an expansive scope, both in terms of the doctrinal bases for liability and in terms of the transnational diffusion of legal norms.

In 2003, further amendments to the British Race Relations Act heightened the justification requirement in the standard for indirect discrimination. The statute required employers to show not only that the justification is unrelated to the sex or race of the persons involved but also that the justification is proportionate to a legitimate aim. In addition, the Race Relations Act's definition of indirect discrimination was broadened: to include a "provision, criterion, or practice," not merely a "requirement or condition":

> A person also discriminates against another if...he applies to that other a provision, criterion or practice which he applies or would apply equally to persons not of the same race or ethnic or national origins as that other, but:
> (a) which puts or would put persons of the same race or ethnic or national origins as that other at a particular disadvantage when compared with other persons,
> (b) which puts or would put that other at that disadvantage, and
> (c) which he cannot show to be a proportionate means of achieving a legitimate aim.[34]

The 2003 Amendment to the Race Relations Act was adopted in order to comply with the European Union's Race Equality Directive of 2000. The Race Directive required all member states to adopt antidiscrimination laws that included a prohibition of indirect discrimination subject to a proportionality test:

> (b) [I]ndirect discrimination shall be taken to occur where an apparently neutral provision, criterion or practice would put persons of a racial or ethnic origin at a particular disadvantage compared with other persons, unless that provision, criterion or practice is objectively justified by a legitimate aim and the means of achieving that aim are appropriate and necessary.[35]

This same definition of indirect discrimination was applied in the EU's Framework Directive on Equal Treatment, which prohibits and defines discrimination on the basis of religion, disability, age, and sexual orientation.[36] The U.K. statutory framework has been revised again, unifying the Sex Discrimination Act, the Race Relations Act, and other antidiscrimination statutes under a single Equality Act. The Equality Act retains the basic definitions of the 2003 Race Relations Act on indirect discrimination. It provides that a "provision, criterion or practice" is indirectly discriminatory in violation of the Act when the following four conditions are met:

a. A applies, or would apply, it to persons with whom B does not share the characteristic,
b. it puts, or would put, persons with whom B shares the characteristic at a particular disadvantage when compared with persons with whom B does not share it,
c. it puts, or would put, B at that disadvantage, and
d. A cannot show it to be a proportionate means of achieving a legitimate aim.[37]

Scholars of antidiscrimination law in Britain have acknowledged the influence of *Griggs* on the Sex Discrimination Act, the Race Relations

Act, and decisions of the European Court of Justice and the European Court of Human Rights.[38]

III. The Disparate Lives of Disparate Impact

In the last thirty years, the CJEU has developed an indirect discrimination doctrine that diverges in at least four significant respects from American disparate impact law. First, the indirect discrimination idea emerged to construe a treaty guarantee of "equal pay for male and female workers for equal work."[39] By contrast, in the United States, the Supreme Court declined to import the disparate impact theory into its construction of the Equal Pay Act.[40] Second, the outcomes reached in CJEU cases are arguably more protective of women workers than are those reached by U.S. courts interpreting Title VII. For example, U.S. courts have declined to extend disparate impact theory to proscribe discrimination against part-time workers.[41] In Europe, early cases established that discrimination against part-time workers disproportionately burdened women, as women were statistically more likely than men to be engaged in part-time work. Thus, the CJEU drew on the concept of indirect discrimination to instruct national tribunals to scrutinize the justifications employers gave for any policies that treated part-time workers worse than full-time workers. Third, the CJEU's case law enables plaintiffs to establish a prima facie case more easily than American courts have permitted. A series of CJEU cases of the 1980s and the 1990s permit the plaintiff to establish a prima facie case of indirect discrimination by presenting a disparity between the advantaged and disadvantaged group, without proving the disparity to be caused by a specific identifiable practice. Thus, the burden on the employer is more easily triggered. Finally, the employer's burden in European indirect discrimination cases is heavier than that in U.S. disparate impact cases. According to the CJEU, the employer must defend a specific practice if one is identified by a plaintiff, or must prove that the disparity was caused by an employer policy with a legitimate aim and that the means of pursuing that aim were necessary and appropriate. The CJEU applied proportionality analysis to the employer's "business necessity" defenses, making it more difficult for the employer to defend itself in the face of a prima facie case.

This evolution appears to have been catalyzed by *Griggs*. The CJEU first cited *Griggs* in *Jenkins v. Kingsgate Clothing Productions, Ltd.*, in construing the equal pay guarantee of Article 141 of the EC Treaty (then Article 119 of the EEC Treaty).[42] The application of disparate impact theory to an equal pay case is itself an interesting contrast with the American doctrinal landscape, as the U.S. Supreme Court has explicitly declined to extend *Griggs* to construe the Equal Pay Act.[43] The CJEU heard the equal pay case through a preliminary reference from the Employment Appeal Tribunal of the United Kingdom, before which Anthony Lester had brought an equal pay claim on behalf of Mrs. Jenkins under English law as well as EC law.[44] Mrs. Jenkins was a part-time employee, and her rate of pay was 10 percent lower than full-time employees performing the same work.[45] All the male employees except one worked full-time, and four of the five part-time employees were women. In the preliminary reference proceedings before the CJEU, Lester argued that paying part-time workers a lower rate than that paid to full-time workers for the same work constituted sex discrimination because of its disparate impact on women, unless such a policy could be objectively justified.[46]

The CJEU highlighted *Jenkins'* reliance on *Griggs* in its decision:

> Mrs. Jenkins also refers to the principle enunciated by the Supreme Court of the United States in *Griggs v Duke Power Co* 401 US 424 (1971), according to which what must be prohibited are not merely practices which are intended to discriminate, but equally those which are discriminatory in their effect, irrespective of the intentions of their authors.[47]

Although the *Jenkins* decision does not elaborate on the meaning and scope of *Griggs*, the Advocate General's opinion in that case is illuminating. It is obvious that Advocate General Warner's understanding of *Griggs* was shaped by Lester's submissions:

> At the hearing Counsel for Mrs[.] Jenkins explained that what that proposition meant "in plain language" was that if, as was clearly the case, women were less able to work 40 hours a week than men, because of their family responsibilities, the requirement that an employee should work 40 hours a week to earn the full hourly rate must obviously hit, in a disproportionate way, at women, compared with men. That did not necessarily mean that there was discrimination, but it did mean that there was prima-facie discrimination in effect, which required "some special justification from the employer." Counsel called this the "*Griggs* approach" after the decision of the Supreme Court of the United States in *Griggs v. Duke Power Company* (1971), 401 US 424.[48]

Griggs facilitated the expansion of the discrimination concept to include employment practices that disadvantaged women because of their family responsibilities. *Jenkins* was the first in a line of CJEU decisions that used the indirect discrimination concept to scrutinize employers' policies toward part-time workers. The court concluded that, where unequal treatment of part-time and full-time workers had a disproportionate impact on women, such treatment had to be "objectively justified" based on reasons other than sex.[49]

From the beginning, the European notion of "objective justification" had some teeth. The employer purported to have a commercial interest in encouraging its employees to work longer hours. The CJEU acknowledged that this interest could constitute an objective justification and left it to national courts to scrutinize whether an employer's allegation of such an interest was convincing in any individual case. At the same time, the court expressed some skepticism of the proffered business justification in this case: "If an employer wished to encourage his employees to work longer hours, he should pay a suitable overtime rate and not reduce the pay of those working part-time."[50] Thus, an objective justification required consideration of other ways of achieving the purported legitimate aims, without the disadvantaging effect on women.

Griggs provided European courts with inspiration and transnational authority to develop an indirect discrimination doctrine that would scrutinize employer policies that disadvantaged women with family responsibilities. Two subsequent cases, both involving unequal treatment of part-time workers, developed this idea. In *Bilka-Kaufhaus GmbH v. Weber von Hartz*, the CJEU confronted the question of whether a German department store had violated the equal pay provision of the EEC Treaty by refusing to pay a pension for employees who had not worked full-time for a minimum of fifteen years.[51] Karin Weber von Hartz, a woman who had worked for the department store part-time for fifteen years, argued that the pension policy placed women workers at a disadvantage "since they were more likely than their male colleagues to take part-time work so as to be able to care for their family and children."[52]

The CJEU built on the logic of *Jenkins v. Kingsgate* and concluded that excluding part-time workers from the occupational pension scheme would violate the equal pay provision where, "taking into account the difficulties encountered by women workers in working full-time, that measure could not be explained by factors which exclude any discrimination on grounds of sex" but rather by "objectively justified factors."[53] Bilka, the department store, argued, as Kingsgate had, that its policy was justified as a discouragement of part-time work.[54] Weber von Hartz pointed out that Bilka could discourage part-time work simply by refusing to hire part-time workers, and the European Commission urged the court to adopt a test that would require pay practices to be "necessary and in proportion to the objectives pursued by the employer"[55] to comport with the treaty's equal pay provision. Here, the CJEU spelled out a proportionality standard, strongly implied in *Jenkins*, for the employer's justification of policies that disadvantaged women. It required the national courts to find "that the means chosen for achieving that objective correspond to a real need on the part of the undertaking, are appropriate with a view to achieving the objective in question and are necessary to that end."[56]

While making the justification burden on the employer heavier, the CJEU stopped short of reading the equal pay provision as imposing positive duties on employers to accommodate workers' family responsibilities. The court concluded: "Article 119 does not have the effect of requiring an employer to organize its occupational pension scheme in such a manner as to take into account the particular difficulties faced by persons with family responsibilities in meeting the conditions for entitlement to such a pension."[57] Advocate General Darmon, in denying the existence of employers' positive duties in this regard, affirmed the existence of positive duties on the part of the state in compensating for the disadvantages caused by family responsibilities: "[A]n employer cannot be required to take over the role of the authorities in constructing a pension scheme which will compensate for the special difficulties faced by workers who have family responsibilities."[58] AG Darmon also suggested that such positive duties, on the part of the state, could even be located in the equal pay provision of the treaty: "Article 119 lays positive duties only on the Member States and not on commercial undertakings, which are subject, within the limits described above, only to an obligation not to discriminate."[59]

Seven years later, in *Enderby v. Frenchay Health Authority*,[60] the CJEU strengthened the proportionality requirement in the indirect discrimination standard in a case challenging the pay inequality between speech therapists and pharmacists employed by a state health authority. Pharmacists, who were predominantly male, were paid more than speech therapists, who were predominantly female. In this case, the state health authority gave two justifications for paying pharmacists more than speech therapists. First, the rates of pay had been determined through collective bargaining processes conducted by the same trade union, and second, the pay reflected, in part, the shortage of candidates for pharmacist positions and the need to attract them with higher salaries.[61]

In *Enderby*, the CJEU concluded that a prima facie case of indirect discrimination could be established by a statistical showing that a job with lower pay is predominantly occupied by women, while a comparable job with higher pay is predominantly occupied by men.[62] Once this prima facie case has been made, the burden of proof shifts to the employer, who must then show that the difference in pay is based on "objectively justified factors unrelated to any discrimination on grounds of sex."[63] *Enderby* requires national courts to apply the principle of proportionality to determine "whether and to what extent the shortage of candidates for a job and the need to attract them by higher pay constitutes an objectively justified economic ground for the difference in pay between the jobs in question."[64] In addition, the mere fact that any pay rate was produced by collective bargaining could not be accepted as an "objective justification" for a difference in pay.

As Advocate General Lenz makes clear in his opinion, the *Enderby* decision does not require complainants to point to a specific requirement or practice of the employer that causes the disparate impact.[65] It appears sufficient for the female plaintiffs to have established through statistics that jobs predominantly held by women are paid less than those held by men in order to make out a prima facie case of indirect discrimination, which then places a proportionate objective justification burden on the employer.

Griggs thus invigorated the evolution of a European doctrine of indirect discrimination, primarily in cases construing the meaning of equal pay between men and women. But *Griggs*'s influence, both directly and by way of CJEU case law, was not limited to the gender context. The European Court of Human Rights (ECtHR) cited *Griggs* in its landmark 2007 ruling, *D.H. & Others v. Czech Republic*,[66] which recognized an indirect discrimination theory to find a violation of the equality guarantee in Article 14 of the Convention, taken in conjunction with the Article 2 Protocol 1 right to an education.[67] The claimants argued that a Czech government's disproportionate assignment of Roma children to special education programs constituted a form of indirect discrimination in violation of Article 14.

In issuing its final decision in that case, the Grand Chamber of the ECtHR closely followed the approach developed by the European Court of Justice. The ECtHR began to scrutinize the Czech government's policies and justifications for them after the claimant's presentation of official statistics documenting a racial disparity in assignments to special school.[68] The claimants had shown that Roma children were grossly overrepresented in special schools, where they received an inferior education. But the claimants had not made any showing that any specific policies, such as the particular psychological exams employed, caused the disproportionate outcomes. The statistical disparity was sufficient to require the Czech government to justify its entire scheme of special education assignment. Based merely on the presentation of undisputed reports that Roma children had constituted 70 to 90 percent of students in special schools since the 1990s, the ECtHR concluded:

In these circumstances, the evidence submitted by the applicants can be regarded as sufficiently reliable and significant to give rise to a strong presumption of indirect discrimination. The burden of proof must therefore shift to the Government, which must show that the difference in the impact of the legislation was the result of objective factors unrelated to ethnic origin.[69]

Following the CJEU's approach, the ECtHR applied a proportionality test to the government's proffered justifications. The Czech government explained the disparities by claiming that they were the result of legitimate attempts to adapt the education system to the capacities of children with special needs. Specifically, they argued that the disparities resulted from the use of psychological tests that measured children's capacities, which were used to make school assignments. Once the assignments were made, the parents consented. Thus, the government attributed the disparities to the intellectual capacities of Roma children and parental consent. The government claimed that parental consent was "the decisive factor without which the applicants would not have been placed in special schools."[70] The court rejected the government's submissions, first by raising the possibility that the tests were biased or that their "results were not analysed in the light of the particularities and special characteristics of the Roma children who sat them,"[71] and second, by holding that parents could not validly consent to discriminatory treatment, which would amount to an impermissible waiver of a Convention right.[72]

The ECtHR's approach in *D.H. & Others v. Czech Republic* illustrates the gulf between current European jurisdictions' "indirect discrimination" concept and disparate impact doctrine in the United States. In Europe, discrimination plaintiffs can shift the burden of justification to the alleged discriminator simply by pointing out a disparity and alleging that the defendant is responsible for it. It is then for the defendant to explain the causes of the disparity, specifically that the disparity results from the pursuit of legitimate aims, and that the means utilized are necessary and appropriate toward achieving those aims. In the absence of this "objective justification," disparate outcomes are presumed to indicate discriminatory causes. The ECtHR's indirect discrimination framework has become firmly established in subsequent cases. In two similar decisions challenging the overrepresentation of Roma children in special schools for the mentally disabled or academically challenged, the ECtHR has required the state to justify the overrepresentation after a statistical showing of disparity, and has then rejected the state's justifications.[73]

IV. Indirect Discrimination before *Griggs*: Free Movement of Workers of All Nationalities within the European Community

Despite the embrace of *Griggs* in the CJEU's early indirect discrimination decisions, the European concept of disparate impact discrimination was not merely transplanting American antidiscrimination law. In fact, *Griggs* was imported to strengthen and give structure to a concept of discrimination that the CJEU had developed in 1969 to enforce a treaty provision guaranteeing the free movement of workers. In this context, the norm against discrimination on the basis of nationality within the European Economic Community was not primarily a protection of individuals from the dignity-harms of unequal treatment. Rather, the EC Treaty prohibited discrimination on the basis of nationality to enable the members of the European Economic Community to work toward the primary goal of their treaty: the creation of a single European market.

The influence of the free movement cases is subtle but explicit in Advocate General Warner's opinion in *Jenkins v. Kingsgate*. In that opinion, AG Warner distinguished between the so-called *Griggs* approach and that advanced by an English case, *Clay Cross (Quarry Services) Ltd. v. Fletcher*.[74] Warner read *Clay Cross* as developing an effects-based test for discrimination as an evidentiary dragnet for intentional discrimination and suggested it was inapplicable to the instant case. He then went on to embrace the *Griggs* approach instead, reading *Griggs* as allowing a prima facie case to be established by evidence of disproportionate effects of an employer policy on men and women and then requiring the employer to provide some special justification.[75] At that point, he noted: "I draw similar comfort from the fact that that conclusion accords with a familiar line of authority in this Court, Case 152/73 *Sotgiu v Deutsche Bundespost* [1974], 1 ECR 153, Case 61/77 *Commission v Ireland* [1978] ECR 417 and Case 237/78 *CRAM v Toia* [1979] ECR 2645."[76]

Article 48 of the EEC Treaty (EC Treaty article 39, and currently Treaty on the Functioning of the European Union art. 45) provided: "Freedom of movement for workers shall be secured within the Community" and specified that "[s]uch freedom of movement shall entail the abolition of any discrimination based on nationality between workers of the Member States as regards employment, remuneration and other conditions of work and employment."[77] Additionally, a Council regulation adopted in the 1960s, addressing terms and conditions of work as well as unemployment and dismissal procedures, stated: "A worker who is a national of a Member State may not, in the territory of another Member State, be differently treated from national workers by reason of his nationality..."[78] The common market created by the treaty in 1958 was based on four fundamental freedoms: free movement of persons, services, goods, and capital. These freedoms were delineated as essential to the creation of a single economic area.

In *Sotgiu v. Deutsche Bundespost*,[79] the first free movement case mentioned by the Advocate General in *Jenkins*, the CJEU developed the concept of "indirect" discrimination in the context of interpreting Article 48 of the EEC Treaty. Mr. Sotgiu was an Italian citizen working in Germany for the German postal service. Postal workers in Germany who were employed away from their place of residence received a separation allowance. However, the separation allowance was higher for workers whose residence at the time of their initial employment was within the Federal Republic of Germany than for workers whose residence at the time of their initial employment was abroad. But the policy did not obviously treat German nationals differently from foreign nationals. The policy did not use the nationality of workers as a criterion for different treatment. An Italian national who was already residing in Germany before taking the job with the German postal service would get the same separation allowance as a German national in the same situation, and a German national who was residing abroad before taking the job with the German postal service would get the same reduced allowance paid to foreign nationals living abroad before the initial employment.

Nonetheless, the CJEU concluded that the policy at issue violated the prohibition of discrimination based on nationality in the free movement provisions of the EEC Treaty. In justifying its decision, the court stated:

> The criterion of the place of recruitment might make it possible to circumvent the prohibition on discrimination based on nationality: in fact workers recruited abroad are normally of foreign nationality and a criterion of differentiation based on place of recruitment of the worker would lead substantially to discrimination against non-national Community workers. Such a criterion is contrary to the principle of freedom of movement.[80]

The inquiry is not a technical one as to whether the distinction made is one of nationality but a question of principle: Does the category at issue, whether it can be viewed as a proxy for nationality or not, contravene the principle of freedom of movement?

The court then framed the problem as one of "hidden or indirect discrimination," taking a very fact-based, consequentialist, practical approach:

> The concepts of discrimination and of nationality must be interpreted on the basis of factual criteria. A purely theoretical idea is not sufficient. Rules

based on other criteria such as residence abroad, language, place of birth, descent or performance of military service in the country may in fact conceal discrimination on the basis of nationality. Such would be the case in particular if the application of certain criteria of differentiation were to result, in all cases or in the vast majority of cases, in foreigners alone being affected without any objective justification.[81]

Here, we can discern the outlines of an indirect discrimination test that was given much fuller articulation seven years later in *Jenkins v. Kingsgate*. If a rule or criterion disproportionately affects foreigners, an objective justification must be present to avoid a finding of nationality discrimination. Further, the court provides some guidance to be applied by the national court as to what might or might not constitute an objective justification:

> The criterion of residence abroad might not appear to be discriminatory in a case in which, unlike workers recruited within the country, workers recruited abroad receive a separation allowance without having to find a home in the country of employment or to remove, and in which they receive the allowance at the lower rate for a practically unlimited period throughout of the whole of their period of employment. The question whether this scheme gives rise to discrimination either in intention or in effect, or whether it is only intended to control one particular situation in an objective way, should be settled in terms of national law.[82]

If, for example, the employer were to require its own nationals to relocate to the city of employment, thereby paying a larger allowance for a shorter period of time, while permitting nonnationals to commute with a smaller allowance for an indefinite period, the court suggests that this could meet the objective justification test. These arrangements would appear to facilitate, rather than undermine, the nonnationals' ability to work in a different member state. Ultimately, what matters with regard to the objective justification is whether, as the court stated earlier, the principle of free movement of workers is contravened.

The *Sotgiu* case was decided in 1974, after *Griggs*. But the indirect discrimination idea that is so robustly articulated in *Sotgiu* does not cite *Griggs*, and there is no indication that *Griggs* played any role. The idea of indirect discrimination derived from a 1969 free movement case before the CJEU. Invoking both the treaty provision prohibiting nationality discrimination as well as the regulations, an Italian citizen who was working in Germany challenged the application of a German law, which entitled workers who had served in the German armed forces to have their periods of military service counted as time employed for the purposes of wage regulations and collective contracts.[83] Salvatore Ugliola, the Italian employee of a German company, sought to have his military service for Italy counted for the purpose of calculating his duration of employment. Again, the policy did not necessarily treat German nationals and nonnationals differently. Germans who did not serve in the German military would be treated the same as non-Germans who did not serve in the German military. The German government pointed out that the law providing for the counting of military service as employment was part of German military law, not German labor law. Thus, the law was presented as a policy enabling the German state to compensate employment disadvantages sustained by persons who had served in their military. Germany argued that, therefore, there had been no discrimination based on nationality.

The CJEU responded to this line of argumentation by focusing on the effects of a policy rather than the intent behind it. Thus, the concept of "indirect" discrimination emerged:

> A national law which is intended to protect a worker who resumes his employment with his former employer from any disadvantages occasioned by his absence on military service, by providing in particular that the period spent in the armed forces must be taken into account in calculating the period of his service with that employer falls within the context of conditions of work and employment. Such a law cannot therefore, on the basis of its indirect connexion with national defence, be excluded from the ambit of Article 9(1) of EEC Regulation No 38/64 and Article 7 of EEC Regulation No 1612/68 on equality of treatment and protection for migrant workers "in respect of any conditions of employment and work."
>
> [A]rticle 48 of the Treaty does not allow Member States to make any exceptions to the equality of treatment and protection required by the Treaty for all workers within the Community by indirectly introducing discrimination in favour of their own nationals alone based upon obligations for military service.[84]

Here, the concept of "indirect" discrimination is not the same as "disparate impact" discrimination. The discrimination in this context is "indirect" in the sense that the law makes no explicit facial distinction between Italian workers and German workers and does not use nationality, as such, as a criterion of differentiation. It distinguishes on the basis of the government for which one has performed military service. The law could benefit a foreign national who performed military service for Germany or disadvantage a German who performed military service for another nation. This is why the discrimination is characterized as "indirect."

The CJEU's reasoning as to why the treaty must prohibit these "indirect" forms of discrimination can be discerned in Advocate General Gand's opinion. He points out that "performance of military service in the army of the State other than that of which one is a national is a hypothesis which even the Government of the Federal Republic of Germany considers to be somewhat theoretical."[85] Advocate General Gand identifies the obvious consequences of the law for Germans and non-Germans: "In fact, the provision in question only benefits German citizens..."[86] But instead of harping on the Italian national's right to equal treatment, Gand emphasizes that "the very purpose of the regulation on freedom of movement is precisely to abolish such privileges."[87] In short, what's wrong with German policies that benefit German workers only is that they hamper the integration of the European market. The wrong of discrimination is located by reference to one of the four fundamental freedoms protected by the European Economic Community—specifically, free movement of workers. Finally, Gand points out that, while indirect forms of discrimination are prohibited, the possibility of justifying policies that undermine free movement is articulated in the limitations in Article 48, Paragraph 3 of the treaty.[88] Section 3 provides that the freedom of movement for workers is subject to limitations justified on grounds of public policy, public security, or public health.[89] Applying this standard, AG Gand concludes that there are no such grounds that could justify the employment policy of remunerating former German military members at a higher rate.[90] In the cases of the 1970s protecting the free movement of workers, the CJEU did not draw a sharp line between direct and indirect discrimination. Rather, national rules or employer policies that disadvantaged nationals of one member state were generally scrutinized to determine whether the interference with workers' free movement and European integration could be tolerated.[91]

V. Conclusion

Thus, the European approach to indirect discrimination originated before the citations to *Griggs*, in cases rooting out member state policies that had the effect of advantaging workers who were nationals of that state. Such policies made sense when markets were national, but they were contrary to the goal of a common supranational market. When the CJEU invalidated such policies, it was aiming not to eradicate racism or national animus but rather to end a prior set of institutional arrangements that supported a different type of market. Thus, the European law of indirect discrimination, unlike disparate impact law in the United States, did not begin as an evidentiary dragnet for racism, ethnic animus, or any other evil that was being repudiated and rooted out by law. Rather, indirect discrimination doctrine began because it was acknowledged that the new and collectively shared goal of European economic integration would require the eradication of existing practices that had been premised on a different, nation-centered economic model.

The amalgamation of *Griggs*'s disparate impact theory with the indirect discrimination theory in the free movement cases highlights the potential and limits of American antidiscrimination law. The free movement line of cases envisions the paradigmatic instance of discrimination as a privilege reserved for nationals, not a rights violation stemming from animus. That privilege is problematic not because it is morally repugnant but because it undermines the fundamental goal articulated by the treaties organizing the European Economic Community: the economic integration of these national markets. Similarly, the *Griggs* Court characterized the policies that it repudiated as "barriers that have operated in the past to favor an identifiable group of white employees over other employees."[92] Does anything significant happen if we say that the target of disparate impact liability—or antidiscrimination law in general—is not black disadvantage but white advantage? What is the difference between characterizing the purpose of Title VII as the eradication of white advantage, as contrasted with the eradication of black disadvantage? If white advantage is to be eradicated by antidiscrimination law, one might argue that this goal can only be achieved by forging a new economic and political order after segregation. Yet Title VII did not deliver the architecture for one.

Sociologists have suggested that racial inequalities today are largely the result of whites' ordinary use of available social networks and resources to amass opportunities for themselves.[93] Most people help their friends and family find educational opportunities and jobs, if possible. (In fact, many people believe this is what it means to be a good parent or friend.) Should civil rights law regard these dynamics as illegitimate "opportunity-hoarding" or desirable methods of preserving much-needed social capital? It would only be possible to render "opportunity-hoarding" as illegitimate if one developed an account of how these behaviors significantly undermined clearly shared social goals, such as the eventual and complete racial integration of American civil society.

The evolution of a robust indirect discrimination doctrine in Europe suggests some limits to the concept of discrimination. When the concept of discrimination emphasizes effects and consequences rather than practices or procedures, those consequences have to be understood in relation to a collective goal. It is only because the European Community was attempting to create a single market that policies undermining the four fundamental freedoms become problematic. Note also that the freedoms that are thought to be "fundamental" are not freedoms in a universalistic human rights sense. They are freedoms instrumental to the project of European integration. Free movement of workers only refers to workers within the European economic community and not to an abstract free labor idea. The freedoms are valuable primarily by reference to their furtherance of the articulated goal of creating a common market. Within fifty years, enforcing the norm against nationality discrimination within the European Community enabled a transnational integration of labor markets. The EU is now the largest internal market in the world, and it exercises enormous regulatory power globally.

By contrast, the Civil Rights Act in the United States did not aspire to the collectively shared purpose of a fully racially integrated workplace. Rather, the American ideal of equal opportunity appears consistent with the absence of integration. In fact, the framers of the Civil Rights Act explicitly avoided defining what the end-state of this body of law should be and made clear that the prohibition of discrimination would never require employers to achieve racial balance. As *Ricci* illustrates, the fear of encouraging the use of quotas motivates courts to limit the disparate impact theory. As we prepare for the next half-century of Title VII in the United States, we must confront the difficult question of whether American antidiscrimination law has any collectively shared social goal. Are we striving for a total racial integration of the workplace by Title VII's centennial? If not, one wonders what the Civil Rights Act is for today.

About the Author

Professor of law, Benjamin N. Cardozo School of Law–Yeshiva University. Many thanks to Daniel Halberstam, Christopher McCrudden, Reva Siegel, and the participants in the University of Michigan Law School Symposium on The Civil Rights Act at 50 for helpful comments on an earlier draft.

Notes

1. Griggs v. Duke Power Co., 401 U.S. 424 (1971).
2. *Id.* at 427–28.
3. *Id.* at 427.
4. *Id.* at 432.
5. *Id.*
6. *Id.* at 433.
7. *See, e.g.,* Michael Evan Gold, Griggs' *Folly: An Essay on the Theory, Problems, and Origins of the Adverse Impact Definition of Employment Discrimination and a Recommendation for Reform,* 7 INDUS. REL. L.J. 429 (1985); George Rutherglen, *Disparate Impact under Title VII: An Objective Theory of Discrimination,* 73 VA. L. REV.

1297 (1987); Michael Selmi, *Was the Disparate Impact Theory a Mistake?*, 53 UCLA L. REV. 701 (2006); Christine Jolls, *Antidiscrimination and Accommodation*, 115 HARV. L. REV. 642 (2001); Amy Wax, *Disparate Impact Realism*, 53 WM. & MARY L. REV. 621 (2011); Richard A. Primus, *Equal Protection and Disparate Impact: Round Three*, 117 HARV. L. REV. 493, 520–36 (2003).

8.   *See Pamela L. Perry, Two Faces of Disparate Impact Discrimination*, 59 FORDHAM L. REV. 523, 529–40 (1991).

9.   *See* Reva B. Siegel, Foreword: *Equality Divided*, 127 HARV. L. REV. 1, 14–16 (2013) (discussing cases).

10. *See* Washington v. Davis, 426 U.S. 229 (1976); Personnel Adm'r of Mass. v. Feeney, 442 U.S. 256 (1979). Reva Siegel provides a textured historical account of the division of discriminatory impact from purpose in her recent *Foreword, supra* note 9.

11. *See* Wards Cove Packing v. Atonio, 490 U.S. 642 (1989).

12. *See* Ricci v. DeStefano, 557 U.S. 557, 563 (2009).

13. *See* Implementation of the Fair Housing Act's Discriminatory Effects Standard, 78 Fed. Reg. 11460 (Feb. 15, 2013).

14. Texas Dep't of Housing & Community Affairs v. Inclusive Communities Project, June 25, 2015, slip op. at 18.

15. Wards Cove Packing v. Atonio, 490 U.S. 642, 651 (1989).

16. *Id.* at 651–52 (1989).

17. *Id.* at 652.

18. *Id.*

19. *Id.* (quoting Albemarle Paper Co. v. Moody, 422 U.S. 405, 449 (1975) (Blackmun, J., concurring)).

20. *See, e.g.*, McClain v. Lufkin Indus., 519 F.3d 264, 275–79 (5th Cir. 2008); EEOC v. Joe's Stone Crab, Inc., 220 F.3d 1263, 1275, 1288 (11th Cir. 2000); Davis v. Cintas Corp., 717 F.3d 476, 497 (6th Cir. 2013).

21. Wal-Mart v. Dukes, 564 U.S. , 131 S. Ct. 2541, 2555–56 (2011).

22. *Id.*

23. *Wards Cove*, 490 U.S. at 659–60.

24. *See* 42 U.S.C. § 2000e-2(k)(1)(A)(i).

25. *See* Susan Grover, *The Business Necessity Defense in Disparate Impact Discrimination Cases*, 30 Ga. L. Rev. 387, 414 n.86 (citing examples).

26. Selmi, *supra* note 7, at 706.

27. *See* JEANNE GREGORY, SEX, RACE, AND THE LAW: LEGISLATING FOR EQUALITY 34 (1988).

28. *Id.*

29. ROY JENKINS, EQUALITY FOR WOMEN ¶ 33 (1974).

30. *See* Lord Lester of Herne Hill QC, *Making Discrimination Law Effective: Old Barriers and New Frontiers*, 2 INT'L J. DISCRIMINATION & L. 161, 173 (1997). *See also* Anthony Lester, *Anti-discrimination Legislation in Great Britain*, NEW COMMUNITY, Vol. XIV, No. 1/2, at 21.

31. Sex Discrimination Act, 1975, c. 65, § 1(1)(a) (U.K.) (as amended).

32. *Id.* § 1(1)(b).

33. *See* Simon Forshaw & Marcus Pilgerstorfer, *Direct and Indirect Discrimination: Is There Something In Between?*, 37 INDUS. L.J. 347, 351 (2008).

34. Race Relations Act, 1976, c. 74, § 1A (U.K.) (as amended).

35. Council Directive 2000/43, art. 2(2)(b), Implementing the Principle of Equal Treatment between Persons Irrespective of Racial or Ethnic Origin, 2000 O.J. (L 180/24) (EC).

36. Council Directive 2000/78, art. 2(2)(b), of 27 November 2000 Establishing a General Framework For Equal Treatment In Employment and Occupation, 2000 O.J. (L 303/18) (EC).

37. Equality Act, 2010, c. 15, § 19(2) (U.K.).

38. *See* Bob Hepple, *The European Legacy of* Brown v. Board of Education, 2006 U. ILL. L. REV. 605, 608–09 (2006).

39. *See* EC Treaty art. 141 (formerly EEC Treaty art. 119).

40. *See* Cty. of Wash. v. Gunther, 452 U.S. 161, 170–71. The Equal Pay Act prohibits employers from "paying wages to employees in such establishment at a rate less than the rate at which he pays wages to employees of the opposite sex in such establishment for equal work on jobs the performance of which requires equal skill, effort, and responsibility, and which are performed under similar working conditions." 29 U.S.C. § 206(d). Unlike the equal pay guarantee of the EEC treaty, the U.S. Equal Pay Act permits "a differential based on any other factor other than sex." The Court has read this language to bar disparate impact constructions of the Equal Pay Act's nondiscrimination guarantee.

41. *See, e.g.*, Ilhardt v. Sara Lee Corp., 118 F.3d 1151, 1157 (7th Cir. 1997).

42. *See* Case 96/80, Jenkins v. Kingsgate Clothing Prods., Ltd., 1981 E.C.R. 911.

43. *See* City of Los Angeles Dep't of Water & Power v. Manhart, 435 U.S. 702, 710 n.20; Cty. of Wash. v. Gunther, 452 U.S. at 170–71.

44. *See* Case 96/80, Jenkins v. Kingsgate Clothing Prods., Ltd., Opinion of Advocate General Warner, 1981 E.C.R. 929, 931.

45. *Id.* at 934–35.

46. *Id.* at 936 (quoting Counsel for Mrs. Jenkins).

47. *Jenkins*, Case 96/80, at 916.

48. Case 96/80, Jenkins v. Kingsgate Clothing Prods., Ltd., Opinion of Advocate General Warner, 1981 E.C.R. 929, 936.

49. *Jenkins*, Case 96/80, at 925.

50. *Id.* at 916.

51. Case C-170/84, Bilka-Kaufhaus GmbH v. Weber von Hartz, 1986 E.C.R. 1607.

52. *Id.* ¶ 6.

53. *Id.* ¶¶ 29–30.

54. *Id.* ¶ 33.

55. *Id.* ¶ 40.

56. *Id.* ¶ 37.

57. *Id.* ¶ 43.

58. Case C-170/84, Bilka-Kaufhaus GmbH v. Weber von Hartz, Opinion of Advocate General Darmon, 1986 E.C.R. 1608, ¶ 14.

59. *Id.*

60. Case C-127/92, Enderby v. Frenchay Health Auth., 1993 E.C.R. I-05535.

61. *Id.* ¶ 4.

62. *Id.* ¶ 19.

63. *Id.* ¶¶ 14, 19.

64. *Id.* at I-05577.

65. Case C-127/92, Enderby v. Frenchay Health Auth., Opinion of Advocate General Lenz, 1933 E.C.R. I-05553, ¶¶ 35–38.

66. Case of D.H. & Others v. Czech Republic, Application no. 57325/00 (Grand Chamber, European Court of Human Rights) Eur. Ct. H.R. 2007-IV (2007).

67. *Id.* ¶ 210.

68. *See id.* ¶¶ 188–203.

69. *Id.* ¶ 195.

70. *Id.* ¶ 202.

71. *Id.* ¶ 201.

72. *Id.* ¶¶ 202–03.

73. *See* Case of Lavida & Others v. Greece, no. 7973/10, Eur. Ct. H.R. 2013 (First Section); Case of Horváth & Kiss v. Hungary, no. 11146/11, Eur. Ct. H.R. 2013.

74. Case 96/80, Jenkins v. Kingsgate Clothing Prods., Ltd., Opinion of Advocate General Warner, 1981 E.C.R. 929, 934, 936.

75. *Id.* at 937.

76. *Id.*

77. Treaty Establishing the European Economic Community art. 48, Mar. 25, 1957 (as in effect 1958) (now Treaty on the Functioning of the European Union (TFEU) art. 39).

78. Regulation 1612/68 of the Council on Freedom of Movement for Workers Within the Community, art. 7, 1968 O.J. (L 257/2) (1968). *See also* Regulation No. 38/64/ EEC of the Council, art. 9, 1964 O.J. 62 (1964).

79. Case 152/73, Sotgiu v. Deutsche Bundespost, 1974 E.C.R. 153.

80. *Id.* at 158.

81. *Id.* at 160–61.

82. *Id.* at 161.

83. Case 15/69, Württembergische Milchverwertung-Südmilch-AG v. Salvatore Ugliola, 1969 E.C.R. 363, 364.

84. *Id.* ¶¶ 5–6.

85. Case 15/69, Württembergische Milchverwertung-Südmilch-AG v. Salvatore Ugliola, Opinion of Advocate General Gand, 1969 E.C.R. 371, 375.

86. *Id.*

87. *Id.*

88. *Id.*

89. *Id.* (citing EEC Treaty art. 48(3)).

90. *Id.*

91. *See, e.g.*, Case 55/77, Marguerite Maris v. Rijksdienst voor Werknemerspensioenen, 1977 E.C.R. 2327; Case 16/78, Criminal Proceedings v. Michel Choquet, 1978 E.C.R. 2293; Case 237/78, Caisse Régionale d'Assurance Maladie de Lille (CRAM) v. Diamante Palermo, 1979 E.C.R. 2645.

92. Griggs v. Duke Power Co., 401 U.S. 424, 430 (1971).

93. *See* NANCY DITOMASO, THE AMERICAN NON-DILEMMA: RACIAL INEQUALITY WITHOUT RACISM (2012); CHARLES TILLY, DURABLE INEQUALITY (1998).

List of Contributors

Kathryn Abrams is the Herma Hill Kay Distinguished Professor of Law at the UC-Berkeley School of Law.

Samuel R. Bagenstos is a professor of law at the University of Michigan Law School.

Devon Carbado is the Honorable Harry Pregerson Professor of Law at the UCLA Law School.

Brian T. Fitzpatrick is a professor of law at the Vanderbilt Law School.

Cary Franklin is a professor of law at the University of Texas School of Law.

Nancy Gertner is a retired federal district judge and a professor of practice at the Harvard Law School.

Mitu Gulati is a professor of law at the Duke University Law School.

Craig Gurian is the executive director of the Anti-Discrimination Center and an adjunct professor of law at the Fordham Law School.

Nan D. Hunter is a professor of law and associate dean for Graduate Programs at the Georgetown University Law Center.

Olatunde Johnson is a professor of law at the Columbia Law School.

Ellen D. Katz is the Ralph W. Aigler Professor of Law at the University of Michigan Law School.

Sophia Z. Lee is a professor of law and history at the University of Pennsylvania Law School.

Patrick Shin is a professor of law at the Suffolk University Law School.

Julie Suk is a professor of law at the Benjamin N. Cardozo School of Law at Yeshiva University.

Theodore J. St. Antoine is the James E. and Sarah A. Degan Professor Emeritus of Law at the University of Michigan Law School.

Robin L. West is the Frederick J. Haas Professor of Law and Philosophy at the Georgetown University Law Center.